AF849644

LAW WITHOUT FORCE

Library of Conservative Thought

America's British Culture, Kirk
Authority and the Liberal Tradition, Heineman
A Better Guide Than Reason, Bradford
Burke Street, Scott-Moncrieff
The Case for Conservatism, Wilson
Céline, Hindus
Character and Culture, Babbitt
Collected Letters of John Randolph to John Brockenbrough, Shorey
A Critical Examination of Socialism, Mallock
Edmund Burke: Appraisals & Applications, Ritchie
Edmund Burke: The Enlightenment & Revolution, Stanlis
The Essential Calhoun, Wilson
The Foundations of Political Science, Burgess
Ghosts on the Roof, Chambers
The God of the Machine, Paterson
A Historian and His World, Scott
Historical Consciousness, Lukacs
I Chose Freedom, Kravchenko
I Chose Justice, Kravchenko
Irving Babbitt, Literature, and the Democratic Culture, Hindus
Law Without Force, Niemeyer
Lord George Bentinck, Disraeli
The Moral Foundations of Civil Society, Roepke
Natural Law, d'Entrèves
On Divorce, de Bonald
Orestes Brownson, Kirk
The Phantom Public, Lippmann
Politics of the Center, Starzinger
Regionalism and Nationalism in the United States, Davidson
Rousseau and Romanticism, Babbitt
The Social Crisis of Our Time, Roepke
Tensions of Order and Freedom, Menczer
The Vision of Richard Weaver, Scotchie
The Voegelinian Revolution, Sandoz
We the People, McDonald

LAW WITHOUT FORCE

The Function of Politics in International Law

Gerhart Niemeyer

With a new introduction by **Michael Henry**

Routledge
Taylor & Francis Group
LONDON AND NEW YORK

Originally published in 1941 by Princeton University Press.

Published 2001 by Transaction Publishers

Published 2017 by Routledge
2 Park Square, Milton Park, Abingdon, Oxon OX14 4RN
711 Third Avenue, New York, NY 10017, USA

Routledge is an imprint of the Taylor & Francis Group, an informa business

New material this edition copyright © 2001 by Taylor & Francis

All rights reserved. No part of this book may be reprinted or reproduced or utilised in any form or by any electronic, mechanical, or other means, now known or hereafter invented, including photocopying and recording, or in any information storage or retrieval system, without permission in writing from the publishers.

Notice:
Product or corporate names may be trademarks or registered trademarks, and are used only for identification and explanation without intent to infringe.

Library of Congress Catalog Number: 00-062925

Library of Congress Cataloging-in-Publication Data

Niemeyer, Gerhart.
Law without force : the function of politics in international law / by Gerhart Niemeyer; with a new introduction by Michael Henry.
p. cm.— (Library of conservative thought)
Originally published: Princeton : Princeton University Press, 1941.
Includes bibliographical references and index.
ISBN 0-7658-0640-1 (pbk : alk. paper)
1. International law—Political aspects. 2. International law—Philosophy. 3. Sociological jurisprudence. I. Title. II. Series.

KZ1250 .N55 2000
341'.01—dc21 00-062925

ISBN 13: 978-0-7658-0640-6 (pbk)

To the Memory of

HERMANN HELLER

The Man · The Teacher

The Friend

CONTENTS

PART THREE

A RECONSTRUCTION OF INTERNATIONAL LAW

INTRODUCTION TO THE TRANSACTION EDITION

Readers who come to this book already acquainted with Gerhart Niemeyer's later writings will find themselves in a terrain both strange and familiar. The latter is the clarity of mind, the breadth of scholarship, and the rigor and thoroughness of argument that were hallmarks of Niemeyer's work. But this is early Niemeyer, published when he was only thirty-four years old and an assistant professor of politics at Princeton. This is Niemeyer the legal scholar and thinker, before the intensive study of communism and foreign policy, before political theory (as he would later teach and write about it), before Voegelin and Christian philosophy. I can remember being surprised to discover that Niemeyer's degree was in law, since by the time I came to know him in the early 1970s he was teaching and writing on many aspects of political philosophy but not on law. Had I read *Law Without Force* then, however, I would have understood how his training and scholarship in law contributed to the precision of his reasoning, and how many of his later philosophical and foreign policy concerns were already present in his theory of international law. As an early, and indeed his first major work, *Law Without Force* provides us with a kind of foundation layer of Niemeyer's thinking, a basic stratum underlying the further stages of his intellectual development. And even though he presents a theory here that he eventually abandoned, aspects of his thinking turn up, explicitly or implicitly, in his later writings, like outcroppings of bedrock on the surface.

Niemeyer's publications before *Law Without Force* were few and relatively brief and concerned with either law or social analysis or both. In 1940 he published two articles that are essentially arguments from separate sections of *Law Without Force*, "International Law and Social Structure," in *The American Journal of International Law* and "The Significance of Function in Legal Theory," in the *New York University Quarterly Review*. His first publication, in 1932, was *Einstweilige Verfügungen des Weltgerichtshofs, ihr Wesen und ihre Grenzen*, a detailed historical and conceptual analysis of the legal status and limits of provisional decrees, particularly in the case of the International Court of Justice. This is a legal analysis of a legal issue, without the sociological context, but his 1935 work *Vom Wesen der Gesellschaftlichen Sicherheit*, a pamphlet-length study of the meaning of security in society as well as in international relations shows the sort of sociological analysis on which the argument in *Law Without Force* rests. It also shows the influence of Niemeyer's mentor Hermann Heller, to whom Niemeyer served as assistant in 1932.

Heller, born in 1891, was a Privatdozent at the University of Kiel, where Niemeyer received his law degree, and a prolific writer on law, politics, intellectual history, and sociology. When he died suddenly in 1933 he left an unfinished major work, *Staatslehre* (Political Theory), which Niemeyer edited and published in 1934. *Law Without Force*, which is dedicated to Heller, frequently quotes from and refers to *Staatslehre* (and occasionally to Heller's 1927 book *Die Souveränität)* and much of Niemeyer's theory follows the lines of Heller's theory and his analysis of society and its historical changes. Rejecting the theories that sought either to reduce the knowledge of the state to a form of natural science or to transform the state into an abstract, universal manifestation of *Geist*, Heller instead insisted that political theory must be understood as "culture-science" and sociology, or as he put it quite succinctly, "reality-science" (*Wirklichkeitswissenschaft*). Reality meant what concretely-existing individual human beings actually chose to do in their living together in specific times and places. Political science is properly concerned not with universal abstractions but with the individual characteristics of political standards and forms, while also taking note of the constants in human behavior and thinking despite the difference in circumstances. It was on the richness, complexity, and concreteness of experience that Heller believed political science must be founded, and therefore he acknowledged that there was something artificial about political science because the state (and politics) is always only a part of a complex life-reality from which political science isolates it. Political science has value only when it constantly refers the isolated state back to the whole of reality (*Wirklichkeitsganze*) in which it alone has life and truth. Similarly, there are no isolated individuals but only individual human beings living and acting together in society, and therefore no true political theory can begin from the solitary individual. Since Heller saw the state, and the individual, as part of the concrete whole of human social life, he could not agree with a natural law theory that opposed to historical change a human nature that was always thought to follow the same laws.

Heller's emphasis on building theory on the basis of concrete human social reality carefully observed and analyzed is a fundamental theme in *Law Without Force*. At the end of the Preface Niemeyer describes the "spirit" of Heller that guided him in writing the book: Heller sought the "rational mastery of political reality" as a profound human responsibility, he sought "to penetrate the phenomena of political association with the clarity of the spirit," and he looked "straight into the face of realities." Always, as in any science, the starting point is an already existing and functioning reality, a reality that the mind seeks to comprehend. Heller's theorizing was driven not by the "wishful thinking" of attempting to conform reality to some previously conceived theory, but instead by the integrity of seeking to understand only what actually existed and to express it exactly, so that, Niemeyer tells us, sometimes he spent an entire day carefully working out one sentence. This rigorous concern with seeing and expressing reality clearly was, of course, for Niemeyer also a lifelong attitude of mind.

Law Without Force appeared in 1941, while Hitler was swallowing up Europe, after the collapse of the League of Nations and all the treaties, pacts, and other devices of international law intended to prevent war. Niemeyer had begun the work several years earlier, when the crisis of international order and collective security was already manifest, and his purpose was, first, to provide some answer to the question how and why this collapse of international order had happened and, second, to indicate a new and more effective way of thinking about international order, "a new direction," leaving the specific details to be worked out in later discussions. What he regarded as an "unflinchingly realistic account of the past" is rather pithily summarized in the title given to the Introduction: "The unreality of international law and the unlawfulness of international reality." His thesis is that although international law worked under different social conditions in the past, the conditions have changed so much that international law has become ineffective and incapable of being improved. Niemeyer's analysis of the breakdown of international law is very clear and precise in pointing out how and why its modern system developed and why this system in place for three centuries had ceased to correspond to the social reality of international relations. What one reviewer called the "unorthodoxy" of the book is encapsulated in the statement that "with our present conceptual equipment we are incapable of redrafting the rules of international order so as to make them fit the changed political conditions." In short, Niemeyer, like others of his generation, finding himself in the midst of catastrophic disorders which the traditional or orthodox theories were incapable of grasping, was forced to search for other conceptual tools with which to come to grips with the changed conditions of reality. In his later essay "Conservatism and the New Political Theory" Niemeyer quotes Eric Voegelin's description, in *Science, Politics, and Gnosticism*, of the intellectual quandary of the European thinkers in the late 1930s:

> Europe had no conceptual tools with which to grasp the horror that was upon her. There was a scholarly study of the Christian churches and sects; there was a science of government, cast in the categories of the sovereign nation-state and its institutions; there were the beginnings of a sociology of power and political authority; but there was no science of the non-Christian, non-national intellectual and mass movements into which the Europe of Christian nation-states was in the process of breaking up.[1]

When he wrote *Law Without Force*, the first work in his more than fifty-year effort to comprehend the twentieth century, Niemeyer had only such limited tools to work with, but his study of communism, his investigation of the historical roots of ideologies in general, his essays on foreign policy, politics, philosophy, and cultural analysis were all further stages in his continuous effort to penetrate reality with the power of reason.

And the power of reason that Niemeyer here applies to law in general and international law in particular is indeed impressive and enlightening. A summary cannot do justice to the richness, complexity, clarity, and tightness of his analysis, but I would like to mention a few points.

Essentially, Niemeyer's thesis that reality itself is inherently lawful in a way completely ignored by traditional international law is the basis of his functional theory that the legal binding principle is contained within the very nature, structure, and inherent ends of the activities in which human beings engage cooperatively. In the first part of the book, Niemeyer traces the development of modern international law over three centuries and argues that the fundamental error was in Grotius' assumption that international law should be based on the Roman legal concepts of person, property, injury, and contract. The consequence of this was that states were considered, from a legal standpoint, as persons, as separate entities, and therefore as isolated individuals presumed to act in their self-interest and restrained only by morality, but without a sense of their necessary connection. In his analysis, Niemeyer shows the weakness of this personalist theory that regarded states as individual persons subject to an international law backed up by ethical rules. This system was viable only as long as all the nations involved acknowledged themselves bound by the same moral principles. The Christian moral restraint on states' behavior eventually was replaced by the international connections of the bourgeoisie which, composed of individuals freely coordinating economic activities in the world marketplace, acted as an international society that checked the antagonisms and aggressions of individual States. This restraint on *raison d'état* began to break down during the world economic crisis of the 1930s when businessmen appealed to their governments to counteract the effects of the crisis, thereby handing over to governments much of their own power and independence, and also when some states became totalitarian and collectivist societies in which the freedom of citizens to engage in activities with citizens of other states was severely curtailed or even completely eliminated. This trend toward state control of the individual, which Niemeyer saw as widespread, removed the economic counterweight to the self-interests and natural antagonisms of individual states. Therefore, as Niemeyer put it, "present-day international law, which had been shaped by the exigencies of an individualistic world-Society, today serves only as a tactical position in the power conflicts of governments. The actual working of this law no longer fits the function of law between states." The problem was, of course, that without the independent bourgeois world-Society pursuing its own interests there was nothing to ground an obligation that states would have to conform to international law, particularly when statesmen calculated their national interest in other terms. Nor could one argue that international law was reason itself because, apart from considerations of ethics, there is rationality inherent in the decisions of statesmen when they are calculating and pursuing their national self-interest.

Niemeyer argues that law, including international law, is not concerned with separate individuals but with relationships, with interrelated and coordinated activities. His theory is that reality, properly understood, is essentially lawful and that international law will work only if we transform it into the lawfulness inherent in coordinated activity among states, just as there is an order built into such cooperative and coordinated activities among individuals as a fire brigade or a stock company. The end of a fire brigade is to extinguish fires and save lives and property, so all individual members, regardless of their own purposes in joining such an organization, have to coordinate their activities in order to fulfill the ends of the activity as such in order to realize their own personal purposes. Similarly, Niemeyer's functional theory assumes that, with a proper grasp of reality, states will subordinate their self-interest to the necessary ends of coordinated activities. Instead of the obligations of Christian morality or the economic activities of a bourgeois class restraining the power and ambitions of states, they would be restrained by the very nature of the activities in which states have to engage in order to pursue their interests. A kind of "Invisible Hand" built into the nature of reality would ensure that states would have to subordinate their rivalries and hostilities to the lawful and orderly ends inherent in the cooperative activities that modern states cannot avoid engaging in. Just as an athlete who wants to achieve greatness can do so only by playing according to the rules and ends of the game or sport and not by making up his own rules, so states can most successfully pursue their interests in coordinated activity with other states. This argument assumes both a "hardness," a facticity, in reality not malleable according to human desires, and, on the part of heads of governments, a rational ability to understand and accept and work within reality. But in the twentieth century ideologies rejected such reality and rationality.

Let me summarize Niemeyer's thesis as concisely as possible: For three hundred years international law as we have known it worked adequately because the self-interest and mutual antagonisms of individual states were counterbalanced by a universally accepted ethics or by the interests of an internationally connected bourgeoisie. But in the twentieth century social conditions have changed to the point where international law has become a "dead letter" and there is nothing to restrain aggression and contain hostilities. Niemeyer's question is: "Is it not imperative to abandon a structure of international law which owes its shape to social and mental conditions so utterly different from those of the present time? . . . Since new criteria seem to dominate the value-experience of modern masses, we must explore the possibilities arising out of them, in order to find ways in which the functions of a legal system can be adequately fulfilled in our time." In other words, the social and mental conditions, the choices and actions of individuals, are the reality, and, since they have changed it is necessary to change international law to accommodate them. The fundamental theory of order spontaneously arising from coordinated activities is the new accommodation since, presumably, even governments unrestrained by public opinion or morality would still be forced to see the necessity of coordinating their activities with others *en route* to the realization of their ambitions.

This brings up two questions that I want to consider briefly: After producing such an ambitious, thorough, and carefully argued work, why did Niemeyer drop the functional theory and indeed abandon law and international law entirely as a central issue of his reflection? And how much of his thinking in this book remained with him in his later works?

I believe the answer to the first question is that he realized that the roots of disorder went much deeper than a disparity between social reality and international law, that, in fact, the social reality was itself fundamentally disordered because there is another, transcendent level of reality beyond that of concrete individuals engaged in specific actions, and also that political rulers did not always act according to any traditional sense of political rationality. The functional theory will not work if someone takes over command of the fire brigade in order to destroy it on the basis of a conviction that fires have been permanently eliminated, for this theory assumes that human beings, at least those with power, have a reliable tendency to calculate their actions on the basis of a rational assessment of reality. The functional theory is helpless in the face of what came to be known as the "second reality," a new and imaginary "reality" forcefully imposed on the truth. The analysis of the problem had to dig down into the disorders of the spirit that had been developing for centuries, hence Niemeyer's later detailed analysis of communism and other ideologies and how they developed into the "total critique" of society.

In a later essay on "The Communist Mind" Niemeyer makes a clear distinction, not yet developed in *Law Without Force*, between substantive and pragmatic rationality. Substantive rationality concerns "basic views of man, society, nature, and life." It is the rationality of the Platonic *nous*, the ability to see and dwell in the truth of existence. Pragmatic rationality concerns "the suitability of means to given ends." Although the communists were generally quite rational in the pragmatic sense they were entirely irrational, even anti-rational, in the substantive sense because their ideology postulated arbitrarily distorted and contrived ends and "realities," and since they were devoted to destroying social structures they were driven by "a militant hostility towards men and existing institutions [and] a desire to subvert, uproot, and destroy everything that exists."[2] Since men and existing institutions are essential components of the reality Niemeyer saw, he found in communism a state of mind that contradicted the fundamental rationality he had assumed among statesmen in developing his functional theory. Niemeyer always believed that there is basic truth in individuals choosing and acting with others in society, but he also came to recognize that human beings have a tendency to fall prey to those who seek to replace this imperfect reality with a daydream of "perfection," and that there is a kind of "political madness" in "a ruler committed to a dreamworld," who can, nonetheless, still bring about impressive technological accomplishments. The emphasis on the reality of what concrete human beings do that is found in his last writings is much the same as in his early writings. What changed was his understanding of how easily human beings can lose this sense of reality. One of Niemeyer's major points about communist ideology was precisely that it set out to destroy reality in order to replace it with a forcefully imposed "second reality." And his resistance to collectivization because of its hostility to the dignity and personal identity of individuals that is evident in *Law Without Force* remained one of Niemeyer's basic reasons for opposing communism.

Although Niemeyer did not publish any other works specifically on international law after *Law Without Force* he did write on international relations and foreign policy, where he maintained the separation between ethics and foreign policy apparent in this book. In *Law Without Force* Niemeyer argues that morality did not properly apply to international relations because morality is actually a restraint imposed on the irrational passions, and so it cannot apply to activities inspired by some kind of social or pragmatic reason, that is, morality is a restraint on arbitrariness but is superfluous where some form of rationality is already in charge. (At this state of his thinking he has not yet distinguished pragmatic from substantive rationality.) In a 1980 essay, "Foreign Policy and Morality: A Contemporary Perspective," he provides a better explanation for separating foreign policy from morality. He argues that government has an intimate connection to ethics in "its foundations in habit, the accretion of common sense judgments and assessments of many generations, and in human nature, the philosophical yardstick for what is appropriate to the good life,"[3] that is, he saw a close relation between the functional political order and ethics on the basis of the reality and the good of human life. However, he did not see the same close relation between states, between "wholes" that are not "natural" substances as individuals are and that have "no center of normative experience resembling the human soul." Therefore, foreign policy is not so directly related to the existential truth of human nature as governments are because foreign policy is not immediately concerned with fostering the good life but rather with preserving the existence and promoting the interests of "an artifacted whole" whose characteristics are not really "given," as human beings have experienced morality as "given." Observing that traditionally, and with few exceptions, European diplomacy has conducted power and trade relations in a morally neutral way, Niemeyer concludes that "in foreign affairs the moral element is, what it has always been, an outsider, an element of culture rather than politics."[4]

The only exception he made to his exclusion of morality from foreign policy—and it was a clearly and forcefully made exception—was in the case of communism, which he called "an historically new form of massively evil power that knows no bounds." Because of communism's hostility to reality Niemeyer believed the West had a moral obligation to resist it, even at the risk of war. This meant, in practice, a distinction in foreign policy between authoritarian and totalitarian regimes, a distinction that Niemeyer found both substantively and pragmatically rational. In a 1966 article, "National Self-Defense and Political Existence," Niemeyer observed that "we take it for granted that nobody today thinks of morality in the terms of that caricature drawn up in the eighteenth century, a body of cut-and-dried abstract principles valid unchangeably for all times and places. Rather, we approach moral problems as Aristotle suggested: as the mature man's rational response to reality, both the fundamental reality of being and his own nature, and the changing reality of time and place."[5] This is prefatory to a discussion of the moral aspects of war in the face of the communist threat, where Niemeyer's argument is that the choice of surrender to communism rather than resistance, the preference for physical existence over the love of truth, amounted to nihilism. That is, Niemeyer subordinated pragmatic to substantive rationality and was arguing for a rationality grounded in the truth of order. Even in *Law Without Force* he had maintained that "the result of arbitrary power inside a system of government can be just as fatal to creative life, to human productivity and progress, and to the development of culture, as the fight between nations." He went on to argue that imposition of a dictatorial world government is not an acceptable means of avoiding war: "Fundamentally this means the disposition to do precisely what the now totalitarian nations have done: to sacrifice the values of personality and autonomous development for the value of security."

For all his insistence on the moral imperative of resisting communism, Niemeyer was adamantly opposed to a universally moralistic foreign policy because it would inevitably be in conflict with reality. It would have to ignore the fundamental distinction between the unprecedented evil of communism and the common "personal-habitual" type of evil so that, like communism, such a foreign policy would be perfectionist and would have to aim at eliminating evil in general, which would require the government to be either a universal avenger or a universal redeemer possessed of perfect virtue itself. Also, a government that sought to bring other people to its understanding of the good life would be acting as though it were the state of which all people in the world were citizens, contrary to reality.

On this basis he was highly critical of the injection of "human rights" into American foreign policy because he saw it as an American pretension to be a "world supervisor, a global governess, chiefly in dealing out punishment to our friends," and he saw the UN as burdened with the expectation that it would function as "a kind of embryonic world government."[6] Both errors were rooted in a dream of perfection caused by mixing pragmatic politics with "misplaced religious expectations," that is, both denied reality.

Also, Niemeyer always rejected the "Robinson Crusoe" thesis that man is fundamentally a self-sufficient atomistic individual, an "autonomous man" existing in a kind of private universe. Niemeyer believed that human beings are social by nature and find meaning only by participating in a divine order of reality. The disorders endemic to conceiving of individuals without connectedness—to each other, to reality, to God—individuals as "autonomous," or, really, solipsistic, and who lack the essential "deference to reality and subservience to truth," are eloquently described in his 1974 essay "The Autonomous Man."[7] While his later thinking had a metaphysical depth lacking in his earlier idea of "man-in-coordination" there is continuity in the thinking. He was always an opponent of collectivism and ideology because of their hostility to the dignity and personal identity of individuals and to the truth of social institutions and practices created by those individuals. But he later came to understand the substantive irrationality of the ideological total critique, which defined the good as essentially the opposite of what exists, that is, it claimed that what is real is actually unreal, at least compared with a future perfection, that the existing institutional structures of society are the source of evil, and that there is no truth in human nature as we now know it. Although Niemeyer in 1941 had not yet conceived of the total critique explicitly, the roots of this concept were already present in his commitment to look straight into the face of realities.

In short, *Law Without Force* remains of interest for several reasons. It shows how a first-rate mind grappled with a legal, historical, social, and ultimately metaphysical problem, even with inadequate conceptual tools and conclusions. Through Niemeyer's analysis it provides much insight into the development of the problem under the aspect of international law and the ways in which legal scholars attempted to deal with it. It provides, in detail, the reasoning behind Niemeyer's rejection of a foreign policy based on morality and his distinction, in foreign policy, between authoritarian and totalitarian governments; and it provides us with the first stage of Niemeyer's lengthy and prodigious effort to understand the problems and disorders of "this terrible century." To slightly paraphrase a comment by one of the book's reviewers, it is a book that no serious student of Niemeyer can afford to ignore.

Michael Henry

Notes

1. Eric Voegelin, *Science Politics, and Gnosticism*, Henry Regnery Company, Chicago, 1968, p. 5.
2. See Gerhart Niemeyer, *Aftersight and Foresight: Selected Essays*, The University Press of America and the Intercollegiate Studies Institute, Lanham, MD, 1988, p. 83.
3. Ibid., p. 139.
4. Ibid., p. 140.
5. Ibid., p. 116.
6. Ibid., p. 221.
7. Ibid., pp. 3-13.

PREFACE

THIS book outlines a hypothesis which applies not only to international law but also to the entire problem of legal order in the present epoch. The general idea set forth in it might be roughly indicated in these words: Law (and social order in general) is concerned only with relationships, and not with separate individuals or groups of individuals. Therefore the standards of legal order ought to be derived from the idea of interrelated and coordinated activities, and not from the idea of the independent existence of persons.

To many this may seem an abandonment of the time-honored values of individualism. Actually, however, it constitutes an attempt to safeguard individuality against the growing threat of collectivization. In a period in which social life requires an increasing degree of rational coordination, it is necessary to emphasize that the "existence" of human beings is not the concern of social organization and legal order. Law's domain consists of the activities through which people are connected with each other; but the integration and perfection of each man's solitary "existence" is a task incumbent solely on him alone. This is the fundamental idea underlying the functional conception of law, a conception which to me seems imperative today, lest in a thoroughly planned society human individuality should become a product of social organization.

This book is not a final result. It does not draft a program of international order; it merely indicates a new direction. Whether progress in this direction is possible is not for me to decide. Not to one person but to an entire generation belongs the task of breaking the ground for a new structure of international law. This realization seems to justify a book on functional conceptions which deliberately withholds suggestions of a scheme of action. It is to the community of my fellow-workers in the international field that I submit this hypothesis for correction. It is their criticism, advice and help that I seek in publishing this volume.

As the book is meant to offer a thesis, and not a complete survey of the problem, it does not contain a full bibliography. The works listed are mainly those from which I derived stimulation, material and ideas. It seemed to me a point of intellectual integrity to give the fullest possible evidence of the German sources on which I fed for so long a time. Space prohibited entering into polemics with other schools of functional thought. Since the presentation of the main features of a theory is the primary intent of this book, not only polemics, but also some of the detailed aspects of the thesis itself, must be left for future publications. It seemed advisable to confine this particular study to the general implications of a functional theory of international law.

The book is dedicated to the memory of the man whose spirit guided me throughout the four years of work. Hermann Heller's teaching inspired me with his ideas; his living inspired me with the example of an extraordinary man, outstanding in qualities both of soul and mind, a man to whom the rational mastery of political reality meant a profound human responsibility and thus a personal task. His urge to penetrate the phenomena of political association with the clarity of the spirit sprang not from a mere intellectual interest in his work but from the depth of his soul, which suffered from arbitrariness and the lack of order in politics much as a man may suffer from the moral inadequacies of his own nature. Yet the strength of his character made him look straight into the face of realities, without flinching from their ugliness or covering their features with the veil of wishful thinking. Hermann Heller's life and death were a constant and forceful proclamation of the idea that to realize a genuinely rational order in the political side of human culture is not merely a pragmatic, but an ethical requirement.

GERHART NIEMEYER

Department of Politics
Princeton University
November 5, 1940

ACKNOWLEDGMENTS

THE completion and publication of this book would not have been possible without the spiritual and material aid which I received from many quarters. The Society for the Protection of Science and Learning, of London, enabled me to find such conditions of work as constitute the prerequisite of any free research. Princeton University generously contributed funds which were needed for the preparation and publication of the book. To both institutions, as well as to the Carl Schurz Memorial Foundation, I am deeply indebted for the general and specific help which they granted me.

Professor William S. Carpenter of Princeton University supported my work throughout the period of writing, not only by his tolerance, his confidence and his understanding, but also by his energetic help in overcoming practical difficulties. It is to him that I owe the opportunity of doing work of this type without being disturbed by intellectual or material pressure from without. To Professor J. B. Whitton I am obliged for a valuable opportunity of testing my thesis, which he provided by making the uncompleted manuscript the object of a discussion in his seminar on international law. Mrs. F. A. Lutz devoted herself with a rare talent of understanding to the task of editing the manuscript and giving to my often heavily involved sentences an adequate English expression. Her conscientious and yet imaginative revision of the text puts me very much in her debt. Equal gratitude is due to Professor D. F. Bowers of the Philosophy Department of Princeton University, for his invaluable assistance in the organization and wording of the third part.

There are many other colleagues and personal friends who have read parts of the manuscript, have offered advice and much needed criticism. There are many who were ready to discuss the topic of the book in long conversations, which often changed essentially the direction of my research. There are many who have aided me on problems of language or by their general interest. It seems to me that to mention their names here would not be in accordance with the warm personal feelings that were established between these helpers and myself. As their contributions sprang from sympathy and kindliness, so my gratitude is an immediate and direct one which does not require any public expression.

Finally—though only in a chronological sense—I wish to thank Director J. A. Brandt and the staff of Princeton University Press for a comradeship-in-work which made of the tedious business of printing and publishing an enriching experience.

Two excerpts from this book were published as separate articles. A condensation of chapters I and II in part I appeared under the title "International Law and Social Structure" in vol. 34 of the *American Journal of International Law.* The introduction to part III was published in its entirety in vol. XVIII of the *New York University Law Quarterly Review* (also series 2, number 2 of the *Contemporary Law Pamphlets*).

G. N.

INTRODUCTION

THE UNREALITY OF INTERNATIONAL LAW AND THE UNLAWFULNESS OF INTERNATIONAL REALITY

INTRODUCTION

THE WAR AND THE PROBLEM OF RECONSTRUCTION

ON THE First of September, 1939, an international disaster marked the end of an epoch in the public order of the world. The generation which had to bury its hopes of peace, security and harmony on that day is called upon to stand up and make a new effort to master the difficulties of international politics. The task demands the energy of unsentimental thinking, regardless of the prejudices which may have to be sacrificed. Two problems have to be faced: The first is to give an unflinchingly realistic account of the past, the second is to try to conceive an alternative for the future.

With the realization that the catastrophe was but the consequence of the crisis that befell the post-war system of collective security and international justice, a gloomy query at once arises: How was it possible for all the provisions, standards and procedures of an entire system of international order to collapse almost simultaneously, leaving to the world only the alternative of national armaments, national self-sufficiency and national power politics, an alternative which was bound to beget war as its *ultima ratio?* And, provided this question is answerable, a second one follows in its wake: What will be the shape of things to come after the struggle; along what lines can a new order of international politics be imagined?

The world began to ask these questions long before the actual outbreak of the war placed them in the foreground of everyone's concern. The development in the post-war period by the great powers of a planned framework of international relations, had added to the traditional rules and principles of international law a complicated system of instruments, institutions, procedures and organizations. This fact had given rise to a general hope for some of that stability, in international politics, which the modern state had accomplished within national boundaries. But when the failure to achieve a world economic settlement, the breakdown of disarmament, the successful invasions of Manchuria and Abyssinia and the unhindered intervention in Spain's civil war disillusioned this hope, doubt began to arise as to the soundness of the standards of order which prevailed. As soon as the crisis in the structure of post-war international order was realized, the question began to be asked: How far does the crack in this machinery reach down into the underlying foundations of traditional international law? Are we witnessing a general "decline of international standards," as Sir Alfred Zimmern put it, or does the breakdown affect only the too ambitious superstructure, leaving intact enough substance at the bottom to enable us to continue on the same basis? This latter opinion has been advanced especially by Professor J. L. Brierly, who points out that in spite of a few spectacular violations, the bulk of international law still functions quietly and steadily. Accordingly, he concludes, we have no real cause for anxiety, any more than we should to despair of law and order in any national community, because of the occasional infractions of the law by criminal elements.

The issue between these two points of view is a vital one. For since we are confronted with the task of reshaping the order of international relations, it is essential to know exactly how much or how little is left of the one that used to exist. If the foundations of the old one are still sound, it will be feasible, and sensible too, to establish a new order on the same lines, though with some technical modifications. If, however, the very foundations are cracked, they will have to be re-laid before we can start to construct the building of another order among the states.

THE BREAKDOWN OF WORLD ORDER OUTLINED

A brief general survey of the extent of the catastrophe may be required before the present situation can be analyzed. The system of international law which through centuries had functioned in the form of a set of rules and standards, had eventually hardened into an elaborate complex of institutions, organizations, precise prescriptions and juristic doctrines. The manifold devices composing this structure may be grouped under five general headings corresponding to the ends they served. In this way we are able to show to what degree the great powers had cast aside the spirit and the letter of each group of laws during the last ten years.

First, there were rules and devices meant to compel states to respect each other's sovereignty, territory and legitimate interests. For instance, several articles of the Covenant of the League of Nations were inspired by this idea, and in addition there were various instruments guaranteeing states and boundaries, such as the Nine Power Treaty, the Locarno Treaties, the guarantees of Austria and Czechoslovakia, and the numerous clauses containing assurances of friendship and mutual respect, which were to be found in countless bilateral treaties. This part of international order was disregarded in principle by Japan (in her relations with Manchuria and China), Italy (in the case of Abyssinia, Spain, Albania), Germany (Austria, Czechoslovakia, Spain, Lithuania, Slovakia, Poland), Russia (Poland, Finland, Baltic States), England and France (Austria, Czechoslovakia). The list does not pretend to be complete, nor does it include any violations of this part of international law made during the war for the sake of military strategy.

Secondly, there were rules and devices that were meant to compel states to abstain from imperialistic aggression and preparation for it. Apart from the provision for automatic assistance against an aggressor under the League Covenant, this group included the Kellogg Pact, the General Convention signed at Geneva in 1931, the naval treaties and other restrictions on armaments that had been stipulated among the great powers. Moreover there was an entire system of non-aggression pacts in existence between individual states, as well as assurances of mutual assistance of a purely defensive character, of which the ultimate aim was also solely that of barring aggression. This section of international law and order was never even completed. Two of the most important attempts to make it into a system of preventive and prohibitive measures against aggression failed to succeed: the Disarmament Convention and the Geneva Protocol of 1924. The Kellogg Pact, although signed and ratified, never became an effective rule of law, its entire history being one of constant violations. Of the remainder, not a single provision stands intact. League security died during its first serious test in 1935. As for the rest, it suffices to point to the general disillusionment both of statesmen and of the public all over the world, without enumerating the various occasions on which countries were attacked, or abandoned in face of an attack, without even so much as a formal denunciation of the relevant legal obligations. There can be no doubt that the law which was meant to safeguard the world against aggressive wars has not merely failed: it has entirely disappeared.

The third set of precepts in post-war international politics consists of those rules and devices which were meant to compel states to submit their disputes to an impartial judge and to refrain from executing the law themselves. This to many people was the most important link in the structure of world order, since it was widely believed that wars resulted from concrete grievances and quarrels. If only such quarrels could be settled by an impartial judge instead of by each state judging for itself, the main source of international disorder would be destroyed. So ran the argument. Modern internationalism, inspired by this idea, was the midwife of the various institutions and legal rules centering around the notion of judicial decision: The Permanent Court of Arbitration and the Permanent Court of International Justice, both at The Hague, the various claims commissions, commissions of conciliation and inquiry, tribunals of arbitration, and so on, established by special agreement between various states. A dense network of arbitration and conciliation treaties, mostly modeled on a common pattern, was established among the world's nations in the post-war period. The so-called Optional Clause, signed and ratified by the majority of the world's states, including the Great Powers, obligated them to submit to the jurisdiction of the Permanent

Court of International Justice all conflicts in which action was brought by one state against another. The idea of judicial settlement of international disputes, however, was profoundly shaken after the fateful decision of the World Court in the question of the Austro-German Customs Union, and it was entirely discredited by the farce of arbitration in the Italo-Ethiopian conflict, and by the failure to arbitrate the Sudeten issue between Germany and Czechoslovakia, despite the invocation of the existing arbitration treaty by the latter. Today it can safely be said that scarcely any real hope for the effectiveness of the arbitration idea is entertained in responsible quarters. States have been destroyed by other nations with which they had signed arbitration agreements, again without even a denunciation of the law. Not merely the respect for, but the very spirit of, this part of the post-war order seems to be dead.

The fourth group of legal provisions was meant to compel states to respect international agreements. There are only a few concrete rules and devices in this section, such as the article of the Covenant which provides for a peaceful revision of existing treaties. As for the rest they consist mostly of doctrines, standards and traditional principles regarding the sanctity of treaties. They have been crystallized in speeches and notes by statesmen, in common resolutions made by international conferences and institutions, such as the manifesto of the Stresa Conference of 1935, and the repeated resolutions of the League (in connection with violations of the law by Japan, Italy, and Germany). In spite of these professions of faith in the binding character of agreements, the law-abiding respect for treaties has been deliberately disregarded in the case of the following major instruments: the Covenant of the League, the Treaty of Versailles, the Nine Power Treaty, the Protocol accompanying the Optional Clause, the Locarno Pact, the Non-Intervention Agreements, the Munich Pact, the Rome Protocols; and in the case of the following bilateral treaties, to mention only some of the more important ones: the Italo-Abyssinian treaty of friendship, the German-Polish non-aggression pact, the German-

Czech treaty of friendship and arbitration, the Austro-German agreement of 1936, the German-British naval treaty, the German-British peace pact, the Franco-Czech treaty of mutual assistance, the Russo-Polish treaty of non-aggression. The list seems impressive enough to warrant the assertion that the habit of observing treaties has given way to a habit of disregarding treaties as soon as they become inconvenient from the point of view of a state's interests, or at best to a habit of abusing treaties by disregarding their spirit and observing the letter for the sake of diplomatic advantage. It cannot be said, under those circumstances, that the law concerning the sanctity of agreements remains in any way an effectual principle of international relations.

The fifth and last group of international legal provisions consists of rules and devices meant to compel states to make compensation for injurious acts and for violations of the law. The main items in this group consist of those sanctions which were not specifically directed against imperialistic aggression, but against any infringement of legal obligations. Of the whole system of post-war order, this part alone seems to have been left unscathed, mainly because of its secondary character.

PASSING SICKNESS OR ORGANIC DISEASE?

Although the crisis seems to have affected almost all branches of the post-war system of world order, although it seems to have brought about an all but complete collapse of its mainstays, some people argue that this is only a passing period of lawlessness, after which there will be a return to normalcy, i.e. respect for the established rules of international law. The fact that the system of international law is violated from time to time, they say, does not destroy the validity of its commands. Such infractions occur daily even in the best ordered community. If the existence of crime and criminals does not shake our faith in law and order, the existence of unruly states should not do so either.

One of the aims of this book is to prove that the crisis of international order which has been outlined above is not merely a series of incidental violations but that it is symptomatic of a world-wide decline of faith, not in international order as such, but in the particular system of international order which has been in operation in the Western world. And this book is meant to emphasize especially that the general scepticism affects not only the post-war scheme of institutions and legal provisions, but the very essence of traditional international law as practised among the nations of Occidental culture for three hundred years. If this assumption should prove true, the conclusion is inevitable that any new international order which is erected on the foundations and in the spirit of this seventeenth century tradition underlying present international law will meet with the same fate of ineffectiveness and defeat at the hands of political reality.

Our thesis is therefore that *political reality has become unlawful, because the existing system of international law has become unreal.* Only a few indications of the main lines of this argument can be given in this introduction.

It is certainly true that occasional violations do not affect the validity of the law. No number of assassinations can ever establish a rule of murder. But a comparison between states under international law and the criminal under domestic law misses the point. The criminal recognizes and accepts the legal order as it stands: he only tries to get away with an exception in his favor. By contrast a state which explicitly or implicitly denies the binding force of an international obligation does not merely infringe the law, but rejects it. If a parallel is to be drawn between international law and the law concerning individuals, the rejection of legal obligations by states is equivalent not to a contravention of the law but to a revolt against it.

As long as such revolts, occurring more frequently in the international field than within the states, are merely directed against a single treaty or some other detail of international order, the world can put up with them. The public has long been resigned to the fact that the violent rejection of some legal provision is the only practical way by which international law can be adjusted to swiftly moving reality. It has been regarded as an unfortunate but inevitable shortcoming of international law that it is exposed to periodic changes at the hands of lawbreakers. But the crisis of the last ten years was not merely a series of revisions of particular rules by force. For the cases of broken obligations, of which some examples were enumerated above, signify only the more spectacular breaches torn in the wall of rules protecting the world against disorder. They were accompanied by other developments which revealed an even more radical destruction of the international sense for order. These were not outright violations, but systematic distortions and abuses of international rules, standards and institutions, under the disguise of lip-service to the letter of the law. The French used the League as a keystone in the building of their own particular system of security; the British disavowed it as soon as it conflicted with their traditional Empire policy; the Russians professed an austere legalism which was calculated, however, to produce not lawful but political results; the Italians attempted to break the League through cooperating within its framework. All the nations participating in the Non-Intervention Committee were agreed that, through the operation of that institution, they were covering and sanctioning an established policy of intervention in Spain. The absence of a declaration of war was seriously held to be the equivalent to the non-existence of a state of war. The avoidance of bloodshed during the annexation of one country by another was considered to fulfil the requirement of respect for the sovereignty and independence of nations. Terms like war, peace, neutrality, intervention, sovereignty, independence, self-determination, self-defense, and so on, which form an integral part of the verbiage on which international law depends, were distorted beyond recognition, and then were accepted at this false face value in the endeavor to twist the wording of the law so that it might fit and cover unlawful situations and illegal procedures. Far more than the sensational cases of open defiance, these and numerous other examples of concealed lawlessness demonstrate how far the real foundations of international law and order have been undermined. They reveal to what extent the sense for law has ceased to be an effective factor in the decisions of statesmen. They show that even the capacity for distinguishing between what is right and what is wrong has largely disappeared, and that a formal observance of legal technicalities, an empty shell without any substance in it, is all that is really left of international order.

This degeneration of the very medium of law—the sense for the meaning of its provisions and the capacity to discriminate between right and wrong, just and unjust, legal and illegal—indicates that the breakdown of the post-war system was the result not merely of an unfortunate sequence of external circumstances. It was symptomatic of a fundamental crisis in our entire conception of international law, going far deeper than what happened to be the historical expression of that conception in the post-war period. This becomes more evident if we recall briefly the basic tenets on which international law has rested since its beginnings in the early seventeenth century.

When at that time some eminent thinkers, headed by Hugo Grotius, conceived a system of law which should govern the relationships between sovereign states, they did so by applying to the affairs of states four fundamental notions, borrowed from the sphere of private individuals, and derived from Roman law. Those concepts were person, property, contract and injury, introduced into international law by Zouch as: *status, dominium, debitum* and *delictum*. These were considered axiomatic categories of law and order in general, and since a state was regarded as a member of the society of states, in analogy to the position of the individual in the society of individuals, it was natural that the standards of international relations should be formulated with the help of these notions.

From these four initial positions, various postulates and principles were derived, which in the course of centuries developed into so many branches of international law. The idea that in the beginning of society there was the *person*, for instance, led to the formulation of the rule that the existence and the independence of states must be respected as a fundamental right. A host of concrete applications of this standard can be found in different provisions of international law. Main derivations from this basic notion are the doctrine postulating the equality of states, the idea that no state can be another state's judge in a dispute between them, the rules forbidding intervention in each other's affairs, and exempting sovereigns, their representatives and, to some extent, their subjects, from each other's jurisdiction and other similar norms of international law.—On the other hand, the notion of *property*, applied to international relations, produced the principle of the inviolability of the territories of states, and the respect for their territorial integrity. Moreover, this notion was extended to include interests as well as possession. Thus the entire law of neutrality is ultimately an application of the concept of property to international situations. Again, the axiom that *contracts* are binding obligations has become of paramount importance for the whole of international law, since it has been made the very foundation of its obligatory force. Under the influence of a school of thought which essentially reduces international law to the tenet that agreements must be kept, public opinion in the whole world has become accustomed to consider as international law that which has been stipulated between states. Accordingly the respect or lack of respect for agreements is, in the eyes of the public and of most statesmen, identical with the test of the effectualness of international law as such. Finally, the notion of *injury* has inspired the principle that every state is responsible for injurious acts committed by its officials, and that sanctions against a wrongdoer among states are a legitimate form of compulsion in international politics.

Throughout three centuries, these basic tenets have formed the core of international law. They have been elaborated, by application to various situations, into concrete and detailed prescriptions, and they have appeared in different practical shapes as social conditions changed. But however modified and developed in the course of this period, international law has continuously rested on these four conceptual pillars. They form its very essence; they represent the fundamental orientation of international order from Grotius to Briand.

The post-war framework of international law was nothing but the ultimate consequence of those original axioms. The idea of collective organization, for instance, follows directly from the concept of *person.* For one cannot think of *person* without at the same time imagining a collectivity composed of a number of persons. And just as the idea of *person* evokes the idea of personal interest, so the concept of community is connected with the assumption of collective interest. Common interest, however, calls for collective organization. Thus the postulate of an international organization is but the logical consequence of the axiomatic notion of *person* in international law. In the same way the other main parts of the post-war system were highly representative of the four basic tenets of international law.

Accordingly, when the statesmen of most of the great powers acted on the idea that some states are not worthy to be respected as independent and sovereign nations, when they disregarded the law of non-intervention and neutrality, when they not only condoned but actually sanctioned the forceful abrogation of international treaties, and when they concluded that it might be not only inexpedient but also unjust to carry out sanctions against an offender, they were really abandoning not only the post-war line, but also the fundamental positions of that law of nations which had been the usage for the last three hundred years. Their attitude toward its basic tenets manifested their innermost conviction—however reluctant they may be consciously to admit it—that the application of these legal axioms to modern conditions in international politics was no longer acceptable to them. They revealed the fact that the fundamental notions of traditional international law have ceased to give effective guidance to them when they envisage problems of international order. They displayed all the symptoms of a fundamental crisis in international law not only as it stood after 1918, but as it was conceived by Grotius and practised by states ever since.

WHERE TO LOOK FOR THE CAUSE

What has happened? Why should international law, which was vigorously surging upward only twenty years ago, have become almost a dead letter now? The picture we have drawn of the role of international law in modern international relations did not show only cases of violation or disregard of the law. It also showed the prevalence of profound indifference toward its standards, often even an entirely cynical attitude, of which the most typical manifestation is the systematic abuse of legal rules, betraying the lack of any sense of obligation regarding its standards. This phenomenon is so general that obviously it would not do to meet it simply with exhortations and admonitions. If the real shape of things is consistently at odds with our ideas about it, the only possible attitude is to accept the facts and try to adapt our theories to their trend. Accordingly it seems futile to insist on the theory of international order which used to apply before the breakdown, and to bridge the gap between it and reality by lamenting the lack of a strong enough appeal of international standards in the present world. Instead it seems imperative to set out from the empirical observation that present-day international law on the whole fails to exert a sufficiently binding effect on some of the most important states.

Now we know that international law depends, for its effectiveness, almost entirely on the element of obligation, or moral appeal. Its rules cannot be enforced systematically. Only to a very limited degree is international law backed by sanctions in the form of physical compulsion. The main basis for its binding effect on the will of governments and nations has been, throughout the centuries, the "age-old principles of morality, as applied originally to the individual," to borrow the words of Professor Reeves. Because it was the universally recognized duty of governments to respect certain rules of conduct regarding the relations between states, and because the content of these rules corresponded to recognized standards of morality, international law was capable of exercising, on the whole, a binding effect on the states.

Consequently the most common explanation of the present inefficiency of international law is that good will on the part of the separate states is lacking. "International law, not being enforced by a collective organization, cannot be realized except by good will on the part of the governments and other representatives of states. Therefore the crisis of international law can only be overcome by spreading the ideal of an international order of compulsory arbitration, of a more efficient league of nations, and of international conciliation": thus runs the argument most frequently heard in both expert and lay circles. However, let us, for a moment, examine more closely the conception involved. The correctness of the factual statement is obvious: there *is* a lack of good will on the part of the states as regards international law. But what does that mean?

The requisite of good will as a condition of the effectualness of international law implies the idea of a moral obligation to carry out legal rules according to their true meaning. If we say that in general there is no longer any good will in the field of international law, we are saying that morality is consistently proving ineffective as a means of securing the adjustment of the states' behavior to the legal prescriptions as they stand at present. So far the tireless preaching of politicians and scholars has not brought about a change in this attitude of governments. Are we really to assume that the world is governed by a set of gangsters who are simply unable to respect the law owing to their lack of moral instinct and their criminal character? Or is it not more reasonable to suppose that the men who head states and represent nations are just as good or just as bad, just as wise or just as stupid, as rulers, with a few exceptions, always have been? Is it not sensible to seek a more realistic explanation for the failure of both international ethics and international law than to assert simply that the quality of the human element has declined? If we are to follow this line, it means starting out from the fact that ethics are no longer an efficient medium for a legal order of interstate relations. Refusing to believe that the moral sense of men all over the world has disappeared, one might therefore conclude that nations could have become so separated from each other that their mutual relations have sunk to a negligible quantity, and that they can afford, from their own point of view, to dispense with international law and order, because it is not required. But such an explanation is ruled out by even a superficial observation of reality. The world is economically and politically interdependent. Events and developments during recent years have proved beyond any doubt that this interdependence, far from diminishing, is actually increasing in proportion to the increase in the number of individuals living by industrial employment in the various nations. The very experience of the self-sufficiency policies of many countries has brought to light their interconnection with the social and economic structure of other countries.

If the world neither can do without an international order nor has suddenly lost its moral conscience, we necessarily come to the conclusion that the reason international law is ineffectual is that in its present form it neither serves the need, nor appeals to the moral sense of, the modern world. Therefore the cause for the breakdown of the international order must be sought in international law itself, in the inadequacy of its concepts, the obsoleteness of its standards, the unreality of its rules.

THE DIFFICULTIES OF REMEDYING THE SITUATION

If the duty to obey the law is consistently disregarded by nations and statesmen, whose sense of obligation is otherwise active and awake, it can only be because this duty is in conflict with another obligation of statesmen: the obligation to act in accordance with reality and with a view to the practical consequences resulting from their acts and affecting countless individuals. In other words: international law is being put aside because it has drifted so far away from the realities of politics that it has become even morally justifiable to defy it.

Governments head states, i.e. institutions exercising practical functions in definite social situations. If the most elementary requirements of their task are at odds with the existing rules of international law, the practical sense of governments comes into conflict with their legal conscience, and, since the practical ends of government are considered to be the primary responsibility of statesmen, necessarily succeeds in winning the victory.

Now there seems to be an easy remedy for such a situation. What we seem to need is a comprehensive revision of existing rules, a redrafting of the provisions of international law, which would reconcile the political with the legal criterion, and would enable governments to abide by the norms of international law without having to disregard the responsibility pertaining to their office.

But here the real difficulties begin. Both the main lines and the details of international law have been thoroughly and scientifically redrafted several times. There is scarcely any suggestion made by statesmen or scholars of international law during the past century which has not been, at one time or another, the subject of some international agreement, convention, conference, research or negotiation. We have no reason to believe that any other variety of the main themes around which the discussion of international law has centered so far would meet a fate different from that of the League of Nations, the World Court, the Arbitration System or the Disarmament Conference. It is precisely these main themes which have been rejected wholesale during the recent crisis. In other words: the possibilities of the existing framework of international law are utterly exhausted. There is nothing we can hope for from a further development of its basic ideas, nothing we can expect that has not already been suggested, tried and defeated.

This book advances the thesis that, with our present conceptual equipment, we are incapable of redrafting the rules of international order so as to make them fit the changed political conditions. The very axioms of our thinking on international law are inadequate to fit the real situation. Whatever legal scheme, device, rule or prescription could be formulated within the traditional framework of international legal concepts will necessarily be in hopeless conflict with international politics, and will consequently continue to be overruled by the laws of that political reality.

The theory on which this book proceeds is, accordingly, that an obsolete and inadequate way of thinking is just as disastrous to the possibility of establishing order in the real world as is war or rebellion. In fact it is even more disastrous than these spectacular events of disorder, because it is constantly producing unfitting concepts and consequently ineffectual rules. The initial standpoint from which we view reality conditions the perspective in which we see it. Thus the fundamental importance we attribute to certain features of reality compels us to see all other things in a specific light, and to form certain ideas and concepts about the nature of the living world around us. To use the words of Professor R. S. Lynd: "The controlling factor in any science is the way it views and states its problems. Once stated, a problem can yield no further insights than are allowed by the constricting frame of its original formulation."

The picture which we have of the world determines our impulses and our initiatives in it. We move in conformity with the world as it lives in our consciousness or subconsciousness. We map our course of action according to the notions through which we comprehend the manifold phenomena of reality. And it is with those concepts that we operate in our reflection on reality. We use them as links in the chain of our conclusions, we employ them as units in our formulations, we derive postulates from them and base legal rules on them.

It seems that the basic concepts with which the present system of international law operates are in conflict with a new outlook on reality which compels governments to reject legal standards and rules. A changed attitude toward things social is making itself felt among individuals high and low, which is the chief cause of the difficulties in applying the traditional concepts of international law. Because our image of reality tends to adopt a new shape, the notions corresponding to a perspective of past centuries fail to fit our world. Thus, for example, we realize the need for international order because of the *interdependence* of states. Yet in thinking about international law we still imagine states as separate units existing in physical *isolation* from each other. We are searching for rules to govern the *common* relations of nations, but we still attempt to base those rules on the *particular* interest and on the subjective will of each. We are intent on finding some principle of *order* in international politics, and all that we can think of is a collective accumulation of *force* to be turned against single states, as if states were wicked boys instead of social institutions.

Why is this so? An attempt will be made in this book to prove that it is the inevitable result of the basic assumptions underlying our ideas of international reality and international order. These initial positions force us, more than any external influence could do, to proceed along a certain line of thought and action, which is precisely that line which leads to the results of the post-war period. Consequently any real reform, any fundamental change, any reconstruction of international law has to start here, at the conceptual root of the shortcomings of the present system. It is not merely a theoretical issue. There is no reality that is more compelling than the tacit premise conditioning all our actions. There is no force that is as inescapable as the images which dominate the subconscious layers of the mind, just because these notions seem so self-evident, so needless of discussion and consideration. And there is no obstacle that more persistently obstructs any practical progress than basic concepts which have been passed down to us, unrevised and unadjusted, from a different age, and which, though outlived, still mold, unnoticeably, a living reality.

LAW WITHOUT FORCE

Accordingly, this is a book about the notions which condition the present system and the actual practice of international law and order. At the same time, it is an attempt to revise those conceptual foundations in the light of the political, social, and mental pattern of our times. There is a negative side to this task, and a positive one. Any construction of a new international order is impossible unless the ultimate reasons for the failure of the present one have been uncovered. The mental roots out of which those ill adapted concepts and inadequate ideas have grown, must be unearthed first. Otherwise they will continue to produce the same schemes of international order which have proved to be futile and even detrimental. But obviously mere criticism, no matter how deepgoing and clarifying, is not enough.

At the time of writing these lines, Europe is engaged in a tremendous struggle, a war which is clearly being fought not so much for the possession of this or that territory, for the prevalence of this or that national interest, but for the sake of the future order which is to govern the international relations of Europe. There is hope in this circumstance. However, this war will have a true and significant meaning only if we know in what direction to steer ultimately. It will mean something more than mere destruction, only if at its end there emerges a lasting and effective order, an order which is organically adapted to the reality of international relations. More important than military efforts are the efforts to recognize and to contemplate the outlines of things to come, once the war is over. That question is already being asked and discussed by the public. However, it must become more than the main topic of general contemplation, it must become the one problem which predominates in all our mental efforts. Readiness for peace is almost more imperative today than readiness for war. This peace is the one great achievement of ordering which the present generation owes, as its foremost task, to the generations that are to come and to those which preceded it.

Public discussion has so far not revealed any new ideas. There seem to be two main trends, already familiar from years of past theorizing: one proposes a union of European states, or even of the world, under a federal régime; the other envisages a revised League, this time equipped with the power to enforce its decisions. The feasibility and the desirability of these plans will be discussed with more detail in later chapters of the book. Of the two, only the League project is a plan of international order in the proper sense of the word. The idea of a federal Europe or a federal World State depends on the capacity of a leading power to obtain from the other nations the consent to be merged into this new giant State. Accordingly it does not depend so much on advance planning, as on political possibilities and feasibilities.

As far as ideas about the nature of a future international order are concerned, however, all projects advanced so far are merely old wine put into new bottles. International order, in the proper sense of the term, cannot be established by organizing an agency of power over and above the separate states, or through any other collective accumulation of force. It cannot materialize in the form of an interstate or super-state police force, but only in that of an effectual system of international law. The effectualness of international law rests fundamentally on its own merits, not on the assumption of some pressure behind it. This is the thesis which this book develops.

States, units of supreme government in human society, are by inherent necessity the highest, most powerful and most efficient organizations in the sphere of social order. Accordingly there can be no effective pressure against a state except by another state. This means that to base international law ultimately on the threat of sanctions is equivalent to basing it on the action, and interest in action, of some great power. This was precisely the fundamental defect of the League scheme, and the reason why it failed in all its practical tests. The same inherent weakness will characterize any system of international order which ultimately relies on force. To threaten states with sanctions means using measures of compulsion against those units which through centuries of social development have proved to be the topmost agencies of power in human society. There is only one form in which compulsion can be employed against these territorial units of social High Command: war. Alexander Hamilton demonstrated this truth with an argument which is of timeless validity.

Consequently an international order which depends on force as its *ultima ratio* is a permanent source of international struggle rather than a medium of order. Grotius and his followers recognized this when they based their system of international law on morality and its binding effect on the minds of men. Those writers regarded it as axiomatic that the law regulating the interrelationship of the most powerful units of social organization could not in turn be secured by organized compulsion. International law was held to be obligatory because, and in so far as, it was inspired by Christian morality. It was effectual inasmuch as the obligations of Christian morality were actually felt by people high and low and influenced their thoughts and actions. The present crisis of international law results from the circumstance that the compelling force of its standards and principles is no longer a real experience. There is no longer any universal moral code which has an equal appeal to all the civilized nations of the world, on the empirical validity of which a law of nations could rest, and from which it could draw a real binding force. Consciously or subconsciously this is being realized everywhere. The very postulate of the necessity for some organized force to secure international law is nothing but an admission that the law of nations has lost its moral appeal, and with it the condition of the directly binding effect of its rules.

Out of this situation there clearly emerges the problem of finding a basis on which a system of international law can function as a set of rules which are binding by virtue of their own merits, and effectual because of their inherent appeal. But if the moral community of the world has been disrupted, if there is no longer a universal moral code, is there anything left which nations still have in common, anything which would appeal equally to men living in different countries? Here lies the main task of the present generation of scholars. Grotius succeeded in establishing not only a theoretical but also a practical system of international law, because he recognized the empirical appeal of rational ethics in the world of his time. An appeal is a psychological reality. It can be observed and analyzed with relative accuracy. It is no less a reality and no less an empirical fact than the action of gunpowder or the convincing argument which lies in the point of a bayonet. To recognize the type of appeal which empirically moves the hands and heads of people in a given cultural pattern is to understand the conditions of law, the fundamental orientation of valuations, which characterize an historical period.

An attempt is made in this book to formulate what seems to be the cultural orientation of our epoch. Past centuries were primarily inspired by the image of the individual "in existence," by the image of *Man Independent.* They felt the appeal of everything connected with the personality, the status, the rights, the sovereign existence of individual beings. Our generation seems to vizualize more the image of the individual "in action," and the corresponding notion of *Man Coordinate.* We feel strongly the appeal not of what separates individuals from one another and from the world, but of everything that enables men to be active, to operate and cooperate, of everything that appertains to the conditions and the forms of meaningful work. The former orientation stressed morality, as a code of inhibitions protecting the status and the existence of individuals. The type of legal order it required was restrictive and authoritative. The new outlook tends to stress organization, as the practical mold of all meaningful coordination. Thus it necessarily arrives at a positive valuation of political functions. For the political institution par excellence, the State, is not only an instrument of the collective interests of a group; it also seems to control the conditions under which men can engage in common activities which are meaningful and socially significant. It is through work that modern man experiences his connection with the world, and the coordination of his existence with the social system. The problem of work, therefore, has become the central preoccupation of our time. This attitude quite naturally tends to place things political, and political reasoning, in the foreground of social values, since the state is the foremost mold of social cooperation which modern society has developed.

It seems that this cultural orientation blocks the functioning of a system of international law based on prohibitive morality, and prevents it from being an effective order of international politics. For the existing law of nations is one that restricts states, inhibits their action, bars their operation.

The new emotional experience, however, reacts positively to whatever enables social institutions to function, and negatively to what prevents them from doing so. It is the valuation of the active function of politics, of the practical meaning of the state in society, which has triumphed over the governments' sense of moral inhibition. Accordingly it must be in this criterion of political function that the basis for a new system of international law can be found.

By virtue of their objective function in social life states are interdependent. Those tasks of social order which they can perform only in conjunction with, or in relation to, other states form the substance of international politics, of conflict as well as of cooperation. It is for handling those affairs with which states cannot deal exclusively within their own boundaries, that international law is required. In other words: connectedness not separateness, interdependence not independence, activity and not mere existence produce the need for an international order. Therefore this order should be conceived not in opposition to, but in accordance with, the ends for which states function.

International law must be more political, if politics is to be more lawful. In this world, in which the political point of view plays such a predominant role internally as well as internationally, there seems to be only one way of an effectual international order: Law instead of acting as a dam, must become the helpful canal, through which functional coordination of states can be achieved, the condition under which states are able to fulfil their functional tasks. Its rules must cease to be abstract commands, they must become the articulations of the immanent laws which govern human activities in the field of political institutions. Just as the law of individuals developed in ancient times as the first *social* science, growing out of the observation and formulation of the standards according to which people actually lived and worked together, so likewise the law of international relations must be made a discipline which studies the inter-connectedness between states, and crystallizes the rules found in it. There is no other way that will lead to an effectual legal order of international politics.

PART I

THE FUNCTION OF LAW IN INTERNATIONAL POLITICS

HISTORICAL INTRODUCTION

A GENEALOGY OF INTERNATIONAL LAW

POLITICAL CONDITIONS SURROUNDING THE BIRTH OF INTERNATIONAL LAW

INTERNATIONAL law covers a field of relationships which first appeared as such in the epoch of the great political reorganization of Europe: the period of consolidation of new political units in the sixteenth and seventeenth centuries. As a consequence of this process, entirely new factual situations arose, for the regulation of which no established rules were available. New norms had to be found, which developed into a whole body of law, destined to provide order for an entire and distinct sphere of social reality. What circumstances brought this new type of relationships into existence? What conditions engendered the need for international law?

Neither Antiquity nor the Middle Ages had a body of international law in the modern sense. Greece, India and China had employed certain rules of interstate intercourse, without reaching the completeness and consistency of our modern system. All that Rome knew, apart from the law applicable to its citizens, was a body of law pertaining to the non-Roman subjects of the Empire. Similarly, the medieval unity of the world admitted only of a law applicable solely to individuals, and centering in the universal authorities of Church and Empire. After the decline of these two universal powers, however, new contenders in the struggle for political power emerged: the Estates on the one hand and the territorial princes on the other. This change produced the historical situation in which the need for a body of international law arose.

The Estates were bodies representing those forces to whom belonged, under the feudal system, the concrete means of power.

Accordingly, the princes, on their part, could rule only by way of the fealty of those elements as represented in the Estates. Thus, when a situation arose in which the princes found themselves under the necessity of carrying on the struggle for political power against the Estates, they could do so only by building up their own means of power in the form of standing armies, which consisted of professional soldiers and were therefore at the disposal of the prince independently of fealty, legal titles and political interests. Professional armies, however, served the purposes of the prince only so long as he was able to pay them regularly. This led to the need for a permanent revenue, and to the introduction of regular taxes, together with the establishment of a permanent, professional and organized bureaucracy.

The first ruler to develop a modern state out of a system of feudal fiefs in this way was the Emperor Frederick II in his kingdom of Sicily. His example proves clearly that the need for a standing army and a permanent navy is the reason for transferring all the regalia of the king, which used to be his private property, to public administration. It is a process of "depersonalization" of the formerly personal powers of the ruler. Instead of legal titles belonging to the king there now appear, besides a public armed force, a public hierarchy of officials, public buildings and ports; this in turn leads to public administration and education. Thus the more or less personal and legal relationship of feudal vassalage gives way to an organized and depersonalized unit of public action: the State.

This development in Frederick's Sicily is only an isolated anticipation of the general European evolution of the State. However, only a hundred years later the Italian city tyrants begin to organize their power in the same way, introducing permanent taxes and employing mercenary soldiers. This type of political order turned out to be so superior to the feudal one that the example of the Italian tyrants, the first rulers to employ it, was soon widely imitated. First in Spain, then in England, France, the German Electorates[1] and other places,

[1] Thus Professor Ziekursch remarks, in an article on the Great Elector: "It was the

the central power of the prince was buttressed by a bureaucratic administration, a system of general taxation and standing armies. After Machiavelli had baptized the new phenomenon with the name *lo stato* and, through the notion of a "Reason of State," had vindicated for the public entity a specific point of view as opposed to personal and private criteria, the idea of the State gradually conquered the entire theory and practice of European politics.

The characteristic feature of the new phenomenon was that it drew a line between political matters and the rest of life, that it separated public affairs, or the "State," from private relationships, or "Society." The feudal system knew of only one comprehensive social order, comprising authority, law and morality in one undifferentiated cosmos of norms. The coordination of all men in a common framework of ordered existence was then achieved by everybody's abiding by the personal duties which pertained to his status and defined his place in the social hierarchy. The ruler had the personal right to demand certain services from his vassals, the vassal had the personal obligation to render certain contributions to his superior's power. This personal and legal tie between high and low, servant and master, lord and vassal, admitted of no distinction between private and public spheres. Every person's entire individuality was linked for good and bad, for peace and war, for what he was and what he had, with the fate of those above and those below him. The new pattern of political order, on the other hand, called only for standardized contributions, to be rendered by the individual to the commonweal. Most of these limited and standardized participations of private persons in public affairs were defined in terms of monetary duties. The commonwealth, in peace as well as in war, ceased to depend on

army which really represented at first the centralized State. For the army's sake the Great Elector undertook the reform of finances and taxes, and consequently the reform of public administration. The power of the Estates was eliminated; the absolute authority of the ruler was established; the foundations were laid for the real union of all his territories. The unified army called for a unified administration, a unified bureaucracy, and a unified financial system." *Frankfurter Zeitung* 1938, Nr. 217 (translation mine).

the active readiness of every vassal, every feudal lord, to fulfil the obligations by which he was responsible to his superior for acts of justice, administration and warfare. Instead it now rested on the action of permanent bureaucrats, who represented the community as such, and who simply demanded from the private individual compliance with their orders, and even that only within the limits of public interest. Thus the individual obtained, apart from his duty of obedience and financial contribution, a non-political sphere in which he enjoyed the freedom of a "private" life, thanks to the "organ-ization," i.e. the separate establishment of an organizational machinery, of public affairs. The corollary of the "depersonalized" order of public affairs, the State, was the "liberalization" of private existence: Society.

INTERSTATE LAW: LAST BEQUEST OF ROMAN UNIVERSALISM

This evolution might not have occurred had not the local consolidation of different states within the orbit of Christianity been counterbalanced by the continuation of the Church as a common and all-pervading element. Notwithstanding the split-up of Christendom into numerous political units, the Church persisted as a common denominator, successfully maintaining its claim to domination of all individual souls. Thus, throughout the realm of occidental civilization the Church maintained a uniform standard of culture, over and against the manifold standards of political power and political interest created by the different states. In this dualism of viewpoints, that of the Church was equivalent to a standard of individual freedom from the requirements of the respective political units, a standard which thus obtained a universal and moral validity. As long as Church and Empire coincided, at least theoretically, in the territorial range of their authority, a dualism between a private sphere of a moral and religious character, and a public sphere of a political and legal character could not arise. The only kind of conflict which was possible under the dual authority of Papacy and Empire was a struggle for competencies and supremacy within the one undifferentiated order. But as soon as the Empire dissolved itself into a plurality of local units, whose respective power interests came into conflict, and whose legal systems became centered in their respective sovereigns, the universal sphere of the Church had to segregate itself from the particular sphere of the State. When this took place, there appeared above the states, quite logically, the doctrine of absolute natural law as the corollary to the relativity of positive law, as enacted by the various states. The notion of the absolute value of the individual soul was adapted to politics in the form of the natural rights of individuals, rights which were conceived uniformly and universally throughout Christendom, in contrast to the changing requirements of political expediency and political power. These "natural" fundamental rights of man were an expression of the universal authority of the Church and its domination of individuals' private lives, which, because of the catholicism of the Church, were saved from being absorbed into the respective laws and interests of the particular states.

It is here that we have to look for the roots of modern international law. The separation of political affairs as a sphere with specific functions and specific laws of its own, from the totality of social life, required a legal boundary-line between the public and the private realms. Since the new order, the State, was essentially a way of administering common concerns by a staff of permanent organs, it was important to secure to these organs the monopoly of political action; and since this new and separate field of politics constituted only a sector of the whole of social life, it was necessary to determine legally how far its function extended into the private sphere of the individual.

It is no coincidence that the first teachers of international law were Spaniards who were, at the same time, priests or monks. For the conquest of America by Spain was the first activity, to be pushed as a state enterprise, i.e. as a public affair, from Europe into the non-Christian world. Here for the first time the distinction between the spheres of State and Society, between public and private interest, between Reason of State and the general human viewpoint, clearly presents itself, not so much in the internal relations between ruler and ruled, as in the external affairs of the state as a whole. In this case the "official" character of the ruler's enterprise is determined by the missionary purpose which, whether actually or only ostensibly, constitutes the motive for conquest. Consequently the rulers of Spain did not display a merely "personal" power, seeking by this expedition to extend their dominion and glory. They functioned, rather, as the organs of a common action, which was a general and objective concern. Thus Spain became the scene of the first external action of a modern state clearly recognizable as such. It became the first functionally circumscribed organization of common affairs. Therefore it is Spain's example which brought to the light of consciousness all the legal problems connected with the new "body politic," in respect to its relations with private individuals as well as with other "bodies politic." There arose two main groups of questions, which may be defined as follows:

1. What relation did his political office establish between the ruler (i.e. the State) and the individual members of the newly discovered peoples?

2. What standards should obtain in such relations, between the conquering state and other states, as resulted from the occupation of new territory which had not previously been subject to Christian rule?

How clearly the leading thinkers of the period realized these problems is illustrated by a significant historic incident. When Columbus, returning from his second voyage, brought home booty consisting of a number of captured Indians, whom he intended to sell as slaves, the king ordered their immediate release. His dictum was that these Indians, being subjects of the crown of Spain, had the same right to personal liberty as every other Spaniard. The conception of the relation between a Christian conqueror and unchristian conquered barbarians as partaking of an official status was something new. At the back of this conception is undoubtedly the idea of authority as a trans-personal office, and that of the state as a territorial organization comprising all people living on its territory, without distinction as to feudal vassalage and fealty. The other complex of questions, too, immediately becomes a practical concern. When Portugal and Spain began to quarrel over the delimitation of their spheres of influence in the New World, it became obvious that the conflict could not be decided by any norms of the traditional Christian order nor by any precedents set by former disputes over competencies or territorial authority. It was in vain that Francis I of France combed the whole Bible in search of a passage which indicated that Spain should own one half of the world and Portugal the other. The famous decision of Pope Alexander VI in 1496, dividing the new conquests into a Spanish and a Portuguese sphere of colonization, is certainly one of the first rules of modern international law.

For international law is nothing but a legal order applying to those relationships which result from the unorganized side-by-side existence of several supreme organizations of social order. The fact that rules concerning these relations were established in the shape of a uniform body of law which was binding on all Christian states, is owing only to the influence of the common Church and its spiritual universalism. It was this universal authority in things cultural and spiritual which made it possible to separate the State, as a relative and local political organization, from the community of all Christians, as an absolute and non-political universe. Without the spiritual counterbalancing of clerical Catholicism against the tendency of the new states to absorb all life into a self-sufficient territorial unit, the rise of a general Christian and European system of law would be unthinkable. The material solidarity of interests transcending state boundaries would never have been able by itself to bring forth a body of international law. Such an interdependence of interests certainly creates a need for international law, but, without a common agency to formulate and elaborate common standards, only isolated and disconnected particular rules would result from this need. A coincidence of interests does not of itself contain the practical possibility of forming a uniform system of law. This is evident by the example of the Greek city-states of Antiquity. There we have a plurality of local political units with a solidarity of culture and interests similar to that which characterized the Europe of 1600. Yet, since every *polis* had its own gods, since religion was intertwined with political order in one undifferentiated system of norms, there was no abolute platform from which to see the relativity of the different states, and no common agency to formulate the rules of common values.[2] Thus, despite the interstate solidarity, it was not possible to overcome the spiritual and religious autarkism of these city-states. Consequently, the Greek community as such never developed a uniform and consistent body of international law, but only isolated usages, treaties and settlements by arbitration, merely practical forms of interstate relations.

Accordingly, it is no mere coincidence that the first writers on international law were Dominicans and Jesuits, the banner-carriers of the Counter-Reformation. The Church, having definitely resigned its claim to temporal authority over the State, insisted energetically on its influence over the spiritual and moral domain. Through the channels of natural law, which as *ius* ranked, with absolute obligatory force, above the State and its *leges*, the Church successfully secured spiritual authority over the whole of Christian territory, under whatever political rule it happened to be.

SPIRITUAL WORLD UNITY AND INTERNATIONAL LAW

This basic idea manifests itself quite clearly in the systems of the great theoreticians of the Counter-Reformation. F. Suarez, for instance, concedes the sovereignty of the territorial princes,

[2] "Not even the fact of participation in a common nationality, culture, religion and speech, not even the experience of common danger . . . , not even the recognition of the endless disaster of intranational division could break the exclusiveness of the city-community." R. McIver, *Community*, p. 293 (by permission of the Macmillan Co., Publishers). The explanation of this fact is simple: in spite of all good intentions, the Greek city-states did not have enough of a common ground to develop a body of standards in which their feeling of solidarity could find juristic expression, each city-state being not only political, but also religious authority.

and their independence of the authority of both Pope and Emperor—which by his time had of course become an undisputable fact anyway. In his mind the notion of Christendom takes the shape of a purely mystical and spiritual community, existing solely in the common faith and in the universal scope of the Papal authority. Among the plurality of autonomous political units the Church remains the one institution of universal range and universal solidarity. The significant conclusion which Suarez draws from this premise is that mankind forms a legal community, which he construes also as a spiritual universalism, but applies to temporal rules. Similarly, the Italian thinker Bellarminus concedes that the political power is autonomous and sovereign in its field. But against a background of ecclesiastical universalism like that of Suarez, he asserts that the officers of the Church have the right to exercise, in so far as the care of Christian souls may require it, an emergency authority in cases in which political government may fail in its task. In the light of these and other lines of thought, which are typical of the Counter-Reformation, it is possible to understand the new notion of international law, as the Spaniards conceived it, as a religious and moral unity of the general human sphere over and against the plurality of political units.

This is the basis on which Spanish legal theory approaches the problem of the colonization of America. In the meantime the universalism of the Church had expanded to embrace the entire world, including all non-believers, the union being purely spiritual and clerical, without a trace of temporal or political claims. Reducing the State to its specific function within this universal community, the great Spanish jurist F. de Vitoria concedes to the warring and conquering political authority certain powers and rights. It was possible to define those competencies of the state, precisely because the sphere of politics had been clearly and sharply separated from the universal union of humanity. War is conceived as an action of the State, i.e. as a specific form of struggle, characterized by its functional meaning. It is a power conflict of political units, not a tussle of men.[3] This notion logically results in the postulate of a law of war, a common set of rules calculated to confine the struggle to the official representatives and the official apparatus of states. States fight each other with their armies, while mankind remains unified in and through the Church. Political units war against each other, but men, being equally valuable and sacred children of the one God, as such live in an unpolitical reservation, a sphere into which this political struggle for power should not penetrate. This is the meaning of the restriction of warfare to military and State personnel, and the exemption from it of the "civil" population—one of the first and most fundamental principles of international law.

But in peacetime, also, this separation of public acts from the civil sphere requires international regulation. Suarez realizes this necessity when he systematically develops a theory of the status of aliens. Every man, as a member of that universal community, enjoys certain rights in whatever political territory he may happen to be. There is a fundamental right of settlement, of work, of freedom of movement, and of a minimum of legal protection. The postulate of such a general status of individuals in foreign countries follows logically from the notion that the State is a human institution with a specific function in society. Consequently it cannot be meant to run counter to the destiny of human life, as embodied in the universal norms of the Church, nor can it be intended to injure the community of mankind, of which the Church and Natural Law are the guardians. The Catholicism of Rome, through its leading thinkers, here performs the last great achievement of its universal domination of the Occident. The last great sway of its scepter sets up a body of universal norms regulating the relations between Man, the universal soul bound to God, and the State, the human institution bound by its function. In so

[3] Of particular significance in this context is the title which the Spanish jurist Ayala gave, in 1582, to his work on international law: *De iure et officiis bellicis et disciplina militari libri tres*. Equally significant is the fact that Ayala defined a just war as a war between sovereign princes, as distinguished from a war between private persons. With regard to this problem of separating war as a public action from all private activities, see also J. Brown Scott, *F. de Vitoria and the Law of Nations* (1934), pp. 206*f*.

far as this grandiose act of legislation introduces order into the relations resulting from the plurality of states, and in so far as it regulates the relations between these states, and their possible effects on individuals, it is the act which lays the foundations of international law.

THE EUROPEAN SOLIDARITY OF THE ESTATES

However, it may be doubtful whether the theoretical structure of the Catholic thinkers would have been sufficient to bring about the general acceptance of a system of international law, had not the historical conditions of those times called for an international order as a social exigency. After all, the idea of the union of mankind, on which the Spanish jurists based their speculations, corresponded, at least in Europe, to a pattern of social and cultural reality. All countries in this area shared equally in the same system of social stratification, the hierarchy of Estates. These Estates had, during the fourteenth century, developed into "international" groups of common interests which "everywhere disrupted and transcended the political enclosure of state territories."[4] The great associations of cities and commercial organizations embraced the whole of Europe with their administrative agencies and their legal and economic relationships. The system of credit, of warehouses and of commercial exchanges, the institution of commercial convoys—briefly, the whole of the indispensable apparatus which had gradually grown up for the satisfaction of material needs all over the Occident, transcended the plurality of states and united them into one common commercial area.

The states as such at first merely served the need for unified military action. They had arisen as a reaction against the insecurity and disintegration of the medieval régime of feudal lords and Estates. To medieval pluralism they opposed the centralized organization of monarchic military power and supreme territorial authority. But the State at first could not, and would not, take over those functions of government which were still adequately managed by the surviving units of the

Hermann Heller, *Staatslehre* (1934), p. 128.

medieval Estates. Such functions were, especially, production and commerce, and also science, education, transport and similar activities. The State replaced the feudal régime, but it did not provide a substitute for the latter's specifically "bourgeois" performances, even where these presupposed the existence of corporate forms of political order, possible rivals of State power. Thus the "bourgeois" aspects of social order retained a vital importance in the social structure, they supplemented the new administration of the State and could not be dispensed with for the moment. Since the State was reluctant or unable to replace the bourgeois corporations in their social function, it followed that they had to be granted a sphere of security and non-interference in which they could operate efficiently and continuously. This condition of security and non-disturbance had to be effected on an international scale, since "bourgeois" activities were themselves international in scope and organization. Inside Europe this requirement was met for the time being by the existence of the Estates, Corporations, and quasi-military commercial unions, such as the Hansa. They formed a European community of interests which, transcending the limits of the separate states, was equipped with its own means of power and protection.

The situation changed, however, when colonies and new commercial areas were acquired and were placed under the immediate sovereignty of the princes. Here the State was confronted with tasks which inside Europe were still performed not by centralized power but by the Estates. How could the security and protection, which were indispensable for the carrying out of the specifically "bourgeois" activities of society, be achieved by the State in interstate relations? The Middle Ages did not know a system of world trade as an integral feature of the social pattern. Thus there were no precedents, no traditional set of standards, no established norms which might secure law and order in this new field of commercial activities. Thus the task of regulating commerce, production and traffic with the new trading areas became a function of the State. The princes began to conclude conventions concerning land and sea trade, commercial settlement in colonies, the protection and privileges of merchants, and so on. The growing frequency of these problems led to the practice, among the sovereigns, of permanent representatives with each other. This again required new rules of law. For just as the new standing armies, being instruments of "public" power, had to be distinguished and separated by law from the rest of the population, so diplomats and consuls, being agents of a sovereign, had to be given a legal position corresponding to the "official" and representative character of their mission. The State, having become an independent apparatus of administration with the function of organizing social order on a territorial scale, could be distinguished as such only if its organs ceased to be conceived in a merely personal capacity, and acquired the trans-personal status of officials.[5]

The foregoing observations on the origin of international law may be summarized by saying that international law was born in the historical situation in which the institution of government, being concentrated in territorially consolidated states, acquired new tasks which called for governmental action beyond the limits of state boundaries. The economic interrelationship of European society became an object of State organization, in so far as it assumed proportions with which the still existing medieval corporations and associations could no longer cope. Inasmuch as this interrelationship transcended state boundaries, it required an international order which could be achieved only by common agreement among the different states. The fact that the sovereigns actually did succeed in setting up a body of international law, however, is owing primarily to the common inheritance of a Christian and humanitarian body of values, and especially to the potent effect of Roman universalism.

[5] ". . . Therefore it would be mistaken to infer from the establishment of a permanent diplomacy that international solidarity and integration were increasing. On the contrary it must be said that the new organization of diplomatic intercourse in the sixteenth and seventeenth centuries corresponded to a growing estrangement of the Courts and an increasing divergence of national political aims." Holtzendorff, in his *Handbuch des Völkerrechts*, vol. I (1885), p. 382 (translation mine).

What is true of the law of peace is equally true of the law of war. The root of the branch of international law which relates to war is likewise not to be found solely in the ideal conception of a spiritually united mankind as against the multiple units of political power. Here also the historical conditions called for a set of norms which the structure of the contemporary conscience was able to provide. The princes, in whom the idea of the state became embodied, gained "their" state not merely by struggling against adjacent rulers, but principally by fighting the feudal and corporate units of power within their own territory. Frequently they depended in this struggle on the help of foreign monarchs with whom they entered an alliance against the Estates of their own country. Thus there resulted a solidarity of interests among the princes as such. Accordingly, since the enemy of today might become the ally of tomorrow, and since all princes shared the identical problem of how to cope with the organized units of power in their realm, their political antagonism among each other could not be allowed to acquire the intensity of a fight to the bitter end. Thus there arose the need for a set of rules which would enable the princes to fight out the conflicts of power between state and state on a purely "objective" scale. Every prince, being an organ of a state, was an adversary, but not a personal enemy. Every prince, being a potential ally, might be weakened, but not annihilated. So there grew up the European States System, with its practice of legislative peace conferences, its limited wars and its complex system of diplomacy. As soon as war was considered as a means of securing a legal settlement, and accordingly was aimed at victory short of complete elimination of the enemy, certain norms became necessary.[6] These norms had to confine warfare to the purposes and limits of a test of power, and had to prevent it from becoming a fight for exter-

[6] "Not only the political conditions, but also commercial competition between the countries gave rise to the idea of a comparative calculation of power; until right down to the eighteenth century the idea of a trade balance was intimately connected with the sister idea of a political balance of power." J. ter Meulen, *Der Gedanke der internationalen Organisation in seiner Entwicklung* (1917), p. 39 (translation mine).

mination. Here the historical conditions of the modern law of war are to be found. The mutual interdependence of the supreme rulers required their mutual preservation during, and in spite of, all conflicts which might arise between them.

The conditions under which international law originated may be summarized thus: The "organization" of political structure by means of the establishment of permanent "organs"—bureaucracy and professional army—and the "depersonalization" of government which this entailed called for separate regulation of private and public spheres. The plurality of such units of organized government in the realm of Christianity required an order regulating their relations with each other, in harmony with the homogeneous structure of the entire society of Christendom. The detailed provisions of this legal order, however, are not a result of these historical conditions, but were formulated by the medieval inheritance of Roman and Christian universalism.

CHAPTER I

LAW IN THE INTERDYNASTIC POLITICS OF ABSOLUTISM

THE THREE ASPECTS OF ABSOLUTISM IN POLITICS

DURING the seventeenth and eighteenth centuries the European states became absolute in three respects: First, the princes succeeded in breaking the power of the *Estates* and in concentrating the unity of the State in the ruler as its highest organ. His political power, by eliminating all other units of political power within the State's territory, became the center of an exclusive and authoritative system of order which everywhere imposed itself with the help of its own organs. It is only by the definite establishment of a single authority of command, characterized both by the strength and the supremacy of its power, that the State becomes an autonomous organization in all respects. Only when this singleness of authority is secured is the State in the position successfully to secure unity of social order within its territorial borders. Thus, in this first sense Absolutism means emancipation of the central power from dependence on other political units and bodies.

Simultaneously with its emancipation from the former local and mediatory powers, the State becomes absolute in relation to *positive law*. During the Middle Ages the function of law in society was determined by the social stratification in Estates. Medieval law was "corporate law, which created and maintained Estates and made them the main props of government, in the sense that each Estate was assigned a special task in respect to public order and authority."[1] In the absolute State, the role

[1] Schotte, "Der Imperialismus oder die Formen der aussenpolitischen Herrschaft," in *Handbuch der Politik*, vol. II (1925-26), p. 60. For a discussion of feudalism in its bearing on the history of international law see also G. W. Keeton and G. Schwarzenberger, *Making International Law Work* (1939), pp. 15-18.

of law is essentially different. For here "the law does not have an independent significance of its own. It is not, like germanic law, an integral part of authority but merely an instrument of authority, working for the most part in the service of the administration."[2] Although this characterization tends to overlook the dependence even of absolute power on a legal basis, it nevertheless points to the essential feature of the relation between law and the absolute State. For under Absolutism, the link between the private individual and the public authority was not primarily a legal one, but it materialized in the form of organization. Being mainly an administrative and organizational relationship it had acquired a certain measure of independence of positive law. Given to this development, the State was able to take over the leadership of the legal order, in respect to which it functioned as the most influential and most efficient unit of decision. By the introduction of this central unit of decision into the legal system, a uniform and standardized system of law could be realized for the first time since the Middle Ages, a unity which, in turn was the condition sine qua non of the political unity of performance. Its prerequisite was the unity of the State's will. By the monopolizing action of political authority through codification, standardization and bureaucratization of the administration of law, the medieval pluralism of the legal order was overcome, and law within the political territory was transformed into a rational and systematic body of rules. The absolute ruler personified the State, until the State itself came to be conceived of as a person whose will was considered the source of the law, and whose authoritative enactment became the criterion of positive law. In this sense the absolute State is characterized by its relative independence of its own creation, the law.

Thirdly the State, during this period, emancipated itself from *religion.* The Spain of Charles V and Philip II still presented the picture of a political body entirely in the service, not of the Church, but of the Catholic faith. The Hapsburg

[2] Schotte, *loc. cit.*

World Empire acquired its meaning and justification only through religion. Its specific mission was held to be the defense and enforcement of the Catholic dogma in the world. Against it a new type of state grew in the France of Henry IV, where the religious indifference of the king was matched by thinkers like Bodin, whose "Heptaplomeres" was essentially a plea for the sovereign's tolerance in religious matters. The assertion of the "Reason of State" over and against religion is by no means to be regarded as a continuation of the medieval struggle between spiritual and temporal power. This was no bickering between State and Church about competencies and titles to authority. The essence of the French development is that the State was put on its own terrestrial foundations, that its specific social function was vindicated as against the former conception of it as a servant of religion, that its meaning in society was explained in terms of immanence instead of transcendence. In political theory this development was marked by the attempts at an immanent conception of politics which made Machiavelli and Hobbes the fathers of the modern sociological theory of politics. This emancipation of the state's own social function from religious determination is not inconsistent with the fact that the French kings were frequently devoted and obedient servants of the Church. They abided by the dogma of the Church and even by the Pope's authority, but only in so far as it was reconcilable with their functions as political rulers. The State, having won its own basis and autonomy in organizational, military, administrative, economic and juristic respects, also cut the ties which bound it to the purposes of the Church. Whereas under the Spanish régime it had still been "Faith in action," it gradually developed, in this process of emancipation from all heteronomous purposes into "Society in Action." So far as concerns the State, the Church and its dogma lost their character of absolute guides to conduct, and became just one of the several social factors comprised in the all-embracing order of the State.

This social and political situation characterizes the majority of those states which convened in 1648 to set up the first general convention of international law. It is this historical pattern, the absoluteness (emancipation) of these states in relation to Estates, legal tradition and Church dictation, which explains the rise of a new order of sovereign states in Europe. However, still other historical factors, particularly in the economic field, had made their appearance in the meantime, and contributed decisively to the rise of the new positive order of interstate law.

THE CONSOLIDATION OF CENTRALIZED POWER

The new type of state, once it was finally consolidated and was functioning efficiently, now took over one by one the administrative tasks which the historical development of society required. First, Spain and England put their national economies under state direction. Political power needed the revenue coming from production and commerce, as the economic basis of its autonomy, for political power mainly rested on the possibility of continuously being able to dispose of considerable financial resources. The Hapsburgs, for example, buttressed themselves by their close relationship with the great banking families of Europe. In order to bolster the financial capacity of these banks, on whose capital the power of European monarchs depended, they were given every possible facility for accumulating immense fortunes. At the same time, in Spain, all income from the newly discovered colonies was made a state monopoly. This required very detailed regulation of Spanish overseas commerce and of activities in the new colonies. The Spanish based their claim to the exclusive title to maintain naval communications with America on the already mentioned arbitration verdict of Alexander VI. According to this decision, the ocean west of Spain was considered Spanish "territorial water." In England the financial needs of the crown resulted in devices designed systematically to increase the taxpaying capacity of the people. The king issued orders which aimed at the accumulation of monetary capital in the country, hampering imports and protecting the native production of export-goods. These policies developed into the theory of mercantilism which gradually permeated the commercial policies of all European states. Its best known manifestation is Cromwell's Navigation Act (1651).

Still more clearly than in England, the new relationship between State and Society, between politics and economics, is visible in the Netherlands. The Dutch merchants had, since the beginning of European colonization, brought under their control practically all the intermediary trade in colonial goods. While Spaniards and Portuguese looked with contempt on such shopkeeping activities, the Dutch supplied from Lisbon the entire European demand for spices and other produce of overseas countries. Amsterdam at that time was the busiest port in the world, and at the beginning of the seventeenth century three-fourths of all seagoing vessels sailed under the Dutch flag. The East India Company, founded 1602, soon began to provide for the security of its overseas communications by ways and means of its own. Equipped with the appropriate privileges, it established fortified warehouses, had armed men-of-war to convoy its merchant navy, and maintained a small armed force to protect the commercial settlements in the colonies. Thus in the Netherlands the development, though heading in the same direction, was inverted: It was not the State which fostered the formation of capital as a prerequisite of its autonomous central power, but it was rather the enormous fortune of a commercial company, and the influence which its merchants thereby acquired, which compelled the political power actively to secure the economic relations of the nation with other areas. Holland became a merchants' and traders' state, the existence of which depended on the accessibility of trade routes and commercial settlements. Thus, for instance, the Dutch trade with Spain went on uninterrupted by the war between those two countries. To Spain it was indispensable as a source of imports, to Holland as a source of income. A significant incident illustrates the social pattern of these times: When in 1603 a vessel of the Portuguese India-fleet was captured by a Dutch man-of-war, the shareholders of the East India Company threatened to resign their membership. They were afraid, not without reason, that such lawless and arbitrary acts of violence would ruin the Dutch trade with the Indies. It was in this situation that Hugo Grotius wrote his "*De jure praedae*," which was the draft of a plan for the international regulation of prize-law.[3]

This picture of Holland shows the same structure as that of all other states at that time. Its main features are that political power is compelled to regulate the interstate commercial relations with a view to securing the most stable and highest possible monetary income for its subjects. For the wealth of a country was then considered to consist in its stock of money. The only way of increasing the nation's stock of money, however, was through international trade and commerce. Agriculture almost everywhere was producing only for home consumption, offering scarcely any possibilities for export and the acquisition of foreign money. The mercantilist idea was later refuted by the physiocrats, but all the same the policies of European states continued to foster the export of manufactured goods. The aim of these policies was to prevent any disturbance of a nation's own trade or of any foreign trade which affected that nation's own exports. Correspondingly, in wartime all action at sea and some action on land was aimed at interrupting the trade communications of the enemy, thereby undermining the financial basis of his capacity for political and military action.

THE INTERDYNASTIC FUNCTION OF IUS GENTIUM

What is the function of interstate law in this historical situation? To answer this question we must take a glance from still another direction at the structure of political organization in Europe. The religious wars had brought about the decisive struggle for power between the absolute central ruler and the feudal entities in most of the European nations. Consequently the center of gravity of political consolidation lay in the international struggle among the various dynasties. As yet the

[3] See Vogel, "Hugo Grotius und der Ursprung des Schlagwortes von der Freiheit der Meere," in the periodical *Meereskunde*, vol. XII, Nr. 4.

dynasties, and not nations as such, were the contending parties in this fight. Their conflict was still to decide the definite territorial delimitations of political power units within which the respective states were to develop into unitary moulds of social life. This shifting of the process of political consolidation from the internal to the external plane is most distinct in the Thirty Years' War. It started as a religious war, but during the latter half of the period it became a purely dynastic conflict which was to fix the power boundaries of the ruling families in Europe. Accordingly, it was ended not by a religious pact, a protocol of tolerance or a document of religious privileges, but by a modern peace treaty which fixed the borderlines of Europe. During this struggle of the European dynasties, the monarchic State of the absolutist brand consolidated the political organization of Europe in the form of sovereign territorial units.

An important feature in this situation was the Turkish threat, which formed a danger common to the whole of Christendom. Although Christendom no longer formed a politically united community, although some nations, like France, maintained friendships and alliances with the Eastern neighbors of the easternmost Christian countries, there was still enough consciousness of the community of cultural values and the common bond of faith left in all parts of Europe to allow a common tendency to develop in politics also. It seems highly possible that the principle of a *justum potentiae aequilibrium*, which after 1648 formed the recognized constitution of the European States System, was a product of the common front of Christendom against the onslaught of Islam. Although no one dreamt any more of restoring the former political unity of Christendom, there survived enough of its tradition to make people realize that Christendom could continue to exist divided into a plurality of states, only if the independence of each formed the common interest of all. How clear this realization is to leading European minds is manifest in this formulation of Fénelon: "Neighboring states are not only obliged to treat each other according to the rules of justice and good will. They should also form a sort of society and a general commonwealth, for their own particular security as well as for the common interest. All the members composing the great body of Christendom owe each other, for the common good, and owe to themselves, for the security of their country, every effort to prevent the progress of any member from upsetting the equilibrium."[4] This seems to be the key to the function of international law during that epoch. The fact of the division of Christendom into a multiplicity of independent territorial units had become an axiomatic certainty in the thirty years' combat of all against all. The specific social function of an autonomous political power already formed the condition sine qua non of social life everywhere and could no longer be dispensed with. Thus, although the absolute rulers in this process of political consolidation fought each other for the expansion of their respective realms of authority, there was yet a general agreement that these wars must not aim at the extermination of peoples or at the destruction of the enemy state as such. The meaning of these dynastic struggles was not the conquest and domination of other countries, but merely the definite delimitation of the spheres of power and authority of different dynasties. The expansion and limitation of monarchic sovereignty in a territorial sense was the objective around which war was being waged in the Europe of the seventeenth and eighteenth centuries.

In accordance with this function of war, interstate law of this epoch on the whole bore the features of an interdynastic order. Its action was not yet that of a law of "nations." Its specific functions paralleled the objectives of the "limited war" of those times. Thus, among its functions was that of preventing those excesses of war which would have gone beyond the inherent aim of the interdynastic struggle for power, such as permanent damage to the civil population and their social order. In other words, since all were tacitly agreed that no ruler would or should expect from the war he waged more than a

[4] Quoted by Dupuis, *Le principe d'équilibre et le Concert Européen* (1909), p. 26 (translation mine).

territorial extension of his power at the expense of another dynasty, all were inclined to confine the action of combat to means sufficient for attaining this end. The concept of "nation" in the modern sense did not yet exist. The population of the territory to be conquered was looked upon as a potential part of one's own people, especially as a potential source of wealth and revenue for the crown. Consequently, the concept of war and conquest did not aim at, nor was any ruler interested in, damaging or exterminating the civil population of hostile territory.[5] The fight was carried against the authority and the title which another ruler had in those territories, with occasional admixtures of the desire for political prestige. Therefore, the sovereigns of this period were inclined to acknowledge a set of rules which enabled them to hit the adversary in that spot and only in that spot. This common interest of dynasties was the main bulwark of international law during the period of Absolutism. Its rules concerning privateering, contraband, prize-law, neutrality of ship and cargo, war and its termination, the conclusion of peace and the acquisition of territory made it possible for the will-for-power of the monarch to meet its contestant on that common plane on which their fight against each other could yield a result in the most efficient way. In other words, the interdynastic law of this epoch was essentially a common basis for the disputes of power between rulers. It regulated the relations between states and princes mainly with respect to their encounter in war and the case of armed conflict.[6] There is no trace of any peace-creating or peace-maintaining function in the international law of Absolutism, such as characterized that law in the latter part of the nineteenth and the beginning of the twentieth century. Nevertheless the political function of international law under Absolutism was highly important, considering that political power, having only just become sovereign and autonomous, had not yet attained a definite external delimitation of its scope.

[5] F. Pratt, *Road to Empire* (1939), p. 68.

[6] See Westlake, *Collected Papers on International Law*, edited by Oppenheim (1914), pp. 30*ff*., especially p. 32.

However, these positive rules of war, prize-law and neutrality formed only a very fragmentary international order in the sense of a regular observance of norms by the states. They were nothing but a crystallization of certain usages which had turned out to provide an adequate framework for purely interdynastic struggles, and which as such appealed to the general consciousness of that epoch. Accordingly, there was no systematic consistency in these customary rules. Thus, for example, a general notion of neutrality was lacking. When we speak now of international law during the seventeenth century, we are thinking less of these customary rules than of the theoretical systems of Gentilis, Grotius, Zouch, Puffendorf and other thinkers. What was the role which their theorems played in the social and political reality of their time? What were the conditions of their effectiveness?

It is not by chance that the theorists to whom is owed the whole modern doctrine of international law, all belonged to the Protestant and "bourgeois" parts of Europe, which had just won their civil liberties and their national self-determination by struggling against the Spanish kings. From the point of view of their social situation, the problem of international order and international politics had an aspect quite different from that of the Spanish jurists. Between Suarez and Grotius there was an essential difference not only in the original attitude of mind, but also in the political and social pattern of the society surrounding them. For Suarez the legal community of mankind was not a mere postulate, but a fact: it was the necessary form of being in which alone the notion of humanity could be conceived. The *corpus mysticum* of Christendom, the religious authority of the Church, the spiritual universalism of the Papal office—all this was for the Spaniards merely a description of an existing structure. It was an ontological realization of the substance of things. Accordingly, the law governing the community of mankind was also conceived as something substantial, in being, immutable. It was the universal truth about the existence of men and states. Human will in this permanent and stable order of law had the role only of giving effect to, not of creating, law. Legislation and contract were not sources but reflexes of the law, temporary attributes of its ideal existence. This approach of the Spaniards corresponded to the realities prevailing in the Spanish Empire. However, it did not fit the case of the English and French kings with their absolute political and legislative will, with their sovereignty which had just been defined as *legibus soluta potestas*. North of Spain there were political organizations in which the ruler's will, emancipated not only from the ties of positive law, but also from those of religion, actually created law. The development of history favored the path taken by the French kings and not that taken by the Spanish Empire. Therefore, the significance of Suarez lies not so much in the concrete norms of international law which he taught, but in his grandiose conception of an all-embracing law of nations as such. It is this universalistic idealism, not his practical system, which exercised a decisive influence on European thinking, while Grotius, who took up his conception in a more realistic way, became the father of most of the concrete rules of the new discipline of law.[7]

The reason for the stronger influence which Grotius exercised on the reality of politics is that he lived in a political community of the type which just at this time was supplanting the Spanish type of State, in the sense of an emancipation of political power from the guidance of theology, the prevalence of religious goals and the ties of traditional positive law. The Netherlands represented a much more "absolute" type of State than Spain. Clearly recognizing the most effective factors in the process of political organization and consolidation, Grotius attributes to

[7] The difference between the ideas of Suarez and Grotius, respectively, is best illustrated by the following two passages, the first from Suarez, the second from Grotius:

. . . humanum genus, quantumvis in varios populos et regna divisum, semper habet aliquam unitatem, non solum specificam, sed etiam quasi politicam et moralem, quam indicat naturale praeceptum mutui amoris et misericordiae, quod ad omnes extenditur. (*De Legibus* etc., II, XIX, 9.)

. . . Illud hic addam, cum omnis Christiani unius corporis membra sint, quae jubentur alia aliorum dolores ac mala persentiscere, sicut et ad singulos pertinet, ita et ad populos qua populi sunt, et ad reges qua reges pertinere.

this absolute will of the State a much more autonomous role than Suarez.[8] The will of the absolute State obviously operated as a creator of law. Accordingly, Grotius distinguishes between positive international law, which is of contractual origin, and the natural law of reason. The latter binds the ruler's will as an ethical commandment, but the former is the practical rule which regulates social reality by fixing rights and duties and by making people behave in a definite way. Thus, the State, having in reality monopolized the enactment and enforcement of law, is given in theory, also, the position of the fountain-head of law and legislation. On this basis the extremely important conclusion which had to be drawn for the theoretical construction of international law was that the states, by common and coincident wills, establish the positive law which is to be in force between them.

Obviously this conception of international law approximated the political pattern of most European communities much more closely than the more medieval one of the Spaniards, in which the subject of law played only an auxiliary role in respect to the eternal being of universal law. For those states and rulers who had won their power by fighting against Spain had actually established for themselves this autonomous and emancipated power which decreed and revoked laws, established social order, and successfully claimed the legal obedience of the whole of their territories' population, recognizing as superior to itself only the principles of *ius divinum et naturale*. In these modern power-states the will of the prince manifested itself daily as the true dynamic force of the legal order. The State, personified by its ruler, presented itself visibly as a law-creating and law-maintaining agent, whose autonomous power shaped the law in the form of positive and effectual rules.

On the other hand, the more "individualistic" conception of

[8] Westlake, in his *Collected Papers*, remarks with regard to Grotius and the Treaty of Westphalia: "Then, for the first time, through the decay of the Empire and of the coercive power of the Catholic Church, it could be seen that the society would be a purely secular one, and would be composed of such a crowd of practically independent states that only general considerations could be applied to their mutual relations" (p. 48).

law and order which distinguished Grotius from the Spaniards, corresponded again to the social structure that surrounded him. And the eminent place which this thinker occupies in the history of international law can, among other reasons, be also explained by realizing that the type of society in which he lived represented the social pattern which in coming centuries was to be characteristic of the whole of the Occident. Grotius wrote for a nation of merchants, traders, scientists, craftsmen—members of the "Third Estate." The core of their social existence was commerce, the core of commerce is contract. In Germany the need of the trading class for legal security and certainty had led to the adoption of Roman law, centering around the axiomatic notions of the legal person and the person's will. The class of commercial people, the professions, the crafts, could thrive only provided the political atomization of Europe, with its countless local laws, was superseded by a "uniform and written system of rules, in which each rule was systematically made to conform to the unity of the whole."[9] The "bourgeois" way of living and working required this standardization of law as a basis of certainty and calculability of commercial relationships all over Europe.

The adoption of Roman law had occurred in the period of early capitalism and individualism. In the meantime, mercantilism had supplanted this more individualistic economy. Accordingly, the trade between nations, especially Dutch overseas trade, required the same conditions of legal certainty and calculability which in the early capitalistic period had brought about the adoption of Roman law. State treaties now fixed the rules of commercial intercourse; but it was also necessary that treaties should be observed, that the vicissitudes of the power struggle should not constantly change the stipulated law, and that the inequality of states should not lead to disadvantages in their commercial relationships. These were the conditions under which international trade might flourish. They

[9] Hermann Heller, *Staatslehre*, p. 134. Also see E. Ehrlich, *Die juristische Logik* (1918) and Below, *Die Ursachen der Rezeption des Römischen Rechts in Deutschland* (1905).

could be recognized especially clearly in the Dutch traders' State. And, moreover, the Dutch theorists' views about international law were bound to carry special weight in the eyes of the world. Three-fourths of the world's sea trade was carried on Dutch boats: this fact explains much of the predominating influence of the Dutch jurists.

Accordingly, the theory of international law which placed the subject's will in a central position was not only in line with the requirements and the sentiments of absolute monarchs, but also corresponded to the consciousness and legal conditions of the Third Estate and its sphere of commerce, which essentially depended on international law. This explains why the Dutch and not the Spanish conception of international law asserted itself in history, and why our present ideas of international law are derived from Grotius and not from the more profound Suarez.

The circumstances mentioned above also determined the real significance which the great theoretical systems proved to have in the political reality of their times. It would have been unfruitful and perhaps even impossible to develop a system of law inductively out of the loose agglomeration of habits and usages. However, it was a most urgent task to set up theorems of international law, on the basis of which an international practice of law might evolve. "The unwritten slogan of the times was the philosophy of international law, not its interpretation. . . ."[10] Thus, for instance, commercial agreements between states increased rapidly. However, these conventions were predominantly political in character, just like any other concessions which are made under pressure and are liable to change with the political situation. The State allowed these treaties to be molded exclusively by the *Raison d'Etat*, i.e. by the ruler's need for money. However, in this form commercial agreements did not fulfil their vital function of providing a secure framework for trade relationships. In order to enable political practice to find a way of introducing more stability and certainty into these legal instruments, it was necessary for

[10] Plappert, *F. Suarez als Völkerrechtslehrer* (1914).

the principles of justice and legality to be formulated. This is precisely what the theoretical systems of international law achieved. They did not directly create law—that being the function of the State's will—but they offered a framework of rules, founded on natural law, to the practitioner of international politics.

Thus in practice as well as in theory the sovereign will of the State, personified by its ruler, had become the law-creating and law-maintaining agent. Precisely for this reason, however, a mediating link was required to bridge the gulf between the idealism of legal theory and the realism of political practice. This connecting link is the principle of good will. The "good will," "good faith" or "*bonne foi*" is the moral postulate which is the indispensable corollary to the subjectivity of the State's will in the legal structure. It is the lever by which the philosopher becomes instrumental in shaping the will of the State. For the Occident at this time is still a moral and spiritual whole, Christendom is still a tribunal before which rulers have to answer for their deeds and intentions, to be judged by the measuring rod of divine commandment and human reason. This jurisdiction of occidental morality is inescapable. Not even the most absolute ruler can avoid it, because the community of faith and values still embraces all Europe, no longer as a glowing Christian conviction, it is true, but still as a code of humanitarian morality.

Thus the theory of international law in this period had the very real function of forming the link between the elaborate legal consciousness of bourgeois society, its standards of justice, its system of concepts and its need for legal certainty on the one hand, and the will of the absolute State, its specific *Raison d'Etat*, and its requirements of power positions on the other hand. In this sense it has been said that "natural law performed, in the older days, the function of a bridge between international and private law."[11] This function was a necessary one, because the bourgeoisie, being the main source of national wealth, had a vital political importance but did not participate in the

[11] Lauterpacht, *Private Law Sources and Analogies in International Law* (1927), p. 34.

formation of the State's will nor have any official position of political command. There was only one way by which the trading and producing Third Estate could exercise its influence on the shaping of international relations: the voice of legal science, which confronted the sovereign State with the postulates of legality, justice, morality and humanity. Through this channel the influence of the Third Estate has actually operated for two centuries as the legal commandment opposing power politics. This vital function of legal theory also explains why international law during the seventeenth and eighteenth centuries was the creation of a small group of thinkers. These circumstances, moreover, account for the fact that international law appeared, during this period, as a complete system, a consistent whole centering around the notion of the legal person, while with all other types of law the process of systematization is only the final step crowning a long development of concrete legal practices.

CHAPTER II

THE ROLE OF INTERNATIONAL LAW DURING THE PERIOD OF LIBERALISM AND IMPERIALISM

THE GROWTH OF BOURGEOIS WORLD SOCIETY

THE social developments and trends of ideas following Grotius and his time did not affect essentially either the function of positive international law or that of legal theory. Consequently the scope of international law remained relatively unchanged until the middle of the nineteenth century. What authors like Pufendorff, Bynkershoek, Vattel, de Martens and others contributed during this time was merely an elaboration of the foundations laid by Suarez and Grotius. A new phase in the function of international law begins, however, when the coming to power of the bourgeoisie, and the industrial revolution created a new pattern of State and Society. To understand the role of international law in this period, a role characterized by an intensive production of international conventions, unions, and other instruments of positive prescriptions, it is necessary to analyze the mutual relations between the political organization and the non-political pattern of social life: the "State" on the one hand, and "Society" on the other.

During the seventeenth and eighteenth centuries the State had imposed its power heavily on the early capitalism of the bourgeois classes. In this period of political consolidation and organization, the "Reason of State" had established its ascendancy over private and non-political criteria. The State accordingly took charge of the regulation of typically "private" activities, organizing the economic system in conformity with its own needs and exigencies. However in that phase of the development of the political unit, which still contained many relics of the medieval system (such as guilds, Estates, and so on), the State's needs in economic respects had not yet embraced the idea of a closed national economic unit. The State, in organizing economic activities of individuals, did not envisage a goal of self-seclusion or autarky. The "political exigencies" which imposed themselves on the economy were rather confined to the financial needs of the crown. For, quite apart from abuses in the form of excessive court-expenditure and the costly institution of royal mistresses, money was the most important requisite of the ruler's political power. Consequently Absolutism fostered, intentionally or unintentionally, the rise of a gigantic empire of private economy, centering in mobile capital working in industry, commerce and finance. Needing capital as a requisite of absolute power, Absolutism engaged in developing capitalism, which was eventually to become the cause of its downfall. Being based primarily on financial power, Absolutism took care to develop the spirit and practice of an "acquisitive society," thereby engendering a bourgeois mentality which soon sought to follow its own laws. Science was again the channel by which this mentality made its way into the State's policies. After Adam Smith, Ricardo, and others had given the bourgeois point of view adequate theoretical expression, after the financial difficulties of governments had brought bankers and economic experts into leading political positions, after the economic orientation of bourgeois thinking had conquered influential circles, especially the leading brains in politics, liberalism began its general sway which was ultimately to lead to complete ascendancy of the bourgeoisie. During this process bourgeois private economy obtained, step by step, almost complete freedom of action from the State. It developed that type of "daring entrepreneurs"[1] which is so characteristic of the period. Large-scale enterprise became possible on a threefold basis: technically by the inventions of the early nineteenth century, organizationally by the liberation of commerce, pro-

[1] Schotte, "Der Imperialismus oder die Formen der aussenpolitischen Herrschaft," in *Handbuch der Politik*, vol. 2 (1925-26), p. 69.

duction and work from the fetters of the medieval guild, legally by the introduction of the limited-liability corporation. Craft-shops could develop into factories, factories into enterprises. The development of communications brought enormous spaces into a system of division of labor within which the possibilities of individual efficiency seemed to be unlimited. The bourgeois was not satisfied with an existence secured and circumscribed by corporate rigidness. He now pursued the goal of the greatest possible efficiency of individual forces: status turned into profession.

The same individualism which manifests itself in economics as free enterprise, in law as freedom of contract, in the State as parliamentarism and party-rule, presents itself in international politics as nationalism. The epoch of bourgeois liberalism and world-economy is at the same time the epoch of the foundation of nation-states and of imperialistic power-politics. This seeming paradox reveals its inner logic when these apparently contradictory phenomena are recognized as different forms of expression of an identical outlook. Such self-contradictory manifestations of the same fundamental outlook are but the consequence of the diversified nature of different realms of activity and their properties. Individualism in respect to economic affairs results in liberalism while in respect to political organization it leads to nationalism. The most important consequence is the situation, so characteristic of the nineteenth century, in which politics and economics maintain widely divergent viewpoints with respect to identical phenomena. This tension between an economic system which inherently contradicts the existing system of political organization, while both systems are mutually dependent on each other for their respective functions, is the essential feature of the nineteenth century pattern.[2] It explains the seeming contradiction between the nineteenth century trends in internal and international politics, respectively.

On the one hand, there is an unheard of accumulation of State power. Both the qualitative aspect of power (popular

[2] Hermann Heller, *Staatslehre* (1934), p. 137.

mass armies, technological development of armaments, naval defense system) and the quantitative aspect of the State (colonial possession, imperialist expansion, spheres of influence, and so on) assume gigantic proportions. But, on the other hand, bourgeois society grows into a sphere of human activity which is essentially free from interference by the State. Here it is not the criterion of political organization, or of collective existence, which dominates, but the criteria of private interest, market situations, standards of trade values, etc. This bourgeois society is accordingly composed not of national units but of systems of economic relations and spheres of commercial interest and divided labor. This is a type of social cohesion which is completely different from that of political organization, and is, moreover, independent of it. Schotte, in his article already quoted, has explained the inner structure of this bourgeois world society by describing the example of economic ascendancy of advanced capitalistic interests over backward peoples; a process by which these peoples are made an integral part of a far-flung economic system. In his example of a not yet "civilized" country this process of economic integration into world society takes the form of "bribing the people with the goods of civilization as such, and provoking spiritual and material needs, on which these people become dependent. At the end of such a period of 'awakening' [*Erweckungsperiode*] we find a complete transformation of production. The colonized nation abandons its autochthonous production and adopts a system of divided labor in conjunction with the European nation. It produces for European needs in order to obtain the means with which to pay for the civilized goods that have become so indispensable to it. Thus the colonized country, by this division of labor, grows into an economic unity with the master nation."[3] And, one should add, this unity not only embraces the colonized country and its European masters, but also includes many other nations and countries. To this "private" and unpolitical system of world-wide economic relations should be added other typical features of bourgeois society, such as the

[3] Schotte, *op. cit.*, p. 62.

habit of studying abroad, the international assimilation of education, the increased volume of tourist traffic, a world-embracing news service, a world literature and other factors of international integration. Thus in the last phase of this development there is, for the first time in history, a sort of "mankind," not only as a mere notion, an idea, or a postulate, but as a real and general field of social forces, a universal intertwinement of interests and a world-wide interdependence of economic factors.

On the other hand, this "international society" of individuals and private associations is possible only because, throughout the world of its time, individuals enjoy a sphere of non-political freedom from the State, within their respective nations: a sphere of "free" activities in which only the laws of peaceful world trade and undisturbed world interrelations have validity.[4] With subtle humor the Swiss poet Gottfried Keller has characterized the character of bourgeois existence in his *Leute von Seldwyla*: "From politics they have divorced themselves almost completely, because they believe that it always conduces to war. Thus they have come to the point where they scrupulously avoid any judgment in political affairs, in order not to base, consciously or subconsciously, any business on such an opinion; for they consider it to be more solid to trust blindly in chance. . . ." This essential "anti-political" aspect of bourgeois society in all countries is the basis for its international homogeneity and its world-wide ramifications. In most countries of the world it produces uniform standards of civil law and thus establishes one of the foremost conditions of world economy.[5]

[4] "The freedom of movement and of business activities, which most legislations since the middle of the nineteenth century grant to individuals, generally without regard to their nationality, has factually taken from the states the control over international trade and commerce: the State can intervene either through lending help or by creating obstacles; but the modern State neither can nor will either create or abolish this intercourse." M. Huber, *Die soziologischen Grundlagen des Völkerrechts* (1928), p. 36 (translation mine).

[5] H. v. Beckerath and F. Kern give special attention to the similarity of the private law systems of world trading nations up to 1914. "Even in former wars people in the belligerent nations constantly remained conscious of the fact that the social and cultural patterns of the world presupposed the unviolability of the private rights acquired through economic activities." *Autarkie oder internationale Zusammenarbeit?* (1932),

However, Bourgeois Society turns its back on politics only *almost* completely. Simultaneously with the sphere of non-political Bourgeois Society arises the idea of the State of National Power as its necessary corollary. For the economically-minded bourgeoisie considers the diplomatic and military apparatus of the nation-state the *ultima ratio* of the competitive struggle against superior capitalistic power. On the other hand the international ramifications of Bourgeois Society create problems of order and organization which, though they transcend the various state boundaries, still call for state regulation. Expanding industries, commercial enterprises and financial institutions establish valuable private interests abroad; foreign production threatens the markets of native factories; the spirit of enterprise and of individual achievement points in the direction of colonial empires; the importance of far-flung communications calls for the effective protection of trade-routes: all these and similar problems make it necessary to extend political authority, political power and political order to the realm of world-economic relationships.

Imperialism is the historic form of this trend. Its essence is inextricably linked to the penetration and opening up of the world by daring and enterprising individuals, to the subjective drive for individual expansion, to the general rush for economic power-positions and means of personal exaltation. However, as the whole century is one of dualism between politics and economics, so side by side with Imperialism it harbors a strong trend toward internationalism. The positions of private economic power in the world are maintained with the help and support of public political power, but at the same time they are jeopardized by the disturbances resulting from interstate power conflicts. Therefore international pacifism arises from the same foundations as the notion of the modern power-state, liberalism springs from the same roots as nationalism, the idea of world-economy grows up together with that of protectionism. The

p. 14. They point out that after the war of 1914-18 this basis of world society was disregarded and was gradually destroyed by socialistic or etatistic tendencies.

common basis of these trends is the movement of individualism, the urge for individualistic self-display, self-expression and self-realization—but their antagonism is the consequence of a divided and disorderly social structure, torn between economic and political, individual and collective, private and public, social and political points of view. The nineteenth century, particularly its second half, is, in spite of all its external forms of order, a profoundly chaotic period.

LEGAL FORMALISM IN NINETEENTH CENTURY INTERNATIONAL RELATIONS

This characteristic dualism between the dynamics of the political nation-units on the one hand and the dynamics of an interdependent world-economy on the other determines the function of international law in this period. For "this economy based on far-flung communications and on a high-strung and ever intensified division of labor, calls for a corresponding rationalization and calculability of not only economic production, but also of political and legal relationships."[6] Characteristic manifestations of this function are the international institutions which arose during the second half of the nineteenth century. Thus were established: in 1865 the Telegraph Union, in 1874 the Postal Union, in 1875 the Meter Convention, in 1883 the International Protection of Industrial Property, in 1886 the Protection of Literary and Artistic Property, in 1890 the Union for the Publication of Custom Tariffs, in 1890 the International Office for International Transport and many other institutions of similar character. They all reveal the same need: to establish among the pluralism of states in the world a uniform legal basis for certain conditions of economy and trade. All these unions, conventions, offices, and so on have the same function. They are meant to induce states to adjust their respective legal systems to a uniform international standard, thus creating a pattern of many municipal laws with identical or similar provisions. The identical provisions and international calculability of the domestic legal systems of many nations is the condition

[6] Hermann Heller, *Staatslehre*, p. 111.

for an "international society," i.e. for the free and direct co-operation of individuals across national boundaries.

The shift of the center of gravity from politics to economics and from the State to Society also gives a different significance to the specifically "political" part of international law, that part which concerns the power-conflicts of states. On the one hand Bourgeois Society now carries to its final triumph the tendency of completely separating war as a public matter from the private existence of non-combatants. The Paris Declaration on naval warfare of 1856, the Geneva Convention of 1864, the Petersburg Convention of 1868, the Hague Convention on land war of 1899 and the London Declaration on naval war of 1909 represent the main phases of this development. These instruments are part of the endeavor to separate as far as possible war and economic affairs, power conflicts and individual existence.

On the other hand the extension of the notions of private law to international relations now assumes large proportions. The idea of arbitration leads to the establishment of the Permanent Court of Arbitration (1899) and to the formation of numerous arbitration agreements between particular states. Formerly the law of war functioned as a common formula enabling states to follow a standard of behavior which was politically expedient, owing to the historical circumstances. In the same way the institution of arbitration exercised a similar function in the realm of non-bellicose conflicts. In both cases the legal rules fulfilled their task not so much because of the justice of their provisions, but rather by their very existence as a common standard of reference. Arbitration owed its increasing popularity not to the truth and value of the various decisions, but to the mere usefulness of a formula coined by impartial judges, which provided the states with an objective basis for the peaceful solution of their conflict—a solution which was required anyway by political considerations.[7] The true function of arbitra-

[7] "The existence of the prize court does not signify an emancipation of the law from its political basis, but it expresses only the fact that the development of world economy has made the "neutral" and commercial interests of the three most important states (Great Britain, Germany, and the United States) come to the foreground, and the antagonistic strategic interests recede." M. Huber, *Die soziologischen Grundlagen des Völkerrechts* (1928), p. 13 (translation mine).

tion was confined to such disputes, the nature of which made a peaceful settlement politically imperative. In these cases the existence of a tribunal of arbitration enabled the contending parties to come together on the common ground of an objective formula.

Arbitration as such was of course not new: indeed it is the oldest type of legal order in international politics. That which was new in the nineteenth century was only institutional arbitration, arbitration as a contractually anticipated and generally accepted form of solution for international disputes. Here, as in all the institutions, unions, and codifications of the epoch, the peculiar style of bourgeois and individualistic Society manifests itself in legal forms. It is important to realize the nature of this bourgeois pattern, since it has molded the type of international law with which we are dealing today. To use the words of Paul Tillich, bourgeois society may be characterized as "divided into countless individual beings, the atoms of society, a society which is held together by economic ends and economic necessities, constituting its natural laws. Conflict of interests and solidarity of interests are the underlying forces of group-formation."[8] In a culture structured according to these laws, all individual differences and inequalities are reduced to the measurable quantities of money and capital. And this formal equality of the subjects corresponds to a formalization of all relationships and institutions. A society based on the exchange of goods calls for a formal calculability of all social affairs, and of all those forces which might possibly disturb the economic system. Owing to the atomistic structure of this society it can master life only when and if life can be reduced to a common denominator and can be expressed in the form of abstract quantities.

All the international conventions and institutions mentioned above serve this vital condition of an international and bourgeois society. Similar to the codifications of domestic law (which were carried out in the same period within the various nations), the "political" part of international law is meant

[8] *Die religiöse Lage der Gegenwart* (1926), p. 19 (translation mine).

to make the actions of political units calculable by setting up a formal and standardized pattern for them. Both in domestic and in international law the method is the same: the construction of a rational system of concepts which approximates as closely as possible to the formalism of mathematical symbols. Thus Lauterpacht[9] has put his finger on the most essential feature of present international law by showing that it was the private law in use within the various nations which was the main source of international legal rules in the last eighty years. International law during this period is the law of an international society of economically minded individuals, and it functioned as a scale by which to calculate the bearing of acts of political power, and the conflicts resulting therefrom, on the relations of world economy. In order to bring about such calculability, this epoch of individualism had no other way than of transposing the elaborate and formal concepts of private law into rules applied to international relations. The systematization and classification of the rules of international law which was thus brought about made it possible, at least in some parts of international law, to deduce legal conclusions with the same formalistic certainty that had been achieved in municipal private law. And since the very availability of a formula in international politics was for the most part just as important as the contents of the rule, the unsuitability of these private-law norms for international relations could be overlooked. The existence of a system of rules and conceptions as such, regardless of whether in themselves these rules were good or bad, enabled Society to calculate to some extent the scope of international relations.

To sum up, it may be said that the function of international law in the period of imperialism is determined by the fact that, as a result of the international interdependence of bourgeois society, the states had to fulfil a great number of organizational, administrative and protective tasks which transcended the realm of their immediate power. For Imperialism not only manifested itself in the expansion of states into colonies and

[9] *Private Law Sources and Analogies of International Law* (1927).

protectorates, but also in the claim that the private property of a state's nationals abroad, as well as all those material values fluctuating and circulating in a nation's international trade, formed objects of political protection. This is the essence of imperialism, that political power follows the paths of expansion of private interests, that the scope of political power, the sphere of political domination, is determined by the initiative of economic enterprise. From this there resulted innumerable occasions for friction, conflict and also cooperation with other nations which sought political expansion with a view to the same functions. In so far as these disputes were not of vital political importance, affecting the existence of a state as such, they were very suitable objects for regulation by international law. Thus the coincidence of the expansionist tendencies of Imperialism with an interdependent world economy of Bourgeois Society was the condition for the specific function of international law in the period of liberalism.

PEACE THROUGH LAW

After the World War this general structure and the corresponding function of international law is reestablished and even further developed. For "international society," world economy, division of labor, capitalistic expansion and its accompanying Imperialism, did not disappear with the war but fell under the blows of the economic crisis ten years after the conclusion of the peace. The cause for this ultimate destruction of the world-economic system and all it stood for may of course be traced ultimately to the war. But all the same the period immediately following the war saw a vigorous revival of essentially the same system of political and economic world-relationships which prevailed in pre-war times. Accordingly, the function of international law remains unchanged in principle. It was merely accentuated and developed further in the direction of the highest possible calculability of political affairs. For on the one hand the war had brutally revealed the whole extent of the potential destruction which politics could bring over the realm of Society. On the other hand the optimistic prosperity of the decade following the World War led people to believe that world economy was heading toward another period of limitless expansion and intensification. At the same time the introduction of the radio, the development of air traffic, and the rise of a new film industry of international extent produced new bonds uniting individuals across national boundaries and created increased interdependence of bourgeois society. One might even say that this period was the very climax of the reign of Bourgeois Society. For it was a decade of general rejection of the antagonisms of international politics, a decade of international trusts and cartels, a decade in which banks and industries, and not states, were the protagonists of international rivalries. Accordingly the whole political and legal apparatus centering round the League had two functions: on the one hand it was destined to prevent international politics from becoming excessively dangerous; on the other hand it was supposed to secure, organizationally and juristically, the vital conditions of international society and its world-economic system.

Thus the League of Nations is Bourgeois Society's own administrative instrument *par excellence*. In its commission the nations are represented by delegates of the various domestic parties, or by non-political experts. In the International Labor Office decisions are made by direct representatives of employers and employees. In the numerous minor institutions and committees surrounding the League proper, it is the League's secretariat which, with its own relatively independent bureaucracy, directly influences social cooperation in intellectual, sanitary, humanitarian, economic, technical, scientific and other respects.

But even in its capacity as a properly political congress of nations, the League's function is one determined by the international intertwinement and interdependence of Bourgeois Society. The Covenant and the associated legal rules aim at the provision of a rational framework of legal precepts and legal procedure for the status quo and the vicissitudes of world affairs. International politics with its dynamics, and its specific forms ranging from diplomacy to war, is referred to a fixed method contained in the Convenant. After the model of former conventions and drafts, this method is defined in formal concepts and abstract rules of procedure. The qualitative inequalities of states are put aside in the formal principle of unanimity and equality of votes. Political conflicts are supposed to follow a rigid and general pattern of procedure, with set terms, after the fashion of private disputes under municipal law. The status quo is protected without any consideration of its inherent value. The revision of treaties is made dependent on the consent of all states. All of these norms manifest by their very structure the task for which they actually operate: the mastery of non-political world Society over national politics, by the means of quantitative, abstract and general concepts applied to political events, and by procedures fashioned after the model of private law suits. This is the function of the League of Nations within the social pattern of its time. It is possible that this function does not wholly coincide with the intentions of the Covenant's authors. However, the position and operation of institutions in social reality is determined by the general pattern of this reality and not by subjective purposes.

This picture becomes more complete if the post-war system of treaties and conventions is included. It is obvious that they all partake of the above mentioned function of the League. This is true even of the Kellogg Pact, which makes sense only in connection with the League and its specific procedure. Again, the development of the legal framework of international trade points in the same direction. Here we find that to the old form of direct political domination over spheres of imperialistic interest, new and less aggressive forms are added: mandates, vassal states, customs unions, dominions, and so on are legal ways of expressing the fact of economic hegemony that are characteristic of this period. The commercial policies of governments are carried out within a framework of standardized treaties of commerce and arbitration, the corollary of the tendency toward codification followed by the League. Finally, the idea of quantitative solutions of the disarmament problem, of naval ratios expressed in tons and army levels expressed in heads and pieces, confirms the general picture of a formalistic, quantitative, standardized system of international order. Realizing the characteristic style of this system, it is obvious that it is functionally conditioned by the dynamics of a bourgeois and acquisitive society, by the atomistic structure of its philosophy, by the role of money as its scale of measurement, and by its reduction of all social relationships to formal quantities.

THE FUNCTION OF LEGAL THEORY IN INTERNATIONAL RELATIONS

It is impossible to recognize the function of international law in the culture of the Bourgeois Society and the imperialism of its politics, without glancing at the specific role of legal theory in this context. This theory shares in the general change of perspective that took place around the turn of the nineteenth century. It may be characterized by two utterances representative of the whole century's intellectual trend: In 1796 George Washington gave expression to the vital law of a bourgeois society in his final message to the American Congress, by establishing as a principle of American foreign policy that while commercial relations should be extended there should be as little political contact with foreign nations as possible. And, on the other side of the Atlantic, St. Simon addressed a famous pamphlet to the parliaments of England and France,[10] in which he derided the traditional political system of a balance of power in these words: "Europe was divided into two groups with the idea of keeping them equal: This is equivalent to engendering war and maintaining it constitutionally; for two groups of equal force are necessarily rivals, and there is no rivalry without war." This opinion, so commonplace with us today, becomes significant as a symptom only when one considers the person of its author. He originated the postulate of the absorption, or rather dissolution, of politics into economics, thus influencing decisively the liberal and socialist trends of thought of the

[10] *De la réorganisation de la Société Européenne* etc. (1814).

nineteenth century. That his comment is symptomatic however, becomes clear only when one realizes that the system of the balance of power had not been inaugurated in the Peace of Westphalia in order to preserve peace in Europe. Its aim was to maintain by a system of power politics the independence of Europe's many nations against the aspirations to hegemony of any one state. In other words, the balance of power not only did not preclude war, it actually presupposed war as its way of functioning. The fact that St. Simon insinuates that the system of the balance of power was a device for the preservation of peace, and that it was not adequate to this task, reveals the fundamental change of outlook. It means that during his time people began to consider the system of the balance of power as a peace system, and that he could undertake to criticize it for producing war. His criticism points to the new social requirement: the elimination of war from a structure of humanitarian, and later world economic Society. Accordingly, after the Napoleonic wars, the European balance of power gives way to the European Concert, the first of the various forms of a peace organization.

At the same time the influence of the American Revolution and its theoreticians spread the idea of "peace through law" to the public opinion of Europe. The idea of perfect security and certainty under the rule of law which resulted from the rationalization and codification of law in domestic social life was transposed into the idea of international politics being dominated by legal norms. And the inspiring example of the natural sciences during this epoch led to the notion, that adequate scientific penetration of law with respect to its relevance for world politics, a theoretical elaboration of legal "types" and concepts and their integration to a comprehensive system of international law, would induce states to subordinate their affairs to the rules of this system. People considered the availability of a procedure drawn up in accordance with general rules as the main condition for the elimination of war. It was believed that in international politics, just as in interindividual society, all individual interests would mutually adjust themselves in harmonious order if only there were a framework of rational and calculable legal rules which would formally enable this adjustment to take place.

Thus legal science began to produce attempts at a codification of international law. Textbooks appeared containing definite rules in the form of sections, or articles, and comprehensive systems of positive law which reproduced the practical experiences of international law as a logically ordered cosmos.[11] However, since the attitude of mind which was characteristic of that period laid stress exclusively on facts, these systems were not derived from some central notions of natural law, but were constructed on an analogy with the domestic law of states and the constitutional law of federal unions. This purely positivistic and yet abstract systematization was buttressed by a doctrine concerning the nature and obligatory force of the rules of international law, a problem in which almost the entire polemics of the period found its subject matter. This separate doctrine proved that the obligatory character of international rules was necessary, precisely because these rules were abstractly conceived with a view to a theoretical system, and thence had to be authoritatively imposed on the unlogical reality of politics.

Whatever the theory of the source of obligation, however, the criterion of the validity of positive law was held to be a formal one. This formal criterion of legal positiveness corresponded to the need of the time for precise and calculable legal forms, parallel to the conciseness and certainty of law within the states. Backed by the doctrine of obligation, and imbued by the conviction that the law, as soon as states had subjected themselves to it by agreement, would bring about pacification in international politics, legal science worked feverishly on the elaboration of a positive system of international law. Its point of view, conquering the minds even of many leading politicians, naturally influenced the reality of law

[11] Proposals of codification were made, among others, by: Bentham, Mancini (1872); the exposition of international law in form of statute sections was attempted by: Bluntschli (1868), Dudley Field (1872), Fiore (1890).

just as much as it was conditioned by this reality. The period called for rationalization of the legal system, and the politicians met this demand from the supply of legal postulates piled up by the theoretical systematization of the lawyers.[12] This explains why the states adhered to legal rules beyond those required functionally by the conditions of the "international Society." They adopted a number of rules and conventions which can be traced only to the idea of theoreticians that world pacification would be effected by a world system of law. Thus the unlimited faith of science in the political effectualness of duly enacted rules, of "positive" norms, and the unchallenged belief that the results of positivistic thinking held the monopoly of truth, gave legal theory a considerable influence over international "legislation." Since the practical tests of international rules usually occur only very infrequently, it is quite possible for a convention which is incapable of fulfilling any legal or practical function, e.g. the Kellogg Pact, to enjoy a long period of unchallenged "positive" existence as a part of the theoretical system which science has produced in the international law of the epoch.

This role of scientific systematization in practical international law is unique. Here a purely abstract theory, based on the criterion of logical consistency, appears in close connection with the actual shape of the law itself, in spite of the discrepancy between its logical system and the unlogical pattern of political reality. In the period of Absolutism the doctrine of international law was to positive law what the absolute postulate is to the concrete will. The epoch of liberalism, however, with its need for calculability and rationalization, had placed science itself in the very center of legal practice. Thus legal theory, based on Grotian tradition and feeding on the sources of domestic private law, attained a considerable practical importance, although the reality of international relations

[12] "While the profound political changes of the nineteenth century demanded creative juristic theory in international law, the conditions of the civil law in that century called for a cessation of creative thought and a period of organizing and systematizing activity." Roscoe Pound, Philosophical Theory and International Law; *Bibliotheca Visseriana* (1923), vol. I, p. 80.

was by no means ripe for systematization and consequently was often simply ignored. Thus there developed a practice of international law which, following scientific guidance, mostly attempted to regulate more than could be regulated, and enacted rules where no abidance by them was possible. Thus international law assumed a function which was determined not only by the actual relations and conditions of social reality, but also by the legal rationalism of the period, by its utopian pacifism and by its faith in the omnipotence of scientific knowledge.

CHAPTER III

THE PLACE OF LAW IN THE WORLD POLITICS OF TODAY

INTERNATIONAL LAW AND SOCIAL STRUCTURE

DURING the centuries in which the modern State was emerging as a territorial organization of social order, the world accustomed itself to seeing all positive law emanate from the State's will. Even the common law countries concede the State full sovereignty in this respect, since its statute law is allowed to overrule ancient precedent. For all practical and theoretical purposes the State, inasmuch as it embodies and represents the "general interest" within the section of society it embraces, is considered the natural source of all general rules concerning social conduct. Thus the "general interest," crystallized in the State, expresses itself in legal standards of behavior, and, on the other hand, the fact that the orders of the State are considered to be the law is a result of the intrinsic connection between the State and the "general interest." Therefore, if states in their turn are to be bound by legal rules, these rules have to be based on a common interest still broader in scope than the "general interest" represented by each state, an interest which transcends the State and makes its role appear relative.

As has been shown in the preceding chapters, the function of international law exists, and is determined by, the nature of such wider-than-state interests in society, and by the weight of the social groups by which they are represented. International solidarity, experienced by certain social groups with respect to common interests of transnational scope, is the real basis for a system of law which calls for restrictions on the international freedom of action of the State. For a restrictive law binding upon the states requires a social power which is capable of compelling states to observe its rules. Therefore, the present type of international law can be effective only if it serves the needs of such groups, institutions or classes as are socially powerful enough to exercise effective pressure on governments, while their internationally ramified interests require the functioning of an international order.

Three different types of such international solidarity of social groups have made possible the effective operation of international law during the various historical phases dealt with in the preceding chapters. At first the church and the spiritual universality of religious institutions provided a social group which had international ramifications and whose influence succeeded in imposing certain limitations on the particular interests of national states. Later the dynasties realized the congruity of their respective interests, and manifested this solidarity in the European balance of power system.[1] This international line-up of the ruling houses of Europe constituted enough of a real influence to carry the main institutions of international law through the dangerous period in which the subjective viewpoint of the individual State had definitely gained ascendancy over religious universalism. Finally, during the last hundred years it was the international class of trading and manufacturing Bourgeoisie, with their world-wide range of intertwined interests and connections, who depended, for their very existence, on the restriction of State action by an international system of law. In all these instances the groups whose international solidarity of interests required a wider-than-State system of law were socially important enough to be able effectively to carry the idea and practice of a system of international law against the specific interests of national governments. By far the most powerful action in that respect, however, was that of the Bourgeoisie who, having obtained a directing influence in practically all

[1] "On the plane of power-politics, therefore, the only realistic alternative for those countries which were neither geographically nor politically in a position of exceptional security, was provided by the principle of the balance of power, the only factor of relative stability in a world divided by alliances and counter-alliances." G. Schwarzenberger, "The Rule of Law and the Disintegration of International Society," *American Journal of International Law*, vol. 33, p. 67.

nations of the world, developed international law into that elaborate system of rules which we know today. The now prevailing pattern of interstate law has been made to measure for an individualistic, capitalistic, interdependent world-Society. Accordingly it is characterized by such features as: calculability, standardization with a tendency toward codification, rigidity of procedure coupled with a laissez-faire attitude as to the contents of the contractually created rules.

It is this specific type of international law, the type resulting from an individualistic world-Society, that has met with such disastrous failure during the past decade. Since its effectiveness depended on the social influence of that class whose interests were inherently international, one way of explaining its crisis is to analyze the social changes which displaced this class from power in most states, or at any rate disrupted its international solidarity. Such changes have occurred throughout the world since 1930. The result is that a system of international law designed to function in an individualistic world-Society is deprived of its social substratum and accordingly of any real basis of effectiveness. We still cling to a determinate structure of international law, although we have already abandoned the social structure to which this system of law is appropriate. This situation needs clarification. What is the nature of these changes? What features are characteristic of the present phase of social and political development?

THE END OF LAISSEZ-FAIRE

Though pointing to 1930 as the turning point, we do not overlook the fact that penetrating social transformations were preparing themselves over a long period preceding that date. However, though the pattern of society had already changed greatly during the war and post-war decade, it seems that there was no general awareness of this fact until 1930. Not until then did people actually begin to feel, to think, and to act in a consistent way that was different from that of the preceding epoch. Not until then did people actually abandon the line of codification, standardization, and formalization of international law which characterized the entire period from the middle of the nineteenth century down to the post-war instruments of standardized legal procedure.[2] The period which came to a close

[2] In this context, the following survey of the development of international treaty-making during the years from 1925 to 1935 is illustrative. The data are from *Politische Verträge*, ed. by V. Bruns (1936).

Year	Commerce and Navigation	General Collaboration	Arbitration and Conciliation	Guarantee	Neutrality and Non-Aggression	Alliances	Ententes	OBSERVATIONS
1925	//		////	///	/			
1926	////	//	//	////	//	///		
1927		///	//	/	/	//		
1928		/	////		//	/		Kellogg Pact; Pan American Conference, Optional Clause; General Act; Resolution about peaceful settlement, with model treaty.
1929			////////		//	///		Young Plan; Convention about prisoners of war. Convention about wounded in war.
1930			////		/	/		General Convention to Improve the Means for Preventing War.
1931		/	//	/	///			
1932			///		/////		//	Reparation agreement; Non-recognition doctrine. Austrian Protocol; Manchuria Resolution of League.
1933			//		////		///	Definition of Aggression by League. Little Entente. Definition of Aggression by Eastern states.
1934			/		/////	/	/////	Balkan Pact. Rome Protocols concerning Austria and Hungary. All "Neutrality and Non-Aggression Treaties" by Russia.
1935					/	//		The two "Alliances" were pacts of mutual assistance.

under the impact of the world depression was essentially one of ascendancy of the *homo œconomicus* over the *homo politicus.* It was a phase of history in which the individual, because of his vital importance for the development of economic possibilities, was allowed to prescribe the criterion of action to the State. International law, the same as administrative law and considerable parts of constitutional law, were typical limitations placed on politics in the interest of *individual freedom of action,* and the unhampered display of individual initiative. The private management of a world economic system presupposed a high degree of calculability in political and legal conditions. The only way of providing this calculability for the individual was both to limit political action and to standardize legal systems in the direction of favoring individual freedom of disposition. The separation between the direction of the political organizations and that of the economic system required a high degree of individual freedom from state interference, in order to allow the individual to perform his functions as a director of economic relations.

This situation could last as long as the economic structure and the importance of individual initiative in it remained unaltered. However, the first fundamental transformations in this respect occurred already during the World War. For the first time in history, obligatory military service in all parts of the world completely subjugated individual life to the exigencies of the State, and that not only by means of law, but also by a detailed organization of daily affairs. At the same time, production and commerce were regulated not for economic, but for political ends. In order to strengthen the efficiency of the State in its foreign relations, the laws of supply and demand were discarded, and political expediency determined production and consumption, wages and prices.[3]

The necessary consequence of such a predominance of state interest over individual interest in nearly all matters of life has been state responsibility for individual welfare and security. For the first time in history, the State not only claimed

[3] Stolper, "Lessons of the World Depression," *Foreign Affairs,* vol. 9, p. 244.

the individual forces of the whole nation to an unlimited degree, but also assumed full responsibility for their material existence. "It guaranteed food and clothing not only to the army, but to the civilian population. As the economic freedom of the individual is gradually and comprehensively extinguished, it follows as a matter of course that all economic, social and political initiatives and complaints must be addressed to the State, as the only collective personality capable of buying, selling and acting."[4] Now every war is accompanied by an accentuated concentration of all national energies and a corresponding limitation of individual liberties, and these conditions last just so long as the existence of the national community depends on the organized centralization of all efforts. Thus even this previously unheard of degree of "politicization" of the whole of social life would not justify the assumption of an historical change resulting from it, were there not certain direct lines of connection between the wartime organization of the different states and the autarky and authoritarianism of the years following 1930.

At first there is, however, a strong movement toward a return to the pre-war ways of world-economic cooperation and toward the disestablishment of politics in economic affairs. Following the slogan "Business before Politics" the problem of reparations was transferred, by the Dawes Plan, from the political to the economic plane. Rathenau's statement "Economy is our destiny"[5] was representative of a general trend of feeling among the public. There is a symptomatic significance in the fact that men like Loucheur, Rathenau, Cuno, Hoover, Mellon—representatives of big business—took charge of politics in more than one state, and that scholars like Keynes, Cassel, Stolper, Rist gained considerable popular influence that had eventual bearings on government policies. These symptoms mark a temporary return to a reintegration of the world economic system, with its ascendancy of private and economic interests, over public and political viewpoints. That this tend-

[4] Stolper, *op. cit.*, p. 245.
[5] "*Die Wirtschaft ist das Schicksal.*"

ency produced forms of legal internationalism and political pacifism in international law has already been shown in the last part of the preceding chapter.

But this apparently sweeping comeback of private enterprise and individualistic internationalism was a pyrrhic victory over the forces of political dynamics. Simultaneously with the renewed assertion of private competency against State organization of social life there were factors at work which were diametrically opposed to this tendency, pushing irresistibly toward a definite preponderance of the State in all social relationships.

First there was a generation of disillusioned war-veterans who had been brought up on the war-time organization and integration of all individual life into a great machine of national power. They came home, accustomed to individual submission to the interests of the community, and imbued with ideals of national preeminence and unity; above all they were used to regarding State-organization under powerful leadership as a means of solving every social problem. While this generation passed away in some countries without gaining decisive influence, in others it crystallized into political movements, finally taking supreme power and imposing its spirit on the entire nation.

Secondly the habit of expecting the State to assume a general and public responsibility for the security, welfare and material existence of individuals persisted, although the corollary of such responsibility, namely individual subjection to State service, had disappeared with the war. This claim on the part of the individual to be looked after by public institutions engendered a new phase in the development of the State which has been aptly called the Social Service State. It was only natural that the State, being burdened with a host of new functions in this respect, began in turn to claim the preponderance of its sphere of activity over that of the private individual.

Thirdly the blow dealt by the war and by reparation payments to national currencies all over the world made the economic systems of the countries concerned increasingly dependent on State regulation of the foreign exchanges. Here again, private interests saw themselves compelled to place their fate in the hands of the State, and to abandon to the same degree their private competency in economic affairs. However, this is only one aspect of the steadily growing importance and necessity of State regulation and organization which inevitably results from the increasing complexity of an industrialized society. This tendency for administrative and political solutions to be applied to economic problems could be observed throughout the second half of the nineteenth century. But while the increasing difficulty of running the modern economic system entirely on the basis of individual initiative and intuition caused people to rely more and more on government action, at the same time individualism, while it prevailed, produced liberalistic checks on this trend. While the administrative functions of the State extended in scope, administrative law again secured that measure of individual liberty which was judged a requisite to the functioning of a capitalistic society.

In the same way the forces working for the preeminence of individual competency and those working for the ascendancy of the State continued to be fairly evenly balanced in the post-war period, thus allowing a continuation of the pre-war tendencies. What finally brought the epoch of a privately directed world-economy to a definite end was, significantly enough, the financial collapse following the year 1929, marked by the Hoover moratorium on debts and the breakdown of the gold standard.

THE AUTHORITY OF THE STATE IN INTERNATIONAL TRADE

It has been rightly pointed out that the gold standard was essentially a legal order, "securing to the individual certain inalienable rights."[6] For the gold standard was the spinal column of an economic system in which prices, production, markets, and so on were determined by the competitive strength of the individual producer. Thus the initiative of the producer, his personal effort, was the most important requisite

[6] Cassel, *The Downfall of the Gold Standard* (1936), p. 128.

of the economic development of a country, and his private liberty was the condition under which initiative could be displayed. But an automatic adjustment of economic values could take place only if credit could be expressed in terms of a generally recognized standard of value, such as gold. It was this common denominator in economic affairs which made possible a system of "trade relationship with the *whole* of the outside world."[7] In it, every country was a world market on which, after surmounting the local protective barriers, the entire world competed on equal terms. This general openness of foreign competition on the various national markets constituted the essence of the world economic system: it was the feature which made it a world system. Such notions as world prices, world production, world demand, and so on became possible only through this relatively free interplay of competitive forces, which in turn could materialize only by reference to a common denominator of economic values, the gold standard.

When, owing to the moratorium on debts and the abandonment of the gold standard, the flow of international payments ceased to be governed by the actions of private competitors, and was placed under the control of governments, the mainstay of individualistic world economy had gone. At the same time there developed, for various reasons, a deep distrust on the part of producers and merchants in their own capacity for solving the problems of the economic system, a weakness which caused them to throw themselves into the sheltering arms of the State. For safety's sake, they pawned their individualistic assets to their respective governments. But it was the control of states over the financial exchanges which had the most far-reaching effects on the structure of society all over the world. In many states the already mentioned disbelief of businessmen in the competence of private enterprise to restore former conditions expressed itself in a general flight of capital and in an individual aversion to investment. Obviously these disturbing phenomena could not be met by any measures of private enterprise, because they resulted precisely from the reluctance of

[7] S., "New Complications in Commercial Policy," *Foreign Affairs*, vol. 13, p. 69.

private enterprise to shoulder the responsibility of the hour and to trust in the productive function of capital. Consequently the State forbade any purely speculative or financial movement of capital, thereby confining capital to its function as an instrument for the exchange of goods. The acquisition of foreign exchange was permitted only in connection with the transfer of goods. However, there is also a form of capital flight which consists in excessive purchases of goods, a flight into so-called "real values" (*Sachwerte*). Accordingly the distribution of foreign exchange had to be made dependent on a distinction between "normal" and "speculative" transactions in goods. But what was to be called normal, and what speculative? This is the point where foreign exchange control necessarily resulted in a planning function of the government in economic affairs. Foreign exchange was granted only for the acquisition of such goods as the government held "desirable" in the "interest of the nation"; everything else was excluded from importation by the refusal of foreign exchange. The necessary consequence is that "the organization charged with centralizing the operations in foreign exchange becomes the supreme and irresponsible regulator of the intercourse between the interested country and the rest of the world."[8]

In all countries this development is accompanied by a considerable enhancement of governmental functions and governmental power. In Germany, even before Hitler, the régime changed from a parliamentarian to an authoritarian structure, the government meeting the difficulties of the situation by decree-laws promulgated over the head of the people's elected representatives. In England a "national government" took over, in order to operate as an emergency committee of the whole nation. Both in Germany and in England the new type of government, more authoritarian in type than would be compatible with an individualistic society, remained for good, indicating that what brought it into being was not a passing emergency but a permanent change in social structure. In 1933 America willingly and readily followed President

[8] P. van Zeeland, *A View of Europe* 1932 (1933), p. 28.

Roosevelt on his road to a State-regulated economy. Similar developments occurred in other countries.

This process, a new social arrangement following fundamental changes in the economic sphere, somewhat resembles the general reorganization which took place with respect to public security and defense during the fifteenth and sixteenth centuries. Conditions in the sphere of public order at that time were not unlike the conditions prevailing in economic affairs in 1932. The breakdown of Imperial and Papal authority jeopardized the feudal system of providing for justice and security, a system in which public order was administered through individual responsibility and on the basis of individual ownership. When this way of administering peace and order began to fail, the public, requiring more political efficiency, turned to kings or territorial princes as the most potent units of government and, enhancing their power, sacrificed liberties and individual titles for the security which it expected from them. The need for a standing army in this connection made the princes create the administrative apparatus necessary to secure public revenue and other conditions for maintaining such an army. This developed into the mercantilistic regulation of economy and the partial politicization of the law. As the central power then took over the task of public defense and security from the crumbling system of feudal individualism, so the modern State takes over the function of organizing the economic system from private enterprise which seems to be failing in that task.

The same sort of process which led, in the fifteenth and sixteenth centuries, to the centralization of security, defense, administration and legislation, set in with respect to the economic process in the 1930's. In the general bewilderment caused by the failure of the privately administered world economic system, the State seemed to be the only organizational unit whose action was likely to secure economic existence, an existence which was in danger as a consequence of the crisis. Private enterprise, which had long been used to enlist the assistance of governmental power in the service of competition, was everywhere ready to place itself under the direction of the State, in order to obtain the protection of its laws and its bureaucracy. Consequently the ascendancy of politics over economic affairs, of public viewpoints over private interest, grew by leaps and bounds in proportion as businessmen appealed to their respective states to use their power in order to counteract the effects of the world economic crisis.

THE DISRUPTION OF INTERNATIONAL SOCIETY

Although governments had been used to being called upon for aid by private interests over a considerable period, this was not a repetition of nineteenth century procedures. This 1930 appeal for governmental guardianship is by no means a new form of protectionism, as many would have it. Protectionism is merely a defensive device against the underselling of the home products by foreign importers on the home market. This kind of defense was on the whole compatible with a world economic system, since it left intact the essential feature: world competition on the various national markets. It merely favored native industries as compared with the rest of the world producers. But since 1931 a new system has been inaugurated, in which the open market of the old system is eliminated. By means of clearing agreements, accounting devices, and highly specialized import quota systems, the general flow of competing goods is interrupted, and only very special trade relations are permitted on the basis of a painstakingly defined reciprocity.[9] The State does not merely protect native commerce from world competition, it directs this commerce into channels which are held to be the best suited to the political situation of the nation. This is not comparable to

[9] According to the International Chamber of Commerce, on June 1, 1936, there were 131 compensation agreements among 34 countries. Of these agreements, 51 were clearing agreements, 11 were pure payment agreements, and 69 were agreements on accounting and payments. The list of the 34 countries was headed by Germany with 32, Italy with 17, Turkey with 18, Rumania with 17 agreements, followed by Bulgaria, Greece, Hungary, Belgium, Yugoslavia, and others. Germany had agreements with all other countries except Brazil, and among her 32 treaties there were 15 clearing agreements, while Italy had 12. Absent from this list are the United States, Canada, Japan, Australia, New Zealand.

"protected trade" as in the old system. It might more adequately be termed "reserved trade,"[10] or better, directed or planned trade. Thus there results a paradoxical situation: individuals appeal to their respective national governments to rescue the world economic system from an international crisis, by using the national means of power; but the results of their action is not the restoration of an international and inter-individual world economy, but its ultimate dissolution and substitution by a state-directed system, the inherent antagonisms of which even aggravate the economic crisis.

This new ascendancy of the State in the economic sphere disrupts the cohesion of that "international Society" which was essentially based on the non-political interconnection of economic activities in the world. We used the term "Society," as opposed to "State," to describe that pattern of coordinate relationship which is regulated by spontaneous individual adjustments, without the aid of State organization. In this sense, the world-wide ramification of individually managed economic activities engendered a world Society of producing, trading and consuming individuals and individual associations whose non-political and autonomous cooperation was only defensively protected by the State. The unity of this Society was based on the unity of the gold standard, on the free mobility of world capital, and on the general similarity of legal and political conditions on all world markets.

When these foundations disappeared, the immediate connection between the economic subjects of the world was disrupted, giving way to a pattern of relationships in which the respective states were the mediators and organizers. Along with this autonomous world-Society of economic subjects there also disappeared the real basis of that system of international law which evolved during the period from 1856 to 1930. It was this world-Society on an economic basis which had called for calculability and stability in international relations, and for rationalization and standardization of world law. When it was superseded by a number of state-directed economic units, in-

[10] A term proposed by S., *Foreign Affairs*, vol. 13, p. 75.

ternational law began to obey the tune of government viewpoints, instead of that of the individual economic subjects. When in one single year (1932) 237 modifications of customs tariffs and 71 increases of customs duties occur in Europe alone, when expired commercial treaties are for the most part replaced by short-term *modus vivendi* agreements, when quotas are fixed month by month and are continually being altered, no trace of the former stability and formalism of international law can be said to have survived.

THE POLITICIZATION OF SOCIAL LIFE

How does this change in the world's economic structure affect the function of international law? If we remember that international law in its present form was the outgrowth of a society in which the individual's free initiative played a vitally important role, and which accordingly established legal barriers against the disturbance of individual activities by political forces, it is clear that the disestablishment of private direction by government direction in the economic system obviously deprives this specific system of international law of its social function. This result becomes even clearer when it is realized that the ascendancy of the State over private liberty is not just a feature of the economic realm of life, but coincides with a general transformation of the moral, cultural and social patterns of many countries. For various reasons the State begins to enjoy a predominant role in social life almost all over the world. Thus for instance in many of the so-called successor states (Czechoslovakia, Rumania, Yugoslavia) the politically unifying element was not a fundamental community of cultural values (the "nation"), but rather the organization of the State itself, its laws, its bureaucracy, its symbols.

During the heyday of nationalism, in the nineteenth century, the nucleus of political unity had been the common adhesion to a guiding notion of culture (cf. "*La Grande Nation*," "*Es soll am deutschen Wesen die ganze Welt genesen*," "*Manifest destiny*," the puritanism in the English national ideal etc.). In other words, the main cohesive force in the State had been a collective consciousness of what constituted the common culture and common ideals of the nation's representative groups. Nationalism was the outgrowth of a non-political pattern, a cultural program prescribing its course to the State as the political association. Accordingly, national policies followed criteria which individuals or groups of individuals, deeply conscious of their own way of living and being, imposed on governments. Nationalism represented the ideas which individuals had of the task of governments, not those which governments had of the destiny of individuals.

This self-realizing community, based on commonly experienced cultural values and interests, this spontaneous union of the politically organized individuals, is disintegrating in many countries. In the already mentioned successor-states it had never existed. Consequently the State itself, not the individual feeling of belonging to a specific community of culture, provides the element of social cohesion in these countries. The same phenomenon appeared in other countries in which the original community of national values disintegrated as a consequence of various destructive influences. Various authors[11] have demonstrated convincingly how the decline of political philosophy, the general breakdown of faiths and beliefs, post-war nihilism, the unsolved labor problem, and other factors, undermined the individual's sense of community in Italy, Germany and other European countries. The average individual in these nations began to feel isolated, his mind became confused, he was incapable of coordinating his own existence to that of society and he lost the feeling of a fundamental community of national will which united him to other members of his people. Thus the individual's own consciousness ceased to work as an active agent of social union and social cohesion.

As always, when individual responsibility fails to yield results, the State had to take over the functions concerned, and to achieve organizationally what did not produce itself organically.

[11] Such as: Hermann Heller, *Europa und der Fascismus*, 2nd ed. (1931), Peter Drucker, *The End of Economic Man* (1939); Hermann Rauschning, *The Revolution of Nihilism* (1939) and others.

The bewildered individual, being unable to prescribe a cultural, social, national program to the State, had to accept whatever the State decided, as being the only available basis of social coordination. The process parallels that already described in the economic field: there is a general retreat of creative individuality from its functions in the social structure. The prewar age was individualistic because the most important decisions were made in the extra-political sphere of life, i.e. by individuals in their own right, guided by criteria of general human values. When individuals began to fail in this task, when their leadership in the economic system, in the integration of the national community, in the autonomous assertion or moral and social criteria, faltered, the State had to substitute for individual initiative in these respects its own organizational unity. Social cohesion, no longer provided by individual free decisions, now had to be "made" by the State.

This gave a new and decisive importance to the State. Now it functions no longer as the mere instrument of preconceived ideas and goals, but as the very source of the criteria of community. Before the World War the State almost entirely followed the lead of those tendencies which developed in the more or less autonomous life of a more or less homogeneous society. In all its aspects it used to operate as a means, not as an end, as an instrument, not as an ultimate value. Since the breakdown of individualistic world economy and the decay, among individuals in many countries, of the self-determining feeling of union, the State has assumed the social function of being the first and only initiator, promoter and dictator of social cohesion. In other countries the State began to exercise the same function in connection with gigantic programs of social transformation and re-stratification. An entirely new social structure was envisaged as the product of State action and State organization in countries such as Russia, Turkey, Mexico. This leaves us with very few countries where the autonomous groups of an individualistic bourgeoisie have not been replaced in their guiding role, not by the power of another social group or class (which is not even true of Russia), but by the power of State bureaucracy.

THE NEW SLOGAN: FREEDOM OF ACTION FOR GOVERNMENTS

This new social pattern entirely reverses that legal and political relationship between the State and the Individual which, during the last century, shaped most of our political institutions. Because of the vital function of autonomous individual decision and initiative within the former pattern of society, the liberty of this decision used to be protected by certain guarantees. Now that the government's decision has acquired a more vital importance for all social processes than the individual's, it is the State's liberty of discretion which is protected by guarantees. Formerly, the government's conduct had to be made calculable and controllable for the sake of the individual's freedom of action. Now it is the individual's conduct which is made calculable and controllable for the sake of the government's freedom of action. Just as the unhampered and undisturbed mobility of the individual used to be the guiding criterion for policies, institutions, laws, so the unhampered mobility of the government has become the central objective of legal and political trends in our time.

However, the method of achieving freedom of action for the State is different from that which secures freedom of action for the Individual. Free mobility of the Individual presupposes a logical and consistent system of law, embracing all walks of life and consisting mainly in generally fixed rules of procedure which enable individuals to calculate with substantial accuracy public and private behavior. Conditions are calculable for the individual in so far as the impersonal and standardized rule of law allows him to forecast the conduct of the authorities. On the other hand, things are calculable for the government in so far as the government exercises direct control through its bureaucracy or other instruments of power. In other words, the State enjoys freedom of movement in so far as it is free from legal fetters, the individual in so far as he is secure from unforeseen acts of authority.

Liberty of action for the individual consists in the rule of legal standards in all relationships; for the government it consists in administrative, or organizational control over the factors that might influence its decision. Lack of formality, standards, principles or rules characterizes the condition of governmental mobility. The adjustment of procedures to changing situations, the ability to take whatever steps circumstances may call for, and to make decisions solely from the point of view of practical expediency, without being hampered by legal or material or ideological barriers—that is the basis for the new "liberty" of the State. To secure this kind of freedom, the domestic and foreign policies of most states in the present world aim at a direct and organizational control over all the personal and material factors that are relevant from the point of view of social order.

The battlecry in this campaign is "Liberty," and only the widespread inability of people to distinguish between the sound of a word and its actual meaning has made it possible to exploit the spell which this term, reminiscent of nineteenth century ideals, casts over minds and souls. The same confusion between letter and spirit enabled governments to misguide public opinion in the world by the use of the word "Peace," and made it possible for dictators to enlist the active support of liberal pacifists in democratic countries. Apart from these psychological smokescreens, the trend of policy, as far as it is determined by the above mentioned phenomena, is toward a consolidation of units of government in territorial, personal and functional respects. The State, being the most important single feature in social existence, tends toward a political set-up in which its government enjoys absolute freedom of action with regard to the individuals involved, the economic means required and the strategic vantage-points available, and a legal set-up which enables it to exercise direct administrative control over all aspects of social life which it might need to organize.[12] The fact that this trend

[12] "*Lebensraum*," the space required for living, is not, in Nazi terminology, the mere space sufficient for subsistence under a system of free exchange of goods. It means a domain sufficiently comprehensive to provide Germany with "absolute" freedom of action. See H. Rauschning, "Hitler Could Not Stop," *Foreign Affairs*, October 1939.

actually prevails in world politics does not, of course, imply that its ultimate ends are attainable. Nevertheless, it must be recognized that, ideologies apart, this tendency toward securing for the government all conditions for unhampered freedom of action, emerges necessarily wherever and whenever the social coordination of individuals can no longer be achieved by means of spontaneous individual decisions, and so becomes entirely dependent on organization by central agencies.[13]

It might be objected that these observations correspond to conditions only in the totalitarian states. It is obvious that government ascendancy over individual affairs, State predominance over Society, has reached its most extreme form in those countries. Nevertheless, to some degree the same trend can be noted in almost all countries. Everywhere govern-

[13] This trend might be outlined in the following way:

To secure the State's organizational freedom of action RATIONE PERSONAE

by:

1. *Aiming at standardization of human material*
   a. through selection (either according to race and blood, or according to political loyalty)
   b. through education (training, propaganda etc.)
2. *Aiming at the highest possible quantity of homogeneous and standardizable human material*
   a. by encouragement of marriage and birth rate
   b. by expansion in order to incorporate in political territory racial kin beyond the border
   c. by exchange of populations

To secure the State's organizational freedom of action RATIONE MATERIAE

by:

1. *Aiming at control of all economic resources within direct administrative reach*
   a. through extension of government control to include entire "*Lebensraum*" (contiguous supplies of raw materials, areas of cultivation, consumers' markets)
   b. through government control over home economy (prices, wages, production, trade, finance and credit)
2. *Aiming at control of objects securing strategic independence*
   a. by control over raw materials, markets etc. in war time
   b. by control of military positions of defense

To secure the State's organizational freedom of action RATIONE FUNCTIONIS

by:

1. *Aiming at an official monopoly of initiative, promotion and regulation of all social relationships*

   (Totalitarian tendency)
2. *Aiming at the exclusion of any but the Government's organized influence on affairs within the State's territory*
   a. through seclusion from foreign countries and foreign Press
   b. through prohibiting or combating any international association

      (Church, Freemasons, Labor International etc.)

ment discretion has been considerably enhanced at the expense of the legal or parliamentary control of the individual over the State. This development is so general that of all nations only the United States still presents the semblance of an old-time democracy. But even here the increasing number of administrative agencies indicates a growing need for State organization and an extension of government functions. There can be no doubt: the trend toward a more organized pattern of social coordination is a general one.[14]

Moreover, even if the demand for more organization did not emerge directly from social conditions in some countries, the appearance of totalitarian régimes among the great powers of the world would force the others, too, into some degree of authoritarian government. Throughout history it can be observed that any new pattern of political organization, arising in some place out of local needs, tends to become, through international contact, a universal standard of régime. A new structure of government may be entirely the result of specific conditions in one country which do not prevail to the same extent in other places. But once it is established other countries are compelled to imitate it to some degree for the sake of their security, even though no internal needs drive them directly to adopt that particular form of government. For new patterns of political organization imply new instruments of power and especially new methods of warfare. To meet this competition, all countries are forced to introduce a pattern of political organization which makes it possible for them to use the same weapons in an eventual power conflict. Thus the reorganization of the Italian city-states during the fourteenth and fifteenth centuries and their employment of mercenary armies was the origin of the general usage of professional soldiers in Europe, together with the organization of a permanent revenue system and the

[14] According to the Swedish periodical *Index* (Nr. 110, Feb. 1935), only four among the following list of states have a more or less unhampered foreign trade: Sweden, Norway, Denmark, Finland, Great Britain, France, Germany, Italy, Belgium, Holland, Switzerland, Spain, Czechoslovakia, Poland, Russia, United States, Canada, Argentina and Brazil. The four exceptions among these are the United States, Japan, Canada and Finland.

administrative bureaucracy which it entailed. Because the trade with the New World was considered to be the spoil of the crown in Spain, it fell under the organization of the State; but other countries had to follow suit, and thus the general structure of mercantilist economy became a European standard. The establishment of democracy in France and the destruction of the Ancien Régime's soldiery caused France to resort to a *levé en masse*, but her device compelled other, still monarchical countries to arm their citizens, thereby fostering democratic tendencies.

This general adaptation of nations to a "standard type" of government accounts for the phenomenon of historical "ages" in political development, such as an age of absolutism, of mercantilism, of enlightened despotism, of democracy, of imperialism, and so on. We speak of an "age" in this context because the historical period concerned is characterized by a type of political structure prevailing in all or most countries during that time. As this same law applies today just as before, it is safe to assume that that trend, of which the extreme manifestation is totalitarianism, represents a general tendency in the development of political structures throughout the world. It is a development by which the organized pattern of social coordination gains decisive ascendancy over the more spontaneous ways of cohesion. The State assumes predominance over Society, organizational mobility becomes more important than private autonomy, the function of government becomes more vital in all walks of life than the function of the individual. To recognize this trend is not equivalent to approving of it. But this is not the place to evaluate historical phenomena. What is needed first is their analysis. One question is whither we are drifting and why; another is how to preserve human values and culture in this drift. Accordingly it must suffice here to summarize the results of observation by stating the hypothesis that this period is one of the organizational consolidation of society both into large territorial blocs of governmental units, and into functional and legal ascendancy of the Government over the individual.

Even if this hypothesis should be wrong, even if this trend is characteristic merely of the totalitarian states, it is bound to affect, if not the structure of government the world over, at least the structure of international relations. For the policies of the totalitarian states—three, or possibly four out of seven great powers—determine the points of contention in international politics. In seeking to obtain the objectives which correspond to their structure of government, or rather to the requirements of their type of State, they determine the types and the places of international antagonisms. It is significant that for these four states the freedom of action of their governments is the one goal of foreign policy.[15] Since the conditions of such State liberty are not given, their foreign policies are necessarily dynamic, with the result that the objects of conflict in international relations depend on the direction of this dynamism. So far as the function of international law is concerned, this is the only important result.

The meaning of international law is order in the relationships between states. Whatever the nature of these relationships happens to be, friendly or hostile, whatever inspires them, influences their evolution and causes them to occur—all this gives shape and content to the function of international law. The pre-war period of individualism saw international conflicts arise out of the expansion of private economic interests and their protection by the State. Now conflicts have their roots in the tendency to secure freedom of action for governments; and this orientation is what gives a specific shape to interstate relations, interstate antagonisms and interstate law. The character of international politics depends on what governments on the whole seek to obtain, and the function of international law depends on the character of international relations. Thus in a world where governments strive for absolute freedom of mobility, international law obviously must be concerned with the function of State organization in the social structure.

[15] For Germany, this has been convincingly demonstrated by H. Rauschning, *op. cit.*

It must take cognizance of the organizational tasks of governments, of the requirements for their realization and of the conditions of functional coordination between different governments. In one word, its orientation must be political, not anti-political. It must not restrict governments, but enable them to function in the service of necessary organizational tasks. Thus a period characterized by the ascendancy of politics over private affairs requires a system of international law which operates not as a restrictive, but as an enabling order of political functions.

THE MISFITTING ROLE OF THE TRADITIONAL LAW OF NATIONS

Clearly the existing system of international law does not fill such a role. Its rules and institutions are designed to check the action of political units, to hamper governments, to restrict states. These provisions were elaborated by an age of predominant individualism, consequently they are inadequate to the function of international law in present-day reality. In its present form the international system of law does not serve as a means of order, but only as a means of conflict. Its possibilities are used, or rather abused, as weapons in the struggle between states.[16] A situation of complete disorderliness in international relations is perpetuated under the cover of a legal façade, the obsolescence of which does not prevent people from falling a prey to its sentimental spell, just as the abuse of ideas like "liberty" and "peace" did not keep them from preserving a sentimental attachment to the mere words.

The development of the law of commercial treaties may serve as an illustration of the spirit which the letter of international law is used to cover today. Treaties of commerce such as had become almost a standard type in the period of world economy had the function of fixing the formal framework within which a free exchange of goods could be effected among

[16] "The main function of morality in the international society does not consist in the control of one's own behavior, but in the use of morality as a keen and powerful weapon against potential and actual adversaries." G. W. Keeton and G. Schwarzenberger, *Making International Law Work* (1939), p. 96.

the interested private enterprises.[17] Long-term tariff obligations and the generalization of treaty terms by means of the Most Favored Nation clause engendered a stable and almost uniform commercial treaty law.[18] Thus the typical commercial treaty served to set up general legal certainty and security, under cover of which individuals in each country could entertain trade relations with the entire outside world. Now this system of general economic relationships has been abandoned in favor of "reserved" segments of international economic intercourse, in accordance with government regulations. The outlines of this development have been described above. It can only be characterized as an all but complete reversal of the former economic system. However, this about face did not affect the letter of the existing commercial treaty law in most cases. Established commercial treaties have not been discarded, but by discrimination of the subtlest kind they are made to serve a function diametrically opposed to that which inspired their shaping. While originally devised to allow world trade to be determined by the competitive forces of the market place, and to provide equal trading conditions for all importers, the viewpoints of governmental economic and financial policies began to supersede this criterion of the "world market." Thus exchange restrictions and accounting provisions, enacted by governments and suspended in favor of certain countries, enable the states to maintain the letter of the treaties while jeopardizing their proper effect. Also, by defining importable goods in a hairsplitting way, or by prohibiting imports for hygienic reasons, and by other administrative measures which are not directly excluded by the wording of the stipulations, governments have succeeded in shifting the national trade from a general basis to the narrow channels of planned and reserved economic relationships.

Similar phenomena can be observed in respect to other parts of international law. While maintaining the semblance, and

[17] Kapp, *Planwirtschaft und Aussenhandel* (1936), p. 96.

[18] H. v. Beckerath and F. Kern, *Autarkie oder internationale Zusammenarbeit?* (1932), p. 15.

even the use, of established legal instruments, concepts, institutions and rules, governments are unanimous in the understanding that they are not bound by the spirit of this obsolete law.[19] Wherever new instruments of international law are set up they deviate considerably even from the external shape of the already existing law. Thus treaties are no longer concluded in the sharp and precise form which was required thirty years ago in order to enable individuals to forecast international relations between states. Instead, these hard-and-fast obligations of former conventions are now concluded in the form of "gentlemen's agreements," protocols, "Axes," administrative agreements, secret notes and verbal understandings.[20] The forms of existing international organization are maintained externally, but their function in actual use is distorted beyond recognition. The example of the Non-Intervention Committee is a clear illustration of this point, and certainly not the only one.

Thus present-day international law, which had been shaped by the exigencies of an individualistic world-Society, today serves only as a tactical position in the power-conflict of governments. The actual working of this law no longer fits the function of a law between states. It does not create order, serving mainly as an instrument of international discord. It may be compared to a church, situated in no man's land between two fighting armies. In a strongly religious period the church would continue to be regarded as a place of worship even during combat, and both armies would respect it as such. In a period of religious indifference however, with other motives prevailing, the church, though obviously built for religious service, would have significance to the armies only as a battle position.

Now obviously this church is out of place, even though it can also be used as a tactical object. It is not fulfilling the function for which it was devised. Similarly the existence of the

[19] One of the most significant admissions of this attitude is Neville Chamberlain's statement in the House of Commons, quoted on page 154.

[20] More instances of loose usages of terms and concepts in international relations and international law are reported by Th. Baty, "The Trend of International Law," *American Journal of International Law*, vol. 33, pp. 653*ff*.

present system of international law cannot be justified on the grounds that it serves as a diplomatic cloak for policies entirely contradicting its spirit. Both for military and diplomatic tactics more suitable instruments can be devised than churches and obsolete rules of law. And on the other hand the respective functions corresponding to churches and legal systems are not fulfilled by institutions which are out of their proper place and therefore can produce only unfitting effects.

This discrepancy between the function of a system of interstate law in the actual world and the legal instruments which an age with a different structure has handed down to us, sets our problem. We have to investigate to what extent the existing system of international law is inherently unsuited to, and therefore cannot function properly under, the present circumstances. As this analysis results in the rejection of the traditional system of law, a further query arises as to what type of law is required by the structure of modern world-politics. Thus the philosophical analysis of the existing law of nations has to be followed by an analysis of the mental and emotional pattern on which a new kind of law might be based. To these ends the following chapters are dedicated.

PART II

LEGAL THEORY AND POLITICAL REALITY

SOCIOLOGICAL INTRODUCTION

THE CONNOTATIONS OF POLITICS

POLITICS AND THE STATE

IF used without discrimination, the terms "politics" and "political" seem to indicate a somewhat general pertinence to the State, as distinct from the affairs relating to private individuals. However, it has rightly been pointed out that not all activities of the State can be considered of political character.[1] The State has a complex structure into which are interwoven more elements than those which are usually called political. Thus the connotations of politics can be found only if we succeed in detecting that aspect of the State which is essentially different from the operation of all other institutions. For it must be the feature in which the State is distinct from other forms of association which has been called political in order to distinguish it from those qualities which the State has in common with business corporations, churches and private clubs. Accordingly, our question is: to which features in the structure and the operation of the State does the term "political" exactly refer? And we intend to answer this question by attempting to isolate analytically the specific type of social integration which characterizes the State, from the vast complex of other types of social order, institutions and molds of human behavior which, though possibly conditioning the State, are clearly of "non-political" nature. Language, custom, ethics, morality, codes of behavior like decency and honor, conventional patterns like the accepted standards of education or economic behavior, the dogma of "it's not done," and so on—all of these constitute media of social integration which are

[1] "Power, Political" in the *Encyclopaedia of Social Sciences*, vol. XII, p. 301 (by Hermann Heller).

evidently distinct from the "political" variety. The law, although practically monopolized by the State, was historically at any rate prior to the State, and to a certain extent retains some features of independence from State direction even today. In addition there are a great number of human associations within the confines of states, or cutting across state boundaries, such as churches, trade unions, economic associations, and organizations dedicated to the most varied human ends.

Among all these different forms of order in social relationship the State is marked distinctly by its character as an *organization*. The word itself suggests the criterion of difference separating the State from the unorganized patterns of human behavior, such as morality, convention, language etc. *Organ*-ization means social integration with the help of instituted *organs*. By organs we understand commissioned officials who permanently and professionally are entrusted with the task of acting on behalf of a multiplicity of individuals. And organization is the process by which, through the action of such organs, a multiplicity of individuals attains a unity of performance and of decision directed toward a common purpose. It is this specific type of social integration which characterizes the State as distinct from other patterns of social behavior. However, there are other organizations besides the State. To discover the distinctive quality connoted by the term "political" we have to analyze the institutional difference between the State and non-political organizations. The main criterion of difference in this respect is naturally the function of the State. But a different function also results in differences of structure and operation, so that we can speak of specifically "political" features of the institution of the State which are not to be found in other organizations.

It is not possible within the framework of this introductory chapter to discuss the role of organization as such in the whole complex of human culture. All that we can do is to state in a general way that social relationships require the specific mold of organization when, and in so far as, the need for common action arises as a result of cultural conditions. Thus it is significant that the origin of the modern State was the need for standing armies, and that its planning and regulative system was extended in proportion as foreign relations, public revenue, export and import management, legislation, jurisdiction, education, social welfare, and so on became problems which called for unitary action on behalf of innumerable individuals who were affected by these problems. Accordingly, the organization of collective action in those respects was entrusted to the hands of professional officials, the bureaucracy of the State. This development has moved, since the days of Frederick II (of Sicily) in the direction of steadily increasing the functions of central planning and organization in social life, as in more and more fields the way of a more spontaneous integration of individual energies became inadequate and intolerable. As the differentiation of civilization progressed, private initiative as an instrument of maintaining order in social relationships was replaced to an ever increasing degree by a rational direction of social cooperation through the decisions of common "organs." There is more organization, consequently more "political state," in our culture than there was in the sixteenth or the eighteenth century. And the recent extension of the organizational form of social integration to include economic activities may not by any means be the last phase in the "rationalization" and organization of social life.

While organization is a mold of social coordination which is found in all fields of social relationships, that type of organization to which the term "political" refers is distinct from all other types by its territorial delimitation. Thus it differs from other kinds of organizations the sphere of which is circumscribed either in personal or in functional terms (e.g. a church is an organization of all those persons professing a common faith; a factory is an organization of all those functional processes pertaining to the end of production.[2] Political organ-

[2] L. Gulick, in *Papers on the Science of Administration* (1937), distinguishes between organization by major purpose, organization by major process, organization by major clientele, and organization by place.

ization is that organization which is established on a territorial basis, i.e. which embraces potentially all activities and relationships occurring on a certain territory. Being territorial in extension, it is not confined to any definite circle of persons or to any particular kind of subject matter. Thus it is the only organization which potentially concerns the whole of social life within a certain territory, in so far as it coordinates all those aspects of social order and social relationships which actually require organization, by virtue of the stage of complexity they have reached.

This is not the place to describe the entire process through which that unity of collective action and decision, which is called State, is maintained and secured in human society, a process which has been more competently analyzed elsewhere.[3] Here we are concerned only with the question: what features in the structure and operation of the State are essentially distinct from all other kinds of organization, constituting the specifically "political" qualities of the State? What specific function does the connotation of "politics" imply? The answer requires a brief analysis of the elements of organization as such. For since by a process of elimination we have found that the State is distinct from some other forms of non-political social order by its organizational quality, it now remains for us to identify more concretely the political species among the genus of the organizations.

THE ELEMENTS OF ORGANIZATION

Three factors may be observed in any organization: the "organs," i.e. the commissioned agents who decide and act on behalf of the whole organization, directing the process of integration and channeling the accumulated energy toward the desired result; the "organized members," i.e. all those individuals whose energies are contributed toward the common action under the management of the "organs"; and finally

[3] Hermann Heller, *Staatslehre* (1934). In English language, there are not many examples of a sociological approach to political phenomena. Notable among them are McIver's *The Modern State* and H. J. Laski's *The State in Theory and Practice.*

the "scheme of order," i.e. the plan according to which the conduct of "members" and "organs" is coordinated, and which usually is laid down in the written form of a statute, a collection of rules or in some similar instrument.[4] However, it would be a mistake to assume that an organization "consists" of members, officers and rules. An organization is a unity of acts not of men. Not the member, nor the organs constitute an organization, but that which connects them; the structure of their relevant behavior. The scheme of order is only a plan; unless individuals actually behave in a coordinated way, as foreseen by this plan, there is no organization. Thus organization is a specific structure of connectedness among individuals, materializing in their behavior.

What are the forces and factors which account for this type of connectedness among individual beings? Any organization owes its existence to the fact that a multiplicity of men can act in a unitary way only by making individual persons act for it. Action requires that unity of will and physical capacity which is the property of individual beings. Therefore many men together can act each individually, but if the need for collective action arises, they have to employ the psychophysical unity of one of them and have to coordinate their efforts with his decisions and acts in order to acquire the capacity for action.[5] Thus the instrument of the organized unit is that individual who acts, as an organ, for and on behalf of the entire organization, deciding and ordering the way in which all individual energies in the group must be actually coordinated in the interest of a unitary effect. Organization exists when and in so far as individual acts of a number of men regularly occur according to a scheme of order, in such a way as transfers their combined energy into the common efficiency of the whole group. Thus organization only exists in and consists of actual cooperation of a specific kind. If individual energies are coordinated by a scheme of cooperation established

[4] Our analysis here follows the ideas developed by Hermann Heller, *Staatslehre*, pp. 231*ff*.

[5] L. Gulick, *op. cit.*, p. 7.

by a common organ, and if the acts assigned to the particular individuals occur regularly, those individuals are "participating" in an organization. An organization does not exist, however, where a group of individuals merely feels united by a community of purpose. Neither does it exist where there is an individual in the position of an "organ," if he fails to obtain the cooperation of the individual "members" according to his plan of coordination, and thus is unable to combine their diverse energies into common action. Organization exists in cooperative acts which take place according to a scheme of coordination and under the direction of an organ, and it exists in those acts only. There are countless other types of integration and unification among individuals, but the organizational type of integration does not exist apart from an ordered structure of actual cooperation, maintained by the unifying guidance of individual organs.

Accordingly, the characteristic and essential feature of an organization is the functioning of an organ as the means of rational unification of action. No collectivity of persons can attain concerted efficiency and unity of decision otherwise than by using the natural psycho-physical unity of concrete individuals as the instrument of action and consequently of their unity. A group does not have a natural capacity to act, it has to acquire it artificially. It can act only by means of a scheme in which an individual is put in the position to dispose of the combined energies of that group. This is the way in which organization proceeds: Multiple energies are coordinated by means of the singleness of will, decision and action of concrete individuals who, in order to fulfill this function, have to arrange for the precise conduct of the group according to the plan of cooperation. Individuals, therefore, cannot act collectively—that is they cannot form an organization—unless they forego, within certain limits, the freedom of their personal will, and accept, as a guide for their conduct, the decision of an organ that indicates the ways and means, the time and place of the action and gives concrete shape to every member's share in the cooperative scheme. Thus, on the one hand, individuals who wish to act collectively are dependent on the functioning of an organ acting and deciding for them all. On the other hand, the individual who is acting and deciding as the organ cannot be instrumental in bringing about the unity of the organization unless his decisions actually elicit response and all relevant conduct is on the whole adjusted to his plan.

THE UNITY OF LARGE ORGANIZATIONS

Now, only a very small or very simple organization can get along with an organ consisting of one individual only. Most organizations require a number of individuals to discharge the functions of a unifying organ. The State, in particular, to the extent to which it is an organized structure, is integrated by a huge body of persons who decide and act as living instruments of the unity of the whole. But we saw that the specific quality for the sake of which a group requires an organ is precisely the ever present readiness for judgment, decision and physical action which distinguishes an individual from a multitude of persons. If the natural psycho-physical unity of an individual is the necessary instrument for any collective action, in order to provide the collectivity with a brain and a will capable of acting, how can this unifying effect be achieved by a plurality of persons functioning as organs? It is indeed true that the natural unity of an individual is the best means through which a collectivity can acquire the capacity of unified action. Consequently, wherever a large number of persons are functioning as organs they must strive to approximate the condition which makes a single individual the ideal instrument of organizational unity: the capacity for integrating judgment, decision and action.

A group of persons who are acting as organs within a larger collectivity, therefore, have to be organized among themselves in such a way as to make sure that they can function at all times and in all situations as a reliable unit of decision and action. This is accomplished by devising and enforcing a hierarchical system of rigid discipline and subordination within this staff of persons forming the organ.[6] Any organ consisting of a plurality of persons can function only on the basis of rules which secure a unity of will and decision within this group. Powers of command, norms about responsibility, superiority of decision, emphasis on obedience and discipline, are the devices aiming at a unification of will which will lead in the quickest, easiest and most efficient manner to singleness of decision and physical performance. This very high degree of coordination within the body of persons forming the organ goes a long way toward molding the total number of these persons into a single unit capable of reaching decisions quickly and consistently, and carrying them into immediate action. In other words, it enables this body of organs to approximate the way in which a single individual would function as the organ of an organization, in cases where a single organ is sufficient.

We call this organization within the organization, this body of organs working in disciplinary, almost mechanical unity, disposing directly of the material means of collective action (such as money, arms, land, buildings, machines, and so on), the *organizational staff*.[7] The "staff" is the body of individuals who function as organs, and is itself strongly unified by an internal scheme of coordination and by a permanent pattern of professional conduct securing its inner coherence. One of the most common errors in political science is to mistake this staff for the entire organization, and to overlook the fact that this body of organs is conditioned, for its functioning, by the actual cooperation of the organized "members," the same as a single individual organ who also can function as such only if his decisions succeed in bringing about coordinate behavior on part of the "members."[8] The staff of organs as a whole is no

[6] "The dominating position of that small circle of persons which we find in every unit of government, with respect to the dominated 'masses,' derives from the 'Advantage of the small number' [*Vorteil der kleinen Zahl*], i.e. from the possibility to communicate quickly with each other, and to be able to bring about at any moment a rationally ordered group action." Max Weber, *Wirtschaft und Gesellschaft*, 2nd ed. (1925), p. 610 (my translation).

[7] On the notion of the staff, see L. Gulick, *op. cit.*, p. 31. Max Weber, *op. cit.*, uses instead of "staff" the somewhat more graphic term "apparatus."

[8] See page 5 of this chapter.

more than the instrument by which a collectivity of individuals obtains the capacity for unitary action. The circumstance that this instrument of organizational unity is in itself composed of many persons does not affect its quality as an organ, nor does it do away with the necessity for effective response and cooperation on the part of the "members" of the organized collectivity. An organizational "staff" that fails to secure the regular effectiveness of its plan of cooperation is no more the organ of an organization than is an individual who tries to act as the leader, secretary or president of a group without being obeyed. Of course the chances that this will happen to an entire staff of organs is infinitely less than in the case of a single individual. However, this does not effect the essentially cooperative structure of the organizational process.

ORGANIZATION IS A UNIT NOT OF MEN, BUT OF BEHAVIOR

Now what, precisely, is it that makes people forego their freedom of action and decision to some extent and submit to the decisions of other individuals who thus become organs of a collectivity? All organization arises out of a collective need for unified action. It consists in behavior of individuals shaped according to a plan of cooperation. This scheme of coordinated action, however, has to be made in accordance with what is understood to be the aim of the group's united effort. Without this common element of a functional "directedness," there would be no possibility of an understanding between the organ and the organized members. The scheme of cooperation must be felt and understood by a sufficient number of people before it can be put into actual practice. Without being aware of the ends of the organization, people would be incapable of realizing the meaning of the cooperative behavior assigned to them and of adjusting their conduct correspondingly. This is what distinguishes an organized collectivity from any other group united by common elements of their living and feeling (for instance, the state from the people): The group, or mass, consists of a psychological homogeneity, it is unified emotionally; the organization consists of a cooperative homogeneity, it is unified by a common intention and for common action.[9]

The common end constitutes the motive that makes individuals incorporate themselves into the system of coordinate behavior decided upon by the organ. It therefore constitutes the limits within which the organ can count on cooperation by the "members."[10] Thus the secretary of a league for peace and good will will be able effectively to urge the members to attend the meetings, to join common appeals, to subscribe to certain periodicals, and above all to pay their contributions to a financial fund. For all these acts will enable him to make the combined energies of the members effective in the direction and toward the ends which they all hold desirable. Or, to take another example: the construction of an irrigation system in a rural community will require the allocation of special duties to the different individuals in such a way that all their activities together will bring about the desired result. Some will prepare materials at home, some will work at the place of the undertaking, some will maintain the transport lines to the next town and the station, and so on. Without an organ to determine everyone's share in this project, the mere zeal of all of them would never achieve the common effect which they envisage. But precisely because they all aim at a common effect, it is possible for someone to function as an *organ*, and an *organ*-ized system of cooperation becomes possible. Accordingly, apart from just that conduct which is relevant to the common end, the individual "member" is not affected by the organization. A member of the league for peace and good will, for instance, may belong to the Catholic or the Protestant Church, he may or may not drink heavily, he may beat his wife or be her slave—all this does not affect his "membership" which consists in the contributions he is supposed to

[9] "Organization is the form of every human association for the attainment of a common purpose." J. D. Mooney and A. C. Reiley, *Onward Industry*, Harper & Brothers (1931.)

[10] "In the last analysis, the efficiency of every administrative system is dependent upon the understanding by the persons affected." J. M. Gaus, in *The Frontiers of Public Administration* (1936), p. 88 (quoted with the permission of Chicago University Press).

make toward the common ends. The construction of the irrigation scheme materializes in so far as the different individuals perform the actions assigned to them, whether particular members of that organization waste their money or save it, whether they live on the first floor and sleep on the second or vice versa, whether they say their prayers at night or not. In this sense it must be repeated that the medium of organization is functionally coordinated conduct, not coordinated individuals. An organization does not consist of men, but of acts. No organization involves individuals any further than the behavior relevant to the end which the organization is understood to pursue.

Because of this fact it is necessary to emphasize again that organization is possible only if and when people are aware of a common goal, or better if they are aware of the fact that a certain result is commonly desired, and only commonly can be attained. The mutual understanding in respect to *something* which is intended in common is the fundamental social condition of organization. The awareness of this fact, however, acts as a restricting and binding force on the wills of the particular individuals. As soon as someone points out to a number of persons an object of common concern (e.g. an enemy, a fire), and some of them realize the aim and the fact that it concerns them all, their individual wills cease to be free in that respect. They are now under the restraint of a common intention, in which their behavior is functionally linked to that of others, and in which the necessity of cooperation acts as an inhibition on their personal impulses. It is the consciousness of a community of purpose with others which makes individuals ready to accept the order, and the duties, of an organization. The realization of an objective "something" in respect to which their intention is linked to that of others accounts for the willingness of individuals to submit to a form of coordination which they understand to be a function of the common goal. It is this binding force of a common intention which gives the organ the power to direct the conduct of the members by his decisions. Such is the structure of organized power, which is always power as a function of "something." Leaving aside the forms of sexual or religious domination of individuals by individuals, it can be said that the basis for social power is always organized direction of functionally determined social conduct. At the bottom of all organization there necessarily lies the restriction upon individual wills and impulses which is derived from the consciousness of certain ends which are also pursued by others and can be attained only by all together.

THE SPECIFIC FUNCTION OF POLITICAL ORGANIZATION[11]

It was necessary to explain briefly the structure of an organized association in general in order to detect in what respects the political species of organization differs from the non-political. It is the question of the functional end of organization which reveals clearly the specific nature and problems of political organization.

In all non-political organizations the realization of the common end precedes the organization as such.[12] People become conscious of pursuing, or of having to pursue in common a goal with respect to which they join with those other individuals in whom they notice the same intention. People who love canaries, for instance, organize in groups in order to be able to raise them on a larger, or better, scale. People who would like to invest their money in a specific productive enterprise join together to run a factory with others who show the same desire. People may organize on the basis of a community of ethical principles, or of common affections, or they may join in organized cooperation with a view only to a specific object (common purchase of a building, etc.). The characteristic note in all these types of non-political organization is that they are no more than an intermediary step between the realization of a common intention by a number of individuals and its materialization in common action. The organization in all these cases is

[11] For a more detailed study of this problem see Hermann Heller, *Staatslehre*, pp. 199-215.

[12] A very interesting discussion of the ends of organization is to be found in: *Groups and Their Administration*, by A Faculty Seminar of The American University (1938), pp. 40*ff*.

functionally determined by an objective realized previous to its existence in the minds of the future "members." It is therefore merely a means to a preconceived end and serves a purpose which lies beyond its own existence.[13]

It is different with political organization. Political organization was described before as that organization which embraces a certain territory, establishing a centrally unified order for social relationships in general throughout this territory. People who share the same space with other people are bound to be in permanent relations and contacts with each other. At a primitive level of civilization, these relations may be rare and simple; they may even be restricted to occasional visits and to combat. Religion and convention are able to provide for what order is needed in these rare and simple relationships. But with increasing density of the population human relations become more frequent and at the same time more sharply differentiated.[14] Out of this process of differentiation of society arises the need for integration of the social order through the unifying action of a central agency. The ends to which political organization is dedicated, therefore, are not freely chosen by people who realize their own intention and their community with others having the same aim. The objectives of political organization are not preconceived by the members who join together because of their consciousness of these aims. While people may want or like to raise canaries, or run a factory, they cannot be said to have chosen to live in common: they cannot help living in common. Wherever they may go, they cannot escape social existence and social relationships. The only exception, Robinson Crusoe, is of no precedential value. Living in common however, presupposes, as soon as a certain level of cultural differentiation has been reached, a planned order of human relationships and a number of common administrative services.

[13] In this sense, Georg Lukács defines organization as "the form of mediation between theory and practice." *Klassenbewusstsein und Geschichte* (1923), p. 302. Also see L. Gulick's definition (*op. cit.*, p. 7): "Organization as a way of coordination requires the establishment of a system of authority whereby the central purpose or objective of an enterprise is translated into reality through the combined efforts of many specialists."

[14] See the description of this process in McIver, *Community*, pp. 242-3.

These depend on a permanent organization for the sake of collective action with respect to both order and services.

Political organization, therefore, is distinct from all non-political organizations in that its "members" cannot choose whether they do, or do not, want to participate in it. The inescapability of political organization, however, is not the same as, for instance, that of a monopoly trade union, into which workers are forced by the threat of serious disadvantages in case of failure to join. The possibility of escape does exist here, although at a heavy price. But human beings, because of the social character of their existence, cannot possibly avoid political organization, since human life, quite irrespective of what men's will may want, unfolds itself necessarily in forms of social order and coordination which are secured by the action of political organization. The mere fact of living together with others—always given a certain level of civilization—imposes the organization of social order as a condition of existence. Thus political organization is not maintained with a view to a specific purpose but as a fundamental necessity; it does not arise from the realization of a community of intention, but in response to basic requirements of social life itself; it is organization not as a function of an end beyond itself, but organization for the sake of its own order. It is the nature and the differentiation of their social existence, and not a purpose, an intention or even a threat, which forces men to submit to a permanent *modus*—or rather *status*—of planned cooperation directed by common organs.

This condition of political organization explains two features characteristic of the State as distinct from non-political organizations:

1. The ends pursued by political organization are not specifically defined by the intentions of purpose-conscious individuals. Arising out of the general requirement of an integrated social order, they are too vague and ambiguous to admit of any meaningful scheme of cooperation without being defined more concretely. Therefore, there is inevitable struggle within the political organization regarding the defini-

tion of its ends. Consequently the State serves as a means to varying ends, and therefore has a tendency to acquire a certain independence from its ends. Organization becomes a means without inherent purpose.

2. The "members" of political organizations have not joined together because they realized that they had a purpose in common. The group of individuals organized in a State is much wider than any purposive groups that might exist within it. Consequently the binding and restricting effect which is exercised, by the consciousness of a community of intention, upon individual wills and impulses, is not operating in political organization. Power in the political sense is thus much more dependant on material means than it is when based on the "taming" force of common intentions.

These statements seem to contradict our previous findings regarding the nature of the organizational process. It is therefore necessary to explain them with more detail.

THE SPECIFIC STRUCTURE OF POLITICAL ORGANIZATION

It has been stated above that every organization is a cooperative unit which becomes possible only by the common awareness of "something" at which "members" aim in common. Human will and human impulses can be bound only by the decisions of a common organ and by the scheme of order, by their own consciousness of being linked to one another for the attainment of concrete objectives. "Defeating that enemy!" —"Combating this fire!"—"Producing coal out of a mine!" —"Raising canaries in common and providing jointly for the accessories!"—these are ends which people can realize sufficiently to submit to a plan of cooperation with regard to them. Because their content is concrete enough to force certain consequences upon the individual wills, they produce a restrictive effect on the wills and impulses of the individual "members." But "Integrating our collective existence!" or "Living in a coordinated way with your fellow beings!" or "Settling social conflicts by common standards!" are not definite enough aims to impose a functional restraint on men's wills. They cannot be realized as bonds of common intention between men, thereby inducing people to submit to a scheme of cooperation, because they do not lead to the consciousness that other people are heading with them in the same direction. Hermann Heller, in his sociological investigations on "*Herrschaft und Ordnung*,"[15] has shown the social ineffectiveness of too vague an end of co-activity. He took as an example the simple order "March!" The subjects to whom this command is addressed would not realize where and how to march, unless aim, direction and formation were determined by tacit convention. They would either walk in all directions, or not stir at all; the effect of the order would be nil. But "March against the enemy over there!" or "March in two columns northward!" are orders which can be understood as a content of common action, and which consequently admit of an organized scheme of conduct.

Thus, in order to coordinate human wills in a scheme of cooperation, the end of that cooperation has to be sufficiently concrete to be understood. The mere fact that some integrating order is required in a differentiated social existence may be recognized by people, but it is not precise enough to make them realize the meaning of common action to be taken in that respect. Social relationships are many and of manifold variety. People who realize that there must be order in social relationships, and that this order has to materialize through organization, do not, by virtue of this general awareness, form that community of intention which is the prerequisite of every organization. Because many ways and kinds of social order are possible, no organization of social order could take shape in society unless there was sufficient agreement as to the concrete type of coordination to be achieved by it. Without such concreteness of the functional ends of organization, the meaning of whatever the organs decide would not be understandable, and no scheme of cooperation could materialize.

Therefore, political organization, not being derived from a community of preconceived intentions, can operate only in the direction of a specific version of its general ends. Those

[15] Heller, *Die Souveränität*, pp. 38*ff*.

ends in themselves—the integration of social life in a general order, and administrative services required for the maintenance of an ordered social life—are too ambiguous to allow people to feel bound to each other with respect to them. Those ends, moreover, are of such self-evident nature that they cannot be visualized by people as a purpose which is freely and deliberately conceived by them: they lie beyond the reach of human willingness or unwillingness to desire them. There is no social existence other than ordered existence. Accordingly, the end for which political organization functions is ingrained in the very existence of all men. But since the actual outline and the materialization of the scheme of order depend on a community of conscious intention among the "members," political organization is always determined by one of several possible definitions of its ends.

Consequently the process of integration and organization within a State hinges on a struggle for the concrete definition of the State's ends. The decision of that struggle in favor of one of the various views about social order furnishes the State with those concretely defined ends which make it possible to maintain a meaningful scheme of cooperative order.

However, since there is always a variety of such views in a given society, the group which is agreed on the prevailing definition of the State's ends does not embrace more than a section, possibly only a minority, of the entire "membership" of the organization. The consciousness of common aims which binds people to one another and acts as a restriction on their individual wills, derives, in the case of political organization, from one particular version about the ends of common action; but the collective action requires the cöoperation of all individuals, not only of those who are united by their adherence to that version. Against their definition of the ends of political organization others will struggle. Accordingly, the "membership" of a political organization does not consist of people who are united beforehand by a community of purpose, but of different groups, each centered around one of the possible definitions of social order and political organization.

Now organization is possible only on the basis of one concrete conception about its functional ends. This is what causes the overruled groups to accept, within certain limits, the version of the prevailing group. It is the unity of common aims among the persons of that dominating group which makes an organization of social coordination possible. Without a precise view of the ends of political organization, held by at least a considerable part of the "members," no organized system of cooperation is feasible at all. Therefore, as long as the overruled groups are at least able to understand the conception of the predominating group, as long as the prevailing version of the ends of political organization can at least be realized by them as a possible mode of action, they will acquiesce in it and submit to the organizational order erected on the lines of that view. For after all, some kind of definition of the functional ends has to prevail, in order to bring political organization about. Thus the definition of the group that dominates in the organization represents in some way the entire "membership" simply because it provides the concrete formulation of the ends of State functions, without which no State organization could operate at all. This is the tragic tension which is to be found in all political organization: Political organization exists because of a general need for social integration and coordination, but it works only on a basis of a partial conception of its ends. Those whose views do not happen to prevail will nevertheless acquiesce as long as the need for an organized social order as such seems more important to them than its particular shape.

Thus political organization differs from non-political organization in this important respect: the latter embraces only people who are united by the consciousness of a common intention and who are thereby inclined to adjust their conduct to a scheme of cooperation by which their common goal can be attained. Political organization, on the other hand, necessarily embraces all the people living in a certain area, but only fragmentary groups within this entire collectivity are united by a common conception of the ends to be attained through political organization. Consequently both the concrete shape and the operation of political organization are determined by a definition of its aims which represents the views only of a partial group. And only within that group do we find that readiness to submit to the scheme of order that comes from the consciousness that the organization pursues ultimately one's own ends.

Naturally, there are differences of opinion about policy in all organizations, in the non-political ones as well as in the political ones. But in the non-political organization the various views of policy concern only the selection of means toward the preconceived common end, with a view to which people have joined the organization. The basic community of intention which constitutes the common bond of their wills is not affected by the difference of views about methods. On the other hand, the operation of political organization is not founded upon an original coincidence of intention of all members, but on the temporarily prevailing definition of its ends by a fragmentary group, which provides the purposive direction of the organization. The members of the collectivity are not bound together by the consciousness of a common intention, but by the inescapable necessity of some sort of organization embracing them all. So they have to be prepared to permit the view of one group among them to determine the ends of the political organization *in concreto*, as long as this dominating point of view contains at least a minimum degree of representation of their own point of view.

Thus political organization, because it is not merely the instrument of a preconceived purpose of all its members, presupposes the formation of purposive groups within its membership. It can operate only if its operation is directed by the concrete conceptions of such a group. Without the existence of such groups of common intention as political parties, pressure groups, and so on, there would be no possibility to shape political organization along meaningful lines. In order to function at all, political organization has to secure and to stimulate the formation of such groups with common political views among its entire membership. Whenever such groups fail to crystallize in a political collectivity, there is a fundamental crisis of political organization which leads to phenomena to be described later.

At this point, a short survey of the analysis attempted on the preceding pages might be indicated.

Among the different varieties of social order which operate in our culture, the State is distinguished by its quality as an organization. Among the different varieties of organizations which we find in our culture the State is distinguished by its territorial circumscription, and by the corresponding comprehensiveness of its functions.

This difference between the functions of non-political and political organizations entails also certain differences in their respective structure. In every organization we find three elements: the "organs," the "organized members" and the "scheme of order." But organization does not consist of these factors. It consists of what connects them, of the coordinate structure of people's behavior.

This structure of behavior is shaped by the decisions of the "organs," who devise and supervise the coordination of all individual acts relative to the ends of the organization. They elicit response in the form of actual behavior of the "members," to whatever degree the decisions and actions of common organs are an indispensable instrument for collective action.

"Members" obey the decisions of their "organs" because they realize that they are pursuing certain ends in community with others. This awareness acts as a restraint upon their wills and impulses which makes them incorporate themselves into a scheme of order which is meant to further the achievement of those ends.

The difference of political organization from non-political organizations stems from the fact that political organization does not originate from a preconceived common intention that binds people together. It arises out of a progressing differentiation of social life, which makes it necessary to provide for an integrating order through the operation of a central agency.

The ends for which political organization operates, are therefore:

1. Not consciously anticipated by those people who constitute the "membership" of the organization;

2. Not sufficiently concrete to admit of a scheme of coordination, which is only possible if the end of cooperation is specific enough to be realized by people.

Consequently, the political organization embraces a collectivity of "members" who have not freely joined because they felt united by a common purpose, but who participate in the organization by reason of their very existence in society.

A political organization, therefore, can operate only if, within its "membership," groups are formed which are united by a conscious definition of the ends of political organization. The struggle for the definition of these ends, therefore, is an inherent feature of any organization which is territorially circumscribed.

The concrete shape and the direction of the scheme of coordination is determined by the views of one of these partial groups which happens to prevail in the political struggle. Its definition of political ends is accepted by the other groups, because of the necessity of some concrete formulation of those ends, and in such measure as it has at least a minimum of representative value.

Because the "members" of political organization are not united by a community of preconceived intention, the power of the organ rests on a different basis. The "organs" are obeyed in non-political organizations because they are instrumental for the attainment of a common purpose. In political organization this is true only of the obedience of the dominating group. The rest of the "membership" is kept in obedience by more material means of power.

THE CONNOTATIONS OF POLITICS

Against the background of this analysis it is now possible to discuss the specific connotations of the term "politics" and "political." The first conclusion is that politics always refers to some sort of collective action. It is a common and fatal error to assume that politics is identical with the process of group living. Political unity is often confused with the feeling and the living of a common culture which brings forth those units of social life called peoples, races, or nations.[16] This kind of common pattern of human culture may be referred to as the *folklore* of those social units. Accordingly we shall term it *folkish community*. Folkish community may exist, under certain conditions, without political organization. We know, for instance, that the Eskimos have not developed any trace of government in our sense. They realize what social order their common life requires, on the basis of traditional and conventional standards, about which the natural superiority of the old and respected among them decides. There is no political organization among them, because there are no permanent and professional organs to whom the function of action and decision on behalf of all is entrusted. A similar picture is provided by many primitive tribes. The Germanic tribes knew a specific organization of their community only in times of, and for the purpose of, war. The conditions of many Indian peoples both in North and South America prove that on a simple level of social development folkish community is felt and lived with great intensity without the need for any common organization. But even on a higher and more differentiated level of civilization, the common patterns of feeling, thinking, evaluating and doing are not produced by the action of political organization but by the emotional intertwinement of individuals responding to each other's existence.[17] Therefore the homogeneity of culture, the unity of social existence, the integration of individual spirits is not the proper field of action of politics, although all these factors may have a strong bearing on the intensity or feasibility of political organization.

Only in so far as collective action in respect to social life is required, does the political collectivity appear as a territorial

[16] The English language knows no specific word to designate that type of felt solidarity which comes from having fundamental cultural features in common. Sociologists have coined the term "commonality" which, however, has not been widely accepted. For this reason I may be pardoned if I use a term ad hoc, in order to distinguish group living from group action.

[17] See the very interesting research, of this process, by Theodor Litt, *Individuum und Gemeinschaft*, 3rd ed. (1926).

organization of action and centralized decision. A political organization thus is not a spiritual or cultural community, but primarily a unit "of military, financial or other performance."[18]

The importance of thus confining the connotations of politics to the field of collective action cannot be overemphasized. It means that politics must not be identified or confused with social life in its totality. Common patterns of living, feeling, thinking, talking are not deliberately engendered, although they certainly may be furthered, protected and destroyed by political action. The community of folkish life grows as a personality grows. It is an irrational and elementary expression of human life. Politics, on the other hand, is a form of rational common action. The circumstance that modern social existence is entirely dependant on political action must not obscure the fact that the community of folkish life and the community of political action belong to fundamentally different categories. While common patterns of human life are the result of processes which cannot be brought about by human intentions, political organization is a method of deliberate collective action by means of a planned and central coordination of energies. Since every organization is composed of acts, not of men, political organization, however "totalitarian" it may be, never absorbs completely the "grown" entities of human life, such as the individual and the community of folkish life. It moves around these centers of creative energy, capturing more and more elements of the various contexts which result from their movements and their needs. But however complete this regulation may be in itself, it has to do only with social relationships, and therefore with partial manifestations of live units.[19] It can never embrace the totality of life as integrated in an individual or a "folk." Politics coordinates behavior, not lives; it brings forth collective action, not collective culture; its unity is one of function, not of being. Politics is performance, not existence.

[18] Heller, *Staatslehre*, p. 89.

[19] The social manifestation of a person is fragmentary, not integral. "We are all fragments, not only of humanity, but of ourselves." McIver, *Community*, p. 302 (by permission of the Macmillan Co., Publishers).

Accordingly, in the center of the connotations of politics is the function of the "organizational staff." For it is through its central planning and its decisions that the combined energies of a collectivity of persons are made to materialize as a unit of practical efficiency. This unity of action in a plurality of individual acts is maintained by constant coordinating activities on the part of the organizational staff, which guides and directs all individual conduct in accordance with the scheme of cooperation. But political organization, as we have seen, necessarily embraces more people than those whose aims coincide with the ends of the political organization at a given time. Therefore, the behavior that corresponds to the scheme of order must not only be decided upon, but also must actually be provoked and arranged for by practical acts and personal contact. Moreover, all behavior contrary to the "official" scheme of order has to be prevented and eliminated. It is obvious that the efficiency of political organization will be proportionate to the degree of actual cooperative behavior which the staff of organs is able to secure among the organized "members." It is equally obvious that conduct in accordance with the "official" scheme of order will be more likely to occur, the greater the common understanding is between the organs and the organized "members" about the meaning of that cooperative system. Such understanding depends upon the realization by the membership of the ends of political organization. The more "members" are able to comprehend the functional ends of political institutions, the more will they understandingly adjust their conduct to the requirements of coordination and cooperation. The degree and the extent of such understanding is influenced by the simplicity or familiarity of the aims, the amount of social and spiritual homogeneity, the possibility of mutual orientation by reference to established standards, and so on.

Accordingly, the absence of these factors will narrow the circle of people who by virtue of their realization of political ends are disposed to behave in accordance with the scheme of the organization. Thereby the regular occurrence of cooperative conduct among the "membership" will be endangered. If this happens, if social decomposition, or the complicatedness of political affairs, or the uncertainty of individual orientation in society, causes difficulties in the self-incorporation of individuals into the organization, then the latter depends on the degree of mechanical control by which individual subordination can be secured. In such a situation, the key position of the organizational "staff" becomes more important than usual, because of its command of technical means by which the actual coordination of social conduct can be established. There then occurs what may be termed the *politicization* of social life.

The ultimate roots of the process of politicization are to be found in the inability of people to agree, in sufficiently large groups, upon common definitions of political ends. It has been said above that the general conditions which make political organizations necessary are in themselves not specific enough to determine the functional significance of the latter, and that political organization becomes possible only through a more definite conception of the ends which it is understood to serve. Such definitions are the object of groups of people within the general "membership" of the State, who join because of their common conception of political ends. It is obvious that the formation of such groups, designed to give a specific meaning to political organization, presupposes a more or less spontaneous decision in favor of concrete aims on the part of the individuals who compose them. However, if the issues and problems which require collective action in a given society become very technical and complicated (e.g. eliminating unemployment, achieving financial stability, industrial recovery, price-regulation, social adjustment), a spontaneous understanding of these objects on the part of individual beings becomes more and more difficult. Consequently, the formation of such groups as agree on a determinate conception of political ends becomes more and more impossible, as groups of common political ideas are based on definite and clear-cut opinions of individuals.

Moreover, in times of cultural transition and transformation, the traditional standards of value usually fail to provide for the orientation of individuals in this world. Accordingly, the average individual becomes every day more uncertain, lacking criteria of judgment and a frame of reference by which to understand the function of political organization in social life. All this jeopardizes the formation of larger groups agreeing on a common conception of political ends and thus making it possible for political organization to function in a determinate direction. However, there must be some degree of uniformity of purpose among the "members" of the political organization. Otherwise it would be impossible for society to be organized in a comprehensive way. For since organization consists in the actual occurrence of coordinated conduct, the entire absence of contact and understanding between the "organs" and the "members" would prevent an organization from materializing. And the contact of comprehension which is necessary between "organs" and "members" can only be in terms of the ends which the organization is to achieve. Accordingly there must be some community of intention in a collectivity, if there is to be organization.

Now we cannot choose whether we should like political organization or not. Political organization exists not because of a desire of human beings, but because of the objective need for integration in a differentiated society. Thus the "organizational staff" has to perform and to act on behalf of the collectivity, even though the collectivity, or parts of it, fail to make up their minds as to the ends it should pursue. Since for the purposes of organization as such, however, there must be some purposive uniformity, the latter is procured by the organs themselves. In other words, the organs, instead of being instruments of purposes previously conceived among the "membership," now create among the "members" that unity of purpose which failed to materialize on its own accord. Thus the political ideas of the "members" become an instrument of the unity of the organization. Since people are primarily unable to agree upon definite conceptions of political ends, the spontaneous unity of purpose among them is supplanted by the mechanical unity of an *ex post facto* acceptance of a course already adopted by the "organs." The "members" who cannot achieve solidarity of their own views, must see the view implicit in the actions of the "staff" imposed upon them. They have to accept it as if it were their own object and intention, because it is the only conception of political ends available for practical purposes.

This is the ultimate reason for both Hitler's *Führer*-principle and Mussolini's formula *L'atto precede la norma*—the act precedes its standard. They indicate that the action of the organs is no longer merely instrumental in realizing an idea that was preconceived among the organized individuals. The "standard" for the operation of the State is no longer set by a community of purpose among the "members." Consequently the necessary uniformity of purpose is created by an *ex posteriori* determination of the members' wills, making them conform to the ends of the organization as actually pursued by the organs. Whereas in a more balanced and better oriented collectivity, organization is the step from the common visualization of an end to common action for its realization, here the action precedes the collective conception of its end, because there are no other common conceptions on a broad enough basis. It is in this sense that Hermann Heller called modern dictatorship the "government of anarchy," because it is the result of disintegration and disorientation among the individual "members" of political organization.

In a "politicized" society, the "staff" seems to hold the only key-position. The whole of social life begins to depend on its performance to an increasing degree. Not only the practical effects of political action, but also the unity of political outlook is provided by the organs in their directing role. Individual persons are induced, by all sorts of influence, to cooperate with the "organs" in actions the meaning of which more or less escapes their understanding, or which they are made to understand in a way chosen by the "organs." Thus it is possible for the "staff" to overshadow the true functional meaning of whatever action is taken. Power seems meaningless, an end in itself; the "staff" seems to function more for its own sake than as an instrument to some ulterior end.

In a fairly well balanced and well oriented collectivity cooperative conduct is secured on the basis of a regular and general realization of political functions, and through the corresponding disposition of individuals to submit to the general scheme of coordination. In a disintegrated and disorientated society, however, collective action becomes more and more dependant on the more or less mechanical compliance with numerous detailed orders and regulations, by which the "organs" have to secure the organizational unity of collective efficiency. It is obvious that this more mechanical way of coordinating social conduct requires an amount of regulative measures and rules which could be dispensed with in the case of a more spontaneous agreement of purposes among the membership. It is equally obvious that owing to all these detailed instructions on behavior, owing to the substitution of "directed" political ends for spontaneously conceived political ends, the entire social complex becomes more and more dependent on the existence and performance of the "organizational staff." The capacity of the "staff" to perform efficiently, its "freedom of action," becomes, therefore, the foremost political postulate in such a system. The coordination of all behavior and all energies lies in the hands of the "organs" to such an extent that the entire social system becomes highly vulnerable in that one point where the "staff" operates. It is this condition which accounts for the tendency, in a "politicized" society, to protect the machinery of government action from every possible disturbance. People begin to feel that their whole existence is tied up with the functioning of the "staff," and they identify themselves more and more with its fate. They actually begin to live for the executive independence of the political "organs." There is only one desire: to make the functioning and the efficiency of the "staff" foolproof, to assure its full control over all factors of possible disturbance, and to place within its immediate reach all the material means conditioning its operation.

The extent of political organization in social life therefore seems to depend on the one hand upon the problems and issues engendered by cultural differentiation. However far the functions of political organization may expand on this account, however, the degree of a full "politicization" of social life is not reached unless the functional meaning of political organization is lost sight of by its individual members. Only in periods of political disorientation does social life actually become a function of the governing "staff." Only then does the single conceivable policy seem to be one that serves the "organizational staff" and its freedom of action as such. Only then is everything which increases the independence of the "staff" from outside conditions considered valuable, while everything that disturbs its performance is condemned. Accordingly, the extent to which political organization is allowed to absorb human life in a given collectivity is determined by the degree to which the functions of political organization are visualized clearly and independently by its individual "members."

DEFINITIONS

If, on the basis of this analysis, an attempt is made to define the meaning of the terms "political" and "politics," it must be accompanied by a warning. Definitions are no more than signs or symbols, representing not a reality but a process of thinking. If used separate from their context, they are exposed to a complete misunderstanding of what their words connote. Brief formulas can do more harm than the best of statesmanship can ever make up for. Therefore, let it be clearly understood that these definitions are a shorthand summary of this chapter of sociological analysis. Beyond this they carry no meaning.

In this sense: "Politics" connotes that organization of energies for the achievement of collective action which is concerned with social relationships within a given territory.

"Political" refers to a quality of inherent functional pertinence to the specific ends which this organization is commonly meant to achieve.

CHAPTER IV

MORAL IDEALISM AND POLITICAL REALISM IN INTERNATIONAL LAW

FACTUAL AND NORMATIVE APPROACHES IN LEGAL THEORY

A MODERN school of legal thinking maintains that the only realistic approach in legal theory is that which studies the function of legal rules within the setting of given conditions and of historical realities. It is doubtless true that without knowledge of existing circumstances and actual facts, no legal problem can be solved adequately. After all, law is not a speculative system of abstract logic, but a scheme of order which is effectual in the historical world of human culture. Yet knowing all the facts and all the circumstances of a given cultural situation does not in itself enable us to reach any conclusions of legal relevance. It is impossible to solve a single problem of legal theory without resorting to normative standards which transcend the actual given facts. The misunderstood "realism" of the modern school of legal thinking is actually nothing but plain materialism which is envious of the accuracy of measurement and the peace of mind characteristic of the natural sciences, and tries to ape them by attempting to draw rules and conceptions from the comparative study of empirical "material."

On the other hand it must be admitted that they are justified in criticizing the abstract speculation of those who believe that law can be found in the statute books and only in the books. A legal science which attempts to study "the law" apart from the concrete structure of existing cultural conditions misses the practical point of every legal problem. But a theory which merely registers observed facts, trying to make law a science of empirical prediction, misses the essential task of law: the corrective evaluation of human behavior. In every legal situation facts and ideas are intertwined. Accordingly, legal science deals with an object of investigation which not only is formed but also is to be formed. Therefore neither the given structure of historical circumstances nor the normative standards calling for its modification may be neglected.

The first part of this book was intended to be a study of factual conditions and forces which have influenced the operation of law in the field of international relations. In this sense it was shown what changes the function of international law underwent through the development of social, political, and economic factors during the past centuries. No attempt was made in those chapters to analyze international law from the point of view of pure ideas. Now the investigation of the empirical circumstances which condition the operation of law may lead to an understanding of what difficulties a legal system encounters at a given time. However, such an analysis does not conduce to any solution. If the problem of international law consisted only in the appearance of new historical factors which had not been assimilated in legal thinking, it might be sufficient to describe the nature of these changes and leave it to practical lawyers to find the formula through which the established principles of law could be applied to the new situation. This, indeed, is what the effort of many writers in our field amounts to. However, it seems to us that not only the practical application of legal principles, but also the spiritual roots of international law are affected by the radical modern transformations both of consciousness and of conditions. If that is true then it becomes imperative to investigate not only the practical difficulties of the present law of nations but the very ground underneath it, and to proceed with a reform of the foundations. While this uncertainty of the basis of international law itself provides an element of discouraging difficulty in our work, it also admits of the hope for an entirely new construction of the building from the cornerstone to the top, doing away with all unsatisfactory patchwork.

While the first part of this book outlined the function of international law from the point of view of given historical conditions, we shall now try to determine it from the perspective of the normative ideas transcending the realm of givenness. The function of international law is a result not only of the factual interaction of social tendencies and the structure of material factors in human culture but, at the same time, of the ideal criteria which guide the writers and scholars on international law. From their conception of ultimate values emerged those postulates which confronted states and governments through centuries of legal thinking, often giving impulse to important developments in the legal order of international relations. It is therefore necessary to analyze international law as a construction of legal theory as carefully as we have to analyze international law as an actually operating factor of social reality.

The origin of international law as a theoretical discipline of its own is generally identified with the writings of Grotius. This fact is significant for the study of the nature of the present theoretical system. For, as indicated before, the essentially new element which Grotius introduced into the study of international law, thereby making it a special discipline, was that he centered his theory around the notion of the State as the subject, and at the same time the master of, international law. The empirical reality of the State became the starting point of his thinking. This perspective forced him logically to found the system of international law on the will of the states as the source of law. It is this perspective which made international law a separate branch of law and a special discipline of legal theory. For it led to the distinction between the legal rules pertaining to, and emanating from, sovereign states, and legal rules pertaining to and emanating from God, single individuals, churches, or one particular state as such. By saying that Grotius initiated the present system of international law, we implicitly make an important statement about the theoretical structure of that law. For we thereby recognize its descent from the personalistic and atomistic ideas of the seventeenth century, and we admit that our present thinking about international law is essentially of the same nature as that of Grotius and his followers. These assertions need to be amplified and tested.

Before Grotius wrote, there certainly was international law and a science which dealt with international law, but that science was not a separate discipline of law. For the earlier writers who treated international questions, notably the Spaniards, did not base their legal thinking on the notion of the particular subject of law and on the subjective will, but on the conception of a harmonious universe. For them the world was essentially a comprehensive order unified by God and culminating in God. The will of human creatures within this system was allowed only the role of an agency concretizing positive rules by an application of the general norms to varying circumstances of time and place. But the will of the subjects of law did not exercise any creative function within this universal system of law. Thus, for the thinkers before Grotius, it was the elementary reality of the unity of all creatures under the fathership of God, not an act of human will or consent, which accounted for the existence of legal rules. *Ius gentium* was in being not because the well understood interests of states caused them to agree on common rules, but because the whole of mankind was a "quasi political society," held together by the spiritual unity of the *corpus mysticum*, which again connoted not just an ideal or a postulate but the real essence of humanity itself.

Certainly the will of the individual subject of law (the person, the state, the ruler) was conceived to be free, but only free to sin against the legal order embracing the universe, not free to create legal rules or to affect or influence their validity. The only will whose action was essential for the shaping of legal norms was that of God, inspiring the entire universal system of law and order. Consequently there was no problem about the obligatory force of law, since law was not a mere obligation, but the framework of the creation itself. There was no dualism between the ideality of objective norms and the reality of subjective wills in this system, because the norms of law were not just ideals but the very core of reality, and the will which violated them was not conceived to be within the system at all, being sin. Because of this subordinate position of the human will in the system of law as conceived by the great philosophers of scholasticism, international law did not appear to them as a discipline apart, but on the same level with other rules concerning the conditions of human relationships. As we would make a distinction between commercial law and labor law, they distinguished international law from other aspects of legal order, but they did not treat it as a special discipline and a separate kind of law. Accordingly, international law, being part of God's universal order of the creation, was dealt with as a part of theology or general jurisprudence. To the pre-Grotian writers it was merely a specification of this universal order, not a legal system of its own.

The emancipation of international law as a system of its own became possible only when the human will was elevated to the role of creating legal rules. While the conception of a universal order, founded on the divine *idea* of law, made international law appear merely as a specific aspect of law, like patent law, for example, the notion that legal rules are a product of acts of will leads to a differentiation of legal systems according to the source of will from which they emerge.[1] This is why the separation by Grotius, of international law from other branches of law is an important clue regarding the underlying conception of legal order. Placing the will of the State, rather than God's universal order, in the strategic center of his system, Grotius had to conceive international law as a separate discipline, distinct from other kinds of law by the type of will which brought about the existence of legal rules. Thus international law, when regarded as a discipline of its own, goes back to a perspective of legal thinking which was first applied to the subject by Grotius. This perspective starts out from the

[1] A. v. Verdross, *Völkerrecht* (1937), p. 42.

assumption that the individual persons are the primary reality in any legal system, and from there proceeds to the notion of the legal order which they establish in their common affairs. We shall call this perspective of legal thought the *personalistic* notion of law. In order to understand the underlying ideas of our present system of international law fully, we shall have to investigate the implications of personalistic legal thinking in general.[2]

THE FEATURES OF PERSONALISTIC LAW

Personalistic thinking has its roots in the mentality of the seventeenth century in Europe. The vain attempts, during the sixteenth century, to achieve a religious peace both of arms and of minds, resulted in a widespread abandonment of the theological approach to problems of world order, and the corresponding growth of a belief in "scientific" methods of solving these problems.[3] Scientific methods meant on the one hand the application of rational arguments instead of those based on revelation; on the other hand it meant that problems had to be analyzed and solved in terms of observed facts and perceivable experience. According to this shift of emphasis from mysticism to "realism," and from religion to science, the main object of analysis and investigation became necessarily the empirical reality of nature. In the case of legal problems this meant the focusing of attention on the empirical nature of man. For the singleness, the individuality of man seemed to be the most basic experience and thus the "natural" element of all things social. Following the discovery of the dynamics of the *Ego* during the Renaissance, and following the anthropological trends in Humanism, the idea was established that the immutable reality underlying all social and legal problems was the nature of individual man. In accordance with this "natural" essence of every order, it was believed that inherent in human nature were certain fixed conceptions, certain laws of social

[2] See also pp. 328 *ff.* in part III of this book.

[3] Dilthey, *Weltanschauung und Analyse des Menschen seit Renaissance und Reformation*, 3rd ed. (1929), p. 90.

structure and relationships, which called everywhere for the same basic forms of morality, legal order and economic conditions. Thus the focal point of all thinking in moral and social sciences became the individual person, typified and standardized through the conception of "man in the state of nature." In the state of nature man was regarded individually, in solitary existence, apart from all social and legal ties. He was isolated from his surroundings "for the purposes of research." In this sense Robinson Crusoe was a book of political philosophy, depicting man "in his true essence." The "true essence" of man could be determined only when individuals were regarded singly and separately from each other. To use the words of Sabine: "Not a man as a priest or a soldier, as the member of a guild or an estate, but man as a bare human being, a 'masterless man' appeared to be the solid fact."[4]

If legal and political thinking begins by positing the notion of a solitary individual and then proceeds to compose society of a multitude of Robinson Crusoes, the first and basic assumption must logically be that of the natural liberty of individual persons. The essential independence and "masterlessness" of the individual's will thus became an axiom of the personalistic approach to legal and political problems. From the notion of originally free and independent wills of originally separate persons to the idea of legal order there leads only one logical way: that of the voluntary submission of the individual person to common authority or to common rules. The idea of contract as the form in which individual persons place themselves under the obligation of the law is the only possibility of making compatible the concept of "natural" freedom with that of legal bonds. The act of consent is posited as the origin of the legal rule.

This approach to legal problems corresponded to the mentality as well as to the experience of people living at the time of Grotius. Their individual self-consciousness had broken free from the universal and all-embracing ties of the medieval idea of order. They had witnessed periods of glorious subjectivism

[4] Sabine, *A History of Political Theory*, Henry Holt & Co. (1937), pp. 432*f*.

displaying itself in unrestrained energy. The first beginnings of modern capitalism had already placed a premium on the initiative of the individual being. *The individual vs. the world* began to be the antithesis dominating their consciousness and replacing the medieval antinomy between the eternal essence of the creation and the un-essence of the sinful will. Thus it was only natural that this basic experience of individual existence should become the cornerstone of legal thinking in that period. The single individual person could not be imagined otherwise but free, and every rule of law thus had to be construed as a creation of human will. If there was limitation upon the original freedom it existed because the individual will had consented to it.

The supposition of the axiomatic freedom and independence of the particular person introduces into legal reasoning an irrational and incalculable element: the subjective interests of those who by their consent bring legal rules into existence. Therefore from a purely personalistic point of view law can be conceived only as a protection of personal interests to the extent that they are compatible with each other. Since the particular person is considered the basic reality, his subjective interests must be given the place of a recognized value in the legal system and must be counted with under all circumstances. Thus the existence of legal rules can be ultimately justified only because the observance of a legal order by all persons means a better safeguard of the interests of each. Consequently, the norms of law cannot be regarded in principle as anything but so many compromises between conflicting personal interests. And since the irrational character of subjective interests does not admit of a rational solution of the conflict between them, the issue can at best be settled only on the grounds of expediency. Thus legal rules, conceived against the background of essentially free and independent persons, are mere formulas of convenience in the relations between these persons, governed only by practical considerations of advantage and expediency. This is the most radical consequence to which personalistic thinking is driven, because it ends with the negation of the obligatory force of legal rules and finally with the denial of law as such.

THE DUALISM OF SUBJECTIVE REALITY AND OBJECTIVE IDEALITY

It was this personalistic approach to legal problems which Grotius applied to international law, and which distinguished his treatment of the subject matter from that of previous writers. On the one hand it seemed quite natural that he should extend an explanation of legal phenomena which was so perfectly suited to the contemporaneous attitude of mind, to the relations between states, looking upon states as so many individuals living with each other *in statu integritatis*. From this point of view international law appeared as a problem of imposing limitations on the free wills of states by the recognition of reasonable and "natural" standards which would appeal to the states and elicit their mutual consent. On the other hand, the practice of international law, far from being systematic or comprehensive, would not yield sufficient precedents for such standards of reasonable conduct. Therefore Grotius, in order to fill in the need for "natural" standards in the new "field" which he detected, had to borrow the principles of another legal system which was already established: Roman law. Thus there arose, in international law, the dualism of the "reality" of its persons (the states) on the one hand, and the "ideality" of objective and abstract rules of law on the other.

This dualism is the result of the two systems of legal thinking which have influenced the theory of international law. On the one hand it was the idea of personalism, the tracing of every legal phenomenon to the will of the persons, and the justification of the law in terms of personal interests. In introducing Roman law into his system, Grotius necessarily embodied the personalistic features of that legal system into international law. The Roman law antithesis between persons and things, persons and property, persons and possession, persons and actions became the logical structure of international law also. Thus the personalistic construction of international law, already emerging from the seventeenth century mentality, was emphasized further through the resort to Roman law. It has remained a dominating feature of international law up to our own days, as every textbook in the field will prove. The treatises on international law invariably start out with a description of the State, defining thus the "person" of international law in terms of its authority, its territory, its membership, its sovereignty and above all, its fundamental "rights" or liberties. Only after having laid down the notion of the legal person and after having defined the person's will, interests and existence, do the treatises pass on to the legal rules developed by the states in their intercourse with one another, usually using the "representative organs" of the state as a stepping-stone of transition from the notion of the legal subject to that of the legal norms.

In accordance with the precedence of the notion of the person over all other legal conceptions, the present system of international law has been dominated since the days of Grotius, by the idea of the "natural liberty" of states. Even when it is not admitted consciously, this feature of natural law philosophy is present in every conception of international law, whether it may be positivistic or otherwise. The doctrine of *domaine reservé* is one of the instances where the idea of the "natural liberty" of states becomes openly manifest. However, in being transferred from the realm of individuals to that of states, the concept of natural liberty took on a different meaning. With respect to individuals it had the practical significance of a sphere of life where individuals were free from the rule of the authorities, being subject only to the will of God. Thus it resulted only in a reservation for the ends of private life, within the framework of a recognized order of law and authority. The idea of the original liberty of individuals did not lead to the rejection of law, but only to its limitation. As applied to states, however, it amounted practically to the declaration of an absolute and complete independence of the states. It led not only to the idea that states were exempt from the exigencies of the common legal order in certain respects, but that they did not in principle recognize any superior authority or law, such as individuals would recognize above themselves. The consequence was that legal rules between states were conceived as an exception to their complete original freedom, instead of liberty being conceived as an exception to the rule of the law.[5] Thus the idea of "natural liberty" in international relations amounted to the idea of a basic isolation of the particular states, from which they emerge, to be subjects of legal rules, only by their own free initiative and free will. To the manifestations of this will, whatever they may be, law lends a merely formal sanction: the interests of states are a value to be protected, and any rule which suits the particular interests combined in the "community" of states enjoys the force of obligation. This personalistic element in international law has led to the phenomenon of positivism in its different variations.[6]

But the personalistic idea of law is not the only root of the present system of international law. The medieval tradition of legal thinking continued to exercise its influence on authors in this field throughout the centuries. It has already been stated that medieval thinking considered law to be the very essence of things, eternally underlying all relationships, independent of personal desires or wills. Law is not made, at any rate not by human wills; it is in being because the creation in itself is ordered and cannot be imagined in any other way but in orderly structure. Law is not created: it is recognized by human reason. It is inherent in the nature of all created things, and has only to be found and brought to light, in which process the human will may play an auxiliary role as an agent of practical formulations applied to concrete circumstances.

It is obvious that the two ways of legal thinking, the "essential" and the "personalistic" approach, represent two systems of theory, each complete in itself, based on its own premises and proceeding with its own peculiar ideas. Neither of these theoretical systems needs the other one; they are self-sufficient and logically incompatible with each other. One starts out from

[5] See Redslob, *Völkerrechtliche Ideen der französischen Revolution*, in *Festgabe für Otto Mayer* (1916).

[6] A. v. Verdross, *op. cit.*, p. 37.

the fact of the existence of the individual person, the other starts out from the idea of order of the creation. One takes it to be the irrational impulse of personal interests which drives the individual to consent to legal rules, the other construes law as the consequence of absolute values which force themselves upon the recognition of all human beings. One construes legal order as a product of personal wills and justifies it in terms of subjective interests, the other regards law as the essence of everything created and of all the relationships in this world, justifying legal order in terms of eternal ideas underlying all human existence.[7]

While these two approaches constitute two independent and opposed systems of legal philosophy, they have been merged into the system of modern international law. However, the fusion has not been a logical one, nor was it logically necessary. It is entirely the accidental product of historical circumstances. The thinking of the sixteenth and seventeenth centuries could not possibly construe any legal system except from the point of view of the person, because the individuality and self-reliance of the solitary person was the great experience dominating the mentality of that age with elementary force. The individual's will and pursuit of his interests which the two centuries witnessed in action with so extraordinary a vigor, had to be the starting point of their legal and political philosophy. At the same time, however, it was mentally impossible for a Christian world to construe the notion of law without resorting to the idea of absolute and objective norms which had validity even without individual consent. A Christian mind could not help recognizing the existence of eternal truths and absolute values, which had to be inferred from the belief in one universal God, one faith, one paradise. The tenets of Christian faith were still too powerfully dominant to admit of the conception of legal order entirely in terms of personal wills and personal interests. A legal order consisting merely in a mu-

[7] M. Bott-Bodenhausen, in his *Formatives und funktionales Recht* (1926), has analyzed the two roots of modern legal thinking with great sagacity. The names which he applied to them are: substantival and individualistic (*substantielles und individualistisches Recht*).

tual adjustment of interests on the basis of expediency would not have appeared as binding to the Christian mind of those times. Thus, torn and undecided between two eras, the seventeenth century mind had to merge the medieval idea of an absolute order as the essence of reality with the Renaissance conception of the individual person as the ultimately moving force in legal order. The merger, as has been said, was not dictated by logical necessity, but by emotional forces which, though conflicting, coincided in the mentality of the seventeenth century.

This explains the peculiar structure of the legal theory which emerged from the fusion of the two ways of thinking.[8] After having discarded the old notion of a divine and universal order of the world, and after having turned the focus of scientific attention to man as the core of all social reality, those absolute ideas, truths and values could be conceived only as the "true," i.e. the original, substance of man's nature. This is where the dual structure of present-day legal thought developed: on the one hand positive rules of law were imputed entirely to human will, to consent, contract and agreement. Here the personalistic idea of law prevailed almost undisputedly. On the other hand natural law common to all men and to all times constituted an objective element of eternal validity, which was not affected by human will or in need by human consent. But, since positive rules were conceived to come only from acts of human will, this objective "essence" of legal order was pushed back to the place of an ideal. Those absolute truths were no longer considered the very core of legal order or the essence of being itself. They became mere postulates, being linked to the omnipotent will of the legal person by way of a moral obligation. The subjective element thus became the driving force, the dynamic reality of legal order; the objective element became its binding limit, the ideal goal. The will of the person provides the specific content

[8] The historical, not logical origin of the combination of personalistic with "essential" (or substantival) elements is overlooked by Lauterpacht, when he remarks, with regard to the two approaches: "The two views are no doubt irreconcilable. It is hardly permissible to speak in one and the same breath of international law as a system of promises, and as a system governed by the objective rule *pacta sunt servanda* obliging states to abide by the rules of international law." *The Function of Law in the International Community* (1932), p. 421.

and the impulse, the general norm represents the formal idea and the confines of the legal system. The reality and the dynamics of the personal will finds its bounds in the existence of objective norms; the abstract ideality of general norms receives life and actuality through the impulse of individual wills.[9]

The link which connects the "natural freedom" of the legal person with the "natural law" of the community is duty. Thus the decision of the individual will carries the whole weight of responsibility for the legal order. Whereas the "essential" system of legal thinking had conceived the legal order of the universe as existing apart from individual acts of will, as the *ens realissimum* behind all appearances, later centuries, under the influence of nominalism, could not imagine an abstract norm as a being reality. To them reality was only what was perceptible: the *ens realissimum* was individual man. To the notion of man's original freedom there corresponded the conception of natural law as a mere ideal. Thus Grotius defines *ius* as the negation of injustice, and injustice is to him what contradicts the "idea" of a community of reasonable beings.[10] And elsewhere he clearly indicates his conception of natural law as a postulate, when he describes it as the commandment of reason, which indicates the ethical value of an action by its conformity or non-conformity with "reasonable Nature."[11] Thus the law of nature reveals itself in individual though objective reason. Accordingly, it is the moral duty of the individual to recognize those "natural" laws by allowing the objective reason in him to speak out, unperturbed by passion, desires and individual interests. In doing so the ideal of action becomes evident, and it becomes the second duty of the individual to subject his will to that ideal. Consequently, the whole structure of legal order, its dualism of concrete human will and abstract natural norm rests on one single pillar: *Conscience*. The objective standards of legal order exist only in dispassionate reason, and it is nothing but conscience which binds the legal person to

[9] Bott-Bodenhausen, *op. cit.*, p. 22.
[10] *De iure belli ac pacis*, lib. I, ch. I, sect. III, 1.
[11] *ibid.*, lib. I, ch. I, sect. X, 1.

reason objectively. The legal order of the community consists only in the observance of those common rules by the legal persons, and it is nothing but conscience which impels the legal person to make reason rather than subjective interests guide his will and actions.

Thus present-day international law rests on a foundation of ethics. Sometimes law and ethics are identified in this system, sometimes they are kept distinct from each other. But whichever view may be taken, and whichever construction of legal theory may be chosen, it is not possible to avoid the intimate connection of present-day international law with individual morality. For a system of law which starts out from the premise of the legal person, its existence and its free will, cannot help being construed as a commandment or a moral postulate addressed to the sense of obligation of the legal person. The legal order is conceived to be a limitation upon the liberty of the legal person, a liberty which is held to be so fundamental that it is termed "natural." Hence the normative basis of the objective rules restricting this "natural liberty" cannot be more than a moral obligation to adjust the concrete reality of personal will to the abstract ideality of the law. The actual force of such obligation is therefore identical with the conscientiousness of the legal person. Thus between the ideal of the law and the reality of the will the only link is in theory ethics, in practice conscience.

THE ANTITHESIS BETWEEN INTERNATIONAL LAW AND INTERNATIONAL POLITICS

It may seem that these points scarcely deserve the attention which has been given to them on these pages. The dualism between the real and the ideal, the moral basis of international law, the original independence of the states, and the nature of law as a normative restriction of that liberty—all this seems obvious and well established. However, it was necessary to dwell on the structure of the theory of international law in order to analyze with more clarity the relation between international law and international politics, not so much in its practical aspects, but as it is conceived in theory. For since we began with the assumption that the crisis of international law was a result not merely of practical difficulties, but of the very nature of its underlying ideas, the place of international politics in the theory of international law must be one of the main roots of the crisis.

The system of international law, as we have shown, is based on the assumption of the separate and independent existence of states. The states are the underlying reality in international law, they are the moving factor, the premise of the entire legal order. It follows from our discussion of the natural liberty of states that the maxim *pereat mundus fiat ius* may be applied to individuals but not to states. For the individual who resists the law opposes himself to an organized community which can continue to exist even without him and therefore claims precedence of its legal order over the individual's interests. But the State is conceived to exist in absolute isolation. Law is just an exception to the natural liberty of action characteristic of the State.[12] The existence of the State is much more fundamental, much more axiomatic, much more of an indispensable feature of the system of international law than the existence of individual persons is to a system of interindividual law.

Accordingly, the theory of international law is working on the premise that the existence, the development and the self-preservation of states is an undeniable reality and also an undeniable right of states. The principle of the State's existence and development has been called the *Raison d'État*.[13] This principle is in its very nature opposed to the idea of an international law. For in accordance with the *Raison d'État* each state is

[12] Cf. page 10 of this chapter.

[13] See F. Meinecke, *Die Idee der Staatsraison*, 3rd ed. (1929). The idea of a fundamental separation between international law and international politics is also expressed by Hall in the following terms: "The ultimate foundation of international law is an assumption that states possess rights and are subject to duties corresponding to the facts of their postulated nature. In virtue of this assumption it is held that since states exist, and are independent beings, possessing property, they have the right to do whatever is necessary for the purpose of continuing and developing their existence, of giving effect to and preserving their independence, and of holding and acquiring property, subject to the qualification that they are bound to respect these rights in others." International Law (8th ed., 1924) p. 50.

looking only in the direction of its own growth and improvement. *Raison d'État,* therefore, is the criterion that determines the states' own interests. The unbridled pursuit of these interests is of course the direct opposite of any legal order. Nevertheless international law, as conceived by the traditional theory, is based on the assumption that the *Raison d'État* is a perfectly legitimate and justified principle of State action, unless it leads to consequences expressly forbidden by international law. International politics was thus placed not under the law but beside the law. The idea of the *Raison d'État* as a valid alternative to international law followed necessarily from the premise of the original liberty of states. And the practice corresponding to the *Raison d'État* could not be regulated by legal rules, because to each state pertained a *Raison d'État* peculiar to itself. Each *Raison d'État* thus represented a unique point of view, which precluded any common rules of law regulating the legitimacy of an action under the criterion of the *Raison d'État.* Therefore the practical materialization of the *Raison d'État,* although recognized as such by the theory of international law, had to be left entirely to practical politics. Thus the role of international law was confined to the formulation of an international ideal. The criterion represented by international law was thus by its very nature opposed to the *Raison d'État* and practical politics. International law did not stoop down to the policies and political actions of the states in order to establish positive criteria of which course of action was lawful and which was not. The world of politics therefore is only guarded, not really ordered by international law (a condition to which someone has applied the term "ordered anarchy").[14] International law set up dams around the realm of political action, it confined politics within certain limitations, but it did not establish guiding criteria of political action.

This means that the ideal which international law erected in opposition to the *Raison d'État* is essentially a non-political

[14] A good example is provided by the Kellogg Pact. It does not forbid the policies which lead to war, but it imposes certain limitations with regard to their pursuit. As to the term "order", it is used in this book in the sense not merely of a mechanical system, but of that inner harmony which sometimes is called "organic" order.

ideal. International law did not set up standards by which states could make a judgment between a politically bad action or a politically good action. The law embodies an ideal not of policies but of human values that seemed to be worthy of protection against the effects of national policies and the *Raison d'État*. Thus, against the background of the assumption that the State and its existence is the essence of reality, international law is something essentially "unreal," because it is essentially unpolitical. It goes without saying that this applies only to those rules of international law which are held to be absolutely valid and do not owe their existence to a compromise of interests between states. But these latter rules do not make up the body of what we call international law.

The very idea that law is an ideal, and not an intrinsically orderly reality, means that legal standards are to be aimed at, but never to be attained. Under this scheme abidance by the law is an attitude of moral idealism, diametrically opposed to the realistic attitude characteristic of politics. Many treatises on international law from Grotius's times to our own bear witness to the fundamental distinction and separation of the ideal postulate of the law from the reality of politics. There are few passages, however, which would better represent the spirit of idealism, and of negation of political realism, in the theory of international law, than the following sentences of Professor Redslob:

"Cependant la question se pose: Ces lois restrictives serontelles fidèlement observées? . . . En soulevant ce problème nous aboutissons à la périphérie du droit, région limitrophe où la loi se confond avec la morale. . . . Ici la loi n'a plus d'autre sauveguarde que la conscience des gouvernants et la volonté populaire. Force nous est donc de reconnaître que la Société des Nations vivra et grandira de pair avec l'idéalisme et la noblesse humaine . . . Et voici quelle est ma croyance historique: Si la seizième siècle a été l'ère de la réligion, le dixhuitième l'âge de la philosophie, le dix-neuvième l'époque de la science, le vingtième sera le siècle de la Justice. Alors on verra ressusciter l'Empire médiéval, transfiguré, rajeuni . . .

Alors l'aiguille s'arrêtera sur l'horloge des siècles et le Galiléen reparaîtra parmi les hommes. Il élèvera ses mains enchainées vers le trône des Puissants et leur imposera, d'un regard lumineux, la Royauté qui n'est pas de ce monde."[15]

Here the connection of the ideal realm of law with that "kingdom which is not of this world" makes it perfectly clear that there is a gulf between the law and "this world," between legal order and political reality.

Such an attitude had been unknown to the Spanish writers. In their view, international law was the real and essential order of practical politics, a part of the world-embracing system of norms and rules. Vitoria wrote his observations on international law mainly for the purpose of finding out what the policy of the Spanish crown would have to be in the New World according to the rule of law. For him, this was not a question of community or international agreement, neither was it a mere ideal of international coexistence. It was the order that God established in this world for all things and all relations, and it implied politics as well as other human activities. Even Grotius meant his first work, *De Mare Libero,* to be an attempt to discover the "existing" order governing international relations in one aspect. But later when he elaborated his law of nations systematically, he abandoned the discussion of political reality, and even refrained from referring to his earlier writings, which were not so much inspired by the notion of the pure ideality of the law. Grotius, like most of his followers, was a practical statesman. All of them had considerable experience in international diplomacy and politics. Thus it is significant that they all sharply distinguish the world of real politics from that of ideal law. Most representative in this respect is Pufendorff. On the one hand he completely idealized international law by identifying it with the law of nature; on the other hand he recognized clearly the independent character and the specific dynamic laws of the political sphere. He studied both sides separately and with equal understanding. Besides his treatise on natural and international law, he published a handbook of

[15] R. Redslob, *Histoire des grands principes du droit de gens* (1923), pp. 560*f.*

practical politics destined to serve as a guide to statesmen in the realm of reality.[16]

Thus it is safe to say that the established theory of international law regards international politics as a field of action which is governed by its own value criteria. It is not considered the function of international law to step into this field, to set up categories of an immanent lawfulness in politics, to regulate the direction and the course of political action. The choice of the ends toward which political action is directed, the motives underlying it, the kind of action to be taken: all this is left by international law to the discretion of the particular states, to be decided according to the principle of the *Raison d'État*. International politics is regulated by international law only in so far as certain barriers are set up which must not be transgressed by the states. Thus international law operates as a boundary line between the action of politics and other spheres of human activity, between the *Raison d'État* and other value criteria in human life. It is not a regulation of political action in terms of political criteria when international law forbids states to enlist aliens in their armies; it is a rule protecting the private lives of individuals from undue interference by political interests. Since international law is operating in the field of interstate relationships, which after all is a field of essentially political character, these non-political barriers erected against an undesirable overflow of political power are necessarily "unreal," i.e. they are a mere postulate, the effectiveness of which is determined by the degree of homage paid to the non-political values it represents. International law is not meant to prescribe to states the policies which they ought to pursue: the only way in which it interferes with the original freedom of the states is by opposing to the "real" will of the states the standard of an "ideal." For the materialization of this ideal, international law had to rely on the strength of a moral appeal.

In this system of order, in which the existence of the State

[16] S. Pufendorff, *Einleitung zu der Histoire der vornehmsten Reiche und Staaten, so jetziger Zeit in Europa sich befinden* (1682). Also see the chapter on Pufendorff in Meinecke, *Die Idee der Staatsraison* (1929), p. 279.

is considered the basic reality and the law an ideal standard to be applied only in the case of a conflict of interests, a clash of duties is bound to result. In the minds of acting statesmen, the "practical possibilities," as seen from the point of view of the *Raison d'État*, struggle against the "ideal postulates" which inspire the rules of international law. This dilemma is plainly manifest in the words of Mr. Neville Chamberlain:

"When we are told that contracts must be kept sacred, and that we must on no account depart from the obligations which we have undertaken, it must not be forgotten that we have other obligations and responsibilities, obligations not only to our own countrymen, but to many millions of human beings throughout the world, whose happiness or misery may depend on how far the fulfillment of these obligations is insisted upon by the one side and met by the other."[17]

Just how effective law can be, when it is conceived as an unpolitical ideal opposed to political realities, is also demonstrated by a statement of the British Foreign Secretary, Lord Halifax, made with reference to the Abyssinian question in the League of Nations' Council on May 12, 1938:

"But when, as here, two ideals are in conflict—on the one hand the ideal of devotion, unflinching but unpractical, to some high purpose; on the other hand the ideal of a practical victory for peace—I cannot doubt that the stronger claim is that of peace. . . . Whether in the affairs of nations or individuals, each of us knows . . . how constantly it is necessary to reconcile that which may be ideally right with what is practically possible. . . . and neither he who forgets ideals in pursuit of practical achievement nor he who, blinded by the bright light of the ideal, loses sight of the possible, will ever make his full contribution to the establishment of conditions under which alone progress can be made."[18]

When judging this view, it should be noted that this statesman is by no means a cynic, but is a conscientious man fully

[17] As quoted by G. Schwarzenberger, *American Journal of International Law*, vol. 33, p. 72.

[18] As reported in the *New York Times*, May 13, 1938.

aware of the validity of the rules of law. Yet in his mind the world of politics is very clearly pictured as a reality independent of, and in principle unaffected by, international law, a law which addresses itself to this reality as a high but unpractical ideal. If this is the best conception of international law available, small wonder that the lawyers in this field consider themselves as preachers who have to overemphasize and even exaggerate the ideal precepts of the law in order to exert at least some influence in practice and to obtain at least a modicum of recognition.[19]

THE HISTORICAL SUBSTANCE OF THE INTERNATIONAL "IDEAL"

We have to come to the conclusion that in the relations between states the *Raison d'État* is considered the subjective, and consequently the "realistic" point of view, which is only externally limited by the existence of an objective "ideal." Thus, even when the obligation under international law is recognized with sincere good will, it inevitably conflicts with the duty of self-preservation, which is an equally recognized value. Therefore international law, when conceived as an ideal, can be effective only through a compromise between the postulate of its rules and the "real" will of the states.

However, there should be no doubt that whenever the values that inspire the prescriptions of international law are actually recognized and felt, international law is really effective, even though it be construed as a mere ideal. The link between the postulate of an ideal and the world of real action is the sense of moral obligation, or conscience. Beyond any question conscience is a real factor in human behavior which has as much actual bearing on the shape of things as has coercion of a physical nature. Provided that in a society there is general agreement as to the standards which are believed absolutely obligatory, conscience is as realistic a foundation for a system of law as can be found. As long as a human being participates

[19] "The law of nations . . . has ever since [Grotius] sought to play the role of the preacher, the teacher, the reformer, the moral idealist, rather than to serve as the jurisconsult, the lawgiver, the practical statesman." P. M. Brown, in: *Niemeyer's Zeitschrift*, vol. XXXIV, p. 6.

in a community, the objective standards of that community will be as much a psychological fact in him as the motivations born of his personal existence and interest. There are degrees of "objectivity," of the proportions between the personal and the universal elements, in the consciousness of every individual. But the common standard has some influence on every individual mind as long as the community actually exists, because there is no consciousness of community other than in the form of the acknowledgement of common standards of behavior. This sense of obligation we call conscience.

For this reason those who deride international law because it is "merely" based on the action of conscience, certainly aim at the wrong point. A system of international law which is construed as an unpolitical "ideal," is effective in direct proportion to the force of conscience in nations and governments. It is true that because of the lack of an international organization enforcing its rules, the degree of efficiency of international law depends entirely on the voluntary conformity of states, but it must be insisted with particular emphasis that in so far as the law does coincide with the universal contents of human conscience, it actually has existence as one of the motivating forces behind individual wills and public actions.

Accordingly, it has to be determined what is in people's conscience in order to find out what is the true law. This is what Grotius, Pufendorff, Thomasius, Wolff, and Vattel did when they explored the human "reason" in their search for community principles. For *con-science* is not merely an individual instinct, it is a *common science*, a knowledge of values and standards which are commonly recognized in a given society. It is not a sliding scale applicable according to a subjective feeling of responsibility, but it refers to definite standards by which we universally measure acts and facts, even though it be in the form of rather general principles and concepts.

The very circumstance that throughout the entire known world a common set of values and standards happened to be recognized, forming the basis for a unitary meaning of "reason" and "conscience" during his time, enabled Grotius to draw up his canons of international law despite the personalistic foundations of his system. A substance of objective criteria, the inheritance of the Middle Ages and of Catholicism, molded the shape of every individual conscience in such a way that there was an almost uniform adherence to certain determinate ideas and principles. On this basis Grotius could assume, and rely upon, an objective reason and a unitary force of conscience that would actively influence reality over and above all differences of national policies and "subjective" standpoints.[20] This is the historical background which alone made possible the conception of a law of nations among states that were imagined naturally free and independent. Grotius drew on what remained of the occidental community of the Middle Ages; he formulated and systematized a body of legal rules out of what constituted the universal element among the Christian peoples of his time: the contents of a non-sectarian Christian conscience.

He drew on three main sources, which inspired the body of principles and standards that were authoritative for his time, and according to which he shaped his international legal rules: The anthropological ethics of the Stoa, as contained in Cicero, Seneca, Plutarch and others; the Hebrew ethics as contained in the Bible; and the Christian ethics as formulated by the Church fathers and the medieval ecclesiastical authorities. Together with concepts derived from Plato and Aristotle, these elements composed the commandments which guided private and public life throughout the Christian world in those times. This was the code that people respected in their private relationships, and although after the days of Machiavelli the exemption of public affairs from its rule was often claimed, it was

[20] "In the seventeenth century there was a moral order as among individuals. Throughout Christendom, men were agreed not only as to its main lines, but largely as to its details . . . Whereas the moral order which was postulated by the theory of international law in its beginning was a reality, the moral order among democratic . . . peoples of today is but a figure of speech." Roscoe Pound, "Philosophical Theory and International Law," *Bibliotheka Visseriana* (1923), I, pp. 77, 79.

See also the remarks of Professor Laun, in "Jus naturae et gentium," *Niemeyer's Zeitschrift*, vol. XXXIV, p. 41. In this context, it is interesting to note the fact that international law used to be taught in American colleges by the president of the college to the seniors. It used to be integrated with ethics and flanked by a course on philosophy.

the only normative standard people had to refer to in state affairs when their conscience was awake.

Accordingly, when Grotius published his law of nations, derived from, and based on authorities which no one could help recognizing, it was necessarily binding on states and princes, because it was beyond their theoretical and practical possibilities to deny values that formed the very essence of Christianity. The law of nations as conceived by Grotius and Pufendorff was obligatory not only in theory, but also in practice, because its contents forced themselves on the conscience of both the people and the rulers. It is true that its standards were those of individual ethics, but these principles were so axiomatic throughout the world of Grotius's time, that there could be no shadow of doubt as to the duty to abide by them in all situations. Therefore, since the moral conscience of Christianity coincided with natural law, Grotius's system was not merely a speculation, but an effective element of order and justice. And what is true for Grotius's period applies equally in a general way to any period in which the law is looked at from a personalistic perspective, and the subjective "real" is opposed to the objective "ideal": In so far as the law amounts substantially to the principles governing people's conscience, coinciding with the contents of moral standards, it always has a real basis for regular effectiveness to the degree to which moral values are universally recognized.

THE ELEMENT OF NATURAL LAW IN THE THEORY OF POSITIVISM

The central thesis, around which are centered all the arguments put forth in this chapter, is that international law could not, and still cannot, be construed without resorting to universal standards of morality and "natural law," as long as a personalistic approach is chosen. The conclusion from this thesis is that the present system of international law stands and falls with a common morality among the nations. This would be rejected as anathema by any positivist, and consequently by the vast majority of living teachers and scholars of international law. To meet their objection, it remains to be proved that the very doctrine of positivism leans heavily on notions of natural law and of universal ethics, having planted its roots deeper in metaphysical soil than most positivists would like to admit to themselves.

The direct and open connection of international law with natural law and ethics, it is true, was gradually severed from the days of Thomasius onwards. Of the two constituent elements of legal theory which we mentioned before,[21] the personalistic idea gained a definite ascendancy over the "essential," or substantival principle. The existence of international law began to be explained more and more in terms of the purposes and impulses of the legal subjects, instead of in terms of absolute and universal rules of natural law.[22] Justice was defined no longer by reference to certain definite standards of natural law and ethics, as Grotius defined it, but as mere reciprocity. Consequently international law ceased to be conceived as a crystallization of interindividual morality as embodied in traditional standards and precepts, and it began to be dominated by the idea of varying purposes of the legal subjects, to which it was supposed to lend merely the external form of peaceful relationships. Legal rules were no longer based on the substance of eternal truths; they began to be regarded as the framework of rational and purposive associations. Even humanity as a whole is conceived as a union *ad certum finem.*[23]

Accordingly, the standards which limited the original freedom of the individual members of a community were no longer found in absolute tenets of natural law and natural ethics, but in a rational analysis of the motives which allegedly had induced the individual subjects to come together. It is obvious that as soon as law was conceived as a mere instrument for the attainment of purposes set *ad libitum* by the subjects of law, legal theory ceased to have any creative significance. Instead of crystallizing, out of the common experience and the most profound knowledge of life, standards that were "natural" to

[21] See pp. 144 *ff*.
[22] Erik Wolf, *Grotius, Pufendorff, Thomasius* (1927), p. 111.
[23] *ibid.*, p. 120.

men and things, its task was now confined to the systematization of such rules and prescriptions as the purposeful human will chose to set up. The collective might engendered by the voluntary and deliberate association of subjects became the source of law, and expediency its criterion of value. Because men united for some purpose, their resolution to come together justified any rules required to govern their union: the law was binding because of their own decision to submit voluntarily to the might of the community. Thus coercibility rather than morality became the characteristic quality of law.

This growing "personalization" of positive law and the severing of connections between positive and natural law left the latter on the high but static pedestal of the "unpractical ideal." Natural law was more and more set apart from the realities of experience and practical knowledge. It indulged in philosophic speculations regarding the purpose for the sake of which men formed associations, and associations united into larger communities. This abstract speculation about human intentions was actually much more metaphysical than the interpretation of the moral order of human conscience which used to be the way of natural law philosophers. Morality is sometimes a practical code of behavior, but it is always an effective one, often more so than a prescription of law imposed by the might of command. Therefore to the same degree to which the science of positive law was "personalized" and technicalized, the discipline of natural law ceased to be a source of juristic wisdom, and consequently ceased to provide the content of actual legal rules. Natural law became a set of general formal tenets in the background of "real" law, obligatory only in a moral, not in a legal sense, and incapable of further development because of its disconnection from the living laws of community.

It was on these foundations that positivism arose in the second half of the nineteenth century. Here natural law was entirely discarded, even as a theoretical background. The will of the legal subject became the exclusive source of the law and the only object of legal science. All reference to the values underlying legal rules was eliminated from legal science proper as metaphysical or rather "metajuristic." The ideal of legal science was the purely formal construction and systematization of the rules enacted by the competent legislative will. But even with its attention concentrated exclusively on the investigation of positive prescriptions, positivist science could not help noticing the enigma of the obligatory force inherent in these rules. The problem presented itself in international law more puzzlingly than in domestic law. How could legal rules establish an objective obligation if they were considered merely the product of the combined rational wills of legal subjects? It was difficult to imagine that there could be any objective restriction of the original liberty of the states, unless the subjectivity of their wills and impulses was limited and bound by an element of absolute universal validity. Since natural law and natural ethics had been officially banned from the realm of "pure science," and since after their elimination only the subjective wills of the individual states were left as a possible source of legal rules, positivist doctrine would have had to draw the conclusion that international law could not exist. And indeed those authors who did not shrink from the most radical consequences of the personalistic conception of law actually took the step of denying international law altogether. Realizing that without the absolute standards of a natural law it would not be possible to construe an objective limitation of the states' original freedom, they either identified international law with might (E. Kaufmann), or with expediency (Lasson), or denied the existence of a law of nations (Austin, Lorimer, Zorn). Other positivists, however, who were temperamentally unable to stand the oppressing vision of a world without a system of law, secretly escaped through some backdoor leading to the safe grounds of natural law—or what was left of it.

In order to realize the problem that these positivists had to solve, let us once more look back on the tacit assumptions underlying the idea of international law. The approach to the phenomenon of international law, from the time of Grotius to our days, has been a personalistic one. In other words: the supposition with which positivism, like every other school of thought, must start out, was that of the existence of a number of free and independent states, whose wills were considered originally unrestricted. On the other hand experience yielded both the fact of, and the need for, a system of law binding the wills of these states by objective obligations. What was required was a systematic explanation of legal rules with results which could be applied to the future behavior of the states. This proposition included the task of proving that legal rules are not only observed but ought to be observed. How could a positivist science find a criterion for this "ought," and how could it prove the obligatory character of legal rules, after having eliminated as metaphysics the idea of "natural," i.e. necessary, law? Any obligation points to the future. Therefore the obligatory force of legal rules could not be construed in terms of empirical realities, which were things of the past. Indeed, the very idea of an obligation could not be arrived at without the reference to such transpersonal standards as were actually acknowledged by human conscience. It is the inescapable conclusion that the obligatory force of any norm comes only from its appeal to the human sense of obligation, which forced positivism to return to notions of natural law, i.e. notions of supposedly self-evident character, which people could not help acknowledging. However this relapse of positivism into a discipline which had been openly dismissed as unscientific did not happen openly. It may be said that in the cases of most positivists it was even a completely unconscious relapse, of which they themselves were least aware.[24] Nevertheless it is highly significant for the theoretical foundations of present day international law.

Positivistic legal science had officially renounced the claim to "invent" legal rules "out of thin air." Paradoxically enough, this became the source of the unrealistic speculation which emerged from positivistic theories in the first part of the twen-

[24] "A positivist, . . . even if there were conclusive evidence in the practice of states of the reception of morality into law would shrink from accepting morality as a sine qua non of international law." Keeton and Schwarzenberger, *Making International Law Work* (1939), p. 82.

tieth century. For jurisprudence had ceased to be the practical wisdom of human relationships. It was considered unscientific for legal theory to interpret the structure of social life and the values which are governing it directly. According to positivistic tenets, legal science must not investigate the conditions of international relations with a view to determining legal norms; it merely could investigate the conditions of positive rules enacted by the states, with a view to determining their meaning for purposes of legal procedure. But in order to explain that states were bound by general obligations to adhere to legal methods of procedure, positivism had to resort to concepts inherited from natural law, concepts which referred not to hard facts but to abstract ideas.[25] Notions like "Family of Nations," "International Community," "Conscience juridique commune," "Legitimate interests," "Fundamental rights of states," "Pacta sunt servanda" and so on are nothing but the indispensable metaphysical foundations of a system of law that had to explain the phenomenon of obligations binding on originally free and independent subjects.[26]

However, since the discipline of natural law had lost its contact with live realities, these general concepts had become formal notions with extremely vague connotations. They no longer referred to a determined set of ethical and traditional principles which were recognized in everyday reality by all individuals. Their meaning had become ambiguous, which made it possible for authors to draw from these concepts almost any conclusion that they held desirable. Thus the unadmitted reference of positivism to natural law concepts opened the door of legal thought to arbitrary speculation on the part of interna-

[25] "The extra-legal yardsticks of judgment which are applied today to questions of international law, are mostly remainders of natural law, from the democratic principle to the invocation of the pretty empty formula of humanity in international treaties." E. Feilchenfeld, *Völkerrechtswissenschaft als Politik* (1922), p. 154. For a thorough criticism of these and other historical criteria of judgment in international law read the pages in Feilchenfeld's book which precede the above quoted one.

[26] "Il est bien certain que, lorsque nous congédions le droit naturel par une porte, un *criterium* semblable entre par l'autre porte; qu'il soit appelé justice, préceptes d'une conscience mondiale, commandements de la nature humaine ou jugement du monde." Jesse S. Reeves, *La Communauté Internationale, Recueil des Cours de l'Académie de la Haye*, vol. 3, p. 76.

tional lawyers. Even in the sober days of positivism this speculative note can be detected. The very title of the fourth book of Rivier's treatise, for instance, reveals it: *Des droits essentiels des Etats, et des restrictions apportées à ces droits par le fait de la Communaute Internationale.*[27] Moreover, Rivier, when discussing the fundamental rights of the states, admits frankly that they are derived not from positive legal rules, but from general notions about the "nature of things": "Ces droits de conservations et de respect, d'indépendance, de mutuel commerce, qui tous peuvent se ramener à un droit unique de conservation, sont fondés sur la notion même de l'Etat, personne du droit de gens. Ils forment la loi générale du droit des gens et la commune constitution de notre civilization politique."[28]

To quote another example, Wilson and Tucker, in their *International Law* argue as follows: "The *right to exist* as a sovereign political unity is the most comprehensive right of a state. From this comprehensive right flow the general rights of *independence, equality, jurisdiction, property,* and *intercourse,* and the obligations which the exercise of these rights imply."[29] How deeply positivistic jurisprudence rooted in these general deductions can be tested by looking at the numerous official and semi-official attempts to "declare" the "fundamental rights and duties of nations," or at the practical and theoretical conclusions arrived at by analogy, or at sweeping definitions like that of justiciable or non-justiciable disputes, as attempted by the *Institut de Droit International* in 1922.[30]

[27] A. Rivier, *Principes du droit des gens,* vol. I (1896) p. 255.

[28] *ibid.,* p. 257.

[29] G. G. Wilson and G. F. Tucker, *International Law,* 9th ed. (1935), p. 77 (with the permission of the publisher, Silver Burdett Company). Also see the remarks of Jesse S. Reeves, *La Communauté Internationale, Recueil des Cours,* vol. 3, p. 44.

[30] Here is a small collection of samples of natural law in the system of positivist thinkers:

"Le droit international public a ses racines maîtresses et profondes dans la nature même de l'homme, dans les instincts et les besoins de sociabilité et de perfectabilité. Sa cause génératrice réside dans la communauté internationale des Etats organisés. . . . La loi de sociabilité est une loi naturelle et nécessaire, non seulement pour les individus, mais encore pour les Etats . . ." Fauchille, *Traité de droit international public,* vol. I, (1922), pp. 6*f.*

"Il est un fait considérable qui, répétons le, domine tout: il existe une société des Etats; les membres qui la composent ont l'idée du droit, c'est à dire de l'usage libre de

The possibility of speculation which was created by this basis of positivism, however, did not become an actual defect of legal science until the ambiguous and formal concepts of fundamental law fell into the hands of an equally vague and meaningless ideal of pacifism. Now scientific self-discipline gave way to the feeling that the pacifist ideal was sufficient justification for almost any conclusion derived from those general ideas about international community, and presented in the cloak of legal theory. It became the task of legal thinking to devise the most ideal system of interstate regulations and procedures that was conceivable. The basis for this type of thinking was an argumentation in terms of the supposed nature of international community, of the type that is represented at its best by N. Politis: "The organization of public justice was . . . the result of the establishment of a powerful and solid order. Its progress has kept pace exactly with the progress of society. The same evolution has taken place in the international community. . . . In an inorganic international community, progress towards compulsory arbitration could, before 1914, be nothing more

---

leurs facultés; ils ont l'idée du devoir comprise dans l'idée du droit et inséparable de celle-ci; ils sont libres." E. Nys, *Le Droit International* (1904), p. 63.

"La norme pacta sunt servanda est un principe de droit naturel que l'on ne peut pas plus détacher des règles du droit positif qu'il domine que des principes plus généraux de justice et de morale dont il précède. . . . Distinctes assurément des principes de la morale, les règles du droit positif ne peuvent pourtant ni se concevoir ni se développer sans ce minimum de moralité sociale et de justice qui est leur fondement dernier." Ch. de Visscher, *Revue de droit international et de législation comparée* 1933, p. 400.

Georg Jellinek, in his *Die rechtliche Natur der Staatenverträge* (1880), speaks of the character of the treaty as a "universal institute of law." On p. 57 of this book, he remarks: "Andrerseits binden die Grundsätze der Sittlichkeit, welche für Staaten . . . ebenso in Kraft sind wie für den Einzelnen, . . . den Staat an das einmal gegebene Wort."

Triepel, in his *Völkerrecht und Landesrecht*, p. 225, states: "Nicht das römische Recht ist es, aus dem das Völkerrecht geschöpft hat, sondern *Vernunft* und *Moral* sind es, aus denen sie beide ihren Stoff entnehmen. Die *naturalis ratio* ist die gemeinsame 'Quelle,' aus der sie entspringen."

Finally an observation which Lauterpacht has to make on the topic of positivism and natural law: ". . . difficult was the position of those positivist writers who found themselves rejecting not only private law but also natural law. Being unable to afford the consistency of totally ignoring both private and natural law, they put in their place 'the reason of the thing,' 'the demands of logic,' and 'the principles of general jurisprudence. . . .' In practice, 'general jurisprudence' is converted into a law of nature of modern garb. . . ." *Private Law Sources and Analogies of International Law* (1927), pp. 33, 37.

than an inspiration. . . . On the other hand, in the international community which is beginning to be organized, compulsory arbitration becomes a real fact and a system. . . . The right of war is no longer unrestricted. Recourse to force, which is now exceptional, is, in principle, unlawful. . . . In case of dispute, the choice is no longer between arbitration and force, but between various pacific procedures. . . ."[31]

In many cases the utopian excursions of legal science were based on the idea of the moral value of a system of law over and above the nations, but the conception of this moral good was too general to be crystallized into precise standards. Capitalizing this recognized, but ambiguous value of "as much legality as is conceivable," the students of this type of positivism felt at liberty to "define" almost arbitrarily the law which they pretended was above the nations. Positivism had dispensed legal science from the necessity to investigate the practical ethics of human conscience as a source of juristic wisdom. But since positivist theory nonetheless rested on ultimate concepts of an ethical nature, without being tied down to the concreteness of practical moral prescriptions, the ambiguity of these ethical foundations provided room for wide speculation of every mediocre thinker who took the trouble to write down and publish his views about the hazy ideal of "international community." That is why the theory of international law, under the cover of the accepted morality of "a" legal order among nations, was in the position to yield to every kind of wishful political thinking, almost regardless of the actual possibilities of interstate relations. Despite the alleged "realism" of positivistic thinking, there has never before been a period in the history of legal science in which scholars have been so oblivious of the actual structure of realities. And this disproportion between legal optimism and the actual existence of common values between the nations was not confined to the world of scholars: Under the leadership of a university professor, even the governments of the world were enticed into the highly unreal structure of the League of Nations; a fact which reveals to what

[31] N. Politis, *The New Aspects in International Law* (1928), pp. 49, 53, 54.

astonishing degree the theory of international law had lost the character of genuine science.

FORMS OF PROCEDURE PREFERRED TO NORMS OF JUSTICE

While on the one hand the subterranean and perhaps subconscious adherence of positivism to the dangerously ambiguous relics of natural law opened the way for irresponsible speculation, on the other hand the responsible and mentally disciplined branch of positivism exhausted its energies on the solution of the problem of the obligatory force of law. It made every effort to establish clearly the link between positive rules of law and those general notions of natural law to which pertained the force of absolute obligation. Positive law could not be tested directly with respect to its binding character, since the question of justification, together with ethics, had been eliminated from the realm of legal science. The will of the subjects in itself did not contain any criterion of obligation. The consequence of this dilemma was an elaborate doctrine of the obligatory character of law as such, i.e. of legality as a peaceful form of human relationships. The external form provided by law, even more than the concrete content of legal prescriptions, was held to be the root of the obligatory character of law.

This emphasis on the formal procedure which is the characteristic of legality, claimed ever growing importance in proportion as the binding force of the concrete substance of legal rules became increasingly doubtful. The substance of legal rules was determined, according to the positivist doctrine, by the will of the states, and not by the absolute standards of natural law or natural ethics. Unlike legal rules derived from the principles of natural law, however, the obligatory character of norms emerging from the will of states, and guided by power-relations, national interests and political expediency, was far from being self-evident. The positivist theory therefore required the utmost intellectual effort in order to preserve the idea of international law at all, and not to lose it in considerations of the *Raison d'État*. Thus there arose those endless controversies about details of theoretical construction which served no purpose other than that of bridging the logical abyss between the idea of an absolute obligation and the positivist conception of law as an expression of will. Failing this construction, no intellectual pretension could have saved the obligatory force of international law.

Thus the doctrine of positivism, contrary to its professed rejection of metaphysics, had to fall back on the "metajuristic" formulas inherited from the natural law of the seventeenth century, because of the obligatory force inherent in them. In taking over this inheritance, however, positivism formalized these notions just as much as it formalized international law on the whole. It did not resort to the concepts of natural law in order to derive from them any knowledge or guidance regarding the substance of rules binding upon states. It did not develop any substantial criteria of right and wrong from them, confronting the states with legal postulates of a concrete nature. Instead, the idea of international solidarity and the "family" principle of international community were used only to derive from them conclusions of a formal nature. To use the words of Professor Baumgarten: "The relation of law to morality lies mainly in the fact that abidance by the law appears as a formal moral duty."[32] The concrete scope of legal commands was left to be determined by the wills of states, but since the states formed a "family" they must under no circumstances quarrel violently. The question of how much reason there might be for quarreling, how to judge the justice or injustice of existing legal rules, was left untouched by positivist theory. Thus the recourse to principles of natural law resulted in the positivist postulate that nations should observe the same forms of legal procedure as were established in the domestic systems of states with so much perfection of technique. Positivism thus applied the idea of seventeenth century thinkers that the norms of interindividual relations are the safest guidance for the law between states. However in drawing from the universal criteria and principles of law among individuals, it left un-

[32] Baumgarten, *Moral, Recht und Gerechtigkeit* (1917).

touched the norms of interindividual morality, taking instead the forms of interindividual lawsuits.[33]

It was then the formal technique of municipal law which received the distinction of being regarded as a moral good in the positivistic system. The security, not the truth of legal norms, was believed to be the value for the sake of which international law was surrounded with the halo of an ethical obligation. For half a century, the scientific discussion in international law centered almost exclusively around the development of methods, mechanisms and procedures. The result was an elaborate system of legal technique which provided a machinery of settlement for every dispute—in theory. The fact that these institutions and provisions of procedure have not always been used, or have been abused in the most serious cases, has been rightly characterized as the breakdown of this system. But it did not occur to positivistic thinking that this might be owing to the development of means without an equal attention being paid to the ends. It was precisely the discrepancy of opinion about ends which accounted for the failure of the means of technical procedure.

The emphasis which positivism placed on the development of legal mechanisms looked very technical and "physical" on the surface. But it must not be forgotten, that this emphasis was conditioned by "metaphysical" notions of natural law derivation, from which the conclusion was drawn that the procedure in legal forms was an ethical good in itself, regardless of the concrete substance of legal rules. In this sense, Professor Baumgarten remarks that "for the majority of men, brought up from childhood on to respect the law, the question is not whether they ought to do what the law demands from them, but only what it is that the law prescribes."[34] Owing to the "official" ban placed on metaphysics, this concealed appeal to conscience is never recognized by positivist authors. But the dependence

[33] Feilchenfeld, *op. cit.*, p. 19, speaks of the unproductivity of pre-war international jurisprudence with respect to truly normative ideas, and attributes to this circumstance the development of international law in the direction of procedural and technical progress.

[34] A. Baumgarten, *op. cit.*, p. 58 (translation mine).

of their conclusions on general formulas like that of the "family" betrays clearly enough that even positivism cannot escape the truism that legal order addressed to "essentially" free subjects can ultimately be based only on the binding force of conscience.

The element of moral approval on which the positivistic doctrine of international law is erected consists in the traditional respect paid to the legal procedures of the various domestic laws. The transfer of the forms used in these legal systems to international law secured for international law the same approval and the same almost habitual recognition of authority on which the domestic systems of law are based. Thus the adjustment of international procedures to the model of the legal technique developed in municipal law is the "ideal" of positivism, the value with the help of which it posits the obligatory force of international law. Fundamentally this is nothing but a repetition of the methods of natural law.[35] It amounts to a generalization of the concepts and ideas about legal order as developed and recognized by individuals in their mutual relations, transplanting them into international relations. It is true that positivism does not resemble seventeenth century thinking in that it dispenses with every criterion of judgment regarding the contents of legal rules. But this formalism of legal theory is only the corollary of the formal and mechanical conception which this modern age has of the ethical obligation that binds each individual conscience to abide by the rules of positive municipal law.[36] In our ideas about the duty to obey the law, the distinction between right and wrong has almost entirely ceased to play a role since the end of the nineteenth century; its place has been taken by the value that is attributed to technical perfection and mechanical security in legal procedures. Thus the formalized "metaphysics" of positivism correspond perfectly to the formalization of contemporaneous

[35] "When we turn to modern international law, we are confronted once more with the same picture of alternate rejection and adoption of the recourse to private law, its repudiation in form going hand in hand with its adoption in substance." Lauterpacht, *Private Law Sources*, etc., p. 17.

[36] Cf. Professor Baumgarten's remarks in the preceding paragraph.

conscience. Without this metajuristic background of a formalized morality, however, positivism could not have maintained the theoretical structure of international law.

THE SEVENTEENTH CENTURY INHERITANCE IN OUR INTERNATIONAL LAW

Owing to the formalization of legal theory under positivism, the substance of those rules which traditionally belonged to the law of nations was left practically untouched by science after legal theory became separated from natural law. Therefore those norms which the investigation of natural law had produced in bygone centuries have been essentially perpetuated. While positivism developed the technique of legal procedures, it contributed very little to the development of the substance of legal rules according to which states were obliged to behave. Therefore not only the theoretical existence of the present system of international law rests on seventeenth century foundations, but even for its concrete precepts it relies on the results of seventeenth and eighteenth century legal science. The general rules of international law as taught in modern textbooks are on the whole the same that were evolved under the influence of Christian ethics during that period. At the time of their inception these norms were accepted for their inherent reasonableness, i.e. as "natural" law. When the criticism of legal rules from the point of view of their justification was banned from legal science, as being metajuristic, those standards could not be questioned any more as to their conformity with the spirit and the realities of new international conditions. They were accepted as "positive" law. Thus the natural law of the seventeenth and eighteenth centuries came to shape the outlines of our modern law of nations.[37]

On the other hand, although the modern theory of international law may seem fundamentally different from the concep-

[37] "Depuis lors, le monde a changé et s'est écarté de cette philosophie; et pourtant, dans une mesure qui, à notre avis, n'a pas été apprecié à sa valeur, le droit international, en tant que système impliquant une société internationale, repose encore aujourd'hui sur les dogmes d'alors." Jesse S. Reeves, *La Communauté Internationale, Recueil des Cours*, vol. 3, p. 42.

tion of Grotius and Vattel, it must be regarded as still resting on the same logical foundations, just as it still operates with the same normative provisions derived from natural law. The basic assumption of theory is still the essential "reality" of the individual subject of law: the axiomatic concept of the isolated person. The supposition inherent in this concept is still the "natural" liberty of the states, and the corresponding notion of law is still that of a body of authoritative rules restricting this liberty by means of an obligation.

Thus, just as in the times of Grotius, it is the receptiveness of human conscience toward the call of this obligation which determines the degree of effectiveness that international law can attain in the present form.[38] The conditions under which international law, thus conceived, can operate, are therefore the following: First, it presupposes an individualistic outlook on life as a cultural pattern which prevails throughout humanity, not being restricted to a few nations. Secondly, it relies on an individual sense of responsibility which must be not only felt but actually practised in the structure of social institutions. Thirdly, it requires a certain cultural homogeneity among the nations sufficient to promote a certain minimum of moral standards and principles of law the validity of which is universally recognized. To what extent these conditions are still prevailing at the present time will be discussed in the next chapter.

[38] "There is no other basis of international law than age old morality as applied to the individual." Jesse S. Reeves, at the thirty-second annual meeting of the American Society of International Law held in Washington in 1938.

CHAPTER V

THE SOCIOLOGICAL BACKGROUND OF INTERNATIONAL LAW

THE HUMANISTIC BASIS OF THE TRADITIONAL LAW OF NATIONS

THE fact that our present system of international law is based essentially on morality, as practised and recognized among individuals, makes this system of law dependent on certain social conditions. For this traditional international law draws its criteria and judgments from a set of standards and principles which are developed not in the interstate "sphere" of reality, but in the interindividual "sphere." Accordingly, international law ultimately is fed by sources that lie outside of its own realm of interstate relations, and on which it depends for its existence. Any change in social structure which affects the principles of interindividual conduct and interindividual morality must necessarily also have an effect on the criteria of international law.

For three centuries, the law of nations has been founded, theoretically and practically, on principles of conduct that were common to all the nations concerned. First this category comprised all Christian nations, then it was extended to all civilized nations, and now there is no limitation or qualification regarding the nations which are supposed to contribute to the standards of international law.[1] What does this dependence on "principles, recognized by all civilized nations" involve? It means that the standards of international law are to be found in those concepts and principles of conduct which are held to be valid by individuals "the world over," irrespective of the interests of their states or governments. It means that the criteria of international law are taken from that which is com-

[1] G. Schwarzenberger, "The Rule of Law and the Disintegration of International Society," *American Journal of International Law*, vol. 33, pp. 63*f*.

mon and universal in all nations, and not from that which is peculiar to each particular nation. Therefore, the criteria and standards of international law are not derived from any notion of the respective interests of governments, but from the notion of "human nature," from the requirements of individual life, from categories of relationship and conduct which are developed in interindividual contact across national boundaries. This is what is general and universal among nations. The basis of international law, as it has been practised and conceived through the last three hundred years, is thus definitely a humanistic one, one referring to concepts of individual life and "private" existence.

This reference of international law to something which was valid and existing over and above the power interests of the various nations, to some "community" which operated independently of the different governments, made it possible for international law to operate as a limitation of political power. In this respect the function of international law was not unlike that of constitutional law. By drawing its criteria from principles which were recognized as values by *individuals* with a view to individual life, constitutional law, just like international law, sets the limits within which state power could be operated without detriment to those highest humanistic values. This is the feature which distinguishes the international law of modern Europe from all other previous cases of legal procedures between states: It consisted not only in occasional treaties and arbitrations, but in a solid body of rules which were neither created nor easily changed by the action of governments. It was a law maintained by a direct understanding of individuals throughout the civilized world—individuals who, apart from the respective interests of their nations, were agreed on certain aspects of human relationships as having a specific value besides, and even above, political interests.

DUALISM BETWEEN PUBLIC AND PRIVATE INTERESTS AS A ROOT OF INTERNATIONAL LAW

Under what social conditions do such common standards of conduct exist among different nations? The terminology of the statute of the Permanent Court of International Justice which expressly refers to "general principles as recognized by *civilized* nations," offers a clue to the answer. Civilization connotes a non-political aspect of social life. Civilization can and does extend beyond state boundaries. It is the cause in the service of which governments operate. It is the link that unites nation to nation in spite of separating frontiers and conflicting power interests. In this sense, the term "civilization" definitely is conceived in contradistinction to such notions as national interests, *Raison d'État* and group-security. "Civilization," and with it the corresponding principles and standards of international law, are products and aspects of social life as generated by individuals in their private capacity, not by governments and public officials. The antinomy between private life and public life, between the ends of individual existence and the ends of the state, is the condition under which there can be "principles common to all civilized nations." For the interests of governments are necessarily antagonistic and mutually exclusive.[2] If individuals identified themselves completely with the interest of their respective nations, with the "public" interest, they would not feel on common ground regarding the standards of international conduct. They would represent the respective viewpoints of their nations, opposed to each other, and would not recognize any general principle binding on all nations. But in so far as individuals draw a line between their private and public lives, as long as individuals feel themselves to be "men," "Christians," "Europeans," "civilized beings," etc., in contradistinction to being "citizens," they experience a community with all other fellow men, fellow Christians, fellow Europeans, fellow beings, which engenders certain standards of universal character, and which limits the exercise of the political power of the different nations by its very existence.

This leads to an important conclusion: International law, at least in the form in which it has existed during the last three hundred years, depends on the existence of a separation be-

[2] Cf. the conception of the State which is expressed in the words of Hermann Oncken: "The very essence of the State consists in the antithesis between itself and other states." *Über die Zusammenhänge zwischen äusserer und innerer Politik* (1919), p. 12.

tween private life and public interest within the nations which adhere to its rules. It might be called, in a way, the line of action prescribed by the autonomous individual to the governments of the countries of which the individuals form a part. Therefore it presupposes an element of liberalism in the political structure of nations, because without this element of individual liberty from the requirements and criteria of political power there is no possibility of the development and recognition of those "general principles," without which the present system of international law cannot be conceived. In this sense, international law, just like constitutional law, means, to borrow the words of John Macmurray, "the limitation of the exercise of political power by the rights of personal life. In the absence of a religious conviction to maintain the values of personal life as the ends for which power may be exercised, there is no possibility of limiting the power of government. Power becomes an end in itself . . ."[3]

International law, in the form in which we inherited it from Grotius and the seventeenth century, can exist only in a society in which political power is relative to some higher ends which are those of "personal life." This dependence on a dualism between private and public life is rooted in the fact that the traditional system of international law draws its criteria of judgment not from the immediate reality which it regulates—the reality of interstate relations—but from a set of values which is essentially opposed to this political reality and thereby serves as a basis for the restrictive and limiting rules imposed upon it as a legal order. Therefore the traditional system of international law presupposes the existence of standards and principles embodying values which are conceived not only apart from but in antagonism to, the criteria of political existence and action. In modern occidental society, these values are the ultimate ends of individual life, in so far as they are held up as the objectives for which political power may operate, and by which it is limited.

[3] From a review of T. S. Eliot's book *The Idea of a Christian Society*, by John Macmurray, in *The New Statesman and Nation* (December 1939).

The dualism between private and public life, and the freedom of personal existence which is connected therewith, is not *eo ipso* an integral part of every nation. It seems to require certain conditions in the general disposition of individuals as well as in the social system. In a general way, these conditions may be summarized as follows:

First, the ultimate ends of personal life, which are to serve as a yardstick for the exercise of political power, must be firmly believed ("with religious conviction") by a decisive part of the individuals of the nations.

Second, the best way to attain these ends must be essentially through individual initiative and spontaneous individual action, free from the regulations and influences of political organization.

Third, this demand of individual autonomy and freedom from the influences of government regulation, for the sake of certain ultimate ends of personal life, must be voiced and represented by non-political institutions with sufficient influence to exercise pressure on the respective governments and to make their voices heard.

The idea of the ultimate value of individual freedom, on whatever reason it may be based, cannot be effective in social order and in a system of government, unless there actually is a domain of social life which is essentially free from political authority, and in which the responsibility of the particular individual is the pillar of social coordination, and autonomous individual judgment the primary agent of decision. Such a "privately managed" sphere of social life however is effectively secured only by the allegiance which men pay to non-political institutions, making of those institutions centers of social power with which governments have to count. Without other non-political allegiances than those which are paid to the state, the demand for individual freedom remains just a pious wish, a desire voiced by powerless individuals without any real effect on social order.

When international law came into existence, the ultimate ends in which all men believed were those of a moral and religious life. Every individual soul had God for its father, and accordingly bore the distinction of absolute dignity, which in turn called for personal responsibility of the individual for the purity of his life and the salvation of his soul. There was nothing that a political institution or organization could do to help him towards these ends. Thus a very important aspect of human life and human works—in fact the most highly valued aspect—was exempt from the governance of the *Raison d'État*. Instead it was entirely administered by non-political institutions and organizations of a super-national character. It is true that the Protestant churches in part submitted to the authority of the respective government, and that the Catholic Church lost much of its influence during the eighteenth century. But the very existence of organizations and associations that embraced all men for the sake of their individual souls, evaluating all individuals alike, and fixing standards of behavior from a general human point of view, accounted for the conception of humanistic ideals extending throughout the realm of occidental culture. The universality of this ideal made it possible to set up a common frame of reference by which to measure the political actions of the different states, in the form of international law. Therefore, as long as the allegiance to the churches was deep-rooted enough to make the pursuit of a Christian life appear the most essential task to the vast majority of people, the clerical institutions were effective safeguards of that moral autonomy, liberty and dignity which corresponded to the function of individual responsibility in the realization of ethical standards.[4]

The religious institutions lost their grip on the individual mind to the degree to which the idea of truth, reason and redemption was secularized. The period of life in the service of religious ideals was followed by a period in the service of reason, of "scientific" truths, of the results of human intellect. Again the State could do nothing to further these ends of life. Again

[4] See the article "War and Peace" (The Failure of the Churches, etc.), *Fortune* (January 1940).

it was the free and unregulated activity of individuals which constituted the only road to those truths which seemed to be the ultimately valuable goal. And again there were institutions with considerable social power, derived from the spontaneous allegiance paid to them by individuals, which protected the sphere of individual autonomy from the absorption by the *Raison d'État:* the courts of justice on the one hand and the universities on the other.

The domain of social life which was exempt from political authority remained a relatively narrow one during this period, and it embraced only the people of considerable intellectual capacity and education. It extended again when, under the influence of utilitarian ideas, the pursuit of individual happiness was elevated to the place of the foremost good in life. So long as utilitarianism was no more than the secularized form of absolute valuation of the individual soul, the ideal of life still centered on the human personality and its ultimate value. Thus the ends of all social order and social institutions remained humanistic ones, but the institutional framework of this individualism changed again. Instead of churches, or of tribunals, it was now capitalistic enterprise which required the spontaneous initiative and the corresponding autonomy of the individual for the discharge of his social functions, and thus served to protect the liberty and other safeguards of that initiative. Again the individualistic orientation of social philosophy and social order, and the practical importance of individual activities were mutually dependent. The individual trader and producer had emerged victoriously from mercantilism, and the gates of the world had been flung open to the daring and energy of every single man. Accordingly, the commonly professed goal of social order had become that of a formal freedom from all disturbing factors, leaving the shaping of individual life to the play of personal will and personal capacities.[5] "Rule of law rather than of men,"

[5] "The individualistic way of capitalistic and liberalistic world economy adapts itself easily to changing conditions; it does not ask the different sovereign states for a universal bureaucratic administration, it only demands from them a relative stability of the legal, political and monetary foundations of international intercourse; as for the rest, it can accomplish it best without the tutelage of the authorities." H. v. Beckerath and F. Kern, *Autarkie oder internationale Zusammenarbeit?* (1932) (translation mine).

the ideal of peace in the world, the emphasis on the legality of procedures rather than on substantial justice: all this expressed demands for individual freedom from the effects of political authority and political organization.

Again this latest version of individual autonomy was effectively seconded by the usefulness of individual initiative in capitalistic institutions. It emerged during the period of industrialization. Capitalistic enterprise as an institution was taking possession of the world's productive and consuming possibilities. In this period of expanding wealth and prosperity, with untold promises to the ultimate fulfillment of dreams about individual happiness, it was individual initiative which was instrumental in opening up new fields of exploitation. At the same time, during this era of economic ascension, individual energy as such was the main source of new material values, for the creation of which it was sufficient to produce as much as possible. In a period of scarcity of supply, production meant prosperity, and production depended on the enterprising spirit and initiative of the individual. This was particularly true of commercial relations transcending state boundaries, with the necessary "automatic" adjustment of capital movements to the flow of goods, a phenomenon which depended entirely on the action and reaction of individual persons and could not be produced at will by authoritarian regulation and organization. Thus, in the social framework of capitalistic world trade, the humanistic ends of social life, although formalized and mechanized, found the institutional protection without which their effectiveness in terms of social order would have been that of a beautiful dream instead of a social standard.[6] Against the background of a world economy based on private property and the use which individual initiative made of it, the value of the individual personality appeared as the primary interest not only

[6] "The gold standard is essentially a legal order, securing to the individual certain inalienable rights. After what has happened in America there will be no possibility of restoring such a legal order. Everybody will be convinced that any rights asserted will be annihilated as soon as the authorities in power find this to be in the public interest." G. Cassel, *The Downfall of the Gold Standard* (1936), p. 128.

from the transcendental, but also from the practical aspect of society.

The foregoing observations, although they merely touch upon the sociological aspects of individualism in society and in politics, already seem to justify some general conclusions. Humanistic standards[7] were acknowledged as the criteria of legal and political order in proportion as the autonomous sphere of individuals' lives was protected by the influence of powerful non-political institutions. Within these institutions, the spontaneity, responsibility and initiative of the particular individual was considered the essential condition for the attainment of the ends for which the institutions stood (thus the responsibility of the individual for his works was the condition of his salvation in the eyes of the church; the free initiative of the individual was essential for the development of capitalistic enterprise etc.). It must therefore be concluded *e contrario* that social ideals centering upon the value of the individual are meaningful in society only when the individual human being actually exercises vital functions in the social structure, and when his responsibility is considered vital, and accordingly is protected, by institutions existing simultaneously with and apart from, the State. Without an actual social need for spontaneous and responsible decision and action on part of the individual person, and without the practical possibility for such free initiative, the mere ideal of individualism does not seem to have any concrete meaning nor will it be socially effective. For the ideal

[7] By "humanistic standards" we mean those norms which are derived from "qualities of the abstract man, whereby it is just and right that he should have certain things or do certain things. The abstract man in the state of nature, i.e. in a state of ideal perfection, would claim only what as a reasonable moral entity he ought to have in view."

During the nineteenth century, humanistic standards became "deductions from the fundamental idea of freedom, and a juristic problem arose of deducing the exact limits of each right so that it could be carried out logically in every direction, and yet there should be no conflict." These passages from Roscoe Pound's *Interpretations of Legal History* (Macmillan Co.) (pp. 158*f.*) refer to the rights of man as applied to constitutional law and political philosophy. But these same individualistic principles have also been transferred, in many cases integrally, into international law, where they are used to judge the relationship between states. Besides, the notion of individual freedom has inspired directly all those branches of international law which ultimately serve the end of non-interference in the pursuit of the aims of personal life, such as the status of aliens, the rights of neutrals, protection of non-combatants, etc.

as such establishes no more than an obligation for men to follow it. It becomes a reality solely through the actual exercise of the freedom of decision by individual wills. It is the individual sense of responsible choice through which every ideal becomes effective in this world. Therefore, when society has no place for actual and practical autonomy of individuals, when individual freedom of decision would not be actually beneficial to society as a whole, and when the freely deciding individual does not exercise a vital social function, there cannot be any humanistic standards of social order. The humanistic ideal, therefore, is intimately connected with the practical reality of self-determining, autonomous and responsible individuals.

At this point, it seems desirable to sum up the argument of the present chapter:

The traditional system of international law rests on a foundation of principles of a humanistic nature, i.e. principles which pertain to the sphere of individual existence and interindividual relations, irrespective of nationalities and governments.

Those principles prescribe certain means and certain limits for the exercise of political power and for the pursuit of state interests, for the sake of ultimately non-political ends.

The transnational character of such principles makes it possible for a law of nations to establish a common order of interstate relations.

Such transnational and generally human principles develop and grow only in a sphere of social relationships in which social functions are essentially managed by individuals in their own right, without the help, the guidance or the intervention of governments. For governments represent state interest, and a transnational, non-political set of standards can arise only out of relations which are essentially not government-managed.

The existence of these principles makes it possible for political power, political action and political interests to be measured by some ultimate yardstick of a non-political nature, and thus to be judged by law.

Whether or not such standards of a humanistic nature develop depends on whether or not there is actually a sphere of social functions in which individuals not only are allowed but are required to act on their own accord; in other words, it depends on a social need for individual initiative.

Moreover, the demands for individual rights and humanistic standards do not become effective standards of social order without the protecting power of social institutions, which for the sake of their own ends must rely on individual responsibility, and which in turn secure the individual's autonomy over and against the political authorities of the world. These institutions, in order to foster the growth of transnational principles of conduct, have to be of a transnational character too.

Chronologically, the last one of these institutions which operated as the practical safeguard of individualism, was capitalistic enterprise.

Thus, the workability of a system of international law such as we have known for the last three hundred years, must be held to depend on the structure of society within the various nations, especially on the degree of individual autonomy from political group-interests. In the same proportion as individual life is destined for and devoted to non-political ends, and dominated by non-political values, there is a social medium for standards of universal, not just national, validity. And in so far as the pursuit of such aims does not rely on the assistance of the respective governments, but is carried on within the framework of non-national and non-territorial organizations, such ideals cross the frontiers of nations, and are understood and recognized wherever individuals can live and meet in their capacity as human beings, regardless of nationality. This community of ideal and non-political principles forms the basis of such international law as the modern states system has so far developed.[8] Accordingly, the extent to which human beings believe in the ultimate ends of personal life, the degree to which they actually do exercise self-determination in society, the amount of their psychological and economic autonomy within their respective

[8] "The universality of a legal norm is always the reflection of universally existing social conditions or social ideals. The similarity of such conditions and concepts among a wide circle of nations produces a law common to all of them, in the same way in which the regular recurrence of certain facts or the stability of actual circumstances shape custom as well as law within the various national communities." M. Huber, *Die soziologischen Grundlagen des Völkerrechts* (reprint 1928), p. 42 (translation mine).

states, are directly proportional to the feasibility of a system of international law based on ethics and humanism.

THE DECLINE OF INDIVIDUALISM

It is through this basis of sociological conditions that the very essence of international principles of law is being affected today.[9] In three respects the social background of individualism, so indispensable to the present system of international law, appears to be on the wane:

First, the institutions which used to protect the demands for individual autonomy in the interest of their own functioning are breaking down or changing their structure;

Second, the ends that individuals ultimately pursue are held more and more to be attainable through the help of the government and the state;

Third, as a consequence the very nature of those ends is seeming to change, collective ends gradually replacing the ends of personal life.

These assertions will be taken up one by one.

The breakdown of the institutions of capitalism has been mentioned in an earlier chapter.[10] The downfall of the gold standard with its implied guarantees for individual autonomy,[11] the shrinking of self-adjusting world trade, and other aspects of the economic crisis have led to exports and imports under government control, directed payments, planned production, controlled wages, fixed prices. Nor is this process confined to dictatorial countries: it merely reveals itself more clearly there than in the democracies.[12] If we take into account the control

[9] "Radical innovations [in international law] can be produced only when external forces push the governments and the most influential groups of society in the direction of these reforms. It is also possible that the foundations of international law are transformed by modifications in the structure of the State itself, through a change in the relations between the State and the various social groups. In any case the ultimate cause for the innovations must be sought in a changed evaluation of the State by the different groups of the people." M. Huber, *op. cit.*, pp. 72*f.* (translation mine).

[10] See Chapter III.

[11] See footnote 6 in this chapter.

[12] See for instance the interesting comparison between the development of English business relations and those in the totalitarian countries, in Eliot Janeway's article: "England Moves Toward Fascism" *Harper's Magazine*, January 1939.

which the government obtained over industry through the rearmament program in England, and through the New Deal policies in the United States and France, it becomes clear that no country in the world is exempt from this trend leading from independent business institutions to gradual subjection of business life to government control. The loss of influence and status by the non-political institutions of capitalism, and their capitulation to political organization, is not a merely temporary defeat in the struggle between two warring powers, either. It is a genuine decline of capitalistic enterprise as an "individualistic," i.e. non-political, institution. If there could be any doubt about this fact, it would be refuted by statements like those of William Hard, made in an address at the stronghold of "individualistic" business, the American Manager Council: "The fight in the world today is not a fight between totalitarianism and individualism. In all countries today we have individualism *plus*. The real question today is the source of that *plus*. It can come from private cooperative effort. But in all countries today, including the democracies, it is more and more coming from the government."[13] The same address quotes a speech made by Matthew Woll, vice-president of the American Federation of Labor, who is reported to have said in 1932: "With the government now at the point of entering every line of business on the grandest scale ever known, we may well say that Labor Day of 1932 marks a policy of abdication by industry from mastery of its own home, the government taking its place." In other words, the non-political institutions of capitalistic enterprise which used to be the safeguard of individual autonomy and liberty from the state, have not lost their power because they were defeated by the agencies of political power in a struggle for supremacy, but because individuals to an increasing degree renounced their allegiance to free enterprise and individualistic business.

This leads to the discussion of the second aspect of declining individualism: the pursuit of desirable ends by collective instead of by individual means. The trend toward organizational

[13] Published in condensed form in *Reader's Digest*, June 1940.

collectivism has been analyzed too often, from Walter Lippman to Hermann Rauschning, from Harold J. Laski to William Rappard, to be taken up in detail again. This trend as such, is not of relevance within the scope of the present argument. The entire phenomenon is relevant only because it has a bearing on the existing system of international law. The connection between the trend toward collectivism and international law is to be found in those fundamental principles of law that used to be commonly recognized among the individuals of the world's nations, and therefore were referred to as a basis for the law of nations. These principles sprung from the consciousness that the individual person had a significance and an importance in world society, distinct from the nation to which he belonged. This consciousness was generated in those spheres of life in which the individual and his initiative were the only and indispensable "manager," in which no other agency would produce results but that of individual autonomy. It is the change which has occurred in this respect that is above all significant for our problem. The trend toward collectivism as such does not concern us, but the part in it which the individual and individual consciousness plays does concern us.

In this sense the most notable phenomenon is the loss of confidence that individuals can achieve social results by their own individual efforts. This development manifests itself in all walks of life. During the economic depression which began in 1929, it led to a general cry for government help. Unlike the reaction of the public in former crises, people began to sign away their assets to the government in order to mobilize government forces for immediate relief, which their own attitude or their own activity did not seem to produce any more. Movements like pacifism, which used to be based entirely on individual initiative and on international, non-political communities among peace-loving people, turned into lobbying groups and pressure organizations, with the result that pacifists even became nationalists and on some occasions went so far as to form the war party in certain countries.

In all these and other instances a general feeling of impotence on the part of the single individual is the root of this development. Without forming part of an organization, without pursuing his ends through an organization, the individual does not feel able to attain anything. This sentiment is well circumscribed by three statements from three different standpoints: Konrad Heiden, analyst of European dictatorships, describes it in the following terms: "The field of decision has become too vast and incalculable for the democratic spirit of the individual being. The individual does not understand this world any more, and is driven nearer and nearer to the desperate conviction that he is incapable of understanding, and that even if he did understand, there would be no use in it because what can one man, even an understanding one, do? In the eyes of this steadily spreading pessimistic philosophy, political decisions are measured by power."[14] In the address quoted once before, William Hard confronted American businessmen with a picture of the statism and collectivism which they had adopted in spite of their professed individualism: "You make the committee rooms echo with your cries for individualism. The fact is that meanwhile you do not represent it yourselves. You operate not as individuals but through corporations. Not content with corporations you have formed trade associations. You now have 7,500 of them. You have your United States Chamber of Commerce. You have your National Industrial Conference Board. You have your American Management Association etc."

And finally, from the point of view of the psychoanalyst, Dr. Frederick H. Allen, in an address before the American Psychiatric Society, explained this increased disposition to think, feel and act in terms of the group rather than in terms of individual efforts, as "the same behavior aberration that causes persons to fasten their attention on members of their own sex." His statement is significant because he traces both phenomena to an inadequate and insecure feeling about one's self, and a fear of accepting the difference of individualities as a creative stimulus: "They both seem to spring from a basic feeling of insecurity and represent attempts to find safer ways of living.

[14] In his book *Europäisches Schicksal* (1937), p. 173 (translation mine).

The more threatened the group, the more intense becomes the nationalistic philosophy, and the more individuals submerge or even lose their individual entity and live through the more apparent security offered by the racial self."[15]

This is not the place to investigate the ultimate causes of this sentiment of individual inadequacy and of the strength of group action. We merely take cognizance of the undeniable phenomenon that individuals, while still pursuing ultimate ends of individual happiness, to an increasing degree seek to attain these ends through the collective action of organized units, discarding the ways of autonomous individual activity. The necessary consequence of this gradually developing consciousness of functional interdependence is an increase in the emotional links and loyalties between the particular individual and his organizations, especially that organization which secures the coordination of all the others: the State. The social system having become far too complicated to allow the average individual to judge the requirements of cooperation by himself, it becomes more and more a task of national governments to organize that coordination of forces which a system based on the free interplay of interests failed to achieve.

In proportion as the individual becomes aware of this vital role of organizational agencies, the initiative in meeting the problems of social order is turned over to them along with the responsibility that used to belong to the individual. Now, bereft of both practical autonomy in the social system and responsibility for independent decisions, and relying for all practical and even many theoretical purposes on the performance of other agencies on his behalf, the individual submits himself heart and soul to the requirements and demands of these organizing agencies. And little difference does it make whether the agency which takes from the individual the burden of

[15] *New York Times*, June 11, 1938. In a report on "The Scope of Political Science," prepared for the 1940 meeting of the American Political Science Association by a group of scholars under the chairmanship of E. S. Griffith, the entire trend is characterized thus: "More and more we are facing the fact that the operative reality in human relations is *associative* action, and that the sharp distinction between public and private action is likely to prove less useful in the future."

decision and responsibility is the government, the party, the political boss or the trade union. For in any case the individual seeks the fulfillment of his dreams about security, happiness and prosperity through the action of organized political power. "The glow of abstract concepts of liberty and freedom dim progressively for the family unable to provide its daily bread; a realized lower standard of living is to them preferable to an unrealized higher one."[16] The higher standard of living promised to the enterprising individual by the idea of free capitalism beckons to them through the efforts of individual initiative, but the security of the lower one, realized in the certain framework of organized cooperation, is more enticing to their disillusioned self.

The individual who thus surrenders his freedom of movement and of decision for the sake of organized security, becomes highly vulnerable to outside influences affecting "his" organization, influences which he cannot control yet still wishes to control. This accounts for the almost hysterical demand for "liberty" and "security" on the part of governments, demands which again are not confined to the dictatorships, but can be detected also in the new battlecry for more governmental power raised by the working masses in the democracies as well as in the demands for heavy armament voiced by former internationalists and pacifists.

It seems as if individuals were disposed to say: Since our government holds a position similar to that of the first engineer in a highly complicated electric plant, since every individual's life and peace of mind depend on the certainty that the government is capable of handling all conceivable emergencies, let the government have all the power to deal with whatever may disturb the social system. Since we all have to rely on its action, let us strive to give the government as much freedom as possible. All efforts seem to be concentrated on removing every possible obstacle to efficient and flexible governmental action. The repeated powers which the French parliament voted its

[16] Harlow S. Person, speaking on the second day of the 1938 conference of the League for Industrial Democracy. *New York Times,* June 11, 1938.

cabinet, the various ministries of coordination which the British created, the ascendancy of executive powers in all the nations of the world during the last decade, bear witness to this assertion. The state consciousness of the masses, which is just one aspect of an increasing disposition to substitute organization for spontaneously concerted individual action, secures a much closer identification of the individual with his state than classical nationalism was ever able to produce.

FROM NATIONALISM TO STATISM, FROM IMPERIALISM TO AUTARKY

If this new state-consciousness of the masses is confused with old-time nationalism and imperialism, we fail to realize the basic change in outlook, a change from an individualistic point of view to an organizational point of view. Nationalism is but the collective expression of typical middle-class individualism. Historically, sociologically and psychologically it is linked to the way of living and the outlook which characterizes the individualistic *bourgeoisie*. It arose from the individual consciousness of group peculiarities and common qualities in speech, ways of life, outlook and tradition, and since national differences in these respects became most apparent in those strata that led a highly individualized form of life, nationalism became their proper political faith. Neither the aristocracy nor the laboring classes of Europe were the breeding places for classical nationalism. Rising historically as an offshoot of the individualistic principle of self-determination, it became politically effective as a dictate of the nationally self-conscious groups of certain strata to the government. The government or the state was not an end, it was the tool of nationalism, by which nationalistic circles of the people undertook to realize their idea of self-development.

Like nationalism, imperialism is also a phenomenon that pertains essentially to the mentality and the social structure of individualism. It is not a movement inaugurated by any needs for expansion on the part of the state as such. As with nationalism, it is the individual who leads the way, extending his own private interests into "backward areas" and calling on the state to follow up with its means of power as far as private initiative has succeeded in carrying its economic activities. The bid for empire is an instrument of individual liberty of action; the state is considered merely a tool for ultimately individual ends.[17]

Instead, the new phenomenon of "statism" presents a different aspect. Unlike nationalism and imperialism, both of which considered the state merely as an instrument in the service of the ends of personal life, following the lead of autonomous individual direction, the present attitude is a straight abdication of individual self-determination. It is rooted in a readiness, on the part of the individuals, to let themselves, their lives, their decisions and actions, be governed by the requirements of organization, especially the omni-comprehensive organization of the state. The smooth functioning of the social machinery, kept in shape by political organization, forms the object of their foremost anxiety. "During the glorious peace of the nineteenth century men had forgotten the price of security; they had believed that other values could be superior to it. But from the moment when they felt their lives and their possessions threatened and inadequately protected by governments which were no longer able to govern, they yearned, as Paul Valéry has put it, for discipline or death."[18]

The decline of old-time nationalism is one of the symptoms of the decline of individualism. From the French Revolution to the war of 1914, wars were led by nations, not by states, by peoples, not by organizations. In other words: the objectives of war, either aggressive or defensive, were the concern of each individual, at any rate among the strata that formed the social core of nations. Wars then implied the personal participation, emotionally as much as practically, of each person in the common enterprise of the nation. There is no such participation of individuals in national wars now. Except where people had to

[17] In an article in *Die Neue Rundschau* (March 1933), Hermann Heller has very appropriately termed this power-aspect of political individualism: "Authoritarian Liberalism."

[18] Significantly enough, this statement comes from the pen of the liberal Frenchman, André Maurois. *New York Times Magazine*, June 19, 1938.

defend their lives, governments all over Europe, including Germany and Italy, had the greatest difficulty convincing their peoples that they did have stakes in a potential war. The policy of appeasement, so characteristic not only of Chamberlain, but even of Hitler before 1939, and practised not only by England and France, but also by a number of the smaller nations, was only the result of the indifference of individuals regarding the objectives of a war. The reason was that the objectives of war in the middle of the twentieth century were those of organizations, not of nationally self-conscious groups of individuals. While individuals had signed away the determination of their lives in society to the organization of the social machinery, they also had resigned that initiative which makes for enthusiastic participation in a common fight for common interests.

In a similar way, imperialism has ceded its place to a policy of expansion which, instead of being dictated by far-flung individual investments and other interests, is determined by the security of organizational action on the part of the state. It is no longer the enterprising spirit of the daring individual which prescribes the extension of state power. It is the interest of the state itself, the requirements of its organization, of its functional freedom of movement, that inspires policies of expanding or narrowing spheres of power. Both are represented in the modern picture: while Germany and Italy are expanding, the United States and England have found it more to their interest to pull in the too far flung ramifications of their influence. The notion of "absolute liberty," meaning completely unhampered freedom of action for the government, is the modern battlecry.[19] "According to our opinion, it is an impossible situation that an important part of our economy should be dependent on foreign decisions over which we have no control. . . . A return to the former so-called automaticism on a basis of the old gold-standard is rejected by the authoritarian states because of the inter-

[19] See Hermann Rauschning's analysis of the objectives of Germany's foreign policy, in *Foreign Affairs*, October 1939.

national dependence that it involves."[20] This statement of Reich Minister Dr. Funk reveals clearly the roots of the policy of autarky, which has been substituted for classical imperialism. It also reveals that the modern reliance of the individual on the action of organization has destroyed, or at least tends to destroy, that sphere of actual autonomy in which individual initiative used to operate as an indispensable agent of the system of social order. The "automaticism" mentioned by Dr. Funk could work only if and when society relied entirely on the "automatic" reactions of individuals to economic changes, i.e., on their free and uninfluenced decision of economic questions. The increasing importance of organized coordination for the existence of society, however, is not compatible with such uncontrollable factors as free individual actions and reactions. Organizational coordination is different from "organic coordination." The tendency to pursue individual and collective ends through the instrumentality of organizations must ultimately lead to the absolute ascendancy of the most central of them all—the State—and consequently to the disappearance of the sphere in which individual initiative and responsibility is, or was, functioning as the determining factor of social relationships.

FROM MAN INDEPENDENT TO MAN COORDINATE

In addition to the decline of capitalistic individualism, and the corresponding state-consciousness of people, or possibly as a consequence of these developments, a profound change in the very nature of individual man can be observed in our time. It is by no means an independent and spontaneous type of individual that has yielded his claim to self-determination unwillingly, in a struggle with superior forces. To make possible the existence of mass-movements like fascism and national-socialism, a change had first to take place in the self-evaluation of the individual personality. That modern totalitarianism is not a usurpation of political power by a decided minority of rulers, but springs from a condition of mind of the masses, is

[20] *New York Times*, March 7, 1938.

proved by the attempts to set up such régimes in countries populated by individuals who actually wanted to be free and independent. Primo de Rivera's dictatorship, modeled after the Italian pattern, fell after seven years of difficult going through lack of general support. And twice afterwards, in October 1934 and in July 1936 the Spanish people prevented by determined resistance the establishment of authoritarian régimes. That they had to yield to the pressure of foreign powers does not modify the significance of this fact. Nothing comparable to that spontaneous defence of individual liberty and autonomy took place to oppose the enhancement of governmental power in Italy, Germany, Turkey, the United States, Belgium, France and Great Britain. Again, the development in the now totalitarian countries may serve as an extreme case of trends which prevail throughout western industrialized society.

The thesis is that the modern individual is not only practically prevented from exercising self-determination, but, even where the practical possibility exists, has renounced determination of his own ends for his endeavors and activities. The causes of the decay of individualism in individuals must be sought in the modern forms of living, and in the features of industrialized society, which have developed mainly without the help or the interference of political agencies. The innumerable forces of suggestion, persuasion, mass-hypnosis and mass-adjustment which work on the individual being every time he comes in contact with the outside world, are elements of a social structure which has not been created by political power, but by the forces of economic individualism. Ceaseless streams of commercial propaganda, mass-production of uniform types of goods, the corresponding growth of uniform types of needs, the standardizing influence of radio, film, syndicated press and mass-level literature must be counted among the main influences which tend to produce the responsive type of mass-man, suppressing at the same time the spontaneous and self-determining type of personality. All political lectures and speakers know to what a surprising degree people rely for their political opinion on their favorite columnist, whose statements are repeated in hundreds of newspapers and read by millions of citizens.

The disposition of the modern individual to renounce his own capacity of judgment in favor of some stereotyped opinion which is served to him "ready for use" by some agency seems to be a phenomenon of universal extension. "The Mass Man means complete uniformity of thought, regimentation instead of freedom, leveling down instead of leveling up. The World War marked the appearance of the Mass Man on the stage of history and opened the way for his demands. He became bewildered and lost and delegated his authority to the dictators." These remarks of the historian, Prince Lobanov-Rostovsky[21] happen to be made with respect to political dictatorship. But if the standardization of individual minds occurred in the political sphere as far as the totalitarian countries were concerned, it developed in other respects in the democracies as well. One of the typical complaints in this respect may illustrate the thesis:

"Lewis B. Traver [President of the American Booksellers' Association] . . . attacked yesterday what he termed the 'mechanized reading of books,' which he said was forced on the public by book clubs. . . . Discussing new contracts designed to protect publishers from the book club method of operation, Mr. Traver said: 'The book clubs concentrate the attention of the public on one or two books for the sake of the economies of mass-production. This means that a great many good books, even superior books, which do not have the promotion, fail to reach a wide market. The public believes it is getting an excellent value. Actually it is not. The public should buy books according to likes and dislikes. Above all, it should not stick to the same pattern. It should grow, and it cannot grow if it permits itself to be dictated to.'"[22]

Here is clearly a case of regular, but non-political dictatorship. On the same topic of literature, V. F. Calverton quoted Pearl Buck as saying: "I wish to heaven that we could do away with the best-seller lists entirely. The best-seller list is not a

[21] As reported in the *New York Times*, November 22, 1937.
[22] As reported in the *New York Times*, May 16, 1938.

thermometer. It is an iron mold clamped on the public mind." And Mr. Calverton continues himself: "It is the reading public which suffers most of all, for what happens is that it becomes so best-seller conscious that it buys relatively few books that are not listed in the best-seller class. I have talked to hundreds of intelligent people within the last ten or fifteen years, who spend nine-tenths of their book-buying money on best-sellers; two or three decades ago those same people would have purchased select literature and prided themselves upon discovering an unusual fiction or a rare, unrecognized genius. Today they wait for the best-seller list to tell them what to read because they have no interest in reading anything which everybody else is not reading. In a word, they have lost their claim to individuality."[23] This example could naturally be matched in other aspects of modern existence. The conditions of modern mass existence seem to generate an inclination to stereotyped thought and stereotyped action. At the same time this involves the decay of the individual capacity for autonomous decision and independent orientation. An increasing number of individuals are coming to rely, for their opinions and resolutions, on the mechanical reflex by which they respond to outside suggestions and stimuli.[24]

Thus modern life, in promoting the habit of mechanically responding to outside influences in daily routine action, rather than resorting to conscious decision, is generating a type of individual who is living for ends not determined by himself. And to the same degree to which the ends of personal life cease to be felt "with religious conviction," to which they become matters of reflex responses, the corollary of self-direction, individual freedom, begins to lose its value. A deep change in this

[23] *Current History*, June 1938.

[24] To what surprising results this reflex habit of conduct may lead, and to what extent it already has become a substitute for conscious decision and rational deliberation, is well illustrated by the experiment of an American scholar. He published on various consecutive days something like the following advertisements in the local papers: at first: "Send me one dollar!" Next he inserted: "Why haven't you sent your dollar yet?" And finally he advertised: "You have one day to send me your dollar!" According to the newspaper report, which I can only quote from memory, he received remittances running into four figures.

respect already has occurred. "The concept of freedom itself has been debased and devalued. It has been proved that economic freedom does not lead to equality. To act to one's greatest economic advantage—the essence of economic freedom—has lost the social value that was placed upon it. Regardless of whether it is man's true nature to put his economic interests first, the masses have ceased to regard economic behavior as socially beneficial in itself, since it cannot promote equality. Hence, curtailment or abandonment of economic freedom is accepted or even welcomed if thereby the threat of unemployment, the danger of depression, or the risks of economic sacrifices promise to become less imminent."[25]

Independence of his personal action was a man's primary goal in times when the price to be paid for it was merely personal danger or the sacrifice of comfort. The means of subsistence being always at hand for the individual, the issue was purely one of character. The economic possibility of independence was secured by the certainty of demand for individual labor or the products of individual craftsmanship.[26] Conscious of the value of their individuality, men of character therefore strove to be free from the bonds of social, political or economic dependence on other people. It was honorable and estimable to do so, because a man who sought the liberty of self-determination was liable to encounter enmity, affront, struggle and danger, at the same time finding opportunity to display the best qualities of his character: courage, strength and perseverance.

But in our modern industrialized mass-society the conditions of individual independence are different. The supply of individual labor is usually higher than the demand. The yield of individual work scarcely produces a livelihood. Employment, on the other hand, involves a high degree of dependence both on the immediate superiors, and on the coordination of a great

[25] P. F. Drucker, *The End of Economic Man*, John Day Co. (1939), p. 77.

[26] T. J. Wertenbaker, "Labor Costs and Democracy," *Princeton University Alumni Lectures* (1938), p. 15: "Just as the insistent demand for labor throughout most of our history has made the American optimistic, self-respecting, energetic, so the present situation makes a large part of the population fearful and dependent."

variety of factors in a complicated system of divided labor. The opportunities for individual enterprise are highly discouraging, confined as they are to a small number of learned professions and the struggling business of the independent shopkeeper.[27] Every individual existence is affected by countless ties of economic interdependence. Breaking loose from those ties does not imply an honorable fate of risk and combat, nor does it provide tests of the high qualities of character, permitting the individual will to triumph or to perish fighting. Today the consequences of breaking away from the connections of social and economic dependence are a miserable existence of starvation and hopelessness, and a life deprived of all positive value by the odium of meaninglessness. An existence of unemployment, being the price for personal "independence," is neither honorable nor estimable nor dangerous, nor productive of character. It is the negation, not the affirmation, of personality.

These conditions have brought about a change in the conception and in the valuation of liberty. There is neither merit nor reward of any kind in gaining independence from the social and economic ties which determine a man's existence in society, and which connect every individual destiny with innumerable other individual destinies. Accordingly, liberty in the sense of personal independence cannot be valued any longer as one of the supreme goals of life. Instead of defying the social ties of interdependence, modern man seeks his freedom within their framework. The efficient functioning of conditions which secure employment, the smooth coordination of productive and consumptive factors, the harmonious balance of social forces, these elements go to make up the contemporaneous notion of freedom. The worker feels free within the trade union, and feels free as long as he is employed; he feels unfree in the state of unemployment, and also when, a lone individual, he has to face the immense bargaining power of huge corporations. Consequently, the ideal of independent individual self-assertion, of a vigorous pursuit of purely personal plans and purposes, is being replaced, as a pattern of life, by the valuation of coordinated

[27] R. S. Lynd, *Knowledge for What?* (1939), p. 92.

activity, the ideal of certainty regarding the functioning of a cooperative social system. The axiomatic concept of man in society is being transformed from one of Man Independent to one of Man Coordinate. The general orientation of standards is not any more in the direction of disjointed personal initiative and enterprise, but is swaying toward the direction of the efficient working of the interrelated whole.

All this tends to show that the conditions under which humanistic principles of law (i.e. principles inspired by the notion of the autonomous, free and responsible individual) can be recognized and kept alive among the individuals of the world's nations, are gradually disappearing.

In proportion as social conditions create a type of individual incapable of autonomous and independent decisions, individuals lose the faculty of judging the value of political actions by a yardstick of non-political derivation. Political power, being the instrument of the centralmost coordination of social energies, becomes identified with his existence. He ceases to be aware of standpoints from which to measure the value of political facts, other than by their political successfulness. All this tends to eliminate the humanistic criterion of value from our system of social standards. For the type of individual who never experiences the responsibility, and at the same time the freedom, of making an autonomous decision on the basis of values of which his conscience is the sole judge, cannot possibly envisage the individual human personality as being the center of all human efforts. For the type of man who readily adjusts himself to an external and standardized pattern of thought and action without claiming any originality for his decisions, there can be no such thing as individual liberty and dignity. Therefore there is symptomatic significance in a statement like that of the Reich Press Chief, Dr. Dietrich: "There is no freedom of the individual. There is only freedom of peoples, nations or races, for these are the only material and historical realities through which the life of the individual exists."[28]

For a sociological analysis of the state of mind of modern

[28] *New York Times*, December 10, 1937.

masses, it is essential to take remarks like these literally. Individual freedom, dignity, autonomy are conditions not so much of constitutional arrangement, as of the individual mind. No law can grant liberty to men who are not free by their own will. The renunciation of the creative faculty for thinking and acting according to spontaneous decision necessarily means the surrender of individuality. This surrender is the more enthusiastic the more the leader or pattern to which the individual succumbs, meets the emotional needs of the disoriented masses. And such absorption of individualities by a uniform political and social pattern signifies the disappearance of the age-old dualism of political power and non-political ideals.

THE ORGANIZATIONAL ORIENTATION OF INDIVIDUALS

We are not concerned in this context with approving or rejecting the value of the tendency just characterized, but with the question whether the traditional system of international law is still based on a real community of values existing among the nations of this period. The common recognition of values throughout the "civilized" nations was possible because of the fact that the sphere of individual autonomy and freedom provided for a frame of reference which was not identical with any one of these nations, and which in actual extension and in ideal significance transcended every single state. It has been shown that not only the domain of practical autonomy of individual decision, but also the individualistic orientation of thinking and valuation is receding in our epoch, having already disappeared entirely in a considerable number of nations. Whether a new non-political criterion of values will emerge, by which political power and its action can be judged, we do not know. But we do know that the basis of interindividual morality, on which our present system of international law is built, has become untenable. It fails to serve as a living guaranty of the rightfulness of international law, because the moral criteria of individuals are no longer experienced, tested and developed in free and autonomous contact with other individuals, but in the relation between individual and nation. Therefore the world-wide community of values which were communicated and confirmed from man to man, apart from national interests and considerations, has ceased to function.[29] All we can do under these circumstances is to try to find the basic value-experience which does inspire individuals of this age, in order to adjust the structure and the orientation of the legal system to this change in social outlook.

The general attitude developed by the masses under modern conditions may be termed an organizational orientation.[30] This term connotes the evaluation of things social by standards of organizational technique and perfection, the satisfaction derived from well organized cooperation as such, without regard to the significance of the ultimate ends of cooperation. It is the reflection of the machine-age mentality in the field of social relations and social order. From this perspective, value is attributed to efficient collective action, but individual action is disregarded in favor of organization.[31] Just as the assembling of parts is the joy of the mechanic, whether amateur or professional, so the efficiency of a well organized human collectivity becomes almost an end in itself, giving a sense of delight to the masses, who feel that this capacity for quick and unitary action is something on which their individual fate may largely depend.

The test of organizational efficiency is usually seen in the swift-

[29] "Economics, financial and social international relations, as well as education and culture, are becoming more and more involved in the turmoil of power politics, where law serves predominantly as an ideology." G. W. Keeton and G. Schwarzenberger, *Making International Law Work* (1939), p. 59.

[30] K. Heiden, *Europäisches Schicksal* (1937), pp. 138*f*.

[31] An illustration of the change of taste in this respect may be found in the public acclamation of various types of ocean crossings. The individual undertaking, in 1927, by Lindbergh, flying alone and on his own initiative, corresponded to the attitude of mind of the masses, and especially that of the democratic United States. On the other hand, Balbo's exploit in 1933, when he flew in formation and executed a coordinated movement, gave expression to the spirit of modern organizationalism, especially that of fascist Italy. However, at about the same time the taste for organization, and its valuation as the condition of efficient action, also was spreading to the individualistic countries. It can be seen, for instance in the difference between the world flight of Wiley Post, which he undertook individually in 1933, and that of Howard Hughes, which was the product of well planned organization and coordination, in 1938. For when in this latter year Corrigan again undertook an exploit of extremely individualistic character, the editorial of the *New York Times* could say about him: "Corrigan returned not so much the conquering hero, but as a mischievous youth who had 'pulled a good gag'."

ness of collective action. It is by no means accidental that the totalitarian countries believe in a military strategy of quick and coordinated movements of mechanized units, trusting to maneuver rather than to warfare of position. The social significance of modes of warfare has been pointed out too often to be discussed here again. Apart from all considerations of military science, this strategy has sprung from the same emotional source which feeds the fascist conception of government: the elementary enjoyment of rapid action by coordinated units. Totalitarian movements in all countries with their taste for "streamlined" organization testify to this basic experience.[32] The organization of power in the dictatorial countries, efficient as it seems to be, nevertheless by far exceeds the actual requirements of the respective régimes. Organization not only serves the end of providing for power, obedience, action, and so on; it also gives direct emotional satisfaction to the mind of modern masses.[33] That this phenomenon is not confined to totalitarian countries is proved by the tribute of envy and admiration paid to them by democratic peoples, on account of this organizational perfection. The travellers returning to their native democracies from totalitarian countries, and converted from bitter enemies into sympathizers with dictatorships by the overwhelming impression of thoroughly organized government action and punctual train service, are already proverbial. The fact that the appeal of effective organization is, even in liberal and "individualistic" countries, so strong as to make people admirers of a régime in which the certainty of coordination has been obtained at the price of personal liberty and individuality, reveals the extent to which the organizational orientation is becoming a feature of modern mentality everywhere. The same sensation of impersonal power and collective superiority, which a machine-conscious individual feels while witnessing the flights of Clippers and Zeppelins, the accuracy of long-range gunfire, the rapidity of streamlined trains, the power of racing cars and

[32] This phenomenon has been exhaustively treated in R. Behrendt's book *Politischer Aktivismus* (1932).

[33] Cf. R. S. Lynd, *Knowledge for What?* (1939), p. 71.

speedboats, the working of a huge and shining electric plant, he also experiences when he beholds the almost mechanical performance of modern organization, which handles human beings like so many screws and levers. The impression of human capacity, expressed through organization, swells the heart of the onlooker with pride, and makes him unconscious of the fact that he himself may be, or actually is, the victim of this "technical" achievement.[34]

Where the idea of organizational efficiency has become firmly enough ingrained, it may even be invoked as a justification of otherwise dubious measures. "Totalitarianism must reject the demand made upon every preceding social order in Europe, to justify itself and its authority. It must maintain that the mechanical, external organization of society constitutes its own justification and that it is a social order in itself. Not only must the mere hull of the social fabric be supreme compared to all social substance: the empty mechanical form must also be the supreme social substance itself. *Organization must serve for creed and order.*"[35] For example, the German purges of 1934 and 1938 show the public reaction to such events to be neither moral disapproval nor approval. The standards by which these actions were judged, were not moral standards at all, but the standards of efficiency and rapidity of organized action.[36] The technical appreciation almost completely overshadowed any other possible value, even the political valuation of the measure. It is obvious that this is an extreme case. But it takes phenomena of extreme character to indicate the direction of a trend which

[34] A good illustration of this mentality is to be found in the remarkable observations of an English girl who married a Nazi German, and who describes her emotional experiences in Hitler's Germany. "A nation guarded by a personal god in brown uniform. Guarded by 'do's' and 'don'ts' as clear as rules and regulations in a home for mental defectives. And there is a real, clean, shining, delicious sense of righteousness and well-being if they are kept. Often I surrender; and sometimes with a kind of rapture. I might as well enjoy passionately what I have got—the feeling that I belong to the mightiest nation in the world, the finest. The open-air cleanliness of simplicity of everyone. The feeling of terrific power." Margaret Schmidt, "I Married a Nazi," as condensed (from *Eve's Journal*) in *Reader's Digest*, March 1940.

[35] P. F. Drucker, *The End of Economic Man*, p. 219.

[36] The popular reaction to these occurrences was crystallized in the phrase, often overheard in Germany at that time: "*Wie er das wieder gemacht hat!*"

might go unnoticed if we sought to trace it in normal and more generally representative features. For this reason, the totalitarian countries, precisely because the social and political crisis of the modern world reached in them a degree of extremity which is not representative of all other countries, serve to indicate what may be happening to a far less radical and therefore less noticeable degree, in the more balanced countries.

Although the organizational orientation of modern mass mind has manifested itself most visibly in those totalitarian countries in which the lack of a more organic unity of cooperation threatened the very existence of the nation, it has begun to spread to the old democracies as well. It is instructive to listen to the overtones in a speech like this of Premier Leon Blum, made in the French Chamber of Deputies on April 5, 1938, as reported in the *New York Times:* "Replying to those who charged that he was setting up exchange control in embryo, he contended that, faced with the problem of how to prevent the metallic reserves from being touched, he found it necessary to depart from pure liberalism. Mr. Blum denied charges that his proposals would push the country toward autarky and dictatorial government, but, he said, there are lessons to be learned from the fact that a great nation under a totalitarian régime can, without gold, without credit and without money, make so astounding an industrial effort."[37] Similar utterances made by leading persons in the democracies in admiration of the organizational efficiency of the totalitarian régimes are legion, and are too familiar to be mentioned in more detail.

It may be too early yet to draw conclusions from observations like these. But it is difficult to close the observing eyes to the fact that modern mass mentality moves and is moved in terms of coordination, in terms of function, in terms of the interconnections making up the whole, rather than in those of the particular qualities of the parts. People are not only beginning to think, but also to evaluate by standards of connectedness, complexity, and cooperation. The orientation of their social consciousness is being determined more and more by the

[37] As reported in the *New York Times,* April 6, 1938.

notion of an interdependent social machinery, kept going by organization, making possible a meaningful existence of individuals only if and when it does operate. Ideas of interdependence, divided labor, organizational distribution of functions, and so on, influence modern social thinking more than could be suspected from surface appearances. But what is essential for the feasibility of the present system of international law is that the standards of individualistic orientation, which used to prevail, are gradually disappearing in this process of social and mental transformation. In this respect, it seems safe to arrive at the following conclusions in this discussion:

The transnational, non-political standpoint from which the traditional system of international law used to judge the value of political action, was that of autonomous, free, self-determining man. In the community of standards developed among the nations through free interindividual contact, international law found a substantial basis for its criteria.

The decline of those social institutions which used to protect the sphere of autonomous individual activities against government interests, and the abandonment of the individualistic outlook by individuals themselves, has interrupted this worldwide interindividual system of human relationships, which used to be the substratum of the law of nations.

The growing state-consciousness of individuals, the appreciation of the security of organization, instead of the liberty of independence, and the corresponding identification of the individual with those organizations on which his daily life depends, have eliminated that attitude of individualism, according to which political action could be judged by the yardstick of the "personal ends of life."

An international law which is built on the assumption that personal life and public life are essentially antagonistic, and that the values of personal life are the standards limiting, directing and ultimately justifying political events, seems to be out of pace with this development of modern social mentality. Standards of general human reference are dwindling under the influence of organizational criteria, especially those pertaining to the state, which today appear more important to the individual than the considerations derived from the ideal of Man Independent. This process destroys the common frame of reference on which international law so far has been based.

Here the question arises: Is it not imperative to abandon a structure of international law which owes its shape to social and mental conditions so utterly different from those of the present time? The task of providing the world with a legal order of international relations must be solved, with or without the help of transnational standards of individualistic morality. Since new criteria seem to dominate the value-experience of modern masses, we must explore the possibilities arising out of them, in order to find ways in which the functions of a legal system can be adequately fulfilled in our time.

CHAPTER VI

MAKING INTERNATIONAL LAW WORK

THE CHARACTERISTICS OF THE PRESENT SYSTEM

DURING the three or four centuries of its existence, modern international law has been based on the dualism of private life and public authority. Within the orbit, first of Christendom, later of the "civilized world," individuals maintained a certain community of ideals which was kept alive through the manifold contacts and relationships among men in their capacity as private persons. In all the nations of the world, people enjoyed a realm of freedom and autonomy in which they had to manage their affairs on their own initiative and responsibility, without the intervention of the public authorities. Within this sphere of life, which used to be the economic one during the last phase of development, individual relations were established and maintained across national boundaries by men in their own right. This circumstance protected an international community of ideals and interests—which were essentially the ideals and interests of private persons, as contrasted with the conflicting interests of their respective nations.

International law was the legal formula that expressed the tension between the realm of individual interests and individualistic ideals on the one hand, and the inherent antagonism of sixty-odd sovereign states on the other. It gave juristic status to the claim of the *common* elements of this world, embodied in the moral, economic or general cultural links between individuals as such, against the *particular* factors, embodied in the interests of each of the various states. Accordingly, international law can be said to have thrived on the conflict between *Society*, being the realm of private contacts, individual relationships, and personal responsibility, and the *State*, being the organization of public power, the realm of centralized administration and authoritative decisions. In this sense, the traditional system of international law was an attempt to mitigate the conflicts arising from the simultaneous existence of various units of supreme power, for the sake of the undisturbed pursuit of personal ends in the framework of those private relationships.

In accordance with this dualism of a privately "managed" Society, materializing in interindividual relations, and the politically organized communities, materializing through the public authority of the State, international law took shape as a system of *ideal norms* opposing their postulates to the *reality of facts*. The essential feature of this system was that those ideal standards were derived from the sphere of private life, inspired by the notion of the natural rights of man, and oriented by the practical needs and requirements of the transnational Society of individual interests. The realm of politics, on the other hand, was conceived as that of pure power, blind dynamics and "vital" forces which had to be kept in check by restrictive commands.

In other words, the criterion of order in international law was not derived from the sphere of politics; it was essentially alien and antagonistic to the nature of political institutions and political relationships. International law was an imposition on international politics; the imposition of an individualistic perspective and private interests on the political outlook and public interests. Accordingly, international law never created a real order of international politics, i.e. it never set up standards of political action *sub specie rei publicae*. It did not establish immanent criteria of political relations, approving one course of action and rejecting another for being *good statesmanship* or *bad statesmanship*. It did not discriminate between different ends of political power, telling governments what to do in order to fulfil their functions of government in the best possible way. It treated politics, political power, political institutions and political relations as some elementary phenomenon, something comparable to the forces of nature, something factual that had its own blind dynamics. Instead of attempting to order political relationships from the point of view of political goods and political evils, it merely took cognizance of the forces of politics, trying to keep them within certain limits. These limits were prescribed for political institutions in the interest of values that were essentially non-political. Thus the "order" established by international law consisted merely in protective walls, raised around the ends of personal life and interindividual relationship in the form of bans, confines and prohibitions against the "evil" effects of political power.

THE UNTENABLE POSITION OF TRADITIONAL INTERNATIONAL LAW

The strength and effectiveness of the traditional system of international law, therefore, was directly proportional to the degree of individual responsibility and private autonomy in social relationships, over and against the authority of the State. A system of international law which operated as a limitation on political interests, imposed on political institutions "from without," had to rely on the potency of those interests for the sake of which it existed. The strength of individualism, the general emphasis on the personal ends of life, the need for transnational relationships of a private nature—all this made for the effectiveness of a law of nations dictated to the nations by the private world-Society of individual interests. Now the actual influence of autonomous individual activities has been fatally weakened during the last decades. In various countries political organization has entirely absorbed all individual initiative and responsibility, leaving to individuals only the role of subjects of the State and agents of political power. The latest phase in the decline of individual self-determination is the invasion of its last stronghold, private business, by government organization and administration. The economic sphere of social life was one of the few realms—and among these certainly the most important one—in which individual autonomy so far had successfully maintained a separation between public interests and private viewpoints. In the same measure in which the individualistic "management" of the economic system is supplanted by public administration, the common ground of a transnational Society, a field of interindividual relationships occurring under non-political and private auspices, is being destroyed. The international community of interests, a community that was knit and maintained between individuals as private persons, is being disrupted.

Simultaneously with the disappearance of the dualism between the transnational private interests and national public interests, the corresponding dualism of the legal "ideal" and the political "real" of international law becomes meaningless and unfeasible. This assertion calls for a more detailed statement of the reasons on which it is based.

A system of international law which is founded on a transnational community of ideals becomes meaningless if and when these ideals themselves degenerate or become meaningless. The humanistic ideals and the standards of morality, as practised and recognized among individuals, constituted the values from which the existing international law used to draw its criteria of judgment. A system of law which is so essentially oriented by the notion of independent, self-responsible man, which derives the very justification for its existence from the idea of protecting the transnational community of interindividual intercourse and private interests, ceases to be meaningful in a world in which there is no longer a transnational community of ideals, or of private relationships. While such a state of affairs has not yet been reached, the trend of political developments points unmistakably in this direction. Private relationships still transcend national boundaries, and in many countries still are considered a normal part of social activities. Humanistic ideals and a common morality are still recognized by the populations of more than one state, forming a community of transnational extension which calls for a limitation of the respective state interests for the sake of its own protection. But it can be asserted definitely that this community of ideals and practical private interests has ceased to embrace all those nations which are held to be bound by present international law. The circle of nations tied together by a relatively common outlook of their populations and by a network of interlocking private interests has become almost smaller than that of the nations which have eliminated individualistic criteria and private interests in favor of an all-comprehensive state-interest.

As critical observers have pointed out, the moral basis of international law was already weakened when the international legal community was broadened to include oriental nations, an extension which was made possible only by a formalization of its principles.[1] Recently the common ground on which nations could agree to legal rules embracing them all was abandoned altogether by Italy, Germany, Spain, Russia, when they abolished the independent initiative of individuals in the social structure of their respective nations. Along with the absorption of all the former functions of private initiative by the State, they disavowed the value of the ends of personal life and posited not only the social structure, but also the ideal of totalitarian collectivism. In such a social system there is no room for non-political ideals. Since every social function is performed by the State, and only by the State, every social standard is also measured in terms of State interests only. Thus the possibility of a community maintained by individuals across state boundaries, overcoming the conflict of State interests, has disappeared as far as the totalitarian nations are concerned. That means, of course, that the community in which common principles of international law were recognized, has been destroyed.

Of the two poles of the traditional system of international law, the "ideal" and the "real," only the second remains. The

[1] See G. Schwarzenberger, "The Rule of Law and the Disintegration of International Society." *American Journal of International Law*, vol. 33, pp. 63*f*.

In this context, it is also interesting to note the conception manifesting itself in an official Japanese statement made recently in China: "When asked about his opinion about the proposal to meet China on a basis of reciprocity and equality, he [Mr. Shiratori, Japanese spokesman] answered: 'It is impossible to regulate Sino-Japanese relations by international law. Orientals have their own national conceptions and political and moral principles. Oriental peoples should be governed by international law peculiar to themselves'." *New York Times*, August 23, 1937.

Keeton and Schwarzenberger, in their book *Making International Law Work*, p. 101, characterize this state of affairs by saying: "We are confronted with the coexistence of an international society and about sixty communities in which the principle 'Right or wrong, my country' is supposed to solve the problem of international morality for the citizen."

international ideal has become empty with the disruption of the world-wide community of individual interests and humanistic ideals from which it drew its life-blood. The now remaining "real" consists, thanks to the definition which it received in the theory of international law, in nothing but naked and unrestricted power politics. The name of a "realist" is claimed today by all those who profess a creed of limitless "selfishness," an out-and-out materialism, a blind faith in national power. It never occurs to these "realists" that ideas and ideals also are social realities, powerful factors with which every knowing statesman must reckon. The modern conception of "realism" does not derive from the nature of politics, or from the hopelessness of our epoch, but mainly from the dual notion of the "ideal" and the "real" which used to dominate our legal and political thinking. This dualism was workable as long as it was a dualism of mutually related notions; but it leads to that complete misunderstanding of reality which is represented by modern "realism," if the reciprocal dependence of the "real" and the "ideal" is overlooked. However, the fact remains that the faith in power politics is the legacy left by the decline of the international community of ideals.

Even from the strictly moral point of view the basis of the present system of international law has become dubious. The rules of international law are binding upon the states by virtue of an obligation which is ultimately derived from morality. It must be remembered, however, that the State, like all other institutions, "behaves" only in so far as concrete individual beings act on its behalf and in its name. Thus the obligation which is incumbent on the State as such will have to be felt and experienced as such by individual beings who serve the State. Now the commandments of international law may demand from those individuals an action which, although in conformity with international standards, is detrimental to the conditions by which states exist. This places those individuals in a conflict of conscience. They must either disregard the law by which the "international community" is believed to live, or the law by which the national "community" of the State is held to work. International law as it exists today has thrown diplomats and statesmen into this dilemma by demanding an "unselfish" attitude on the part of nations.

The present existing system of international law is supposed to be essentially a standard opposed to the "selfish" actions of nations. There is a formula for the criterion by which those "selfish" acts are inspired: the "Reason of State." Reason of State really means nothing but the laws of existence of the particular state, the conditions enabling a state to function on a certain territory. International law, with its background of individualistic morality, made it a moral and even legal duty of the states to indulge in "self-denial," "altruism" and the curtailment of the Reason of State in the interests of the "international community."

But the moral appeal of this position is necessarily a weak one. For it is ultimately addressed to those individuals whose decisions constitute the action of the State. Now individuals acting in public office are not necessarily selfish. On the contrary, they are fulfilling a social and moral duty when they work for the organization of human activities, for the order and unity represented by the State. Therefore, it is impossible for the concrete individual acting in public office, to regard something he does for the growth of his state, as "selfish." From his own point of view both duties—that which derives from the command of international law and that from the principle of the *Raison d'État*—are equally "altruistic" and self-denying. Between the two duties, however, that toward his own country is nearer to him and easier to comprehend.

Accordingly, the antithesis *state vs. international community* is not such a clear-cut moral issue as the antithesis *individual vs. society*. In the latter case it is merely a problem of decision between desire and duty, but the decision between national and international criteria of action presents itself to active statesmen as a decision between two moral duties. This collision of duties might resolve itself in a universal moral order in which the relative value of each duty is determinable by reference to the whole. But there has been no such all-comprehensive system of value-standards except the one which originated in the Middle Ages. Since it disappeared, even the theoretical possibility of a decision between such conflicting duties does not exist. Therefore, it is no cynicism to say that now it has become even morally justifiable to defy international law with the plea of service to the State.[2] It has clearly become an untenable system which bases the authority of legal rules on a morality that is diametrically opposed to the functioning of the states.

If the existing system of international law has become meaningless, owing to the social developments heretofore described, it also has become unfeasible in a practical sense. To the same degree to which individuals and their activities and interests are becoming identified, in various countries, with the interests of the State as such, the restrictive rules of international law are deprived of the transnational forces which by the pressure of their interests could back the legal commands. A system of law which imposes itself on political institutions "from without" becomes unworkable in the moment in which all social forces are absorbed in the political institutions. Political power, political relationships, political organization have ceased to be relative for a considerable number of peoples. Accordingly, it has become impossible to "dictate" the limits of political action to these nations, since they do not recognize a standpoint outside the realm of politics from which any "authoritative" judgment could be made on the value of political action. Governments and peoples of these nations reject the idea that political institutions ultimately serve the ends of personal life; consequently they refuse to submit the political actions of their respective states to the rules of a law which derives its criteria from the personal and not from the political aspect of life. The growing state-consciousness of individuals, especially in the totalitarian countries, thus renders practically unfeasible a system of law established on the idea of the ultimate ascendancy of personal life over state interests.

[2] See footnote 19 in chapter III.

Theoretically and practically, morally, politically and sociologically the existing system of international law seems to have come to its end. While it would be a mistake to confuse the decline of one historical form of international law with the defeat of the whole idea of international law, nevertheless two questions must be asked at this point:

Is there a practical possibility of a system of international law under the present circumstances?

Ought there to be a system of international law under the present circumstances?

The second question will be discussed first. It is the grave mistake of most international lawyers to omit this question in the present situation. The existence of a system of international law is apparently so axiomatic to them that they cannot visualize any historical situation in which a system of international law might not apply. International law, being a special branch of law, is required whenever social circumstances call for a legal regulation of this type, just as the law of corporations, for instance, is needed only under certain social and economic conditions. If there were no corporations, and no need for corporations, it would be senseless to devise a law applying to corporations. In the same way international law is not an absolute value, but is required and brought about by certain circumstances in the development of human society and the forms in which it crystallizes. Accordingly, in a situation like the present one, when international law obviously fails to fulfill its function, it is meaningful and necessary to raise the question whether such a law is really required.

Many of the shortcomings of the present theory of international law seem to stem from the anxious endeavor, on the part of scholars, to avoid this fundamental query. Instead of coolly testing the foundations of international law in the structure of present-day society, most theorists escape from reality by an invocation of the "virtues" which "held together" the community of international law in the past. "International law is based on morality and the recognition of individual ethics. Unless the moral ties of the national consciences be strengthened, there can be no international law. If only governments can be persuaded to acknowledge the moral value of a conduct in conformity with international law, everything will be well."[3] This attitude more or less characterizes the reaction of scholars in the present crisis of international law. Without stopping to ask themselves whether international law possibly may have outlived itself, or whether the existing system is in need of complete readjustment, they fall into a helplessly preaching tone that betrays a deep lack of confidence in their intellectual power to penetrate the problems of modern politics. They reproach historical development for marring the structure of international law, and demand that past conditions be restored so that the world may function once more according to the theoretical schedule of scholars. Thus it is maintained that return to the past—, namely, a return to international morality, to the economics of laissez-faire, to the individualism of the eighteenth century, and so on—is the only way out of present difficulties. To these minds, what the world needs above all is adjustment to their scientific explanation of it.

It seems more sensible, and at the same time more in accordance with the spirit of science, to accept the result of empirical observation and to adjust the theory to the changed structure of society. Experience shows that the present system of international law fails to regulate the reality of politics with regular effectiveness. Confronted with this fact, we must conclude that the reality of modern politics requires a different law, not that the law requires a different reality. As long as only single acts,

[3] An utterance representative of this attitude is the resolution adopted by one of the foremost research organizations, the Carnegie Endowment, on December 13, 1937: "At a moment when the force and power of treaty obligations between nations are broadly challenged, the Trustees for the C.E.I.P. wish to record their conviction that there is no path to permanent peace, no hope for the reign of law and order in international affairs, save by an insistence upon the observance by nations of the solemn covenants which they have made. They hold that a world in which no distinction is made between those who keep their word and those who break it . . . is a world foredoomed to anarchy and the rule of the sword alone." Note the terminology: "permanent peace," "solemn covenants," "foredoomed," and the generally moralizing tone of the resolution.

and those few in number, of conduct are committed in violation of the law, it is certainly the law which must impose itself on reality. When, however, the entire system of law fails to function adequately, when the spirit which manifests itself in the reality of facts is so utterly out of line with the spirit of the legal system, then the law must be adjusted to the social structure. Accordingly we shall have to discuss problems of international law not against the background of its past theoretical conception, but against the background of an up-to-date sociological analysis. The most important empirical observation in this respect is that the institutions and the functions of political organization are moving into a place of uncontested primacy both in the system of practical social activities and in modern consciousness. This development of things social will have to be accepted as the starting point for our reasoning about international politics and international law.

With this supposition in mind, we have to ask our question: Is a system of international law needed in this present world? Ought we to work for its success?

If we offer an answer to this query, it is based on certain hypotheses regarding the structure of modern society and the trend of social and political development. Most of the major nations in the world have attained a population figure which makes it exceedingly difficult, if not impossible for them, to sustain their people with what their native soil produces. The density of population and the standard of living attained make it necessary for people to live in urban centers, and to export manufactured goods in exchange for food products. It seems unlikely that a purely internal division of labor could solve this problem in all of the great powers. Consequently, the division of labor will have to be international. Moreover, even if most nations could succeed in establishing an internal system of balanced labor division by which their rural areas produced for the needs of the metropolitan centers and vice versa, there still would be important international relations. For such a development would presuppose in some nations an increase of their industrialization and their machinery. As long as the raw materials required for modern industry are not found in every single one of the great powers, and in sufficient quantities, there will have to be exchanges between the different parts and regions of this earth. And as long as the functions of legislation, administration, jurisdiction, transportation, communication and general security are discharged by states (i.e. territorial units of supreme power), the need for economic exchange will bring forth all sorts of relationships among these different units of sovereignty. In other words: as long as human society continues to exist at approximately the modern standard of living, with approximately the same system of economic production (industrialized mass-production) and with approximately the same population figure, there will be international relations, if and as far as modern states likewise continue to exist.

On the basis of this assumption we have to examine the consequences of a continued weakness, or even absence, of international law. In whose interest, for the sake of what end—in short, why—should there be international law regulating these international relations? The question in itself is more important than the answer. For the answer to a fundamental query like this depends on a decision which ultimately has to be made by each individual himself. Therefore the answer presented here is more in the nature of an axiological confession than of a scientific hypothesis.

The continued absence of international law would lead to a sweeping idolization of power for its own sake, and this would be destructive of all culture. The reason for such a development is not to be found in the nature of power, or of the state as such, but rather in the conception of political power which has been an integral part of our social philosophy since the Middle Ages and since Machiavelli. The bid for national power has always been considered as essential for the State, and this inherent tendency for its own assertion on the part of each state has been termed *Raison d'État* ever since Machiavelli gave it eloquent expression. But the pursuit of national power interests was only one side of the traditional notion of international relations, the other being the "common" interests of "world society," and the norms representing those interests. These international standards were considered as the "objective" aspect of international relations, while national power was held to be of purely "subjective" character. In this tension between the will of the "subject" and the order of "objective" standards, between the interests of the national state and the values of international order, our civilization found one of its mightiest impulses of evolution.

This conception of political power, which identified political power with subjectivism, exclusive "possession," and with material means of force, would work as long as it was coupled with the counter notion of objective norms binding on all states. But as soon as the obligatory force of these norms declined, as soon as the "ideal" aspect of international relations failed to appeal to nations, peoples and governments, this "subjective" criterion of national power interests became the exclusive driving force in international relations. According to that conception of politics, a conception which has been engendered by the century-old habit of divorcing might from right, and facts from ideals, the "reality" remaining after the decline of the "ideal" is no more than a free-for-all struggle for material power positions.

According to the ideas which have been implanted by generations of scholars, this political "reality," left to itself, can be nothing more than the dynamics of blind forces and "selfish" impulses. The disillusionment about the past "ideal" of international law leads people to turn "realistic," i.e. to surrender unconditionally to the criterion of the efficiency of material power. Confronted with a world in which states are dealing with each other without a common standard of reference, they begin to believe that the only possible criterion for international relations can be the "national interest" in the sense of national possessions of material means of force. And since with the idea of international standards the illusion of a protective higher justice is gone, people dedicate themselves with heart and soul to a life in the service of material power. In the same way in which all values of culture, the standard of living, the leisure of individuals, the prosperity of families, the education of children, are being sacrificed to this goal of national power in the present totalitarian states, so a sacrifice of culture will be the price for the cult of power in the whole world.

Many are inclined to assume that such a development cannot take place because they do not wish it to take place. But idolization of state power, with the ensuing consequences of the complete denial of progress, is within the practical possibilities of the present situation. The State as the personification of power may be deified once more if power in the material sense continues to be the only desirable value in international relations. In this role, the State may once more become the mold of all human life, separating nation from nation in tribal seclusion and narrowing human consciousness to the primitive horizon of one's own people. Already there are symptoms of a development in this direction. The call for an exclusive state religion has been heard from persons highly placed in occidental nations. Signs of a new archaism have appeared in art. A tribal consciousness has manifested itself in the denial of humane treatment to racial and political strangers. Boundaries have been turned into no man's land, as in times when they were not jurisdictional delimitations but borders between mutually exclusive worlds. These and similar phenomena point to possible tendencies in the present epoch which would cause the surrender of all human life, energy and devotion to the one purpose of state power, if the conviction continues that power is the only certainty in a world of international chaos. This prospect implies the justification of a system of international law. The international field is one of the focal points of the political crisis of our epoch. Here one of the main causes of this crisis will have to be removed.

WANTED: ORDER IN INTERNATIONAL POLITICS

With respect to the possibility that the present crisis may eliminate altogether international law from international politics the answer, therefore is: Yes, the present situation may actually lead to the end of international law. But it should not be allowed to come to that point, since international law, or rather, order in international politics, is one of the vital conditions of the maintenance of culture in the present world. Then the other question arises immediately: What are the practical possibilities of realizing legal order in international politics?

Although it means repeating much of what has been said before, we must recall the practical foundations of the traditional system of international law. Considering politics a dynamic "reality," it operated essentially as a restriction and limitation upon the pursuit of national state interests, imposing on them the restrictions of the international "ideal." This idea of certain objective and international standards which limited the exercise of governmental power, made international law appear as an authority above the states. Accordingly, international law had to be founded on the practical power of some social factor of international extent which was strong enough to impose itself on the various governments, and consequently could lend real emphasis to the commands of international law. This factor was what we called transnational Society, i.e. the network of relationships maintained by individual persons and associations in their private capacity all over the world, across national boundaries. This interdependent, self-relying system of private relationships was a factor which governments could not ignore as long as the economic system of the different states needed these interindividual contacts in order to function. As long as the period of capitalistic expansion lasted, the individual with his initiative, his contacts, his relations, his widespread interests alone could produce the prosperity of nations, and thereby secure the financial basis of government power. That is why this world of interindividual and transnational relationships necessarily was taboo to the governments of the world, and why a system of international law which claimed authority over the powerful ones of this earth could operate effectively, seconded by the social weight of this international factor of economic individualism.

Now that the transnational Society of individual enterprises, dealing with each other in their own rights, has been disrupted, now that political institutions and political functions are no longer considered the mere instrument of other, non-political ends pursued by individuals, this type of international law obviously can work no longer. The social center of gravity is now almost entirely in the field of political institutions. No longer do governments have to rely on the activities of individuals to promote the financial aspect of state power. Individual initiative in the economic field is considered not beneficial, in fact actually harmful, to national prosperity in a considerable number of states. The social factor of international character, the social weight of which would counterbalance the particular interests of the nations, has disappeared. If we can think only of the type of international law which issues authoritative commands to the states, if we cannot adapt our juristic imagination to the realities of a world in which political organization has actually superimposed itself on economic processes, then indeed we shall have to proclaim the end of international law.

However, there is a widespread belief that chaos in international relations is impossible as long as nations are mutually dependent on each other. By the pressure of this interdependence of interests, it is argued, nations will be forced to conclude international agreements even if it is only by reason of their own self-interest. This is undoubtedly correct. But the question is whether such agreements, based on the reciprocity of state interests, represent any sort of order in international relations which will prevent the destruction of our culture by the blind action of political forces and the resulting cult of state power.

If states negotiate international conventions without reference to common standards the validity of which creates binding obligations beyond what happens to be their interest, the only basis for such treaties will be the expediency of a transitory situation. Neither the respective interests of different states nor the situation which induces them to come to an agreement, involve any elements of a lasting character, providing for real order. States are group entities in their own right and with their own "individual" interests. Above them there is no other organized unit of will, behind them there is no general and universal ideal, beyond them there is no common rule, which might serve as a common standard of reference in their mutual dealings. Being supreme in their respective territories, states are, as collective entities, unrelated to each other by organization or by ideal standards. What relation there may be between them derives from social relationships, not from that of states as such. Consequently their respective interests, lacking a common denominator, cannot be reconciled in any rational way. They reflect the ultimate essence of unrelated wills, conflicting with each other in an elementary antithesis, of which Mowat has said that "nothing but the violent tussle between the two, and the defeat of one by the other, can solve it." In the absence of a common standard of reference there is no possibility of a rational principle of order to which the conflicting interests of states can be reduced. "These conflicts of interests are necessarily of an elementary intensity, because among the factors influencing them are the fundamental conditions of existence, and the political, economic, and ethical convictions of the contendants. In regard to these conflicts, a legal order is not possible, until a form has been found and firmly established which combines the essential elements of the diverging interests into a unity. Until then there are no criteria either of right or of wrong in the situation."[4]

Accordingly, the agreements concluded under such auspices do not embody the elements of any objective and stable order of international relations. They merely reflect a factual situation of relative power or weakness, which, through its formulation in a written instrument, receives a certain perpetuation.

[4] H. Heyse, *Über die geschichtlichen und soziologischen Grundlagen des modernen Schlichtungswesens*, in: *Archiv für Rechts-und Wirtschaftsphilosophie*, vol. XVII, p. 54 (translation mine).

Also see Small, *General Sociology*, who expresses the same view: "Suppose, for example, we are in the midst of a labour conflict. It is proposed to arbitrate the difficulty. Representatives of the conflicting parties meet. A looker-on, if he happens to be a philosopher, soon discovers that the issue cannot be decided on ethical grounds, for the conflicting parties, and perhaps the arbitration board, have each a different standard of ethics. The employer's ethics are founded upon conceptions of the rights of property. The employee's ethics take as their standard certain conceptions of the right of labour. The arbitrator's ethics may vary from the lawyer's interpretation of the civil code to the speculative philosopher's conception of the ideal rights of man. There is no common ethical appeal . . . The decision has to be reached either by resort to force or by a compromise of claims, each of which continues to assert its full title in spite of the pressure of circumstances." *General Sociology*, Chicago University Press (p. 659).

Instead of providing for stability, they obey the vacillations of changing power relations between the contracting parties. Of such stipulations it has been said that they "rest on a basis of irrational conditions. These conditions are nothing but the compelling force of actual circumstances. Neither the arbitrary will, nor the rational evidence of law, but only the compulsion of facts brings forth the adjustment of power-relations in the legal document."[5]

It is obvious that just as certain situations have compelled the states to conclude an agreement on the basis of a certain ratio of power, a different situation, especially a weakening of the power of one of the parties, is bound to jeopardize the "order" arrived at by such a convention. The merely formal "sanctity" of treaties has proved to be an ineffective, and indeed inadequate, protection for legal instruments whose contents as such do not represent any value or rational principle of greater significance than that of a momentary constellation. Therefore a system of treaties which relies merely on the interdependence of state interests and the expediency of peaceful arrangements will result in a number of compromises, but not in a system of international law and order.

Moreover a system of mere treaties lacks the qualifications of an objective and stable order because it consists only of legal "rules" which have been established in the form of subjective rights. In other words, such a system is essentially composed of legal claims of one state against the other. Now every subjective right is a legal title only as long as it has not been renounced. Accordingly, there is no violation of the "rules" derived from a system of treaties which could not be legalized by the consent of the party whose interests and legal rights are

[5] H. Heyse, *op. cit.*, p. 64 (translation mine). Cf. also the comparison between arbitration in labor conflicts and in international conflicts made by A. Loria, *Les bases économiques de la justice internationale* (Publications de l'Institut Nobel Norvégien, vol. II, fasc. 1), Professor Loria explicitly remarks: "Dans le champ industriel comme dans le champ international, le jugement ne peut être effectif, c'est-à-dire effectivement respecté, qu'à la condition d'exprimer le résultat naturel de la force respective des parties en présence, indépendamment de toute idée de justice; s'il veut au contraire faire abstraction de la force pour obéir à un principe de justice, il devient nécessairement platonique et privé de toute application pratique." (p. 85).

invaded. As a consequence, any international "order" which materializes merely in the form of stipulated claims of states against each other, is entirely at the mercy of the readiness of governments to avail themselves of their rights, a readiness which will be unlikely to exist in the case of a politically weak nation. Thus the very nature of this type of legal "order" puts a premium on political power, because superior strength is able to legalize any infraction of the "law."[6] The inadequacy of such a legal system is felt most seriously when the violation of its "rules" ultimately hits the rights of third persons (e.g. individual beings), in whose interest the rule had been agreed upon. The validity of their "rights" and titles is as great and no greater than the will and the capacity of their respective governments to oppose any injury to them.[7]

Accordingly, a legal system consisting only of treaty stipulations is not only no alternative to the cult of national power but actually calls for the highest possible enhancement of power as the only condition under which favorable agreements can be negotiated or unfavorable ones successfully broken. Therefore, on the basis of "enlightened self-interest" and expediency, no stable order of international relations can materialize. Without a common standard of reference there is no rational possibility of deciding conflicts, but only a practical possibility of temporary truces.

Obviously, no legal instrument, no agreement, no semblance of "order" can bridge the abyss separating the different collective entities and their subjective wills, unless it be by reference to a common element transcending their particular interests. Past centuries found this common transnational element

[6] In this context, "it is essential to remember that, in a system of power politics war is neither a misfortune nor a supernatural event, but only the culminating point in an ascending scale of pressure; and whatever form it may take, the functions of pressure are essentially the same as those of diplomacy." Keeton and Schwarzenberger, *op. cit.*, p. 40.

[7] For this argument I am indebted to E. Feilchenfeld, *Völkerrechtspolitik als Wissenschaft* (1922), pp. 4, 30. About the principle of reciprocity as a basis of international law, Keeton and Schwarzenberger, *op. cit.*, p. 58, have this to say: "Principles of reciprocity can only be applied *formally* unless the structure of the states is roughly similar, at least in so far as the division of competence between the State and the individual is concerned."

in the affinities, convictions and contacts of individuals. Since this extra-political sphere of social life has become too insignificant to serve in this role today, we cannot have reference to non-political standards as a basis of international order. Consequently the only way open to us is to find transnational elements within the very domain of political functions. International law must become functional with respect to politics, since there is no longer a social basis for a system of international law conceived and maintained in essential antagonism to political organization. The standards of reference by which states are bound in spite of their respective interests have to be derived from the inherent lawfulness of political institutions and their functions. Law has to operate not merely as an ideal which relies on the governments' sense of moral obligation but on the necessary functional order in the structure of political relationships. To modify a phrase of Treitschke, one might say: Law must become more political if politics are to become more lawful.[8] The field of political action and political power, so far abandoned to the rule of irrational motivations, must itself be conquered by the ordering mind.[9] We must elaborate rational categories and conceptions with the help of which a system of international law can be conceived not as a prohibitive limitation on political functions but as an organic order enabling the fulfillment of political tasks. Only on this basis can international law operate effectively as a vehicle of order in present-day international relations.

FUNCTIONAL APPROACH AS A WAY OUT

Legal principles which are functional with respect to political institutions and political organization offer the only possibility of a standard of reference among the states, and accordingly

[8] Treitschke said: "*Die Moral muss politischer werden, wenn die Politik moralischer werden soll.*"

[9] "The legal order does not keep pace with the increase of conflicting interests which call for legal regulation. The law is, as it were, a garment that has become too small for a growing body of social relations. The policy required in this respect is that legal order should be made to expand and penetrate those problems of collective life which it did not embrace so far." D. Schindler, "Werdende Rechte," in *Festgabe für F. Fleiner* (1927), p. 403. (translation mine).

of international law. For the decisive significance of political organization for every individual existence, and the corresponding state-consciousness of the masses are social realities in this modern world, just as the moral sense and the rationalism of people were potent factors in the world of the seventeenth century. And just as international law was founded then on the compelling effect of the appeal of moral principles to individuals, so international law today must be based on the mass-appeal emanating from the idea of organization and from the importance of political institutions. Thus, basing international law on the function of political institutions means adapting it to the orientation of the contemporaneous mind. It means invoking the only idea by which modern consciousness throughout the entire orbit of modern civilization feels irresistably moved: The necessity of organization in order to secure the meaningfulness and the material conditions of every individual life.

Obviously, it is insufficient to invoke the idea of political organization and political institutions without demonstrating in what way these notions can contribute to a transnational standard of reference and to legal principles. To this end, it is imperative to overcome the traditional conception of politics, political power and political institutions. Within the framework of past legal theory we have been accustomed to think of politics essentially as a game of power. This idea is logically connected with the concept of the "personality" of the state. For personality and individuality connote compact entities whose existence is regarded as the axiom, and at the same time as the ultimate end of a legal order oriented by these notions. The traditional idea of international law pictures the state as an "individual" and bases the entire theoretical construction on the "reality" (i.e. on the interests, the power, and so on) of this individual state-person.[10] In accordance with this "personalistic" construction such phenomena as territory, population, prestige, interests, and so on figure as "objects" which can be acquired and "possessed." Group "interests," i.e. desires or necessities of possession, are considered to form the core of

[10] For a more detailed discussion of this point see pages 139 *ff*.

political "reality," and political "realism" is unable to see in international relations anything more than the conflict of these group "interests" confronting each other in absolute subjectiveness, leaving material power as the only conceivable criterion for a "solution" of the controversy.

Our thesis is that above all it is the lack of differentiated thinking about politics, the inadequacy of notions like that of the personality of the State, the "object" quality of its constituent elements, which produce this attitude toward power politics. Therefore a thorough revision of our fundamental conceptions about political institutions and their structure is one of the conditions of progress. Similar problems have arisen with respect to the modern labor questions. For in labor relations, likewise, we find the conflicting interests of contending group-entities, for the conciliation of which no legal principles are available.[11] Now it has been pointed out long ago by students of labor questions that the only fruitful approach to these problems was one which emphasized the common function of employers and employees, while at the same time putting aside the conflict of interests as being of only secondary importance. This is what one of these authors has to say: "Most of our concepts are abstractions of things. Modern philosophy, in accordance with the tendencies of our times, has discovered as a more fundamental notion the concept of Function. The difference between the two approaches is that the concept of the thing stands for the symbolic representation of an isolated object, whereas the concept of function (more precisely: concept of system) analyzes the particular reality as conditioned by the whole context and by the system of which it is a part."[12]

The implications are obvious. Focusing them as "things," or material entities, we see states or labor interests only in their subjective aspect. We fail to see the bridge connecting them with other entities in society: operation. Material existence is the isolated aspect of phenomena, it is that perspective which

[11] D. Schindler, *op. cit.*, has made an interesting comparative study of the similarity of problems in international law and labor law.

[12] H. Heyse, *op. cit.*

shows us phenomena in their separateness. Function refers to operation, and therefore is the perspective in which things appear as coordinate. Accordingly, instead of making the substantial "existence" of states the center of our legal and political thinking, we have to arrive at a concept of political institutions which defines them in terms of their operation, or their function.

As has been pointed out previously, political power and political institutions exist only in view of specific functional ends.[13] In other words, political power and political institutions are related to social reality as a whole through the medium of their operation. Consequently, it is this functional aspect with respect to which there is a common ground transcending the immediate "interests" of political institutions, and linking them to society-at-large and to other states. Therefore international law can materialize only as an immanent order in international relations by developing its principles out of the function of political institutions. On this basis it can evolve into an order in which not the conflicting "interests" of group entities, but the functional connections between them are the ultimate end of legal rules. Thus conceived, international law can be made an order which not merely is binding on the moral conscience, but actually lives in political institutions and their "will."

FUNCTIONAL CONNECTEDNESS AMONG STATES

The question of modern labor relations, which presented problems so similar to those of international relations, has been answered by pointing out the functional solution. How does this solution present itself? The characteristic feature in it is that the standard of reference by which the conflict is approached consists in the objective end of the coordinated efforts. Instead of trying to reconcile conflicting interests, the attempt is made to facilitate the achievement of an objective task for its own sake. Thus Mr. Heyse has stated: "Work in the modern sense is a process of divided labor; every special

[13] See pp. 113*ff*.

activity is determined by a system of functions. Instead of starting from the notions of employer and employee, and of defining labor as a merchandize for sale, the functional system as such must be taken as the primary basis, with reference to which employers and employees must be conceived as functionaries, as it were, of the cultural system of labor. Outside of this system the two entities are meaningless, within it they are necessarily dependent on each other."[14]

However it seems as if the functional principle could be applied more easily to labor relations than to international politics. While it is fairly obvious that employer and employees are but partial functionaries in the total system of labor production, there is apparently no similar functional "system" uniting different states in a common "purpose." In labor the objective unit of the plant or the enterprise provides for an organizational center toward which both employers and employees gravitate, while states are separate organizations concentrated on different territories and each devoted to its particular tasks.

It is obvious that states appear functionally disconnected if our thinking about them is dominated by the concept of the State as a "body" of material substance (territory, people, arms, and so on), expressing itself as a "person" in manifestations of its own will and of its "national interests," through the medium of power. If we look at international politics in this way, from a perspective in which each "body" politic appears in the foreground of our picture as the essence of reality, then the whole picture dissolves itself of necessity into a plurality of different states, each existing for no other meaning than its own sake, and each indulging in a completely irrational display of power, force and "nationalism." The scene changes completely, however, if we look at it in the light of the question: What is the meaning, what is the function of political organization? This does not imply that the state is to be understood as instrumental to some ultimate purpose derived from speculations about the alleged course of history of human nature, such as "progress," "happiness," "self-expression," and so on. The

[14] H. Heyse, *op. cit.*

fact that human beings live together in the order of an organized commonwealth is certainly not the result of some such ultimate purpose of mankind or of history, but is merely a consequence of a process of differentiation in human culture, and of the ensuing necessity to provide for forms of organized coordination. But it is precisely because the State is a result of social differentiation that there is an intrinsic functional connection between the State and all other forms of social life. For they all are produced and reproduced by individuals who in their own personality integrate the different manifestations of community and society. The "meaning" of political organization thus is embodied in its actual operation within the entire social system. The function of political institutions in the social system is not determined by a single ultimate end of that system, as in the case of labor. But the absence of a single "purpose" does not make the system of culture any less a system in which the different forms of life, institutions, patterns of conduct and modes of acting, influence each other and depend on each other. In this system of institutions, organizations and differentiated activities the State performs functions which are circumscribed by the totality of social life and of individual consciousness with respect to this cultural system.

Thus the emphasis of political thinking is shifted from the merely secondary aspect of political power to the only essential criterion of political function. Political institutions are viewed from the perspective not of a senseless accumulation of people, territory, military, financial and economic force, or from that of an irrational set of "national interests," but within the setting of the totality of social life, in which they merely form local units of organization. The functions of each state therefore are not limited to facts, objects, people and life within its own territory. If we follow the definition of the political function, which Hermann Heller formulated as the "autonomous organization and actualization of social cooperation in a certain territory," it is evident that under modern conditions "social cooperation" is not confined to the group of people living in that territory. "Social cooperation" involves the entire system of divided labor, the complicated network of traffic and communication, the exchange of goods and values of all kinds, on which modern society necessarily depends. Therefore, the function of the State cannot be merely that of preserving the "existence" of the group of individuals united under its organization, it cannot be merely a service to that concrete "body" of persons called nation. For the coordinating activities of a modern state do not affect merely its own citizens, exempting all others from its order. The order materialized by the State rather embraces all acts and relationships bearing upon, or taking place within, its territory, no matter from what persons or from what places they may have emanated. The regulating and organizing function of the State concerns the trader who may live overseas but has to sell his goods under the order established by the authorities of the marketplace. It produces its effects on the traveller who passes through that territory without being a citizen. The exchange of goods, the type and kind of production, the transportation across its realm, the currency in use, the credit of faraway regions—all of these processes and relationships are partly conditioned by what different states perform in the way of law and order, although they may not pertain to the interests or the life of the "groups" living permanently within those states. It can be said, therefore, that, although its order is locally limited, the function of the State embraces the ecumenic. The State is not only the organized form of a "people," but at the same time the local center of organization for all social relationships touching upon its territory, and therefore a local agency of order concerning the whole human society.[15]

We do not mean to assert that this has always been the function of political institutions. In a world where nations live spatially and personally apart from each other, coming into

[15] "Il en resulte, pour les gouvernants et agents nationaux qui deviennent ainsi gouvernants et agents internationaux, *un dédoublement fonctionnel* caractéristique des relations intersociales." A. Scelle, *Précis de Droit des Gens* (1932), p. 43. Scelle remarks later on: "Les agents étatiques possèdent, en principe, une *compétence globale*, parcequ'historiquement ils ont tendu à monopoliser la gérance de la solidarité collective." *ibid.*, p. 82.

contact only in time of war, the regulating and organizing activities of the political organization will work only for their own group. Its function will then, not only with respect to its economy but to the entirety of its life, assume the character of autarky. That type of political organization, which we are accustomed to call State, however, is comparatively young. It came into existence precisely when social life grew more complicated and differentiated, at the same time extending its ramifications beyond the local sovereignties of the Middle Ages, and calling for the establishment of order and security for ever widening areas. The division of labor and functions has in the meantime embraced virtually the ecumenic. At the same time it has become so intensified that one might say that "humanity," formerly merely an idea, has nowadays become a reality, woven of shipping and radio, raw materials and manufacturing industry, currencies and credit, education and research. Thanks to modern traffic, the press, communication, the mutual concern of nations and regions has entered the daily life of every individual as a part of his conscious picture of life. Human society has become definitely super-national, although society does not know of any other mold of organization than the pluralistic one realized by a multitude of states in a number of different territories. In this sense it becomes clear that in many aspects states are merely the local agencies of international social relationships, sharing the mandate for realizing an order of social cooperation with other organizational units of local concentration.

THE WAY OF RECONSTRUCTION

It is in conformity with these immanent laws of social structure that legal theory has to develop its categories. It must analyze the social functions of political organization, in order to find the criterion of the objective element, of the social tasks common to all states. It is impossible to arrive at any such criterion so long as our conceptions of State and international relations are looking toward the "existence" rather than toward the operation of political institutions, as long as a "reified" idea of territory, people, means of power and national "interests" constitutes the basis of our legal system. Accordingly, a new orientation of thought rather than a new organization of power is what is needed to make a reconstruction of international order possible in our days.

As a result of our investigation it was stated above that international law in this epoch would have to be in conformity with the immanent laws, the inherent dynamics, of political institutions and organizations. At the same time international law has to be based on a standard of reference transcending the particular states. Only in so far as there is a congruity of functional ends among the various states are these two requirements met. The function of an organization is something so inherent that it constitutes the very law of existence of any institution. And if the function refers to a task which is shared with other organizations, this immanent law of existence transcends the particular organization and its incidental "interests," linking it with inescapable necessity to the operation of those other institutions. These interstate laws of functional necessity have to be found, formulated, brought into the clear light of consciousness.

The theory of international law must follow the path of legal science in its earliest times. The science of law then was a form of social science[16], which investigated and analyzed the various patterns of relationship, coordination and transaction among individuals. It gave theoretical expression to the laws which inherently governed these empirical forms of social life, it found the law in the actual behavior of living people. In the same way, the science of international law has to penetrate, investigate, interpret and formulate the structural laws of international relations today. Legal theory consists thus essentially in the analysis of patterns and forms in our social system and the recognition of the rational lines which human beings acknowledge as guides of their coordinate behavior.

The formulation of legal rules is not oriented, in a functional system of law, toward the interest and the "existence" of the different states. Interests, whenever they are in conflict, are

[16] This idea has been developed by Wurzel, *Das juristische Denken* (1904).

rationally irreconcilable, while different functions, instead of contradicting each other, merely overlap. Therefore the emphasis in the functional system is not any more on the question "*To whom* is this thing due?"; a question which only leads to an impassable conflict of interests. Instead, functional law starts out from the idea that all social relationships are meant to accomplish certain objective ends, and accordingly concentrates on the question: "How can *this task* be solved?" In other words, it approaches legal problems not from the angle of the interests of persons, but from that of the function of the relationships between persons. In international law, if functionally conceived, this would mean the orientation of the legal system toward the objective ends for the sake of which there are international relations rather than toward the things that states "desire." The problems which the law is meant to solve are not those of distribution and prohibition, but those of securing the coordination between social activities and institutions within a system of functional interdependence. What is required, therefore, is the realization that not the respective subjective interests but only the objective functional tasks form a common reference, by virtue of which a system of international law and order is possible. But what is more, not only are the functional tasks of international relations the ground on which a system of international law becomes possible, they also constitute the very reason for which international law is required at all. Wherever political organizations function in the service of ends which transcend the range of their own territory, there is the need for international relationships and there are laws of functional interdependence which in significance and weight range above the respective "group interests."

To a future study must be left the task of elaborating some of these functional dependencies among states. Here the problem is one of demonstrating the principle rather than applying it in detail. It also must be reserved for future publications to show already existing tendencies toward a functionalist conception in international law. It is significant that, throughout the present crisis of international law, those agreements that were conceived along functional lines have proved to be immune against political disturbances. Thus the Postal Convention, although nominally it could not be applied in Manchukuo because this state does not belong to the international law community, actually did provide the rules under which the transit and transport of mail was carried out on Manchukuan territory. And again, although the wave of general international conventions that was characteristic of the Locarno and Geneva period broke in 1933, and newly concluded treaties were mostly of a bilateral and political character, there was one exception. This was the Sugar Convention of 1937 which regulated world conditions of sugar production and sugar consumption, i.e. centered around the problem of a task rather than that of interests. And, finally to name another example, in 1938 an agreement was concluded between Great Britain and the United States which avoided a possible conflict of national interests by concentrating entirely upon the function of the object of contention, and by providing for cooperation for the better attainment of this end. It was reported in the Press in the following terms:

"The United States and Great Britain today reached a partial settlement of the dispute about sovereignty over the tiny Pacific islands of Canton and Enderbury by agreeing formally that each should have equal privileges in using the island for commercial air transport and communication facilities. This settlement, which pushes aside . . . the question of actual sovereignty and nationality, was believed the first of its kind in modern history. The islands provided a new problem in recent months with the sudden discovery of their potential value as air-communication bases. Each government felt that it had a valid title to them by right of discovery and past settlement. A dispute was threatened, but before it materialized the two governments agreed to discuss the question on a formulation in which the question of 'use' would be made superior to that of 'title'."[17]

[17] *New York Times*, August 10, 1938. See also the editorial note, on this agreement, by Jesse S. Reeves, in the *American Journal of International Law*, vol. 33, pp. 521*ff*.

This is as clear an illustration of functional treatment of a legal question as is available. Among the functions of political organization in the two nations was the task of securing the lines of air communication. By emphasizing this task instead of their respective and conflicting interests, they were enabled to fulfill their respective functions. Wherever social life is conditioned, in a nation, by international contexts and connections, there the functions pertaining to the organization of the State transcend the range of its own power and make it a co-functionary with other states. The creation of some mold of order that permits the cooperation of social activities as far as they are interdependent, is therefore an objective which is necessarily common to all the states involved. An international order of functional type, accordingly, would facilitate rather than limit the proper activities of political institutions. It would be effective, because it would not be in contradiction, but in organic conformity with the *raison d'être* of political organizations: with their objective function in the system of modern society.

Summarizing the foregoing observations on the relations between legal theory and political reality in the international field, the general conclusion is that no system of international law and order can be expected to develop from the occurrence of new historical conditions. To hope for an automatic adjustment of the factual conditions is the idealistic disguise for an attitude of resignation and inaction. It is only by taking the world as it is and rationally analyzing it from a new perspective that we can discover its inherent possibilities of international law and order. The precondition for the establishment of an effective system of international law today is therefore not re-formation of political forces, but reorientation of political thinking. No conceivable device of legal machinery, peaceful procedure or limitation on power will prevent chaotic conditions in international politics, so long as the essence of political organization is seen in power, and so long as states are generally regarded as so many reified and personified separate entities.

The new situation requires a new perspective, and a new

perspective will result in a new picture. We are experiencing the decline of the age of individualism or better of atomism. Just as in its beginning the Renaissance detected the significance of the individual will, emancipating the personality of the individual man and the sovereignty of the individual state from the universal order of the medieval cosmos, the time has now come for another shift in our outlook on this social world.[18] Searching for a principle more in accordance with the structure of modern culture and contemporaneous consciousness than that of atoms and separate individualities, we begin to see the significance of contexts, systematic interdependence and social connectedness as such. Through this change in orientation in the treatment of international affairs, our awareness is focused on function instead of power, interaction instead of interest, meaning instead of prestige. It is with the aid of these new viewpoints and the corresponding approach to political reality, that we can achieve an international order founded on the immanent lawfulness of international relations.

[18] "We are today living through the end of that phase of our cultural history which was dominated by the quest for the conditions of individual liberty. Heavily laden with institutions developed to that end, we are reluctantly moving into a new phase in which we must somehow manage to rewrite our institutions in terms of organized community of purpose." R. S. Lynd, *Knowledge For What?* (1939), p. 87.

PART III

A RECONSTRUCTION OF INTERNATIONAL LAW

PHILOSOPHICAL INTRODUCTION

THE SIGNIFICANCE OF FUNCTION

THE CRISIS IN LEGAL THEORY: THE IDEAL DISCONNECTED FROM THE REAL

LEGAL theory is a science of systematic evaluation. Its logical constructions, mathematical and abstract as they may seem, are not inspired by the indifferent aloofness of mathematical concepts, but by the idea of achieving consistency in the evaluation of living realities. Legal theory, therefore, is a science which operates not with abstractly fixed and measurable entities, but with changing value-judgments. The question of the source and the ascertainment of these values is one of the cardinal problems of legal theory. Moreover, legal theory, again unlike mathematics, is not concerned solely with the logical consistency of its notions and constructions. It aims not at a system of formulas, but at a given pattern of actual social behavior. Its judgments are systematized not for the sake of their own inherent consistency, but with a view to their application to decisions of human wills. They have the function of determining the real conduct of individuals. The most fundamental question of all legal thinking, therefore, is that of the relation between value and facts, between norm and will, between the "real" and the "ideal." What is the place of values in the facts of social life? Whence does the theory of law draw its knowledge of legal postulates? What connection is there between the actual conduct of men and the norms which guide them?

This problem is approached by traditional theory in a way which is governed by an axiomatic dualism of outlook on things social. On the one hand we see a complex of cause-and-effect relations between physical forces and objects. If we focus our attention on what is considered "real" in this sense, we notice only material facts—men and their impulses, instruments of power, means of inducing people to take certain actions, physical and biological conditions of living, thinking, feeling and doing. This approach to things social, originating with Machiavelli and Hobbes, derives ultimately from the naturalistic concept of "reality" which has prevailed in occidental thinking since the days of Nominalism. For most thinkers on social problems it is an axiom that "reality" is equivalent to material existence and what is sensually perceptible. In a "reality" thus conceived there is no place for the values which are to guide social life. According to the scientific ideal set by the natural sciences, true science cannot know of any qualitative distinctions between better or worse actions. The science of social reality thus takes cognizance only of empirical "facts," defining as such material happenings connected by a naturalistic causality.

Consequently our recognition of social reality, if it proceeds in this manner, cannot possibly be in any way conclusive in regard to questions of value. Since those questions do arise in connection with actual social life, however, there has to be another, completely different approach to social problems. This second approach regards social phenomena not "as they are," but "as they ought to be." However contemptuously it may be criticized for its "unreality," this other way of looking at things social is only the inevitable consequence of a naturalistic concept of social reality, which equates the "real" with the "physical."[1] The second, or normative, approach is certainly not more unreal in itself than the first, or factual approach. There is neither a purely naturalistic causality nor a purely spiritual norm to be found in the realm of social phenomena. The separation of the normative from the factual is justified only so long as we keep in mind that actually they are but two

[1] In this sense, Hermann Heller insisted repeatedly that "*die naturwissenschaftliche Erkenntnistheorie der gesamten heutigen Staatslehre gestattet ihr nur einen materialistschen Realitätsbegriff, sowie dessen Korrelat in Gestalt eines Als-Ob-Idealismus*" (The natural-science method of modern political theory only knows a materialistic notion of reality, and its corollary is a mere As-If-Idealism).

aspects of the same phenomena, two aspects which in actual social life are intertwined, and which are dialectically separated only in our consciousness. But it is precisely this awareness of the relationship of separate notions of the ideal and the real that has been destroyed under the influence of positivism. It now has become a commonly accepted pattern to conceive of "what is" as something entirely disconnected from what "ought to be."[2] The real and the ideal have become two different worlds, held apart from each other not only in our language but also in the "barren divorce between normative theories . . . and the natural and social sciences."[3] Kelsen's attitude in banning from his thought any trace of social actuality is merely symptomatic of the irreconcilable duality of norm and fact, spirit and nature, which pervades the entire realm of occidental political thinking.

In consequence of this situation, legal theory has been forced to confine itself to the self-sufficient sphere of those purely spiritual phantoms: the realm of values absolute. They are absolute and spiritual because of this disconnection between the world of factual life and that of normative standards. Since our concept of "reality" has no place for norms, the science of norms has to take its clues from purely ideal positions kept radically apart from all reality. Here legal theory finds standards, meant to be applied in actual social conduct, but which are held valid apart from living reality. Thus an inherent antagonism results between the real and the ideal. Standards which are found in the absolute, are imposed on reality "from without." They are bound to appear heteronymous in social reality, since they have not been conceived in connection with it. Therefore their relation to reality is necessarily that of authoritative commands clamped upon the structure of social life. A science of social norms which finds its criteria of evaluation not in an interpretation and investigation of actual social conduct, but strictly apart from all reality, at best can but

[2] Cf. R. Pound, "Fifty Years of Jurisprudence," 51 *Harvard Law Review*, p. 804.
[3] See F. S. Cohen, *Ethical Systems and Legal Ideals* (1933), p. 9.

preach a sermon to an antagonistic reality, to which it always remains a stranger.

THE SHORTCOMINGS OF MORALITY AS A BASIS OF LAW

The system of absolute values, to which legal theory in our days resorts as a basis for most of its judgments, is primarily that of interindividual morality. However, social life has innumerable aspects for which this type of morality makes (and can make), no provision.[4] Even in a purely interindividual relationship there are many problems about which the moral code is silent, such as, for example, the problem of work. Current morality bids us to do our work well, but it fails to tell us what is good work and what is not. Above all, however, the affairs of organizations and institutions as such present situations which are not covered by the rules of morality as applied to individuals. It is good for an individual to sacrifice his interests for those of another individual. But is it also good for an organization (which does not exist for its own sake, but for that of numerous human beings) to sacrifice itself for the sake of another organization? Would not the self-sacrifice of an organization be a violation of its moral duty of service to the individuals on whose behalf it is operating? Evidently, conventional morality fails to provide an answer to these and similar questions.

With respect to these amoral aspects of social life, legal theory during the last three hundred years has adopted two different attitudes. On the one hand, it renounced any claim to a legal judgment on such problems, leaving them to an entirely technical or practical type of adjustment. Most economic questions (investment, prices, production output, industrial work, and so on) have been treated in this way. It would not occur to many people that these relationships should or could be

[4] F. S. Cohen, *op. cit.*, claims that there can be no legal valuation without ultimate reference to morality. "Non-moral law is impossible." This view grows out of his all-embracing definition of morality. If any ultimate value judgment is a moral judgment then indeed there can be no amoral law. However, in the present text the term morality is used as connoting merely the traditional occidental morality of interindividual relations, which has historically developed into a unique body of rules based mainly on a Christian conception of life.

measured by standards of a legal character, because from the moral point of view they seem to be indifferent. On the other hand, wherever legal theory did not choose to abandon the regulation of those amoral relationships to chance or to requirements of a technical nature, it construed standards of law in analogy to moral commandments and with the help of some accomplished system of law such as Roman law. In these cases, the details of legal postulates are provided by the system of law, to which reference is made, while morality serves as the cloak of obligation hung around concrete prescriptions of that legal system.[5] This is true, above all, of international relations. Morality, referring to the details of Roman law, provided the criteria of judgment for the theory of international law. However, since these value standards are not derived from the sphere of international, but from that of interindividual, relations, they are not homologous to the reality to which they are applied. Consequently they have to be imposed on that reality "from without", as a heteronymous command.

Now in a world which in itself is strongly permeated by respect for moral values it is entirely feasible to base a legal system on the motivating force of a transcendant morality. Under such circumstances, the legal system, although based on abstract value criteria which are imposed on social reality "from without," is effective, because the reference to moral value criteria coincides with a psychological taboo which compels people to respect these values. But that only means that a legal system may be actually effective under certain circumstances in spite of the fact that its value criteria are not derived from an immanent evaluation of social reality. The mere effectiveness of law which is based on abstract value standards, however, does not make such a legal system a satisfactory one. The fact remains that law so grounded still has to impose itself on an antagonistic reality by the authority of command. Therefore, even in a practically effective legal order which is derived from abstract criteria, the problem exists of how to overcome the gulf between actual reality and legal value criteria, by virtue

[5] F. S. Cohen, *op. cit.*, pp. 29*ff*.

of which law operates only as an authoritative command. That such a dictatorial role of legal rules fulfills the function of law only in a very inadequate way, is obvious. The task before us is therefore to find a way by which legal theory can arrive at value criteria which originate within reality instead of without, thereby avoiding an inherent antagonism between reality and ideality, and the resultant necessity of imposing legal postulates on reality by authoritative command. In other words, what we are seeking is a principle of immanent evaluation of reality by legal theory, instead of the transcendent evaluation now in use.

Here the question might be raised whether the value standards of morality do not after all fulfill this requirement. Does moral evaluation of social relationships really mean imposing heterologous standards on reality? One might argue that since morality is undoubtedly recognized and respected in some aspects of human life, the moral code of values must be connected with social reality at some point. On this assumption it might be concluded that a law based on moral value criteria does not have to impose heteronymous commands on social reality, but merely hands back in everyday coin the treasure which is harbored somewhere by actual life.

This argument, however, misses the point. Interindividual morality, even when generally acknowledged and respected, does not fit every situation in social relationships. Moral rules are not suitable standards of behavior for all aspects of social life. They seem to envisage only those relationships between individuals which are brought about by the essentially "unreasonable" impulses of human beings: passion, greed, appetite, lust, and selfishness. From the social point of view, these springs of individual action are irrational and incalculable. They are elementary patterns of "unreasonable" behavior, to which moral rules oppose the commandment of a similarly elementary and general social "reason," a sort of "minimum-program" of reasonable conduct. Thus morality opposes its postulate of a general and elementary "reason" of social behavior to such types of conduct which are not inspired by "reason" from the social point of view, but by impulses of an unreasonable character. That means that morality cannot apply to activities which are inspired by some kind of social reason anyway. Morality does not seem to be the only "reasonable" alternative to an "unreasonable" behavior. When for instance we speak of a "Reason of State", we imply that the conduct of statesmen in office is not passionately impulsive, but reasoned, although the "reason" inherent in their action is different from that of morality. Similarly we might formulate a "Reason of Economy," a "Reason of Religion," a "Reason of Law" and so on.[6] It will be shown later that all these specific "reasons" refer to specific standards of conduct, just as morality, forming a general and elementary social "reason," represents general and elementary rules of behavior. Our thesis is that through these specific "reasons" are manifested values which are distinct from those of conventional morality and which are immanent in social reality.

To the degree to which we become aware of the fact that not all behavior which fails to be guided by the standards of current morality is *eo ipso* "unreasonable" and unlawful, it is possible to extend the scope of legal value criteria beyond those of morality. Interindividual morality comprises only that set of elementary norms of social "reasonableness" in behavior which applies to the most general class of human motives. It is a general standard of "reasonable" social behavior which opposes its commandments to only the most typical human impulses of "unreasonableness." But in so far as individual actions are shaped not by irrational and subjective passions, but by transpersonal ends toward which individual efforts are directed in coordination with others, a transpersonal "reason" of coordination is inherent in these individual acts. For the coordination of social activities operates in individual wills as a transpersonal law of "reasonable conduct" which opposes itself to the arbitrariness of those wills.

Accordingly the framework of social institutions and re-

[6] For the inception of this idea see H. Heller, *Staatslehre* (1934), p. 226, where he opposes to the Reason of State (*Staatsräson*) a specific "Reason of Law" (*Rechtsräson*).

lationships operates in the same way as morality in restricting individual subjectivity: it bids individuals to observe a socially "reasonable," and forbids a socially "unreasonable," line of conduct. But while the social "reason" of individual behavior contained in morality is abstract, general, and simple, the inherent "reason" of all coordinate and institutional behavior is concrete, specific, and differentiated. Since these inherent standards of "reasonable" behavior are also social norms, they must enter into competition with the general rules of morality. This explains why the commandments of morality have been rejected publicly and candidly by people acting on behalf of social institutions. The experience of what happened to international law during the last decade, seems to bear out this thesis. It is the "Reason of State", i.e. the inherent reasonableness of politics, which revolted against the too moral commandments of international law, because these commandments insisted on treating political action on the same level as the irrational and impulsive conduct of an uncontrolled egoism. It was precisely because of the inherent prevalence of a specific political "reason," different from the general social "reason" embodied in morality, that moral values came at all to be regarded as strange intruders in the field of high politics. Because political action is both reasoned and organized, international law with its "altruistic" code of value-criteria, came to appear as an unreal and artificial order precariously imposed on a reality of different structure. The discrepancy between those types of conduct which moral standards are suited to meet, and those to which they were applied in international relations, has finally led to the wholesale rejection of international law by the dynamics of reality.

To summarize the foregoing arguments: The antagonism between the criteria of legal order and the inherent dynamics of reality in international relations has created a crisis which cannot be explained sufficiently by the assumption of ill will on the part of governments. What is required is not only good will on the part of states, but also a legal order which is essentially in accordance with the inherent laws of international politics.

This situation calls for a new type of value criteria in international law. What is wanted is a standard for judging reality which is immanently derived from the structure of international relations, replacing the reign of those values which are conceived as having abstract validity regardless of any social reality. As shown above, this means abandoning the purely moral basis of international law, and widening the scope of the values from which legal judgments are drawn. Modern society is too complicated to be governed solely by rules derived from the Decalogue. It presents a host of problems which entirely escape the simple measurement of traditional moral right and wrong. These problems legal theory can treat only on the basis of non-moral values which are found operating in the actual structure of social relationships. Since values which were conceived apart from all social reality and then authoritatively imposed on that reality, have proved to be inadequate foundations of international legal order, legal theory has to attempt to evaluate social reality on immanent lines.

However, it is here that the main difficulty arises. Legal theory is forced to resort to abstract and transcendant value criteria as long as social reality is conceived of as a realm of purely material existence and naturalistic causality.[7] As long as we continue to regard social reality as being on a par with physical data, thereby denying that it embodies an intrinsic set of values, there is no possibility of legal judgment of reality apart from that based on a system of absolute and transcendent norms. Of such norms the only systems which are practically available to us at present are Christian morality and Roman law. The theory of international law will be forced to continue along the lines of these two abstract schemes of order, as long as direct evaluative interpretation of social reality is barred.

OVERCOMING THE GULF BETWEEN THE "REAL" AND THE "IDEAL"

The radical separation of the world of values from the world of social reality proved to be the ultimate root of the crisis

[7] See footnote 1.

which has overtaken the practice and theory of international law. The overcoming of the axiomatic dualism between these two approaches to the same phenomena is the prerequisite of any progress in legal thinking. Law is a normative science, a science of judgments, but legal judgments evaluate concrete realities of human conduct. Unless legal theory can keep its criteria in close contact with the pattern of social actuality, its results cannot be experienced in that reality as significant judgments. They will appear as bloodless commandments from another world, from an unreal world, and thus will fail to produce order in reality. The problem of an immanent standard of legal values hinges on a change in our conception of social reality.[8] Modern philosophy, in conjunction with modern sociology and psychology, has attacked the problem of a new conception of social phenomena. Thus, for example, Hermann Heller points out that "scholars of so different an approach as Husserl, Rickert, Simmel, concur with the Dilthey school represented by men like Spranger, Litt and Freyer in assuming a specific sphere of sense, or of meanings (*eine Sphäre des "Sinnes," der Bedeutungen*) which overcomes this rigid dualism."[9]

In what ways does this new approach conduce to a solution of our problem? If social reality is conceived as an agglomeration of mere physical objects and forces, viewed like natural facts, we cannot possibly find in it any more meaning than we are able to find in a rock, or a tree. A tree, or any other part of nature, may have a sentimental, religious, or some other meaning for him who looks at it in a specific mood. But these meanings exist only in the subjective perspective of particular individuals; they have no validity or effect beyond the minds of these persons. If social reality is pictured as an array of material data, it is therefore meaningless as far as scientific recogni-

[8] "From these and similar difficulties we can escape if we get rid of the nominalistic prejudice in favor of atomic facts, and recognize that in the world of reality existence and the relations which constitute its logical implications are inseparable." Morris R. Cohen, "On Absolutism in Legal Thought," 84 *University of Pennsylvania Law Review*, p. 696.

[9] *Die Souveränität* (1927), p. 78. Also see Pound, 51 *Harvard Law Review*, p. 803 on this trend of modern thinking.

tion is concerned. As far as legal theory is concerned, it is simply a series of "facts," which carry no import apart from physical causality. For this reason the naturalistic conception of social reality is obliged to find the meaning of social actions in the postulates pertaining to the entirely separate sphere of values. It can attribute to social occurrences a sense only from the point of view of abstract goals at which they "ought" to aim.

Here modern thinking has introduced a radical change. There is a growing awareness of the circumstance that social phenomena carry their own inherent meaning, and that there are social phenomena only on the basis of meaningful facts. We are coming to realize more clearly today that social reality is nothing but human activity.[10] In other words, material facts as well as general "factors" (such as culture patterns, conditions of nature, and so on) do not have relevance for human society except through the activities of individuals.[11] While this realization ought not to blind us to the shaping of individual conduct according to institutional influences, it helps us to understand the peculiar character of "meaning" in social phenomena. To conceive social reality as human activity is to focus attention on the fact that all social reality is inherently "directed," in the sense that social phenomena are always tending toward goals that are willed by human persons. This is what makes social activities meaningful in a transpersonal sense. The meaning that social phenomena have by virtue of the direction that is necessarily an element of human activities, makes it possible to realize the connection between social "facts" and social values. If social reality consists of human activity, and if human activity is directed toward various goals, standards of value must be operative in shaping the very facts of social phenomena. For how can goals be conceived and willed without values that are attached to them? Therefore the sphere of "meaning" constitutes that aspect of social reality in which spirit and nature converge into culture.

It seems that this new approach to things social is capable

[10] Cf. H. Heller, *Staatslehre*, pp. 69*ff*.

[11] R. S. Lynd, *op. cit.*, p. 24. Cf. also note 18 in chapter VIII below.

of opening a way out of the dilemma of legal theory. Owing to the idea that reality is a sphere of merely material existence and causation, we have become unable to find a place for values in our picture of social reality. Thereby the intermediary position between pure ideality and pure factualness which is proper to law has become untenable for lack of contact-points between the empirical and the normative elements of our consciousness. To the degree to which law is relegated to the completely spiritualized realm of ideal norms, it is losing its real significance in actual life. This situation has caused people to ask whether the place of law and legal theory is not precisely in this sphere of "meanings," in which spirit and matter have become intertwined and mutually conditioned. This question, significantly enough, arose first not in the heads of the intellectual few, but in the practical minds of untrained, but bewildered, individuals "in the street." Unable to follow the "guidance" of abstract value-standards whose absolute commands did not seem to have any relevance to social reality, people have rightly begun to ask, whenever decisions concerning social relationships had to be made: What is the sense of this institution, or of that activity? Instead of trying to measure the value of social conduct by the yardstick of an abstract idea, instead of questioning whether a certain conduct was "right" in the sense of timeless absolute criteria,[12] they began to query whether it was "meaningful." The German scholar Feilchenfeld has condensed this general attitude into the categorical statement "Normative science is the science of tasks. To judge means to examine a process with regard to whether it fulfills an envisaged task. To judge therefore means to compare a process with its task."[13] This kind of questioning, which has become characteristic of contemporary thinking,[14] is in itself only meaningful if people expect to find a normative standard, a real guidance of their

[12] For criticism of this type of legal valuation see F. S. Cohen, *Ethical Systems and Legal Ideals*, pp. 62*ff*.

[13] *Völkerrechtspolitik als Wissenschaft* (1922), p. 131.

[14] See F. S. Cohen, "Transcendental Nonsense and Functional Approach," 35 *Columbia Law Review*, pp. 826*ff*. for a survey of functionalism in non-legal fields of thinking.

conduct, in the ultimate "meaning," or better in the *function* of social institutions and relations. It has to be shown in what way this is possible. To do so we have also to be clear as to exactly what phenomena and features this important notion of *function* refers.

It is to Karl Marx that we owe one of the most precise definitions of what distinguishes the conduct constituting social reality from naturalistic phenomena: "A spider conducts operations that resemble those of a weaver, and a bee puts to shame many an architect in the construction of her cells. But what distinguishes the worst architect from the best of bees is this, that the architect raises his structure in imagination, before he erects it in reality. At the end of the labor-process, we get a result that already existed in the imagination of the laborer at its commencement. He not only effects a change of form in the material on which he works, but he also realizes a purpose of his own that gives the law to his modus operandi, and to which he must subordinate his will. And this subordination is no mere momentary act. Besides the exertion of the bodily organs, the process demands that, during the whole operation, the workman's will be steadily in consonance with his purpose."[15]

Accordingly the activities of human beings imply something beyond mere physical, biological and neurological facts. Human activity is characterized by its inherent tendency toward what is conceived by human minds as the end of their efforts. This inner forecast of the result towards which action is destined bestows on human activity an essential quality of *directedness*. Human activity is "directed" inasmuch as it is destined to serve a goal that exists in human imagination. The objective of our doings is realized by the mind before it is realized in action: that it is what makes human activity meaningful. The anticipation of the objective, however, also imposes a certain rule on human action, by dedicating it to a task which it is to perform. It is in this sense that Talcott Parsons speaks of the "normative

[15] The passage is to be found at the beginning of part III of *Das Kapital*. Quoted here after the translation of Samuel Moore (1889), p. 157.

orientation" of social action.[16] Since social reality essentially consists in nothing but human activity,[17] these findings about the structure of human action are conclusive for our conception of social reality.

Human conduct is socially relevant only in so far as it manifests an inherent functional destination. Or, to state this thesis in different words: Social reality consists only of such human behavior as can be defined in terms of function. For a phenomenon of human behavior is social in proportion as it transcends the intraindividual realm. It is an interindividual phenomenon in so far as it enables a reciprocal orientation of action and reaction to take place. To use R. Pound's terms, we might say that social activities are those activities of men which are "oriented to the activities of others." Such a reciprocal orientation among individuals is based on an understanding of the meaning of the action, which makes it possible to take a responsive reaction in the same sense. Understanding of a human fact, however, is equivalent to realizing its inherent *directedness* toward a human end, the ideally conceived "task" of human action. In other words: Human conduct is socially relevant in so far as it can be understood, and it can be understood in so far as it is meaningful. It is meaningful by being inherently and manifestly directed toward specifically human ends. We understand human activity by grasping its relevance to an effect preconceived in human minds; we realize the meaning of something by experiencing its functional destination toward a consciously anticipated goal. It is obvious that understanding in this sense is limited to a common background of culture, since it implies the actual experience of ends of typical activities as well as the intuitive imputation of observed facts to those ends. It is perfectly conceivable that aborigines in some back-wood area may be unable to understand the functional meaning of a chair, never having experienced the use to which it was meant to be put.[18]

Only what is meaningful is socially relevant, but not all that

[16] *The Structure of Social Action* (1937), p. 44.
[17] See Hermann Heller, *Staatslehre*, pp. 69*ff*.
[18] See R. S. Lynd, *Knowledge for What?* (1939), p. 40.

is meaningful has social relevance. Behavior which is apparently senseless to other individuals may have a perfectly rational meaning to the person who acts. But such behavior is not a socially relevant phenomenon. An action, an institution, an object, a type of conduct, is part of a specifically social reality by virtue of the fact that its established meaning transcends the individual mind, and that its directedness is commonly understood. In this sense, we can restrict our definition of function to those types of meaningfulness which form part of social reality. Accordingly, meaning, or function, connotes co-ordination to ends which are evident in the eyes of most individuals, which are manifest without the need of explaining the intentions of a person's mind. If a man takes off his hat to me I do not have to ask him what this movement means: without knowing his thoughts I understand that the act has the function of conveying a greeting. I understand it because the meaning of this type of conduct is empirically established within a certain orbit of culture. But what is more: the act becomes a phenomenon of social relevance only to the degree to which it is understood and understandable. Thus this type of behavior has acquired a certain independence of the accidental intentions of the respective "actors." Accordingly we have to draw the conclusion that social phenomena, in order to become social phenomena, necessarily must transcend the volition of particular individuals.[19] For if a certain type of conduct is empirically understood to imply the meaning of salute, someone who is desirous of greeting another is under the necessity of behaving in this typical way, or otherwise he will fail in his intention.

Thus we find that all social reality is pervaded by the

[19] Cf. Ramiro de Maeztu's formulation of this idea in the very original and stimulating book *Authority, Liberty and Function* (1916), in which he attempts to establish a similar theory of law. Not having at his disposal the findings of modern psychology and sociology, however, he was not in the position to develop concepts that were adequate to his task. Very clearly he states the transindividual nature of social relationships: "Every society is a society for common ends. In places where the individuals speak in monologues and act for purely personal ends there is no society at all" (p. 109); "Men do not associate themselves without something in which they find that their aims are in common" (p. 139).

inherent meaning of acts, types of behavior, relationships, institutions.[20] By recognizing this we are able to overcome the fatal separation of natural facts and spiritual values, of reality and ideality. For if only that which manifests an inherent meaning is relevant as a social phenomenon, it is obvious that facts and values, givenness and requiredness[21] are inextricably intertwined in social reality. Meaning is nothing but directedness toward a preconceived end, at any rate as far as the meaning of social activities and social institutions is concerned. The foreseeing of the effect that is to be brought about by actual facts constitutes this element of directedness. Accordingly, in things social there is no reality which is not ideally destined toward some functional end, and there is no idea which does not have the tendency to materialize in the reality of facts. This element of destination in all things social is the transpersonal frame of reference enabling subjects to act and react upon each other. But this ideal directedness only becomes a basis for mutual orientation and social relationships in so far as it is embodied empirically in actual human behavior. This is what Hegel expressed in the formula: "*Was vernünftig ist, das ist wirklich; und was wirlich ist, das ist vernünftig.*" In this sense function, or meaning of social facts, implies a goal as well as the real acts working in the direction of this goal.

THE CRITERION OF LEGAL ORDER: FUNCTION NOT PURPOSE

Once it is recognized that an element of intrinsic "directedness" is inherent in all social reality, there exists the possibility of an immanent evaluation of social relationships. During the last fifty years a general trend toward sociological thinking in legal theory has produced many attempts to find criteria of legal judgment within the scope of social reality, instead of looking for legal standards in the clouds of absolute norms. Men like Roscoe Pound and Benjamin Cardozo in America, Duguit and G. Gurvitch in France, Jhering in Germany,

[20] See R. S. Lynd, *op. cit.*, p. 55.

[21] I have borrowed this expression from W. Koehler's book *The Place of Value in a World of Facts*, New York, Liveright (1939). For a detailed discussion see pp. 277*ff*.

Ehrlich in Austria, R. H. Tawney in England, R. de Maeztu in Spain have searched consciously for criteria of value which might be derived directly from social reality.[22] However, these and other similar attempts to develop a principle of immanent evaluation of social reality cannot be said to have yielded satisfactory results. The common deficiency of all these attempts consists in the fact that they retain an individualistic or atomic conception of society. Against the background of such a conception, any theory explaining or criticizing the law in terms of social "contexts" must take as its criterion of value the desires, intentions or needs of the concrete persons that "compose" society. For the individualistic conception of society thinks of social relationships as being entirely determined by the subjective motives, impulses and purposes of independent individuals.[23] With such an idea of social reality in mind, "function" can be conceived only as the purposiveness of individuals in "entering" social relationships.

From the perspective of this theory, legal standards would be criticized from the point of view of individual desires, typified in good nineteenth century tradition. Or, at best, "function" is used in the sense of "service" which is supposed to be the measure of individual rights. But the idea of service presupposes the notion of the needs and wants that are being served, and so this conception of "function" also refers, ultimately, to what individuals desire in society. Thus, all of these theories can be reduced to the attempt to employ one of two basic value criteria: either the *purpose* of, or the *benefit* to, legal persons. Theories vary between these two viewpoints of evaluation, and within each of them, between relating the

[22] I am not discussing here the various schools of "functional approach" which might be classified under the general heading of descriptive sociological jurisprudence. Scholars like J. Frank, K. Llewellyn, Thurman Arnold, for instance, are more concerned with a realistic knowledge about the practical question of how law-suits are decided generally, than with the problem of where to find the value criteria for measuring and criticizing such decisions.

[23] On the basis of this conception of society, "the criterion of values, the test for the reasonable, the guide for law making" is "the maximum of abstract individual free self-assertion." R. Pound, "Fifty Years of Jurisprudence," 50 *Harvard Law Review*, p. 563. See also above, note 8.

purpose criterion or the benefit criterion to the particular individual or to the collectivity personified (society, the nation, etc.[24] These two ideas seem to be the substance of the manifold formulas coined by various authors in trying to set up a yardstick for legal judgments—formulas such as: social engineering, social ends, function of the individual in society, social welfare, social solidarity, the idea of service, and so on. As against all these constructions our thesis is that a functional theory of law and legal judgments can establish immanent value criteria only by reference to the transpersonal ends of social relationships, and not by referring to purely individual purposes and benefits. Moreover, it is maintained here that those functional ends are distinct from the purposes of either single or collective persons. In other words, the above mentioned theories deserve to be criticized for assuming that the yardstick of legal judgments can be a criterion of purpose. Obviously a standard of legal values cannot be found in this direction: obligation would be dissolved into utility.

The attitude which is common to most of these thinkers may be represented by the following passage from an article by M. J. Aronson: "To affirm the teleological principle is to recognize that human conduct is purposive, that it derives its meaning from the goal it consciously pursues. Legal rules, being guides of conduct, should be envisaged, therefore, as means adapted to the attainment of ends and values . . . By their *fruits in social welfare* shall legal rules be appraised.[25] The fundamental error underlying this view is the confusion between the *ends* that constitute the meaning of social phenomena, and purposes as set by individual wills. The very concept of purpose

[24] "Duguit's denial that there are such things as rights and his idea of legal protection of social functions are a *sociological theory of the basis of legal recognition and securing of interests,* not an analysis of the complex of institutions by which they are secured." R. Pound, 50 *Harvard Law Review,* p.577 (italics mine). Cf. the position of Feilchenfeld: "*Im Gegensatz zu denen, die irgend eine Gemeinschaft als Selbstzweck anerkennen, und so schliesslich doch Menschendienst anordnen, kennt das sachliche Ideal keinen Menschendienst als Selbstzweck, sondern nur 'Dienst am rechten Werke.'" Völkerrechtspolitik als Wissenschaft,* p. 144.

[25] M. J. Aronson, "Cardozo's Doctrine of Sociological Jurisprudence," *Journal of Social Philosophy,* vol. IV, pp. 36*f* (italics mine).

connotes the intentions of a person's will. In the realm of social phenomena, only individual subjects can set purposes. In this sense Hermann Heller remarks: "Purpose refers to the anticipated effect of a will, in other words to that which a concrete subject in his concrete mind, either consicously or subconsciously, intends to attain."[26] It is true, that the term "purpose" is also used loosely to designate the trans-subjective function of an institution, *e.g.* in such sentences as: "The purpose of the State is to secure the happiness of individuals". But even in this sense it is impossible to speak of purpose without producing the image of the concrete willing of concrete persons. Whether we are aware of it or not, the concept of purpose compels us to visualize a subject, either real or fictitious, to whose will the purpose is imputed, and in relation to whom the purpose is interpreted. We can grasp a "purpose" only in terms of the will of someone who has set the purpose. Thus the statement that the purpose of the State is the happiness of individuals implies the tacit assumption that the ends of the State are identical with the will of the concrete subjects who created it or who are its beneficiaries. Consequently, as long as no clear distinction is made between what is willed by concrete persons and what is the function of social institutions and relationships, the functional "directedness" which we observe in social reality will always be imputed to some subjective will. This logical necessity is so compelling that whenever it is impossible to impute some "directedness" to the purposes of real individuals, our mind has to picture, as the author of that purpose, some unreal being, such as the People, Humanity, Nature or God.[27] Thus the associations implicit in the very term "purpose" compel us to make such an imputation consciously or subconsciously.

It is this underlying image of a subject and a subjective will

[26] *Staatslehre*, p. 44.

[27] "The term 'functional approach' is sometimes used to designate a modern form of animism, according to which every social institution or biological organ has a 'purpose' in life, and is to be judged good or bad as it achieves or fails to achieve its purpose." F. S. Cohen, "Transcendental Nonsense and Functional Approach," 35 *Columbia Law Review*, p. 822.

which makes the criterion of "purpose" useless for legal theory. For in assuming the content of a subjective will as the basis of a criterion of judgment, we are forced to interpret the will. The interpretation of a will of which we do not know the bearer is, however, not science, but guess-work. It is exposed to the most arbitrary speculation on the part of the interpreters of the alleged purposes. As soon as we trace the function of social institutions and relationships, and the ends of legal rules, to the purposes set by some ultimate will, be it human or superhuman, legal theory becomes the easy prey of political ideologies. These conjectures about the contents of the will which ultimately has set social purposes, range from Hegel's World Spirit to the maxim "Right is what profits the people." On their basis, function is confused with "mission" or "mandate," and the objective theory of legal values ends by preaching the personal political convictions of its author to an unbelieving world. This ultimate consequence of even a tacit assumption that purposes, attributable only to subjects and their wills, constitute the essence of social reality, becomes manifest in the last sentence of the above quoted passage from Aronson's article on Cardozo. Since Mr. Aronson is thinking in terms of purposes, not of social functions, he inevitably makes the individual's well-being the value-criterion of law, thus introducing into legal theory the purely ideological measure of "social welfare".[28] Accordingly, unless we can find a notion of function which is different from that of a subject's purpose, we shall have to abandon altogether the attempt to judge social reality by immanent standards.[29]

Evidently it is not science but bad metaphysics if, in seeking

[28] "The current notion that the function of the jurist is simply to secure adequate enforcement for the expressed demands of society derives from a dangerous metaphor. Society is not vocal. The expressed demands of society are the demands of vocally organized groups, and indiscreet deference to the power of such groups should not lead us to confuse their demands with 'social welfare.' . . ." F. S. Cohen, *Ethical Systems and Legal Ideals*, p. 20. See also p. 89.

[29] "Function and purpose, varied function and invariant purpose, have always been paired together. But the real animus of functionalism lies in the conception of function without purpose." H. M. Kallen, "Functionalism," in *Encyclopaedia of Social Sciences*, vol. VI, p. 523. (By permission of the Macmillan Co., publishers).

a meaning in social institutions, we feel urged to explain these institutions by inferring the existence of a subject to whose will their "purpose" is attributable. In principle such a conclusion is not different from the belief that all otherwise unexplainable events are caused by the action of spirits and demons. If any relevance is to be found in the notion of function, it is imperative to realize that the meaning of human activities is just as little attributable to the wills of concrete persons as the meaning of human words. The social sense of an institution or a type of conduct derives not from the concrete psychological intentions of individuals' minds, but from the transpersonal effect to which the conduct or the institution is coordinated with empirical regularity, just as the sense of certain sounds produced by our vocal chords resides not in individual intentions, but in the regular transpersonal effects pertaining to them.

Social relationships and institutions, the same as words, are inter-subjective forms the meaning of which is relatively independent of subjective purposes, interests or desires. The recognition of this fact is the keystone of the functional theory of law. It is therefore necessary to support this argument with more detailed reasoning. Meaning of social conduct consists in directedness toward specific ends. To say that the meaning of social relationships is relatively independent of subjective intentions is equivalent to asserting that individuals are not free to set the functional ends of their social activities. Individuals are free in setting their purposes, but they attain these purposes through activities-in-society the ends of which they cannot determine at random. This is true not only of social relationships, but of any human activity which can be termed constructive in the widest sense of the word, any activity which involves a relationship between the individual will and factors beyond the individual will, and which is directed toward the attainment of a positive result. All human efforts to give shape to things, to arrange, build, construct, achieve, all activities tending to bring forth some form, material or non-material, are governed by necessity, not by subjective discretion. Human will is not at liberty to choose, pick or reject the functional ends ruling those activities: the individual has to will them or he has to refrain from acting altogether.[30]

This relative autonomy of functional ends with respect to individual purposes may be demonstrated by an example from the sphere of sport. A man who wishes to ride on horseback has to undergo a certain training. During this practice he is acquainted with "what matters" in riding, in other words, with the "end," toward which he has to orient his behavior: the control to be exercised over the horse's movements by means of his thighs and his weight, the reins and the bit. This "end" is necessarily the same for every rider. It pertains inherently to the relation between a mounted man and a horse. He who desires that relation cannot but will the end. Both the end and the shape of conduct that leads to its attainment are thus relatively independent of the subjective purposes of individuals. For whether a man desires to ride in order to lose weight, or because of a practical need for transportation, or because of a fondness for horses, or simply because it is "the thing to do," does not make any difference to the structure of conduct he has to observe, and to the end governing that structure and its inherent laws. He has to direct his behavior toward certain ends in order to be able to ride, and this necessity exists for every rider, whatever his subjective intention in riding may be.

The same applies in social relations and institutions. It is not, for example, within the discretion of an individual to set or to modify the meaning of such an institution as a fire brigade. When a fire brigade pours water from a hose into a building, everyone understands that the meaning of this action is not to water a lady's flowerpot, but to combat a fire. Thus the meaning of this activity is manifestly established regardless of whether every single individual realizes it or not. Consequently the function of a fire brigade's activities cannot be arbitrarily shaped by individual intentions: it imposes itself even upon those individuals whose intention it is to counteract its ends through their participation. The existence of a trans-

[30] The binding and restricting force of constructive ends on human will is clearly recognized in the analysis of the labor process as defined by Marx (see quotation on page 253.

personal meaning in this institution binds the wills of all those who form a part of it, because it makes it necessary for them to direct their activities toward those specific ends which constitute the characteristic mark of a fire brigade. Whether the innermost intentions of all individuals are in accordance with these transpersonal ends or not, does not make much difference. They have to will the functional ends of a fire brigade, or else their actions will fail to be coordinated with the fire brigade, that is, they will not participate in it.

To participate in an institution means to perform acts in accordance with the functional ends of the institution. This "binding" force exercised on individuals' wills by the functional directedness of social institutions compels individuals to pursue their personal purposes through the medium of the objective functions of the institution, even if these subjective intentions run counter to the meaning of the institution. For example: a man may have joined the fire brigade in order to show off the uniform or to loot burning houses. A student may have applied for admission to a university not for the sake of acquiring an education, but for the sake of the social prestige connected with the university's name. A soldier may have desertion or espionage in mind when entering the army. A judge may intend to humiliate a personal enemy in making a legal decision. In all these cases the subjective purposes of individuals are even contrary to the objective function of their official activities. Yet they can be attained only by serving the ends which objectively constitute the social meaning of their institutional acts. They have to will these ends; they have to behave according to the transpersonal functions of a fire brigade, a university, an army, a tribunal, if they want to attain their subjective purposes.[31] Thus it is the functional ends pertaining to the institution or relationship as such, not their private intentions and purposes, which necessarily govern the social conduct of individuals. In this sense Dilthey, speaking of the distinction between function and purposes, points to the "functional structure governing particular wills. By virtue of

[31] See footnote 30.

this structure the ordinary doings of people, although only occupied with their own purposes, nevertheless bring forth what they should."[32]

Only by willing the transpersonal ends which constitute the function of social relations and institutions, can individuals effect that coordination of their energies to those of others, which ultimately may lead to the fulfillment of their subjective purposes.

The independence of these transpersonal functions from individual intentions is, of course, only a relative one. Certainly individuals are not free to deny or to acknowledge the functional ends which are the property of the institution "army". They find those ends embodied in the objective meaning of that institution. The meaning of an institution is just as little at the free disposal of particular individuals as the meaning of words. But individuals may be free to join the army or to stay away altogether. In other words, the realization of those functional ends pertaining to the institution is entirely in the hands of individuals whose subjective interest in that institution will determine their decision to participate in it or not. In this sense, social institutions and relations do depend on individual motivations. But once a man finds that he has to, or wants to, engage in a soldier's activities, for whatever reasons his decision may have been made, he can do so only by directing his will to the pursuit of those ends which are commonly held to constitute the function of an army.

The forms of social interaction and interrelation are thus characterized by an inherent directedness toward transpersonal ends which cannot be invented, disposed of, or rejected, by single individuals.[33] Social relationships materialize only by

[32] The entire passage runs: "*Alles, was in dieser gesellschaftlichen Wirklichkeit vom Menschen bewirkt wird, geschieht vermittels der Sprungfeder des Willens: in diesem aber wirkt der Zweck als Motiv. Es ist . . . das Allgemeingültige und über das Einzelleben Hinausgreifende in ihm, . . . auf welchem der Zweckzusammenhang beruht, der durch die Willen hindurchgreift. In diesem Zweckzusammenhang vollbringt das gewöhnliche Treiben der Menschen, das nur mit sich selber beschäftigt ist, doch, was es muss.*" *Einleitung in die Geisteswissenschaften* (3rd ed., 1933), p. 53.

[33] In an ingenious book on the function of the State (*Der Zweck des Staates*), published a hundred years ago (1842) F. Murhard shows clear understanding of the fact that

reference to such transpersonal ends as give them their meaning. Unless an individual's mind realizes, and his will aims at, these commonly established ends of social relations and institutions, he cannot participate in any of them. Accordingly, the functions of social relationships constitute the frame of reference which enable individuals to act with social relevance.

FUNCTIONAL STRUCTURE IN SOCIAL RELATIONSHIPS

What is the relevance of these investigations for the problem of legal standards of judgment? We set out from the assumption that the rigid and radical separation between legal ideals and social reality was unsatisfactory and untenable. If we can prove that social reality is not a chaotic agglomeration of physical facts and material forces, but that it is structured according to an order of its own, then the way is open to a legal order which operates not against, but in conformity with the inherent laws of reality. To this end we tried to show that under the point of view of function, social relationships are not governed by the impulses and interests of the single individuals, but by meanings which are not attributable to any single person, and which therefore impose themselves on the particular individual wills. What remains to be proved is that these functional ends establish a standard of order, by which individual conduct can be judged and measured.

We must leave to sociology and social psychology the task of explaining how it is possible for there to be ends of human activities which cannot be attributed to the intentions of any single individual, and which nevertheless are realized by the deliberate acts of many individuals. In itself, the problem does not seem to be more difficult than the question as to how it is that verbal sounds have a meaning which cannot be traced to the will of any single individual. However, this is

function cannot be identified with individual purposes. He says: "Das, was die Staatsgewalt als *solche*, unmittelbar oder mittelbar bewirken *soll* und allein bewirken *kann*, um dessent willen sie schlechthin *notwendig* ist und *errichtet werden muss*, was mithin auch ein jeder Staatsgenosse von ihr zu fordern ein Recht hat, ist alsdann allein der *Zweck* des Staates" (p. 400).

not the place to investigate the nature of this phenomenon.[34] Accordingly the fact that the ends of social institutions and relationships exist apart from the subjective purposes of individuals is the supposition on the basis of which we are proceeding. The question that arises next is: what significance does this circumstance have for the problem of legal order?

If specific relationships occur within a framework of reference to transpersonal ends, all the single acts which constitute the relationship must be in a system of order with each other. This conclusion is justified for the following reasons: Any individual act forms part of a social relationship or a social institution by manifesting its directedness toward such ends as are characteristic of the respective institution or relationship. Now all acts which conjointly are directed toward a common goal, stand in a certain functional relationship with each other, whether they are acts performed by a single person only, or acts performed by a multitude of individuals. Any goal the attainment of which requires a multiplicity of acts, entails a functional "structure" of all efforts directed toward it. Thus any complex activity, any undertaking, is essentially a functional "organization" of the relevant acts. Consequently, social relationships and institutions, which according to our supposition exist only in reference to transpersonal ends, imply a functional order of the individual acts of which they are composed. Such a connectedness in fact as well as in ideas between different acts of behavior we shall call a *context* of social conduct, in order to avoid the ambiguous term "relation".[35]

It is important to realize that it is only the functional end common to a number of individuals' acts which establishes a

[34] The best analysis of the processes by which common patterns of culture arise among individuals seems to be that of Theodor Litt (*Individuum und Gemeinschaft*, 3rd ed., 1926), whose explanation is condensed in his concept of "reciprocally intertwined perspectives." For the purposes of this book it must suffice to take cognizance of this and other similar results of sociological and psychological research. For a representative discussion of the problem see H. Heller's *Staatslehre*, pp. 81-101, with ample quotation of literature.

[35] I follow the terminology chosen by Professor Koehler to represent the German word "*Zusammenhang*." See his footnote on p. 74 of his "The Place of Value in a World of Facts" (1939).

functional order of conduct, a structure of relationship among them. For what is it that causes the acts of all the separate members of a fire brigade to appear as a coherent whole? Only the directedness toward the same end which is inherent in each act. What enables us to coordinate the behavior of an individual with a social institution? Only the realization that the behavior has the same functional meaning that characterizes the institution as such. What makes it possible and sensible to conceive of certain acts of various individuals as a "relationship"? Only the awareness of a common and reciprocal orientation to specific transpersonal ends that pervades these acts. In other words: there is no possibility of coordinating individual acts with each other, or of imputing them to social relationships and institutions, except on the basis of those transpersonal ends which constitute the meaning of social relationships and institutions. What "contexts" of conduct and action there are in social reality are brought about by such transpersonal ends, by reference to which individuals realize the connectedness of what they are doing. It has already been said that social relationships and institutions have ends of their own, irrespective of subjective individual purposes. Consequently it is the function of social contexts as such that determines the "structure," the order of coordination of relevant individual conduct.

The most important conclusion to be drawn from this analysis is that we can find immanent criteria of order in social reality only by reference to the functions of social connectedness as such. This is in sharp contrast to the criterion universally recognized at present. For what we now do when we need a yardstick for legal judgment, is to look toward the separate individual, his wishes, intentions, wants, purposes or services. We interpret social relations merely as radiations emanating from fixed psycho-physical units, the individuals, interacting with one another. Consequently our criterion in defining and measuring things social is derived from the notion of these psycho-physical units—independently "existing" individuals. Accordingly, subjective purposes, wants and interests are all that we can imagine as determining the function of social institutions. Even most of the so-called functionalist theories adhere to this scheme of social interpretation. The shortcomings of such an approach to social theory have been demonstrated elsewhere. What matters here is to realize that what determine institutions and relationships are transpersonal ends by which they have meaning independently of varying individual purposes. The functional criterion pertains to social connectedness as such.

An example may illustrate the basic difference of approach: A joint-stock company is an institution which serves the end of uniting separately held units of capital in a common enterprise. The end governs the inherent orderliness of all the parts, relations and units which make up such a company. It is the common point of orientation by reference to which all relevant conduct is coordinated. We can recognize the function of this institution by realizing the transpersonal effect which this specific connection, or combination of, individual acts as such is destined to achieve. It is the function of the interindividual connectedness as such, without reference to subjective individual wishes. Only from this criterion can we draw conclusions with respect to the orderliness of individual conduct in the social context. But we cannot arrive at any transpersonal criterion of order on a functional basis if we define the function of institutions in terms of what individuals expect from it for themselves. Thus if we say that it is the function of a joint-stock company to provide funds for the private purposes of an entrepreneur, such things as the stockholders' meeting and their control over the policy of the enterprise would be senseless and unjustified. And on the other hand, if we assume that a joint-stock company serves the end of obtaining the highest possible return on individual capital, we again get a false perspective which does not account for the position of the managing directors. Neither is it possible to understand the function of an institution in terms of the sum, or the resultant, of the different purposes of participating individuals, or groups of individuals. For actual and ideal connectedness between individuals does not exist with a view to their respective private purposes, but only with a view to such transpersonal ends as are to be effected by their relationship as such.[36] The notion of function centers, therefore, around the phenomenon of social connectedness in and of itself, around the ends determining contexts of action, around the criterion of envisaged effects of a transpersonal nature.[37] Function refers not to the performance of individuals in the pursuit of self-interests, but only to individuals as connected by, and for, the bringing about of objective results.[38]

It is clear that the functional approach involves a radical change of outlook on things social. It focusses attention on social connectedness as such, as a meaningful nexus of social conduct.[39] Social reality is no longer conceived as an agglomerate of individuals, but as a multitude of contexts of interaction and cooperation. Amid the endless varieties of acts, intentions, purposes and individual persons, the contextual structure of social relationships and institutions is the relatively stable form, the *Gestalt* in which dynamic life takes shape. However, one reservation has to be kept in mind regarding the use of the concept of *Gestalt*. While observing a certain "structure" in social relationships which is a result of the coordination of individual acts to common ends, we must not overlook the

[36] It was E. Ehrlich, *Fundamental Principles of the Sociology of Law* (translation, 1936) who first pointed to the fact that "the inner order of associations is not only the original, but, down to the present time, the basic form of law. . . . Law is always concerned with human associations: it determines the position of the individual in the group of working human beings and the relation of the group to its tools." Quoted with the permission of Harvard University Press.

[37] "So we can say that every society is a society in a common object. Its center of gravity lies in the object. . . ." Ramiro de Maeztu, *Authority, Liberty and Function*, p. 138.

[38] "The ethical fallacy which confuses the purpose and the effect of an act is not restricted to the field of law. Most people, being more confident of their goodness than of their wisdom, prefer to be judged by that phase of conduct which least involves scientific calculation, by their choice of ultimate ends, their final motives or purposes." F. S. Cohen, *op. cit.*, p. 68.

[39] According to F. S. Cohen, functionalism is the approach which "seeks to discover the significance of the fact through a determination of its implications or consequences in a given mathematical, physical or social conduct." "Transcendental Nonsense and Functional Approach," 35 *Columbia Law Review*, p. 829.

fact that social contexts have not the same structural independence of their constituent parts as characterizes the *Gestalt* structure found in natural reality. Since social contexts consist of the behavior of living men, they are subject to changes in time and space. But the forms of language undergo transformations at the hands of successive generations in the same way, and yet no one would deny that language represents true structure, that its laws constitute an element of transpersonal necessity by which individuals are bound as long as they wish to make themselves understood. Like language, the structure of social relationships is a framework of interaction between individuals which, though not attributable to any one individual, nevertheless takes shape only in the acts of living men. And just like forms of language, these molds of action and reaction are subject to historical change: "*Geprägte Form, die lebend sich entwickelt.*"

Thus it is solely in these relatively stable structures of social interaction and coordination that immanent criteria of legal judgments about social reality can be found. Recognizing this fact, it is difficult to understand how legal and political thinkers can believe it logical to derive the standards of legal order from the notion of the individual self, from the criteria of his needs, interests, purposes and impulses. It is precisely these self-centered aspects of human personalities that are not capable of being coordinated with each other—which by their indeterminable quality and their power of random decision defy any reduction to a universal standard of legal order. This seems so obvious that it hardly needs to be emphasized. Yet most authors on the subject believe it imperative to start any discussion of the principles of law with the basic assumption that these elements of human life which are, and by their nature must remain, uncoordinate, are the "ends" to which all social order is dedicated. In view of this attitude, is it surprising that in a social reality so conceived no criteria of value and legal order can be detected? Is it to be wondered at that such a "reality" appears as a senseless and incoherent mass of mechanical forces, objects and facts? We can put the house of legal theory in order only by realizing which aspects of social life are coordinate and therefore inherently orderly in character, by realizing that whatever structure exists in social reality exists not in individual purposes, but in transpersonal ends, for which and through which individual acts are connected, and, finally, by realizing that individuals are social beings only by virtue of those transpersonally necessary elements which shape their conduct. Social and legal order is the order ruling individuals-as-connected; the self-centered aspects of individual lives are of no concern to it. They concern the theory of individual self-perfection: philosophy and religion. Legal and political theory has to do not with the rules of individual perfection, but with the rules of social contexts. It must therefore be based on the notion of "man coordinate", not on that of "man separate."

FUNCTIONAL STANDARDS OF LEGAL ORDER

Up to this point our argument may be briefly summarized thus: Individual acts are reciprocally relevant. In other words, they are social acts, in so far as they are socially meaningful. Meaning is immanent directedness toward a transpersonal end. All acts directed toward the same common end stand in a certain necessary relationship to each other. Whenever we observe the immanent necessity of a relationship between various parts we speak of structure. Structure is a complex order of multiple elements which inherently and stably fit together by virtue of their behavior. The immanent necessity of relevance to each other within a dynamic structure we call function.[40] Before investigating the norms of social order which derive from functional relationships, it is necessary to throw some light on the implications of the term function itself.

Function, in whatever sense it is used, connotes dynamic

[40] Cf. Koehler's formulation: "Some objects are essentially *structures*, inasmuch as their parts depend upon each other for their existence. In all the more interesting objects of this kind, however, such interdependence has, let me say, a *direction*. . . . I might say the same of function; as a matter of fact with such objects it is extremely hard to distinguish between structure and function." *The Place of Value in a World of Facts*, p. 17 (italics in original).

coordination. Three meanings of the term function may be distinguished for the purpose of this thesis. In the first place we speak of function in the sense of *task*, or ideal destination, e.g., "The function of the army is to defend the country". In this connection the structure, or the system, which determines this function of the army is not expressly mentioned. Nevertheless, it is clear to everyone that the term function implies the coordination of the task of the army with the structure of the state, within which the army is supposed to perform one of the activities required for the operation of the whole. Therefore, function employed in this way means the task which ideally corresponds to a part in a coordinated whole. In the second place, we speak of function in the sense of *action*, or actual performance (e.g. "The legislature is functioning," "the function of Hamlet," and "the function of the heart").[41] Here we refer to what is empirically done or performed by an entity in a regular way; we envisage a factual operation which can be observed continuously. But again the coordination involved in this performance is implied in the meaning of the term function. For in designating an operation as function, we indicate that we observed not an isolated activity, but activity-in-coordination. We imply in our statement the reference to a larger context of which the observed action forms part. In this second sense of the word function the feature of coordination is not inferred from an ideal "plan" of the whole, but merely from empirical observation, from a recognition of continuous causal interrelationship. Finally we use the term function to indicate the *interdependence* of certain phenomena (e.g.: "X(f)Y," "Prices are a function of supply and demand," and "Freedom is a function of economic conditions"). In the two previously mentioned meanings the word connotes the shape and direction imposed on either ideal or factual operation by its coordination with a larger structure. In this last sense the concept of function refers not to the performance of the parts, but to the relationship of coordination

[41] Cf. Charles W. Morris, *Six Theories of Mind* (1932), pp. 275*f.*, where several definitions of "function" are given.

itself, by which variables depend upon each other. "X(f)Y" means that a phenomenon called *X* is variable in its structure and appearance, and will follow any changes occurring in another phenomenon called *Y*. Therefore, when we say: "The function of *X* is *Y*," we presuppose a notion of the whole structure to which this part *X* is coordinated. When, however, we say: "*X* is a function of *Y*," we are trying to circumscribe in a formula the system of coordination as such. Function in this latter sense connotes not merely the position of one part, but the interrelationship of all the various elements of a context; it indicates the nature and circumference of a structural whole by referring to the connectedness of all those entities which are dynamically associated with each other.

Now the major problem arises whether this coordination, which the concept of function connotes in any one of its meanings implies standards which are significant from the point of view of legal order and legal judgment. This most crucial question of a functional theory of law may be defined thus: Does the element of function embody a merely sociological or technical coordination of parts in a whole, or does it imply a coordinated system of value criteria as well? If this question could not be answered in the latter way, then the functional approach would be entirely untenable in the theory of law, for which it would then fail to provide any conclusive answers. However it seems that not only do functional values exist, but that they have a most potent normative appeal for the modern mind.

Professor Koehler has recently shown that every "context," every structure, contains an immanent element of "requiredness."[42] Given a structural context, so he found, we are able to judge whether a relevant fact is "fitting" or "unfitting" from the point of view of the properties of the whole structure. A fitting fact is felt to be "right", or "better" than an unfitting one. It is true that Professor Koehler's experiments moved mostly in the field of physical and mathematical structures. It seems however that the results of his investigation

[42] *The Place of Value in a World of Facts*, pp. 95*ff*.

have a wider application; it seems to be a typical and necessary reaction of human beings, when they are aware of structure, to experience an inescapable urge to "fit" the intrinsic standard of a context. Since this necessity is rooted in the perception of a structural whole as such, it applies to contexts of every kind, whether their structure is composed of physical facts, of geometric symbols, or of social conduct. It follows that wherever there is a structural whole, in the sense of a specific and necessary coordinatedness of elements in one context, there is also an immanent criterion of judgment.

Accordingly, it is possible to discriminate, without resorting to any abstract definition of values, between "fitting" and "unfitting" facts, between intrinsic right and intrinsic wrong, provided we are aware of the contextual structure as a whole. There is a necessary connection between the feeling for structure and the capacity for immanent evaluation. Hence an essential conclusion about the form of a legal order based on functional standards can be drawn at once: Since legal judgment by immanent standards depends on the perception of structural contexts, and since contexts of social relations are formed by reference to transpersonal "ends," the consciousness of such ends is of basic importance in a system of functional law. To put it in other words: The conduct of individuals in relation to other individuals is guided by common reference to the specific transpersonal effects constituting the "meaning" of their relationship. Thus it is the functional end of social connectedness which governs the laws of coordinate behavior. Therefore, without being aware of those transpersonal ends of social contexts, it is possible neither to become conscious of the structure of social contexts as a whole nor to judge them by immanent value criteria. A functional law thus has to aim primarily at producing a consciousness of the ends of social relationships rather than a knowledge of means alone. The present type of legal order entirely ignores ends. It prescribes rigidly fixed means without any public reference to the ends to which they are destined. It measures the requiredness of these prescriptions not by the inherent standards of social coordination of behavior, but by abstract definitions of good and bad. In other words: it conceals the functional meaning of its legal commands.

Such a system does not require, from the subject of the law, an attitude that embodies the spirit of the law. It even makes it almost impossible to comprehend the ultimate end of legal rules. The subject of the law has to adhere to, and obey, the letter of the law. This in turn makes it necessary to enforce such obedience by the threat of power and compulsion. The law, under the prevailing system, tells the subject to comply in a passive way with the words of the authorities. His initiative is not required, nor is it appealed to. Therefore our notion of law, against this background, is that of the letter of authoritative commands. In a functional system the concept of law is that of orderly conduct of individuals-in-connectedness.

On the other hand a system of law which prescribes merely means without making the ends equally obligatory, provides the possibility of abusing the law by a conduct which is in accordance with the letter though contrary to the spirit of the law. This kind of "legal," although really unlawful, behavior, which is particularly characteristic of the law of nations, becomes possible when the meaning of legal rules is hidden away in the minds of political and judicial legislators, and is not made an integral part of the legal norm. If instrumental measures are prescribed by the law without making known the ends that inspire them, they can be abused for widely varying ends. Using means in an inherently lawful way requires the awareness of their functional destination.

Finally, the present system of law, by withholding the ultimate ends of legal rules from the subjects of law, and by merely publicizing the measures on which the legislator has decided as means, foregoes entirely any appeal to the intuitive sense of evaluation and judgment which operates in individuals. It fails to appeal to the capacity of discrimination with respect to their own actions which human beings possess. It claims only obedience and submission. This requirement of passive compliance on the part of the subject is characteristic of any system of law the rules of which are based on ultimate considerations that the subject ignores.

The unsatisfactory character of a legal system in which lip service is paid to the letter of the law, while its spirit is being put aside, is obvious. Functional law therefore emphasizes the inherent lawfulness of social conduct, not passive obedience to prescriptions, as the essence of legal order. In order to enlist the support of the subject's capacity for judgment, in order to make individuals active agents for lawfulness, the law must consist of rules whose value criteria are actually felt and experienced by those who are to realize them. Now the value experience of which each individual is capable is that of the immanent right and wrong pertaining to the function of social contexts. These inherent standards of requiredness are governed by the transpersonal ends toward which social contexts are directed. Consequently only the invoking of the functional meaning of social institutions and relationships by the rules of law can enable the individual to measure for himself the lawfulness of social conduct, and to become an initiator of legal order instead of its passive slave. Thus functional law calls not for mechanical obedience, but for constructive and active judgment on the part of individuals. It operates as a guide orienting the evaluation of individual actions. It aims at a social order which exists in the inherent orderliness of actual behavior, not in the mere authority of prescriptions and legal commands.[43] The only agency that can bring about this lawfulness in actual social conduct is the sense of immanent evaluation working in the acting individuals themselves. Legal rules should, therefore, serve to point out the functional ends of social connectedness, suggesting means at the same time. They should serve to direct the evaluating sense of individuals toward those ends. They should induce individuals to evaluate

[43] Even the so-called functionalists of the "realist" brand (see note 20) adhere to a conception of law as a command, an authoritative statement, in spite of their criticism of this view in Austin. Thus, e.g., J. Frank maintains that "until a court has passed on those facts no law on that subject is yet in existence." *Law and the Modern Mind*, New York, Coward McCann (1931), p. 46.

their conduct in the right way, enlightening them about the immanent laws which govern social contexts.

DO FUNCTIONAL STANDARDS REPRESENT TRUE VALUES?

The problem of immanent value criteria in social relations would be a simple one indeed if all that it amounted to were the recognition that there are functional ends of social contexts, that these ends entail a certain structure of relevant acts, and that all structure implies standards of immanent "requiredness," by virtue of which we are able to discriminate between inherently "fitting" and inherently "unfitting" conduct. It certainly is essential to realize that social relationships have a structure of their own which is not attributable to the intentions and desires of any single individual. But if we were to stop here, the quality of "value"-criteria in social relations would not be distinguishable from a merely technical ends-means relation. It would be sufficient to state the respective ends of social institutions and relationships in order to infer invariable and "scientific" criteria concerning the rightfulness of acts leading to the attainment of those ends.[44] Such a conclusion might indeed be drawn from the notion of functional standards, if we were to yield to the temptation of transferring integrally the concept of *Gestalt*, or structural context, as elaborated by Wertheimer, Koffka and Koehler, into the realm of social behavior. The fallacy of using analogies from the natural sciences in analyzing social reality has proved fatal to most of the positivistic attempts to find an "objective" criterion of values for legal order.

The admirable definition of the difference between human activities and natural facts by Marx[45] should be sufficient warning against this mistake. It is not possible to treat the question of values of social relationships along the lines of an analogy with the immanent requiredness pertaining to physical

[44] In other words, the functional approach would not solve our problem if it would lead only to a "conditional" criterion of value, formulated in terms which in turn are ultimately subject to moral evaluation. See F. S. Cohen, *Ethical Systems and Legal Ideals*, p. 16.

[45] See above, p. 253.

and mathematical structures. The specific features of *Gestalt* which Wertheimer, Koffka and Koehler observed in physical and mathematical contexts were rooted in the circumstance that the structure as such remains the same while the elements composing it may change (as in the case of a tune which is transposed from one key to another). While Koehler's observations concerning the properties of structural contexts have certainly a general validity, the specific concept of *Gestalt* with which he operates cannot be transferred integrally into the sphere of things social.

The structure of a tune may not vary by its transposition into another key, and by a complete change of the particular notes of which it consists. But social contexts are not so independent of the quality of their composing parts. Social relationships consist of, and exist only in, the actual conduct of human beings. True, their structural laws are not determined by the purposes of single individuals, but nevertheless they are put into effect only by individual decisions and motivations. Individuals are not able to create these laws, but their action and reaction can influence them positively or negatively. Like the rules of language, the rules of social connectedness-in-action have reality only in the comprehending and deciding minds of individuals. Therefore, they are subject to change and development together with the totality of individual consciousness. Therefore the functional ends that govern the structure of social relationships cannot be conceived apart from the totality of the concrete individuals who carry them into effect by their decisions. Their way of experiencing the social meaning of human conduct is what determines the ends, the structure and the immanent requiredness of social relationships and institutions.

This is what distinguishes values in the cultural sphere from the merely formal requiredness observed by Koehler in the sphere of natural and logical phenomena. The requiredness of physical and mathematical contexts derives from a structure that is given to one's consciousness; the immanent order of a social context, however, derives from an end that is put up to one's active decision, and that requires that person's adherence. Discrimination between "fitting" and "unfitting" facts relating to natural and mathematical structure is a reaction of consciousness which is inescapable; discrimination between right and wrong in respect to social structures is a deliberate assertion of the ends of social connectedness. It calls into action the totality of an individual's selecting and postulating faculties.

Social contexts are composed of acts which require decisions of individual wills. While it is true that an act of individual behavior pertains to social reality only by virtue of a socially understandable meaning that is manifest in it, it is equally true that this meaning consists in directedness toward a specific end, and that such directedness derives from the minds and wills of concrete individuals. Consequently the way in which an individual, or rather individuals in general, realize the coordination of social relationships to transpersonal ends, influences the structure of social contexts. For the realization of such coordinatedness is not a more or less automatic reaction of individuals, not a somewhat mechanical reflex, but a conscious decision, which may vary according to the differences of cultural "climate" conditioning it. In social contexts, unlike the *Gestalten* of mathematical or physical character, the immanent requiredness is not entirely a property of the context as a formal structure, because social contexts have no formal independence of the elements composing them. Accordingly, we cannot find the criterion of social requiredness in an abstract conception of social relationships and their functions. Immanent standards of value are contained in the coordinate structure of social action, but they can be found only by a scrutiny of the way in which such coordinatedness is actually realized by concrete individuals in a given historical situation. The element of structure deriving from transpersonal ends, *as it figures in the experience and the actual conduct of individuals,* is conclusive for the immanent standards of social order.[46]

[46] Jerome Frank, in 26 *Illinois Law Review* proposes a program of "patient observation and description" of "what courts do in fact." He shows that "formal law frequently

Accordingly, what is, in non-social reality, "requiredness" deriving from a formal structure, is, in social reality, "interestedness" deriving from concrete elements of consciousness.

"CONSUMPTIVE" AND "CONSTRUCTIVE" VALUES

Value in social reality is experienced as "interestedness" (not to be confused with "interest"), because there is no such thing as a behavioristic *Gestalt* which would exist apart from acts of will decided upon by individuals. Does that mean that all evaluation is subjective, that there is no transpersonal criterion of value inherent in social relationships? Such an assumption would be in flat contradiction to our most elementary experience. The conclusion that the standards of an immanent "good," "bad," "better," "worse," cannot be found in a formal structure of social contexts apart from the individual experience of "interestedness" does not equate values with random predilections of a subjective character. Were it so, no structure of social activities would be possible at all, for there could not be "structure" in things social without the consciousness of transpersonal ends, which in turn implies standards of discrimination not attributable to the merely personal desires of individuals. The circumstance that we do observe such structures in social reality proves, then, that their immanent criteria of value, although existing in individual experiences only, are governed at the same time by transindividual necessity, just as forms of social conduct, although brought about by individual acts of will, are ruled by the functional necessity of coordinate parts.[47]

Thus we have to assume that there corresponds to a trans-

---

conceals what judges do in fact and what makes them do it." However refreshing his criticism of the formal lawyer's notion of law may be, his realism is too "cynically acid" to be still real. Had he proposed "to go, look and see" not what courts are doing, but how men conduct themselves, and feel that they ought to conduct themselves, in their associations and interactions with other men, he would have been closer to the knowledge of the real rules of law. See also Ehrlich, *op. cit.*, p. 11, for the same criticism of Frank's position.

[47] Unlike F. S. Cohen, *op. cit.*, I am not proposing a philosophical theory of value, or a new criterion of the ethical good. I am merely trying to show through what social medium that which is valuable—whatever it is—manifests itself in a legally relevant way.

personal necessity of behavior a similar necessity of evaluation. Not every human value-experience is ruled by such necessity. But only those value-experiences which are governed by trans-individual necessity are at all relevant from the point of view of legal order. Those value judgments of individuals which have significance exclusively for the individuals themselves do not form part of legal order from any point of view. Accordingly we have to distinguish between an "interestedness" which is subjectively-accidental and an "interestedness" which is trans-subjectively-necessary. Only those values which individuals experience with trans-subjective necessity can guide the rules of a legal order.

What is the nature of those values? "Every element of consciousness, whether it be a feeling or a thought, is awareness of something, is knowledge. It may provoke the knowing individual's interestedness, or it may leave the individual disinterested. In the latter case it is irrelevant to him. In case the individual's interestedness is evoked, however, it may be of two kinds. Interestedness may be directed toward 'consumptive' or towards 'constructive' qualities. Both represent a value to the individual, because otherwise the object would be valueless. But the two classes of values are of different kinds. The first class of values corresponds to interestedness from the point of view of 'consumption' (pleasure), the second class corresponds to interestedness from the point of view of 'construction' (production, creativeness)."[48] This distinction between values of a "consumptive" and those of a "constructive" character corresponds to a distinction which modern philosophy, reacting against the sweeping generalizations of modern hedonism, has made in many different forms. It is a distinction between what is relevant to satisfaction of the senses in the widest meaning of the term, and what is relevant from the

[48] M. Bott-Bodenhausen, *Formatives und funktionales Recht* (1927), p. 32: "*Jeder Bewusstseinsinhalt (Gefühl oder Gedanke) ist ein Kennen von etwas, eine Kenntnis. Er kann von Interesse oder von Desinteresse begleitet sein. In letztem Falle ist er für das kennende Subjekt bedeutungslos. Ist er von Interesse begleitet, so kann das doppelter Art sein. Es kann auf Genuss oder Gestaltung gerichtet sein. Wert hat beides für das Subjekt, andernfalls wäre es wertlos, nur einen verschieden gearteten Wert. Einmal dient der Wert dem Verbrauch (Genuss), und das andere Mal dem Aufbau (der Gestaltung).*"

point of view of our creative urges and possibilities. It is a differentiation of the potential significance of things, according to whether they are interesting for the sake of individual wants, needs, appetites, or for the sake of individual constructive impulses, of the desire to bring forth, produce, create. The distinction carries with it an important conclusion for our problem: Interestedness relative to the sensual gratification of individuals (consumptive value) is an accidental phenomenon. It is accidental in the same way as the reflexes of our senses are incalculable facts of infinite individual variety, not allowing of any social standard or of any social coordination. He who follows the guidance of sensual reflexes discards any consistency of conduct, and is ready to act upon whatever unpredictable clue may come from his senses. There may be a biological law in the way in which individual senses record enjoyment or repugnance, pleasure or displeasure, but there certainly is no social lawfulness in it. Kierkegaard, in drawing his famous distinction between an esthetic outlook on life, according to which everything is relevant only to the senses and their gratification, and an ethical outlook, according to which the dominant criterion is the creative shaping of life, describes the arbitrary nature of the "consumptive" values as follows: "In so far as a man lives in a merely esthetic relationship to things, everything has only an accidental significance to him."[49]

On the other hand, values which are relative to constructive urges, are not experienced in an accidental, but in a necessary way. This is quite generally true, even apart from the specifically social aspects of life. It makes no difference whether the constructive urge is directed toward an achievement of material character or toward the creative shaping of immaterial elements. Whether interestedness is experienced with a view to the order which a man endeavors to achieve in his personal life, or with reference to a practical accomplishment to which he devotes himself, or in connection with the ends of social relationships: he is not free to evaluate at random. His value experience obeys a certain transindividual necessity. The most conspicu-

[49] Translation mine.

ous example of this trans-subjective lawfulness of constructive values is to be found in the inner necessity which makes the artist create according to certain laws, whether he is conscious of them or not, and which, at the same time, give his creation a validity transcending his person, his situation, his time and even his culture. But the laws of artistic creation are only a specific case of the necessity of evaluation to which we are subject in everything we do, will or envisage constructively, in every effort we make to bring forth a shape of things not yet in existence. There is no element of individual arbitrariness, no incalculable predilection in the evaluation of phenomena relevant to creative activities: laws of transindividual necessity pervade the emotional reactions of individuals with respect to whatever is constructive in its essence.

In social reality, these transpersonal laws of evaluation can be observed as an empirical regularity of "interestedness." Now wherever such empirical regularity of appraisal occurs, legal rules can be founded on it as a house on supporting rock. Thus Bott-Bodenhausen continues the argument quoted above[50] by pointing out that "gold is a measure of economic value because of the empirical reality of its being regularly valued. It is not up to the discretion of an average individual to hold gold to be valuable or not valuable. He is compelled to acknowledge the value of gold, and this compulsion is a social law which forms one of the bases of the capitalistic economy."[51]

Now social relationships and institutions exist, as has been shown above, only in reference to specific transpersonal ends, toward which they are functionally destined. Accordingly, all social contexts are of a constructive character. It follows that the criteria of value which are immanently pertaining to them, are not subject to the accidental "interestedness" which is characteristic of values relating to sensual pleasure and satisfaction. What individuals want, need, covet for the sake of their consumption in the widest sense of the word, does not determine the value of conduct which is inherently directed

[50] See page 281.
[51] *loc. cit.*

toward some form of construction. Here the profound unreality of all political theory which attempts to find social value-criteria by reference to the appetites, the sensual gratification, the "consumptive happiness" of individuals, becomes strikingly clear. Ignoring the accidental quality of all those values which are of the "consumptive" kind, a popular school of political thinking still believes it possible to base law, government and all political institutions on those values as the ultimate justification of all things social. However, transpersonal laws of evaluation exist only with respect to the functional ends of social contexts as such, not with respect to the "consumptive" advantages resulting from them for the particular individuals. That "interestedness" which relates to the effect to be accomplished by a social relationship, is a value of the constructive kind, with regard to which individuals are empirically subject to transpersonal laws governing the emotional layers of their consciousness.

It was stated above that constructive values cannot be inferred from an abstract conception of the social context. Individual evaluations with respect to social relationships obey a certain transpersonal necessity, but this necessity is conditioned by the typical ways of reaction and reflection which have developed in a particular society. In other words: it is relative to the cultural "climate" which shapes individual emotions and relations. Therefore, we cannot conceive of any pattern of social evaluation apart from a social situation definite in time and space; we can observe them only as empirical regularities in emotional processes. The fundamental fallacy of the natural law philosophy was its attempt to establish values having no historical validity. Laws of evaluation are features of social reality which can be observed in given historical situations. Some of these laws are of practically permanent duration and universal extension, simply because there is little or no change in the typical situations from which they arise. But others are restricted, being tied up with emotional patterns which are of only local validity. While recognizing that the experience of constructive values obeys certain laws of transpersonal necessity, we must not be blinded to the fact that it is an experience of concrete individuals in a definite social and historical situation. Their ways of producing and creating are certainly not subjective or arbitrary, but they are relative to emotional patterns which may pertain only to their type of culture and society.

Therefore, in so far as individuals, because of their common pattern of living and the common background of their cultural situation, do react emotionally in a common and typical way, a community of values exists. It is this empirical regularity and necessity in the process of evaluation which is the only real basis for an immanent legal order. Since law is essentially a system of evaluative judgments of social behavior, it can be immanently evaluative only by reference to a common emotional structure, of a common pattern of culture. In a functional system of law, with its emphasis on the ends of social relationships, the criterion of value is the inner necessity, by virtue of which individuals regularly experience "interestedness" in certain constructive ends. The inner necessity of functional ends, and of the means selected for their attainment, is the measure of judgment in a functional system of law.

SUMMARY OF THE THESIS

The argument that has been developed in the preceding pages might be summarized as follows: The notion of function is a desirable criterion of legal order because it implies the possibility of an immanent evaluation of social reality, i.e., of an evaluation by the standards which inherently govern the shape of social conduct. To recognize these standards it is imperative to realize that social behavior of individuals is possible only by reference to specific transpersonal ends. These ends are not attributable to the desires of any single individual; they are both the envisaged result and the frame of reference of socially interrelated activity. They constitute the objective meaning, or function, of social relationships and institutions. Individual acts are a part of a relationship or an institution in so far as they are inherently directed toward its functional ends. Because of this common directedness toward the same ends, all acts forming part of a specific relationship or institution are coordinated in a structure of functional order. This structural context of individual acts implies standards of inherent rightfulness. They enable us to discriminate between what is functionally right and what is functionally wrong. Consequently functional law refers above all to the ends of social relationships, thus fostering in the individual a consciousness of the functional coordination of his conduct. It strives to bring about in individuals the inner orientation toward the ends of social relationships as such, by virtue of which individuals can immediately experience the immanent "fittingness" or "unfittingness" of their behavior. The ultimate criterion of value in functional law is to be found in the inner necessity by which, in a given cultural and historical situation, individuals empirically feel compelled to acknowledge certain social ends and to select the means thereto.

EPILOGUE: THE WAY OF ASCERTAINING IMMANENT STANDARDS OF VALUE

One final word is necessary about the way in which knowledge about the function of social contexts and the inner necessity of evaluation is to be obtained. It is scarcely necessary to repeat the truism that no "scientific" accuracy in the sense of physical measurement is possible in the study of social phenomena. Social reality is the realm of the "meaningful," and the proper approach to it is through "comprehension."[52] We cannot know anything about social reality unless we proceed on the basis of an understanding of the meaning of phenomena. The question of what is the function of an institution, a legal rule, a relationship, is the most essential one in all problems concerning things social, including problems of legal order.

But the essence of social phenomena is not exhaustively described by the ideal comprehension of their meaning. Social reality does not materialize in the sphere of the spirit, but in that of meaningful facts. Therefore, in all social reality ideal destination is intertwined with factual operation. The function

[52] Cf. Roscoe Pound, in 51 *Harvard Law Review*, p. 803.

of things social has two aspects: a conceivable task and an actual performance. Both aspects are inseparable in reality. When speaking of the function of an institution we refer just as much to the causal effects of its operation as to the idea of its end. For the ideal task is just as likely to be influenced by changes in the system of causal coordination as the other way round. Therefore the mere intuitive comprehension of functions must be accompanied by causal explanation.[53] The intuitive grasp of "what the function of *X* is," must be verified by an empirical investigation of "X(f)Y." The meaning of things social which we can ascertain immediately must be sustained by a study of the causal coordination which characterizes this function in the totality of social life. For a legal order the normative aspect of function is naturally the only relevant one. But the end which human consciousness experiences as the guiding motive of a social institution or relationship can be recognized only by analyzing the relationship of this function to other social phenomena. It is with this in mind that Hermann Heller says with respect to the state: "The meaning of the state can be found only in its social function, i.e. the task which the state has to perform as an operative unit in the operational structure of society. To understand this meaning is equivalent to explaining the state in terms of the coordinated totality in which it functions."[54] Therefore the criteria of functional standards of law cannot be found merely by looking for ideal meanings. We must also take into account the causal coordinatedness of institutions as factors in social reality. We are searching for the meaning of that actual performance which is the property of specific social relationships and institutions in a given totality of social life. The discovery of this meaning contains the key to a legal order based on immanent evaluation of social reality.

[53] F. S. Cohen, *op. cit.*, also pleads for a verification of value criteria by the findings of positive science, by which "we will have to learn how these . . . objects are related to the larger wholes that we seek to value" (p. 44).

[54] *Staatslehre*, p. 44: "*Der Sinn des Staates kann nur seine gesellschaftliche Funktion sein, also die Aufgabe, die er im gesellschaftlichen Wirkungszusammenhang als 'Faktor,' als Wirkungseinheit zu erfüllen hat. Diesen Sinn verstehen heisst aber nichts anderes, als den Staat aus dem gesellschaftlichen Gesamtzusammenhang, in dem er steht, zu 'erklären'.*" See also above, footnote 52.

CHAPTER VII

THE NOTION OF THE STATE

THE functional reorientation in legal theory, far from pretending to offer patent "solutions," is nothing more than a new way of forming conceptions about phenomena in the field of law and political reality. Concepts have to do with the general connections we discover between things. Obviously the criteria according to which we find phenomena to be connected depend on the fundamental orientation of our consciousness, and this again follows the pattern of culture by which our entire being and thinking are formed. Conversely, "the diversities in behavior and culture are the results of different interpretations of experience."[1] Thus there is a necessary connection between the concepts of a legal theory and the basic attitude of mind, the *Weltanschauung*, which is characteristic of a certain period of cultural history. Accordingly, when the issues of polemics in a field of theory have worn themselves out, when they become petrified in deadlocked discussion, it is no longer enough for scientific theory merely to criticize from within. It must go back to the most fundamental "tacit assumptions" underlying the issues, and, instead of criticizing one of the two sides in the different controversies, must seek the causes of their fruitless struggle in the original premises.

This is the situation of international law at present. The present theory of that law has apparently exhausted all the possibilities of development which were inherent in its philosophical foundations. It has gone as far as criticism from within could make it go. The discussion of theoretical questions has been moving in the same tracks for decades, the problems have become static, the ideas routine. In order to find the way to

[1] W. J. Thomas, *Primitive Behavior* (1937), p. 7.

new legal conceptions which are more appropriate to the changed social, political and cultural conditions of our time, we must criticize not any one of the theories adhered to within the framework of the present system, but the very foundations of all of them. We must trace their conceptions to the fundamental attitude, to the "tacit assumptions" out of which they grow; and change must be allowed to take place at the roots.

THE IDEA OF THE "SOCIETY OF NATIONS"

Practically all of the more important concepts in the present theory of international law center around the notion of a society formed by different national states. In almost every comprehensive treatise or textbook dealing with the subject this idea appears in the introductory chapter in a form of which the following statement of Brierly is more or less typical: "Law exists only in a society, and a society cannot exist without a system of law to regulate the relations of its members with one another. If, then, we speak of 'the law of nations' we are assuming that a society of nations exists. . . .[2] The following statement by Oppenheim is also typical: "A community may be said to be the body of a number of individuals more or less bound together through such common interests as create a constant and manifold intercourse between the single individuals. This definition of community covers not only a community of individual men, but also a community of individual communities, such as individual States. . . . The single States make altogether a body of States, a community of individual States."[3]

This notion of society is one of the most axiomatic concepts in the whole theory of international law. Its axiomatic character manifests itself in the fact that scarcely any author attempts to prove the assertion of the existence of a society of nations. Brierly even begs the question when he concludes that there must be a society of nations because there is a law of nations, and then proceeds to use the concept of society as a justifica-

[2] Brierly, *The Law of Nations*, 2nd ed. (1936), p. 34.

[3] Oppenheim, *International Law*, vol. I, 5th ed. The last sentence is borrowed from earlier editions.

tion of the social obligations of its members. Oppenheim simply asserts the fact by means of a definition; others confess that the idea of society is the starting point which in itself must be accepted as self-evident.[4]

Now the concept of an international society as used by these authors is not identical with the one employed in the course of this book. We spoke of Society in contradistinction to State, i.e. of unplanned, interindividual relationships as contrasted with the centrally organized cooperation directed by the State. The idea of society to which the above mentioned authors refer, however, connotes a "body" composed of individual units, a coherent group, a collectivity. A society thus conceived presupposes, on the one hand, "members," separate units whose very essence involves notions of self-sufficiency and separateness, and, on the other hand, a coherent whole having these units as its composing parts. In this sense, the international society is considered as a composite whole whose units are "independent" states.

Accordingly, the very idea of society as such, and so the idea of international society, embodies a paradox. Two incompatible elements are contained simultaneously in the same notion. On the one hand, international society is posited as involving the separate existence of many independent states side by side.[5] On the other hand, it postulates that these "separate" and "independent" units form a coherent whole, which by its very nature can only consist in mutual dependence and subordination of these units within the community. It is these two poles: individual existence and social cohesion, and the fact that they are both postulated in the concept of society now prevalent, which account for the contradictory theories characterizing present-day international law.

The reason for this is easy to see: By definition there can be no whole without parts, no society without individuals. The

[4] Such as, e.g., Westlake, *International Law* (1904), p. 7, also Chs. G. Fenwick, *International Law*, 2nd ed. (1934), p. 83.

[5] "Die Idee des Völkerrechts setzt die Absonderung vieler voneinander unabhängiger benachbarter Staaten voraus." Imm. Kant, *Complete Works* (ed. Vorländer), vol. VI, p. 147.

existence of individuals, on the other hand, cannot be imagined apart from individual interests and an individual will; apart, that is, from a program of values and actions the source of which is the individual *per se*. But no society can materialize without certain limitations on these individual interests and wills, and without, therefore, nullifying or negating—at least by implication—the very essence of the individual. In this way, a theoretical impasse is reached. Between these two incompatible poles to which it is committed by its conception of society, the theory of international law swings back and forth, moving restlessly between the two extremes, and never able to fix on one side or the other. Thus, the structure of its most basic assumption produces for international law a problem which by its very nature cannot be solved.

To legal theory this problem presents itself concretely in the question: By what formula can states "live" with each other in a sociable way? Since each state, by supposition, is a unit which exists "independently," i.e. by its own strength, with its own will, and on condition of its own interests, developing and growing according to its own dynamics, the problem is how to make so many individual "existents" compatible with each other. For the concern of each individual unit about its "existence" produces needs which are inspired only by the desire to exist and to grow individually.[6] These needs are called interests, and the interests of individual units, focused separately, are mutually exclusive or at any rate antagonistic. Coexistence in a sociable way, on the other hand, presupposes certain restrictions on the subjective will to self-assertion, and on the pursuit of their own interests by the different "member" units. Thus by virtue of the assumption with which it starts out, interna-

[6] "Dans toute société humaine, l'organisation de la justice répond à un besoin primordial, c'est à savoir à la satisfaction des intérêts individuels et collectifs." N. Politis, *La justice internationale* (1924), p. 1.

"L'Etat qui sort de son isolement . . . pose d'abord lui même la loi de ses rapports avec les autres Etats. Il se laisse inspirer par son seul intérêt, bien ou mal compris. Envers lui, les autres Etats tiennent une conduite semblable. Des conflits se manifestent entre les intérêts opposés. Se fait bientôt sentir la nécessité de concessions mutuelles. . . . Une loi, commune à plusieurs Etats, s'établit. . . ." Fauchille, *Traité de droit international public*, vol. I (1922), p. 8.

tional law becomes a permanent and never ending attempt to decide the undecidable issue between the interest of the particular state, or the individual "member" unit, and the standard of the collectivity. The rules of law represent the ceaseless endeavor to strike a balance between that restriction of the liberty of each particular unit, required if they are all to exist together, and sufficient freedom for each unit to exist individually. For this reason the problem of "existence" and whatever is required for existence, forms the core of discussion in international law.[7] It is back of every conflict, whether between the interests of two states, or between the interests of a state and a legal rule that stands in its way. It is even back of conflicts regarding particular legal rules to say nothing of the differences of opinion with respect to construction and of interpretation on broader issues. For all such differences spring ultimately from a discrepancy of opinion regarding certain key problems which themselves stem from the basic antinomy between a society and its individual members—such problems as:

Does the society "exist" for the individual members, or do the members exist for society?

Is the particular interest of each superior, in principle, to the collective interest, or does this latter take precedence in case of conflict?

Who shall determine what is due to every member and what is right according to the standard of the collectivity, in a "society" formed by "independent states"?

Thus in its very foundations, the present system of interna-

[7] "The community of States rested on the idea of a social pact freely entered into. Each state kept the liberty which it possessed naturally, except that portion of it which it had formally alienated in favor of the community. Like man in Jean Jacques Rousseau's theory of the social contract, the State possessed rights anterior to and superior to the society of which he was a member. These rights, called fundamental, were held to be absolute and inalienable without the formal consent of the one that possessed them. . . . This was a doctrine of pure individualism, in which the sole mission of international law was to reconcile the fundamental rights with each other." N. Politis, *The New Aspects of International Law* (1928), p. 11.

"Das geltende Völkerrecht geht von der Souveränität der Staaten aus, erkennt somit jedem Staate und dessen Interessen, welcher Art sie immer seien, unbedingten Wert zu." M. Huber, *Die soziologischen Grundlagen des Völkerrechts* (1928), p. 73.

tional law harbors insoluble antinomies: individual vs. community; nationalism vs. internationalism; isolationism vs. collectivism. The problems arising out of these antinomies can in themselves never be solved, just as little as those posed by the antinomy: Temporal Power vs. Spiritual Power in the Middle Ages, or by that of Capitalism and Socialism in modern times. Their historical function is essentially to express, in a manner comprehensible to the age which formulates them, the vital tension which they designate but cannot relax, and thus also to serve as stimuli to practical efforts toward higher and higher forms of social order. Their historical destiny, in other words, is not to be resolved, but to be replaced, once their stimulating quality has exhausted itself, by antinomies of a newer significance and more vitality. Thus the medieval issue between the Church and the Empire, for instance, has never been "settled," but it fails to stir us any more as a vital question. Similarly the antinomy between the State and the "Society of Nations", characteristic of the present system of international law and political thinking, cannot be solved, but will simply become insignificant in the light of a changed outlook.

THE PERSONIFICATION OF THE STATE

To discover the ultimate reasons why our political thinking moves between the poles of the antinomy described above, we must go still deeper in our search. The concept of society, which underlies the present conception of international law, was shown to be a paradoxical one. It was paradoxical because it embraced two mutually exclusive ideas: that of the "independent" existence of individual units, and that of the collective existence of all of them in a group. The present difficulty has its origin at this point, in the notion that society is composed of "individual", i.e. indivisible units. Therefore we must now inquire into the origin and the rationale of this idea. Society so viewed is a concept of Roman Law. Ever since Grotius, whose legal notions were derived almost exclusively from Roman sources, the concept of society has been used in this sense as the accepted starting point for all arguments. Now Roman law was essentially a system of private law, centering around the individual subject of law and his private rights.[8] One of the basic unit-concepts of Roman law was that of the *person*, while society was theoretically construed as an agreement made by "independent" persons to provide a basis for the adjudication of conflict between respective personal interests. Hence in applying the Roman conception of Society as a voluntary union, as they did to the union of states, it is clear that early students of international law could justify their procedure only on the assumption that the concept of *person*, as defined in Roman law, was fundamentally analogous to the State, conceived in relation with other states. Thus, a plurality of states dealing with each other voluntarily could be and was conceived as forming a society just as the voluntary combination of individuals for a common concern could also be so construed. Accordingly, it is the attribution to the state of the qualities peculiar to the private person as a legal subject which accounts for the resort to the Roman idea of society in international law.[9]

What, then, is the essence of this notion of *person*, and to what in detail can its application to the institution of the State be traced? Roman law was a law "for the single individual" because it appeared to the ancients that the "natural unit" was the individual man, that his existence was the basic fact of all social relationships, and that therefore, he and he alone could be the core of all legal rules. And *person* was the central notion of law because it seemed to be the central empirical phenomenon of community life. It is really thus the ancient idea about what constitutes "reality" which accounts for this selection of the natural individual as the cornerstone and ultimate end of the legal system. In accordance with the antique logic of science, which on the whole operated only with the

[8] See R. Sohm, *Institutionen*, 17th ed. (1924), §10. Also remember Ulpianus' famous definition of private law, which, according to him, "*ad singulorum utilitatem spectat.*"

[9] "Il a été possible de considérer les Etats comme les sujets du droit international seulement parce que nous les personnifions." Brierly, *Recueil des Cours de l'Académie de la Haye*, vol. 23, p. 526.

concept of *res*, the Roman idea of reality was one oriented by concreteness and compactness.[10] Only what physically existed, what was tangible, visible, perceptible, was real. According to this notion the only substances of any reality in the realm of social relationships were the bodily existing individual and the equally concrete tangible thing. Everything else—the less tangible phenomena of community, and social relationships such as cooperation, the phenomena of common standards and purposes—all had to be explained ultimately in terms of persons and objects.[11]

What the Romans, with their sense for material and compact substance, saw was the human being as a separate entity. Their attention being focused on the corporeal existence of things, individuals appeared to be nothing more than isolated and complete biological units. What they did not see, because it was not physically perceptible, was the connectedness between individuals, and thus they were led to explain all relations between men in terms of the will and interests of particular persons. Community and society became for them a mere function of those separate psycho-physical entities, while the problem of community itself was reduced to one of distributing private power among persons.[12] Thus the paramount question in this legal system is that of *to whom* the rights over things are due: *suum cuique tribuere*; a legal conflict is an issue between different subjective interests, claiming the power of personal enjoyment of certain objects; while the only question to which an answer is sought is: *whose* interests shall prevail, *whose* will

[10] "There is a certain materialism in a doctrine which knows only of relations between subjects and subjects, or between subjects and objects, but not between subjects and ideal ends." Feilchenfeld, *Völkerrechtspolitik als Wissenschaft* (1922), p. 113 (translation mine).

Feilchenfeld also speaks of "the modern theories which everywhere only want to see legal relations between human persons . . . and which are closely connected with the epoch of materialism, because materialism knows only of material bodies and the relations between them" (p. 121).

[11] Feilchenfeld, *op. cit.*, p. 117, characterizes the Roman style of legal thinking as one which "only knows of *dominus* and *res*, and of creditor and debtor, every legal relationship being conceived as a relation of domination, of power. The Romans had only bilateral legal relations: between the *dominus* and what he dominated, between the legal subject and the legal object."

[12] Sohm, *op. cit.*, §7.

shall be sanctioned? Thus in Roman law the separate existence, and accordingly the will, of the individual person was the fixed point around which all legal constructions revolved. Accordingly, the concept of the person in this system is one of a separate corporeal unit, an isolated entity of will, interests and power.

Only if the institution of the State is looked upon in a similar way, can the Roman legal concept of *person* be applied to it. If the features of physical substance and separateness, of independent will and power, of a "naturally" given unit of existence and interest, had not appeared to constitute the essential characteristics of the State, it would not have occurred to anyone to resort to the notion of human individuality in devising a legal formula to express the idea of the State. It is this way of looking at the State as primarily a substance having a separate physical existence of its own, which makes the personification of the State in international law not only possible, but actually inevitable. It is this standpoint from which the reality of international relations appears as a "society," a body composed of separate "individual" units, whose relations are merely a function of their physical existence and their subjective wills.[13]

It is easy to understand how this interpretation of the State and its relationships originated in modern times. When the modern State supplanted the medieval structure of personal bondage as a basis of political power, the essentially novel feature about it was the concentration of political power over a certain territory in the hands of a single authority. Not illogically, the absolute monarch himself came to be identified with the State, a process evident in such facts as the use of the name of the country itself as a designation of the monarch's person and in Louis XIV's celebrated phrase, *L'Etat c'est moi.* The identification of the State with the person who held the supreme power in it also received support from the patrimonial theory of public power and public office inherited from the Middle

[13] "In international law, as in private law, we are concerned with the 'persons' for whose sake rights are recognized." Holland, *Studies in International Law,* p. 152. This kind of substantival conception of the State has indeed prevailed from the period of Grotius to the present day.

Ages. In this way the physical singleness of an individual who visibly united in himself the supreme power and authority within a certain territory, much as a private person might represent a unit of control over a certain quantity of property, suggested the notion that the State was like a person. Thus when Gentilis proclaims: *principes bella gerunt*, it is evident that he regards the international society as being composed of rulers and it becomes clear by what logic the substantival conception of the State, as a psycho-physical unit of will and "natural" substance, entered into the theory of international law. For once this idea of the State was established, it became natural to apply the Roman legal concept of a person to it, and the corresponding notion of society to the plurality of existing states.[14]

This conceptual inheritance from antiquity and sixteenth century humanism still completely dominates present-day theory of international relations. For all purposes of legal construction, the state is regarded as essentially a unit of land, people and autonomous power[15]. In other words, we define the State by the marks of its external appearance,[16] just as if we were to define a fire brigade as "people in long helmets, riding in a car that is red and brass and makes plenty of noise". Thus it is by

[14] "The classical international law was a law governing men, . . . Its obligations were the obligations of personal sovereigns as individual men, and its rules were imposed on those sovereigns in their capacity as individual men." Roscoe Pound, "Philosophical Theory and International Law," *Bibliotheca Visseriana*, vol. I (1923), p. 76.

[15] "For example, the question of sovereignty over a portion of territory is decided by application of the rules of prescription; certain restrictions of territorial sovereignty are construed after the analogy of easements or servitudes in private law; recourse is had to private law rules of inheritance and succession for the purpose of determining certain rights and duties of States in cases of changes of sovereignty; the responsibility of States for international delinquencies is measured according to principles of private law. . . ." Lauterpacht, *Private Law Sources and Analogies in International Law* (1927), p. 3.

See also the definition of the State in the Convention of Montevideo (December 23, 1933): "The State as a person of international law should possess the following qualifications: (a) a permanent population; (b) a defined territory; (c) government, and (d) the capacity to enter into relations with the other states" (art. I).

[16] "Le droit de domination, les sujets et le territoire, telles sont les caractéristiques de l'Etat moderne; le droit international n'impose aucune recherche sur le point de savoir comment elles se sont réunies; il lui suffit de constater que les caractéristiques sont là et partant qu'il y a un nouvel Etat." Nys, *Le droit international* (1908), p. 69.

reference only to the tangible, and what are in effect merely auxiliary, features of a political organization that our legal concepts about it are constructed. Small wonder, then, if the State's material interests habitually get the better of voices enjoining obedience to international ideals!

It is true that this personalistic conception of the State has been criticized repeatedly and severely. But in spite of this, the theory of international law still seems to be, positively or negatively, dependent on it. The very authors who object to the conception, cannot, seemingly, avoid using it when they deal with practical questions. Thus, e.g., Brierly starts by arguing: "We have accepted a false idea of the state as a personality with a life and a will of its own, still living in a 'state of nature' which is contrasted with the 'political' state in which individual men have come to live. But it is a notion as false analytically as it admittedly is historically. The truth is that states are not persons, however convenient it may often be to personify them; they are merely institutions, that is to say, organizations, which men establish among themselves. . . ."[17] But in spite of this forthright rejection the author, throughout his treatise continually falls back on the use of substantival and psychological categories when dealing with the State. Thus he says: "A new state comes into existence when a community acquires . . . the essential characteristics of a state, namely an organized government and a defined territory. . . ."[18] From this definition of a state as a substance, having a separate corporeal existence and equipped with a will of its own, it is but a short step to the stage where it is personified. And this step Brierly in fact takes, for we find him treating, among other things, the problems of territorial sovereignty exactly as if they were questions of personal ownership and distribution of property.[19] In the same way, another severe critic of the substantival conception of the State, Hans Kelsen, also argues against the notion without overcoming it. While rightly reject-

[17] *The Law of Nations*, 2nd ed. (1936), p. 45.
[18] *ibid.*, p. 102.
[19] *ibid.*, p. 119.

ing the idea that a state represents the same sort of reality as a man,[20] he himself is so unable to escape from the grip of the idea that, rather than surrender it, he is driven to eliminate the State from his system altogether[21].

Thus the theory of international law continues to operate, however reluctantly, with a substantival notion of the State, conceiving it as a compact and individual entity having will and substance of its own, and referring to it mainly in terms of its "existence". In accordance with this fundamental approach, international law, as has been shown above, inevitably centers round problems of State interests and of the distribution of power and "property".[22] The main shortcomings of international law do not result so much from the weakness of its sanctions, but from the fact that the problems and conflicts it considers are essentially incapable of rational solution. And, if the analysis presented in the preceding pages is correct, there is no doubt but what it will continue to labor under this difficulty as long as reality is identified with the substantival and the sensually perceptible. It is this notion of reality which makes any social phenomenon intelligible only in terms of the person, thus leading to the paradox from which ultimately our difficulties arise[23]. It is the naturalistic notion of "reality" in things social which engenders the personalistic conception of the State, leading to its personification in legal theory, and to the atomic notion of society with its inherently contradictory structure.

NEW VIEWS OF THE NATURE OF REALITY

In recent years, however, a new notion of reality has gradually been emerging not only in scientific thinking, but also in art and other manifestations of contemporary culture. The idea that the material substance of things is the essence of their reality has been abandoned. It has given way to the notion that it

[20] *Juristischer und soziologischer Staatsbegriff* (1922), p. 3.

[21] See Hermann Heller, *Die Souveränität* (1927), p. 63.

[22] "The Law of nations is but private law 'writ large.' . . . In international law, as in private law we are concerned with the persons for whose sake rights are recognized; and with the 'protection' by which those rights are made effective." Holland, *Studies in International Law* (1898), p. 152.

[23] See page 290.

is the effect produced by things, the action peculiar to them in their specific connectedness with other entities, which constitutes reality in the proper sense. Thus, for instance, John Macmurray goes so far as to identify reality with significance.[24] The emphasis in our conception of reality is shifting from material individuation to functional connection. The idea certainly is not new,[25] but it is new within the realm of occidental thinking, dominated as it has been by the Greco-Roman substantival mode of thought.

The fact that in all fields of thinking the same tendency is noticeable, proves that there is now a general trend toward interpreting the world in terms of interconnection of operation rather than in terms of separate substantial units. Albert Einstein in physics, Claude Bernard in physiology, Alexis Carrel in biology, Frank Lloyd Wright in architecture, A. N. Whitehead in philosophy, Wolfgang Koehler in psychology, Theodor Litt in sociology, Hermann Heller in political science, Benjamin Cardozo in law: these are men representing different cultures, different countries, different aspects of human life and the human spirit, and yet all approaching their problems with a sense of "reality" which is looking not to material substance but to functional interaction for a comprehension of phenomena.

Thus when Frank Lloyd Wright sets out from the idea that the essence of a house is not its walls, ceilings and roof, but a formed space to be lived in,[26] he realizes that the "reality" which is visibly represented by the brickwork of a house is not confined to the limits of those walls. The house is not "really" something separate from the outdoor world, although materially it is set off sharply as a separate unit; indoor and outdoor space are "really" interconnected, namely by the functional use of

[24] *Freedom in the Modern World* (1934), pp. 118*f.*

[25] Twenty-five hundred years before our time, Lao Tse observed that the essence of reality was not to be found in the material, but in the immaterial aspect of things. In the eleventh chapter of the Tao he said: "There are thirty spokes in a wheel, but its utility lies in the hole of the hub. The potter forms the clay into jars, but their usefulness depends on the enclosed space. A carpenter builds the walls of a house and cuts out windows and doors, but the value of the house is measured by the space within the walls." The translation quoted is that of Bhikshu Wai-Tao and Dwight Goddard (1935).

[26] *The Architectural Forum,* January 1938.

space for living. Accordingly, the visible substance of the house ceases to limit its "existence." A house, viewed as functionally defined space, ceases to be a separate material entity. The walls are no longer the essence, but only a functional part of the total reality of living space. Thus reality in this view is no longer identical with the visible materialization of a unit, but rather with the non-material unity of functional destination. Corresponding with the shift of emphasis from the *reification* of phenomena to their functional *action*, it might be useful not to speak any more of *reality*, but of *actuality*.

Similarly, Alexis Carrel[27] and Theodor Litt[28] give evidence of this change in our conception of the reality of the individual. From the biological as well as from the socio-psychological aspect they prove that individuals are not like islands, connected with fellow islands by relationships which are merely regarded as accessories that can be added to, and withdrawn from, the substance of individuals at their will. It is now recognized that the individual is not a "unit" grown by himself and "possessed of a private 'soul,' 'mind' and 'will,'"[29] but that the very structure of the individual is shaped by interconnections and interactions without which no empirical human being can be conceived. It may, in fact, be misleading to speak of individuals, and it might be preferable to insist that a human being, instead of being "in-dividual," is really a synthesis of the most diverse interrelations.[30] Biologically as well as mentally we seem to be beings interwoven in manifold conjunctions which do not spring from our own will or our own impulses. An individual, according to the modern conception, is not constituted by the biological unity of his body, but actually lives in and through far wider conjunctions and ramifications.[31] The individual body and the individual "mind" are synthesizing factors within these differentiated interconnections, but they

[27] *Man The Unknown* (1935).

[28] *Individuum und Gemeinschaft* (3rd ed., 1926).

[29] R. S. Lynd, *Knowledge for What?* (1939), p. 153.

[30] See M. P. Follett, *The New State* (1918), p. 75. Also Bott-Bodenhausen, *Formatives und funktionales Recht*, who says: "Individuality, in a logical sense, is a synthesis of all the systems of reference" (pp. 24*f*.).

[31] Lynd, *Knowledge for What?*, p. 162.

do not represent the whole of an individual's existence. Thus today we no more conceive of the individual's material separateness as the essence of his reality than Frank Lloyd Wright sees the reality of a house in its stony substance. The psychophysical separateness of individuals is merely the substantial appearance of a partial aspect of individual human life. We have learned to seek the essence of reality in the non-apparent actual core of phenomena, abandoning the naturalistic concept of reality.

It is by means of this line of development that we are able to overcome that substantival conception of social institutions which inspires the notion of the State adhered now to in international law. Thus, for instance, Hermann Heller[32] has pointed out that a state "consists," not in a certain number of people plus certain "outside" factors like a defined territory and government, but in the actually coordinated behavior of individuals within territorial limits.[33] Thus the modern conception of the State does not see the essence of this, or of any other social institution, for that matter, in the material factors through which it becomes perceptible. A state is not made up by people, land and power, its physical substrata, but by the specific pattern of connectedness between these factors. The sum of the citizens plus territory plus an agency called government do not make a political institution; it is the non-material factor, that for which and through which these elements are held together in a structure of behavior, which constitutes the proper "reality" of the institution. The visible substratum of people, territory, material means of power, are merely what the façade is

[32] *Staatslehre* (1934).

[33] Similarly, Lynd, *op. cit.*, p. 67, speaks of the State not as a substantival entity, but as a structural form of culture, viz.:

"Structuring along geographic lines which bestows upon the citizen the right to vote if he chooses.

Structuring of a few highly selected functions such as lawmaking, taxation, policing, and the administration of such things as courts of justice, postoffices, national defense, and a public treasury.

Structuring of property rights.

Structuring of public education.

Structuring of the family to the extent of legalizing marriage, retarding divorce, and insisting upon the support of minor children."

to the house: the material which acquires meaning and sense only through the function it is destined to serve. Thus the "reality" of social institutions consists in the regular occurrence and recurrence of human actions coordinated according to a common plan. Therefore it is logical to say that the reality of institutions is to be found in their "actuality,"[34] this actuality being a planned form of connectedness in *actual* human conduct.

This new way of looking at things social makes possible new developments in the theory of international law. It has been shown above that the fundamental notion of society which dominates the present theory of international law, derives ultimately from a conception of "relationships" and "person" which was inspired by the assumption of essentially "independent" individuals. In accordance with this perspective, the separate "existence" of individuals was the root of all social relationships and the essence of society. It was the fundamental premise, the ground, and therefore also the end, of legal regulation. Against the background of this notion the criteria of interest, property, distribution of power and so on were the primary concern of the law.

Now we realize, however, that "the effort to build a separate science of 'social relationships as such' is barren. Social relationships do not exist as a separate datum, but only as a part of doing something. The attempt to view them as things apart is to lose sight of the only thing that can give them meaning. Institutions are the behavior of always and inevitably interrelated and interacting individuals."[35] Accordingly it becomes meaningless to oppose society to individuality, and to try to distribute power among particular and collective interests. If social relationships cannot be separated from individuals and individuals cannot be imagined apart from their interrelatedness, it is senseless to construe society as being "composed" of atom-like individual units, and to weigh the "existence" of these units against a supposedly different "existence" of society.

[34] Heller, *Staatslehre*, p. 99.
[35] Lynd, *op. cit.*, p. 154.

Consequently, the focus of attention is shifted from the problem of existence to the problem of function—to the questions, for what end, for the sake of what task, is individual behavior coordinated in this or in that structural aspect. The task of the law ceases to center round the insoluble conflict of interests, and is oriented toward the promotion of social functions. Thus, for instance, "Profound juristic insight into the essence of sovereignty can only result from a recognition of the specific social function of the State. A political theory whose positivism bars the extremely positive question of the meaning of the State can neither understand its own conception of the body politic, nor the absolutely unique function of the State in its full relevance."[36] Thus the new notion of the nature of social reality becomes the source of a new orientation foı legal thinking.

THE FORMATION OF FUNCTIONAL CONCEPTS

The new orientation of legal thinking becomes practical in the formation of new concepts about things, and these concepts in turn become the basis for a new line of action. What are the criteria and what the methods by means of which functional concepts are constructed? The important difference between the functional and what may be called the substantival approach is this: the latter begins by asking what is the *essence* of the different phenomena and aims at finding out the nature of their specific *existence* which is considered the core of reality, as was shown above.[37] The functional approach, on the other hand, focuses its attention not on the existential separateness of things, but on the functional connectedness of behavior.[38]

[36] Hermann Heller, *Die Souveränität.*

[37] "The fiction-theory is based on . . . the mistake of not asking simply what is prescribed, but of asking for the allegedly existing 'essence' of a legal phenomenon, as if every empirical phenomenon had a specific 'essence' of its own." Feilchenfeld, *Völkerrechtspolitik als Wissenschaft*, p. 114 (translation mine).

[38] In this context, the following report in *Time* (June 19, 1939) on psychological experiments conducted by Dr. Kurt Goldstein, leading world brain-specialist, is significant:

"Contrary to popular opinion, the brain does not grasp simple single objects first, but understands things only as parts of larger patterns. For example, certain patients who have brain injuries but who appear normal in their behavior, when handed a knife, are unable to give it a name. But when handed a knife with a potato, they promptly

Accordingly, instead of asking for the essence of observed phenomena, it starts out by asking what is the *functional action* peculiar to the observed interrelatedness of things, and it does this in order to detect the inherent *meaning*, or the objective effect which is the proper aim of a particular conjunction of living energies. In the legal sphere, the substantival approach regards the separate individuals as the basic units, the starting point of all relationships, and consequently forms legal concepts by reference to the "essence" of "the individual," to individual "existence" and its accessories: will and interest.[39] The physical separateness of individuals suggests, to the substantival mind, a natural "independence" of individuals which calls for the imputation of social relations to these individual elements as the "authors" of all collective phenomena. The functional approach, on the other hand, sees significance in the connectedness of human beings rather than in their singleness, and regards human existence as consisting of interrelations and interactions of individual energies, in structures determined by common ends. From this perspective, the conjunctive operation of human energies is the nature of social life.

Accordingly, social phenomena can be understood, described and analyzed only in terms of a transpersonal connectedness, by virtue of which alone human energies are socially relevant. It is the element of interrelatedness which is the key to the social meaning of individual behavior, not vice versa. Therefore the given experience, the focal point of social reality is not the single individual and his existence, but the different social contexts of individual behavior from which no particular element can be singled out without destroying the whole. It is because

---

cry: 'That's a potato peeler.' Other patients when shown a triangle and a square and asked to draw them, reply that they do not know what the abstract symbols are. But instead of a separate square and triangle they draw with facility a crude house, with a square body and a triangular roof." These results seem to indicate that it is more natural for human beings to grasp things-in-connectedness than things-in-separateness.

[39] "A further mistake was that people in general started out onesidedly either from the concept of the juristic or from the concept of the so-called natural person, and thus mostly construed the one after the analogy of the other, instead of starting out from a general . . . theory of legal relationships." Feilchenfeld, *op. cit.*, p. 113 (translation mine).

of the functional interdependence of the individual elements in these units of connectedness, making each single element a function of the others, that the approach to social phenomena from the angle of their connectedness rather than from that of their separateness is called the functional approach. A functional context is a unit of social life in so far as the unifying factor of an objective meaning governs the coordination of individual energies: by reference to this common element, they are socially effective and united in the directedness toward a transpersonal end. Thus it seems more sensible to accept the functional contexts of individual behavior as the basic units of social reality, than to assume that separate individuals constitute the "elements" of social life.

And this element of connectedness and coordinatedness between individual energies is, indeed, the only aspect of human life which makes legal conceptions and rules both necessary and feasible. For the "essence" of an individual, his "existence" as a separate and unique biological and psychological unit, is an experience which is accessible only to that individual himself, and is relevant only in his strictly personal sphere of integration. From the standpoint of his social environment the individual is "real" not in his integral unity, but in the differentiated aspect of specific social contexts through which his behavior is interrelated to that of other individuals. Thus John Smith, steelworker, member of the steelworkers' trade union, of the local bowling club, of a Masonic lodge, of a consumers' cooperative, voter, taxpayer, housekeeper, picture-goer, customer of many shops, etc., never appears in the integral totality of all these activities and experiences except to himself. As far as his part in social life goes, he is now the worker Smith, then the trade unionist, here the bowler, there the Mason, and then again member Number XX of the consumers' organization, etc.[40] In all of these respects his behavior is certainly deter-

[40] "A manufacturer of ferroconcrete who treats his wife badly, lies to his children, bullies the servants and cheats at cards, is not on that account placed in a disadvantageous position in regard to a building. A woman who is negligently run down by a motor-car is not prejudiced in her action because she has squandered her father's fortune, or ruined her husband's life." Robson, *Justice and Administrative Law* (1928), p. 197.

mined by his subjective "existence" as far as his ultimate motivations are concerned. But his behavior, and also his motivations for that matter, are relevant in a social sense and relevant to social order in so far as they are imputable to a transpersonal context of human conduct, to the meaning of a specific structure of interrelatedness. It is not the bowler Smith who attends the union meeting, it is not the Mason Smith who purchases a new washing machine. Smith is a social phenomenon only through his socially relevant behavior, and his behavior is socially relevant only in so far as it is inherently directed to some transpersonal effect.[41]

This is true even of transitory and occasional social connections. When two individuals "come together" to carry out a transaction, e.g. an economic exchange, it is this transpersonal meaning of their connectedness which determines their behavior. They do not tell each other their intimate viewpoints, or their self-centered motives, but they advise each other of the objective effect they hope to achieve through the coordination of their behavior. Even if they do reveal their personal interests, this communication is mainly irrelevant to what is going to take place between them; it does not essentially affect the meaning and the shape of the respective conduct which corresponds to each of them in bringing about the commonly realized end. Thus the "existence" of individuals is essentially a private concern[42]; it is neither the medium nor the origin of social reality.

Consequently it is only the transpersonal context of behavior as such that can be regulated, and it is only this functional connectedness of individual energies which needs to be regulated. The individual personality in his integrity is irrational and inaccessible from the point of view of legal order. The connectedness of human beings in itself is the subject of legal science and the criterion which guides the formation of legal concepts. Concepts of law are arrived at with a view to the objective effect for which a specific coordination of individual energies is meant. Legal decisions, whether in the legislative, or in the judicial

[41] See part II, Sociological Introduction.

[42] Cf. the role of the notion of "existence" in Sören Kierkegaard's philosophy, where everything is centered on the singleness and the uniqueness of individual personality.

stage, are made from the perspective of the *task*, or the functional end, to be attained by coordinate behavior. Consequently the question that is proper to the functional approach is not "*Who* shall get this?", but "*What* shall be done?", not "*Who* has a right?", but "*What* is right?", not "*To whom* is something due?", but "How can this or that *effect* be achieved?"[43]

Functional concepts are not symbols for the "nature of things", they do not refer to absolute "existents". They are formulas for a dynamic actuality, describing the coordination of its factors from the point of view of its meaningful end. They are formed in terms of tasks or effects, rather than in terms of substance.[44] In other words, functional conceptions are made by reference to performance, not by reference to essence. This way of looking at things is the *leitmotif* of the functional approach. It yields notions that are workable in social actuality, because they are conceived with a view to the working of social actuality. It is capable of leading to a rational order in social life—in so far as any such order is feasible—because it does not undertake the impossible task of reducing the irreducible subjective impulses of individuals to a "common denominator." Instead of vainly struggling to make irreconcilable interests compatible with each other, it provides rational formulas for the laws under which individual energies are interrelated in social behavior.

THE CONCEPT OF THE STATE IN INTERNATIONAL LAW

It is from this new perspective that the concepts of international law must be reformed if they are to be efficient instru-

[43] Feilchenfeld points out that the problem of the subject of law contains two completely separated problems: "The one problem is the question 'Who shall or may do something?', the other one is the question 'Toward what end shall an action, when it occurs, be directed?' " *op. cit.*, p. 117. "The first question in functional law is not 'Who is to be legislator?', but 'What shall be law?' ", p. 159.

[44] An identical piece of material substance, e.g., may be conceived differently in different functional contexts. Thus a board of a certain size, moving in hinges, will appear as a door when it operates in connection with a wall and an opening in it. The same board, when it is removed and placed horizontally on two supports, must be conceived as a table, when it is operating in connection with chairs and a tablecloth. The example is borrowed from Bott-Bodenhausen, *Formatives und funktionales Recht* (1926), p. 29.

ments in the order of international relations. The revision of legal concepts must necessarily begin with the notion of the State. The importance of an entirely new legal approach to the phenomenon of the State lies in the central significance of this notion for the existing system of international law. Only by overcoming that idea of the State which is the main pillar of the traditional theory of international law can we move forward to new and more appropriate legal standards. The concept of the State which underlies the present theoretical structure of international law results from the idea of the separate "existence" of the State and of the "essence" of this independence. Thus it is bound to center round the notion of sovereignty as the "essential" quality of an independant will, a separate "existent" or a supreme material power. The necessary consequence of these ideas is to conceive of international law as the free expression of that "independent" will. The theoretical and practical shortcomings of this way of looking at international law have been discussed throughout the chapters of this book.

To take the notion of separately existing states as the starting point means putting the cart before the horse, for from the standpoint of international law there is no need whatsoever for a concern with the single state's isolated "existence." It is not the separate existence of states that requires international rules and calls for international regulation: international law is needed in so far as there are problems of order and relationship transcending the single state, in so far as there is interrelatedness between nations. International law is concerned only with states-in-connectedness, not states-in-singleness; with states-in-operation, not states-in-existence. Accordingly, the conception of the State that is necessary and appropriate in the construction of international law must be one which centers round the functional operation of the state in international relations.

The substantival approach, seeking the "essence" of the State as a separate entity, and consequently compelled to conceive international "society" as "composed" of the different state-persons, looked upon people, territory and independent power as the features which make up the "individuality" of the

the State. From this viewpoint, the most significant feature of the State as the subject of international law was the separateness of its territory (conceived in analogy to private property),[45] and the capacity of its government to enforce a unitary will throughout its territory (construed in analogy with the individual's "independent" will). Using these notions, the rules of international law can indeed be construed only as mutual concessions between independent units of will, power and interest, as compromises between conflicting subjective standpoints. In other words, the substantival conception of the State necessarily conduces to a system of law based on the will of its subjects and depending entirely on that will's being "good".

Now the autonomous power, the defined territory, and the "body" of people are no doubt elements within the State. The question is, however, whether these elements are relevant from the standpoint of international law. It has been shown above that social reality is not equal to the sum of different individual persons, that the "existence" of the individual never enters in its integrity into the social picture. Social reality consisting of a functionally determined interrelatedness among individual energies, the relevance of the individual to his social order can be grasped only through the medium of the functional meaning of these contexts. In the same way international relationship is not a "creation" of the states' free wills. It is connectedness-in-social-life-transcending-state-boundaries, it is the interrelatedness of different states by virtue of common or mutual concerns resulting from the congruity of tasks they pursue. Thus international law cannot and should not attempt to reconcile the conflicting "interests" of states, because, on the one hand, interests are by their very nature irreconcilable, and because, on the other, international relations themselves consist of connectedness with a view to functional tasks, not with reference to subjective "interests."

It is not feasible within the framework of this mainly critical

[45] Thus Lauterpacht remarks: "The territory is construed as an *object* of the state's right. . . . The exclusiveness of enjoyment and disposition which is in law the main formal characteristic of both private property and territorial sovereignty." *Private Law Sources* etc., pp. 92, 95.

chapter to elaborate a complete theory of the legal subject in international law. Besides, the very notion of the subject seems to belong to the conceptual structure which we are on the point of abandoning because of its logical and practical inadequacy. Only indications can be given as to the lines along which the revision of legal concepts in that respect will have to take place. The premise of all further reasoning is that international relations are not made by states as independent and free "agents", but that international relations exist as a connectedness between states and result from the complexities and the ramifications of human culture and from the structuring function which states fulfill in this culture. International law is instrumental in introducing order in international relations. Therefore it has primarily to do with international relations as such, and with states only in so far as they are agents of international relationships and interstate contexts. Accordingly, the most central notion in functional international law is that of the functional end that determines the meaning and the character of the different relationships among states.

Here it is that a concept of the State as such is required in international law. For there is connectedness between states only by virtue of the function that states exercise in human culture. As soon as a specific field of social activity and social interrelatedness requires planning and coordinating agencies, the states acquire a regulatory function with regard to that aspect of culture. And if that function cannot be fully exercised by each state with its own organizational means because of the spatial extension of the problem, then states, by virtue of the functions inherent in them, become functionally interdependent and interrelated. Accordingly the key to the understanding of international relationships is the understanding of the cultural functions[46] of states in a given situation. A state is not a free "agent" or an independent "actor" for a state is an institution, and institutions operate according to their inherent functional meaning.[47] Institutions consist of structured individual be-

[46] For the concept of "cultural function" see pp. 267*ff*.
[47] See part II, Sociological Introduction.

havior, and individual behavior is structured by the functional meaning of the institution as it is understood and realized by individuals. Therefore the state, like any other organized unit, is active only in that sort of directedness which constitutes its cultural meaning. In that it is quite unlike the individual person.

Accordingly, the concept of the State that is needed in international law is essentially one of the functional meaning of that institution. In a formal way, this meaning has been defined by Hermann Heller as follows: "The function of the State consists of the autonomous organization and actualization of social cooperation within certain territorial limits."[48] Thus, in the most general way, it can be said that the organizational synchronization of culture, so far as organization of culture is necessary and feasible, and within certain spatial limits, is both the condition and the task of the State. The State functions by constantly producing and reproducing a comprehensive coordination of social activities, and at the same time its own being consists in that comprehensive organizational structure of social life. This immanent function of the State (the central organization of social cooperation to obtain certain unitary effects and actions required by the pattern of social existence) is therefore the necessary "motivation," or better, the inevitable "directedness" of all functional contexts between states. How much organization is required by a culture, and in what sense and in what form, will ultimately depend on the complexity of specific cultures: on their technological level, on the standard of living they produce, on the density of settlement and the pattern of existence of the people who live it. It is not the State itself which sets its own "purposes." The State as an institution merely performs tasks the necessity for which is embedded in the very pattern of the civilization. It is up to the State merely to provide the organizational form necessary for the realization of collective action among a plurality of concrete individual acts and energies. Thus the State is a unit of organized social energy which takes shape in the form of a centralized

[48] *Staatslehre* (1934), p. 203 (translation mine).

territorial order. In this role that unit of organization also functions in the international contexts of social life.

THE NOTION OF STATE TERRITORY IN INTERNATIONAL LAW

The concept of territory, together with the corresponding notion of boundaries between states, is intimately connected with the role of the State as the most central organization in social life. From all other organized institutions the State differs in that it is meant to bring about a comprehensive coordination of individual energies—as far as required—and consequently is necessarily superior to other institutions. The State is not so much the organization of any specific social undertaking as it is the organizational aspect of culture in general[49]. In order to function as a comprehensively coordinating agency the State must be the central organization of social life. There can be no "central" organization, however, without determining the area of which it is to be the center. And to operate as a central agency of coordination in that area the State must be supreme in organizational power and legal authority. Thus the notions of territory and sovereignty are closely connected. Sovereignty is merely the legal formula for the idea that the general synchronization of social life requires a unified scheme of planning by an organization which may potentially extend to all aspects of culture, and which therefore presupposes an organizing agency potentially superior in power to all other forces within the social area concerned.[50] The need for a comprehensive order of all social activities at a certain level of cultural development can be met only by centralizing the function of general coordination in an agency whose organizational competency is exclusive within its territory. The circumstance that social life in a certain area is structured in a scheme of order which is exclusively maintained and secured by a single central unit of organization —this circumstance is termed, in the language of the law, sovereignty.

[49] See part II, Sociological Introduction.

[50] "A governmental unit is by nature a monoply, and is thus not subject to the purifying influence of competition." L. Gulick, in: *Papers on the Science of Administration* (1937), p. 43.

The exclusiveness of the organizational function of a state in a certain territory is the origin of the problems connected with the delimitation of one state's organization from another. In the traditional system of legal theory, this question is dealt with under two distinct and independent headings: property and authority, territory proper and jurisdiction. Since in that system attention is focused primarily on the "existence" of the single state, it is concerned mainly with problems of distributing property and limiting power, as between the different nations. Viewed from the functional point of view, however, the problem is one of delimiting the area over which the planning organization of states functions regularly for the end of bringing about a unitary synchronization of social life. Instead of being regarded as property, the "realm" of the State is seen as the range of general social coordination which is organized from one common center of planned social order. Now organization is essentially a kind of stable structure of individual acts, an institutionalized scheme of behavior.[51] Accordingly, the delimitation of one organization from another can be conceived not only as a definition of exclusive competence in terms of space, but also in other ways allowing the imputation of individual acts to one or the other organization. Thus instead of circumscribing a section of the surface of the earth and thereby marking off the material "possessions" of an alleged state-person, the functional approach to the problem of boundaries looks at the actual extent of organizational centralization which characterizes the specific political unity of social life.

Organized structure does not only spread out in a territorial sense. Organization extends as far as individual acts are shaped according to its planned pattern. Thus the limits of organizational unity may be defined in terms of space ("acts occurring on a certain territory"), but also in terms of persons ("acts performed by certain persons") and in terms of function ("acts of a certain functional type, or acts meant for certain ends"). In each one of these dimensions: territorial, personal and functional, the sphere of competency of one organizational

[51] See part II, Sociological Introduction.

center may be delimited from the sphere of another, but the criteria of delimitation may be different not only in the various dimensions, but also in different respects within each of them. The general function of the State is the leading criterion in each particular case. The organizational requirements of the complex machinery into which modern culture has developed determine where and how individual acts should be governed by this or by that system of central organization, should be imputed to one state or to the other. Thus the "personal" dimension of a state's organized structure may be delimited differently from the territorial dimension, and the functional dimension may be defined apart from the other two.[52] Thus the notion of boundary ceases to be one of mere territorial circumscription. The State's boundaries extend just as far as the State's actual unity of planned social order is effective in the various dimensions of social reality. Boundary becomes a concept of juristic imputation, and the visible demarcation which is necessary for its recognition in daily life is a function not of property or possession but of organizational structure in social life.

THE DUAL ASPECT OF THE STATE'S FUNCTION

These considerations point to an element in the functional operation of the State which cannot be entirely reduced to terms of internationally intertwined functions even from the standpoint of international law. If it is the function of the State to secure a unitary structure of social order within a sector of the ecumene, the State will be bound by its own institutional "directedness" to pursue this end even through its international "contacts". In other words, the very function of the State seems to prevent the State from dedicating its activities to a specifically "international" end, to cooperating solely as a "functionary" in bringing about results which do not fall within the scope of its own unitary organization. The State, seen as a

[52] In this context it is interesting to remember that, during the winter of 1939-1940 plans were discussed among the statesmen of Europe which envisaged a post-war Europe with political boundaries which would be different from the economic boundaries.

factor of energy in international relations, will necessarily operate in the interest of its own maintenance and its own "reproduction", since that is part of its inherent function. Accordingly, the question arises: can the State be conceived at all as functionally bound in international contexts, under these circumstances? Can there be a function of the State's organizational energy which is determined not by a "national" but by an "transnational" task?

There certainly is a "substantive" element in this institutional concentration of the State's function upon its own perpetuation, a self-centered directedness which resists any attempt to conceive the State entirely, or mainly, in the role of an international co-functionary, even if the irrational categories of power, prestige, interest are disregarded. However, while it must not be overlooked that inherent in the institution of the State is the task of reproducing and maintaining itself as the condition of a unitary social structure, it is futile and entirely inappropriate from the point of view of international law to define this irreducible "substance" in the operation of the State as an irrational "will for power", or as an equally irrational "self-interest". Such definitions would completely bar the way to an understanding and a legal regulation of this aspect of the State which resists any definition in terms of international relevance. Interest is not a legal, but a psychological category, and simply is not amenable to legal arguments and conceptions. From the legal standpoint, the State is only comprehensible as a functionally determined institution, a specific structure of organized co-ordination. Its operation and its action can be reduced to legally manageable terms only by reference to this functional meaning. Accordingly, it is here that the key to our problem must be sought.

In this sense the "irreducible substance" in the operation of the State is not irrational subjectivism but a partial aspect of its function in human culture. Modern civilization requires organization of many concrete activities of human beings, but at the same time it requires a comprehensive and unitary framework of order which can be secured only by a supreme central organization. The State exercises both kinds of function. On the one hand it is dedicated to the organization of concrete tasks, relationships, and services; on the other hand it operates as the medium of a comprehensive synchronization of social life. It provides for education, it sets up a scheme of social security insurance, it maintains and protects waterways, it undertakes the "business" of postal communication etc. Simultaneously with serving thus as an agency of cooperation toward some definite common ends, it procures the incorporation of all of these special undertakings into the entire structure of social order, to secure the comprehensive coordination of the whole. However, this all-embracing coordination takes shape only through the organization and regulation of specific types of social co-activity.

Thus the function of the State is dialectically split into a duality of effects. And this dialectic duality in the function of the State also determines the respective role played by the State in international contexts. While acting in functional interdependence with other states for the end of achieving specific organizational tasks, which can only be attained through interstate cooperation, it is at the same time functionally tied to the requirement of maintaining its own structural unity. In this dialectic duality the State's function merely mirrors the ramifications of social life itself. For the various individual activities and interrelations with which international law is concerned have the same dual relevance: they are embedded in local conditions as well as intertwined with international circumstances. Being nothing more than the central organization of social order in general, the State, though functionally involved in international conjunctions, is nevertheless concerned with the unity of coordination in its own domain of organizational effectiveness. And while functioning as the central organization which secures the ultimate cooperation of all social activities it is necessarily concerned with tasks of international extension also.

At this point the question arises: What criterion marks the difference between these two aspects of the political function? By virtue of what circumstances are states functionally interdependent on one another? What aspect of the State's operation is internationally relevant? These questions, also, can be answered only by referring back to the functional meaning of the State as a cultural institution. International interrelatedness of states is a consequence of the state's function in organizing social cooperation. States, constituting the organized unity of social reality, are concerned with the pursuit of numerous ends which are realized in interdependence with factors outside the orbit of each single state. The question as to what aspects of the social system are functionally interconnected with social activities and political order in other states can be answered only with a view to the concrete, particular circumstances involved. The structure of civilization which determines the various functional ends of the State also accounts for the necessities of international coordination or cooperation, the organization of which accordingly becomes a functional task incumbent on the states concerned. In this sense, order in international relations constitutes a direct fulfillment of the functions of the State. International connectedness is inherent in the institutional structure of the State in so far as the conditions of social life in each state depend on outside factors. It is one of the tasks proper to states to secure a planned structure of order in social relationships, and if social relationships transcend the range of a single state-organization, the function of structuring becomes the task of a plurality of states. Thus we arrive at the conclusion that, contrary to the assumption of traditional thinking, it is the function of the State proper, not the idea of a "society" of any kind, that requires a structure of order in international relations. International law and order is just an extension of that coordination of all social activities which states are destined to secure. The need for international law arises in the State, it emerges together with the institutional function of the State, not in contraposition to the State or as a denial of its functional operation.

Thus the State, by reason of its inherent meaning, is functionally involved in the solution of international tasks of a kind that is determined by its own function in human culture. While these "international" tasks of organizing social order are essentially the same as those discharged by the State within its own realm, they differ from the latter in that they can be solved only in combination with other states. The exclusiveness of one single organization cannot be maintained in these transnational aspects of human culture for the simple reason that no organization happens to exist, that is large enough to regulate them by its own means. As regards this particular kind of task, a solution is not possible through the means of one central and supreme organization, but only through a functional coordination of several organizational centers. Accordingly, the State's exclusiveness, i.e. its sovereignty, is modified in the sense that the discharging of its institutional functions in many respects is not possible on the basis of complete organizational centralization, and through the instrument of a supreme unit of organization. Thus the sovereignty of the State, its exclusiveness in the function of structuring social relationships comprehensively, also participates in the dialectic duality which is proper to the State's function. To the same degree to which the exclusiveness of a single organizational unit fails to cover the organizational requirements of human culture, the function of social order is one which devolves upon two or more states in common. In these respects, the exclusive competence of the different political organizations is suspended to the extent to which the task of establishing social order calls for the cooperation of several of them.

Sovereignty, accordingly, has a dual aspect. The term connotes the supremacy of that organization which is meant to secure the ultimate coordination of all other institutions and activities in social reality. As far as this function can be exercised only in coordination with other states the organizational supremacy of the State is bound by the laws of interstate functional cooperation to serve certain ends which are internationally relevant. In so far as the function of the State concerns ends falling entirely within its own range of action, its energy is bound only by its own functional laws. This does not mean that there are two sovereignties, one national and one international, nor does it mean that there should be two notions of the State, one regarding its international function and one its national one. The two aspects are merely two ways of looking at the same picture. The State functions as the organization of unity in social coordination. This organization operates now in exclusiveness, now in coordinatedness. In so far as the State is organizing internationally intertwined relationships, its sovereignty is comprehensive-organization-in-coordination, supreme but functionally bound to cooperate, unitary but conjunctive in its operation. Its proper operation involves coordinatedness, its organizational sovereignty appears here as supremacy-in-conjunction. On the other hand the State is free from such international ties where its action is concerned merely with cooperative unity within its direct social range. From the point of view of international law, the organizational energy of the State is not subject to laws of coordination in so far as it is concerned with the unity of social activities that fall entirely within its orbit, but it is subject to such laws in so far as it is concerned with the order of social relations transcending its immediate sphere of action.

Against this background the notion of *domaine reservé* appears in a new light. According to traditional concepts, *domaine reservé* connotes a field of affairs which are *taboo* to international law because they are so charged with political tension and national self-interest that states are "not ready" to submit them to legal judgment and legal rules, preferring to put their trust in power and prestige. Looked at from the functional point of view, there is no matter, no field, no complex of "interests" which pertains as such to the "domestic" sphere of the individual states. Potentially everything can be of "international relevance".[53] Whether or not something actually is relevant from the international viewpoint depends entirely on the ramifications of social relationships, the existing links of cultural dependence, and the respective organizational tasks of the various states. The question is not: which matters should be excluded from the authority of international law. It is: what functional ends can be attained by the action of one single political organization, and what functional tasks can be solved only by the cooperation of several states? Thus "domestic" and "international" are categories not measured by "interests," and not referring to different classes of affairs, but to different functional aspects of political organization in respect to all "affairs". It is obvious that the effect of comprehensive unity in social life can be achieved only by the exclusive action of one single organizational unit. This type of efficacy therefore is necessarily one which appertains to the "internal" sphere of every single state. No interstate coordination can facilitate this task, no combination of efforts between states can produce this particular effect. On the contrary, the attainment of this effect would be jeopardized if one single organization did not coordinate all social life in supreme exclusiveness. In so far as the action of the State is directed toward this functional end of the unity of all social life, it is of "domestic" concern, because the unity of social order is essentially the product of the exclusive operation of one single political organization.

But, on the other hand, the State functions not only in the service of the unity of all social structure, but also in the service of specific common "undertakings"[54]. It may be that the same "affair" is relevant from the point of view of both of these functional aspects. In respect to the identical matter, the State may operate as a collective agency for the attainment of

[53] The Permanent Court of International Justice has pointed out, in its decision on the question of Tunisian and Moroccan nationality (Series B, Nr. 4), that no absolute line can be drawn between what belongs to the jurisdiction of the State and what to the jurisdiction of international law, the question being an essentially relative one.

[54] See page 317.

certain practical ends, and at the same time as the agency of a comprehensive and unitary social order. Therefore the same "matter" can be relevant both from the viewpoint of "domestic" regulation and from that of interstate coordination. In other words, there are no such things as "domestic affairs" and "international affairs." The "domestic" or "international" relevance is not inherent in affairs or matters as such. The criterion of difference between the two categories lies in the functional objective toward which the operation of the State is directed. Directedness of the State's functioning toward the end of unity in social order calls for the exclusive action of the State as a single central organization; directedness of the State's functioning toward the organization of certain definite and concrete common action may call for coordination with the energies of other states if the problem is of international extension. While the function of securing the unity of social life is necessarily the task of each single state within its range of action, the function of arranging for the practical solution of certain social problems is possibly a task belonging to a plurality of states.[55] Thus not a certain group of affairs but a certain function with respect to social order is reserved to the single state. It is reserved not as a matter of honor, prestige or national "interest," but because this particular cultural function is by its very nature one that can only be exercized by the exclusive action of a single central organization. Accordingly, *domaine reservé* is not at all a domain, but a specific type of efficacy pertaining to political organization, conceived in contradistinction not to a different class of matters, but to a different functional effect which is also peculiar to the institution of the State. One of these functions can be exercised only by the exclusive action of central organization, the other only by coordination of different organizational centers: it is along this line that international law is separated from the "internal" aspects of states.

[55] See the discussion of this problem by Alexander Hamilton in No. XV of the *Federalist.*

INTERNATIONAL LAW AS THE WAY OF FULFILLMENT OF POLITICAL FUNCTIONS

It is obvious that from the functional point of view the classical antinomy between state interests and international standards becomes insignificant. If the substantival concept of the State is abandoned, if the State is seen as an institution governed by its inherent functional meaning, then it is more logical to impute the actions of the state to the functional ends for which they are instituted in human culture than to irrational interests and desires. If states exist by reason of the function they perform then they are not possessed with a free will and an independent status. Institutions follow the laws of inherent functional necessity. Thus it is senseless to construe a conflict between the "will of the State" and certain norms of conduct, as if the will of an institution had any tendency to be normless and arbitrary. If the essence of international relationships is seen in the element of connectedness inherent in the very structure of the different states, then it is unwarranted to speak of a "society of nations" which is "composed" of independent units, and in which the interests of the single "member" are in conflict with the "collective" interest. All of these antitheses: that between the individual will and the common standard, that between desire and duty, that between individual and society, become irrelevant in international law as seen from the functional perspective.

The functional approach, however, does not mean that there can be no conflict between lawfulness and lawlessness. It does not mean a denial of the fact that there is arbitrariness in the operation of institutions as well as in the actions of individual men. However, the conflict between lawfulness and lawlessness does not take place as between the State and an alleged "society of nations". The functional approach transfers this conflict into the very structure of the State itself. International law, if functionally conceived, is the condition of coordination through which states can fulfill certain aspects of their functions. Now it is possible that individual persons use state power arbitrarily and not according to the laws of functional necessity. Functional frustration is the consequence. Lawlessness, or rather arbitrariness, amounts to inefficacy from the institutional point of view of the State; lawfulness, or the inherent necessity of functional action, means efficacy in the discharge of political functions. The antithesis is one between irrational, arbitrary desires, and the inner necessity of orderly behavior, between arbitrary conduct of individuals in the institutional framework of the State and a mold of conduct shaped after the immanent laws governing the functional structure of the State. As far as the inner necessity of its own functional laws governs individual acts within states the State will fulfill its task of merging individual energies into cooperative creativeness.

Consequently the antinomy between order and disorder no longer appears as an antithesis between the state and international law, but as one between irrational power and functional necessity within the structure of the State, between the State as an accidental accumulation of blind forces and the State as a structure of social cooperation. The problem thus arises not between the State and "the world," but between the possibilities of lawful and of arbitrary actualization of energies in the State itself.

This notion corresponds to the idea of a system of international law conceived in accordance with political institutions and political functions, as postulated at the end of the second part of this book. It construes law not as a rule devised apart from reality and consequently antagonistic to reality, but as the immanent necessity in reality itself. Just as decency, for example, is a mold of personality inherent in the "structure" of an individual, and not a mere external postulate to which that person's will is or is not adjusted, so international law, conceived as functional necessity, is a mold of the functional institution of the State. It is functionally necessary in so far as it is in accordance with the laws of cooperation and coordination by virtue of which the institution of the State operates. Achieving the lawfulness of the actual operation of the State means fulfilling the destiny of the State. Thus international law ceases to be a regulative system based on the restriction of political institutions and becomes a way of fulfillment of their functional ends. Functionally conceived, international law does not impose itself through the authority of a moral command but through the force of immanent necessity.

CHAPTER VIII

THE CONCEPTION OF THE LEGAL RULE

"IUS EST QUOD IUSSUM EST"

THE traditional but still prevailing theory of international law conceives of legal rules as commands prescribing a certain conduct to the members of the "International Community." Oppenheim is as representative of this idea as any other writer, positivist or non-positivist, would be, when he defines law as "a body of rules for human conduct within a community which by common consent of this community shall be enforced by external power"[1]. The same concept is to be found in Hall's formulation: "International law consists in certain rules of conduct which . . . states regard as being binding on them in their relations with one another with force comparable in nature and degree to that binding the conscientious person to obey the laws of his country, and which they also regard as being enforceable in case of infringement. . . . The only fundamental distinction, it is said, which separates legal from moral rules, is that the former are . . . commands given and enforced by a determinate authority."[2] Again, Brierly speaks of "rules and principles of action which are binding upon civilized states in their relation with one another,"[3] Charles Cheney Hyde regards international law as "common rules of restraint . . governing their [the states'] mutual relations."[4] Le Fur, finally, uses the term "law" as connoting "a rule imposed by an organized society on its members."[5]

[1] *International Law*, vol. I (4th ed. 1928), p. 9.
[2] Hall-Pearce Higgins, *International Law* (8th ed. 1924), p. 1.
[3] Brierly, *The Law of Nations*, p. 1.
[4] Chs. Cheney Hyde, *International Law* (1922).
[5] *Précis de droit international public* (2nd ed. 1933), p. 156.

In all these and other definitions the common element is the dualism between the law on the one hand and the conduct it is supposed to regulate on the other. Legal rules are conceived in contradistinction to the facts of reality; they are standards "imposed on the particular members by an organized society". Reality and Ideality, actual conduct and normative law are pictured as antagonistic forces: the law trying to keep the forces of reality within the confines of prescribed standards; dynamic reality attempting to free itself from legal restrictions and to escape into unbridled liberty of action. The law and reality are conceived apart from each other: legal rules can be imagined apart from the conduct which is, or ought to be, determined by them; the reality of social existence and social behavior can be visualized apart from the action of legal rules. Accordingly, the conception of legal rules is that of formulas written or unwritten, which prescribe a certain behavior. The existence of such rules is conceived independently of whether "reality" conforms to the prescription or not. A legal rule "exists," according to the prevailing theory, as soon as it is evident that some authority bids us behave in a certain way, as soon as an ideal postulate has been formulated as a precise command. The declaration of will as such, the prescribing formula in itself is considered to be the legal rule: *ius est quod iussum est.*

At this point numerous authors on international law will object that this is a confusion between the views of one particular school of thought with other definitions of the law. They will claim that our assertion is true as far as the voluntaristic theory of Austinian and Continental positivists is concerned, but that it is refuted by the adherence of the great majority of authors to some theory of consent. Construing the legal rule in international law as a product of free consent between the nations seems to be directly opposed to any conception of the legal rule as a command. It is submitted here, however, that within the present philosophical framework of legal thinking, the legal rule is actually construed as a command not only by the voluntaristic, but also by all other schools of legal thought. Although the tracing of every legal rule to the command of some authoritative will may not be admitted, although it may even be subconscious in some theorists, it is nevertheless implied in the very foundations of our present legal philosophy.

It is the theoretical starting point of our legal thinking which ultimately compels us to regard legal rules as commands. In the preceding chapter it has been shown that the notion of the individual subject forms the basis, and also the nucleus, of the prevailing legal theory. The very assumption that social reality is composed of individual subjects who in themselves constitute the irreducible core of reality, implies the idea of an "original" liberty of those subjects. One cannot visualize individual subjects as such without endowing them with a freely initiating will bent upon the satisfaction of individual interests. To borrow a remark of R. S. Lynd: "Present-day thinking is still heavily influenced by the folkways of an earlier era when it was common to think of the individual as an entity apart from society. This was dictated by the view of the individual as one possessed of a private 'soul,' 'mind,' and 'will.' Thus endowed, he was independent, deriving his motivation from within himself through esoteric, rational, hedonistic processes; and when he learned something from the world about him, or when he acted as a member of a group, these things were acts of rational choice of a different order from the isolated integrity of his life as an 'individual.' "[6] This "isolated integrity of his life as an individual", the separate "existence" of the individual subject was held to be the center of dynamics of the legal order. "Pas d'intérêt, pas d'action" is the inimitable formula with which Professor Scelle has characterized the "subjectivistic" orientation of our legal structure. Accordingly the whole of our legal thinking is built upon the assumption of "independent, self-starting willers and doers,"[7] whose will is essentially free to make its choice between all possible courses of action. Without this assumption of the subject's intrinsic

[6] *Knowledge for What?* (1939), p. 153.
[7] *ibid.*

liberty, there is no sense in centering the structure of law around the notion of the subject. Thus the starting point of traditional legal theory is the premise that the subject's individual existence is the essence of social reality, that the subject's interests are the source of his motives, and that the subject's free will is the dynamic force which moves and changes all things social.

On the basis of the assumption that in the center of reality there exists the subject's free will deciding independently between various ways of action, the main problem of a legal order must be conceived as that of erecting such barriers against the free use of that will as will prevent individual subjects from acting to the detriment of their fellow-subjects. Thus a law which centers around the notion of the individual subject necessarily has to be a system of restrictions, of prohibitions, prescribing certain ways of behavior and forbidding others. It can be realized only as an antithetic dualism between the "real" forces of life (held to be essentially unbridled and unrestrained), and the "ideal" rules of conduct (essentially visualized as limitations upon this "original" freedom). Law against this background is only a formula of what ought to be, while the unrestricted forces of will and impulse constitute what is. Upon this essentially disorderly reality law works by imposing the standards of common existence, telling the individual subject: Do this! Do not do that! In other words, the law consists in commands restricting the original freedom of subjective will to certain objective limitations. This is the meaning of the term "binding rules", a notion which will seldom be missing from a treatise on international law. The idea of binding rules presupposes on one side the idea of the original liberty of the subject, because there is no sense in binding that which is not free. On the other hand it indicates that what is to be bound is the free will of the subjects, for conscience, lacking freedom in itself, cannot be bound, and consciousness can only be made to recognize, but does not respond to any sort of authoritative limitations. Thus we arrive at the conclusion that law, if theoretically centering around the notion of the individual subject, is conceived as a set of rules imposing restrictions on the subject's will, in other words: as a body of commands.

But is a command the only conceivable form of restriction upon an originally free will? Is not the assumption of the essential independence of the subject compatible with principles of order which are not authoritatively imposed? Obviously, rules of lawful conduct may emanate from the subject's own conscience. Cannot the behavior of a subject be governed by these rules and thus be restricted without being under the compulsion of a command? There are two fallacies in this seemingly convincing argument. On the one hand, the assumption of an original liberty of the individual will forces us to conceive even the rule of conscience as a command issued from the individual's "super-ego" to the individual's will. Thus Kant clearly characterized the rule of conscience as an authoritative order by calling it the Categorical *Imperative.* On the other hand nobody would maintain that the command which emanates from every individual subject's own conscience is sufficient to maintain legal order in social relationships. Legal rules are rules which are not submitted to the judgment of every individual's conscience. Conscience may bid individuals to obey legal rules, but the rules of law as such emanate from a source "outside" the subject's own individuality. This source must necessarily be conceived as a unit of will, and the prescriptions emanating from it, as commands. The reasons for this are as follows:

Any order addressed to human wills "from without" must be understandable by the subject in order to produce an effect on the subject's will. In order to be understood, a prescription must be sufficiently precise and concrete. Now it is true that norms of conduct are sometimes expressed in very general terms. However, effective restriction upon individual will can be exercised only by a definite formulation of what should be done and what should not be done. A formula like "Thou shalt not kill!" is too ambiguous to provide for those limitations of free human wills which are necessary for common existence, for it leaves open the question of killing in war, in self-defense etc., not to speak of the complicated problem of negligence. Any command requires a concrete decision regarding the various possibilities contained in a situation or in a general principle. There must be a concise specification of *do's* and *don't's* by which the wills of individual subjects can be ordered to abide. "All rational order comes into existence and is maintained by a unification of wills. This unification of two or more wills is necessary for every single rule of order as well as for the entire body of rules. For order is only possible in accordance with a single determinate standard, i.e. every rule of conduct has to prescribe implicitly or explicitly that a certain man in a certain situation shall behave in a certain way."[8]

A decision, however, can be made only by a will or a unit of will. For this reason, the necessary concreteness and "decidedness" of every command addressed to supposedly free human wills presupposes a will from which the precise formula or legal rule can issue. It is impossible to imagine a command without imagining also the will from which it flows.[9] Consequently, if the fundamental assumption of the original independence of the legal subject forces us to construe the legal rule as a command, it also forces us to impute the command to some unit of will that issues it. Only two kinds of rule binding supposedly free wills are conceivable: either it can be a rule of conscience or it can be a rule prescribed by the authority of another will. Both are essentially commands. The command emanating from conscience is called ethics, the command emanating from the authority of another will is called law.

[8] Hermann Heller, *Die Souveränität* (1927), p. 37.

[9] In this context, it is interesting to read Nietzsche's remarks about the general tendency to attribute every doing to a doer, every action to an actor. He maintains that this is a fundamental error implied in the structure of our language. In reality, he says, there is no "existence" behind an action, a deed or a growth; the "doer" is only a fictitious being which our imagination adds to the "doing": in reality there is nothing but "doing." *Genealogy of Morality*, I, 13.

This recalls Thurman Arnold's words: "Law represents the belief that there must be something behind and above the government without which it cannot have permanence and respect." *Symbols of Government* (1935), p. 44. One might reverse these words and say: "There must be something behind and above international law without which it cannot have permanence and respect," which would explain the theories about a legislative will in international law.

This logical structure is inherent even in the present-day theory of international law in spite of all pretenses to the contrary. To base international law on the consent of states does not mean to deny that its rules are commands issuing from a unit of will outside of the legal subject. It means only that this unit of will is constituted by the coincident wills of two or more governments. The theoretical construction of the notion of the legal rule is not affected by the circumstance that the will to which the legal command is attributed is a fictitious one. For the theoretical system of international law it makes no difference whether the law-issuing will is located in the State, a combination of agreeing states, in the "International Community", in "Nature" or in God. For whether the will behind the law is real or imagined, the problems and difficulties arising out of this construction are essentially the same. Therefore it is sufficient to state, at this point, that the conception of the legal rule as a command, and the imputation of that command to an authoritative will, are not specific features of the voluntaristic school of thought, but are integral elements of all schools within the prevailing theoretical framework of international law.

RIGHT AND MIGHT

What is it that lends to the prescriptions of a commanding will the force of binding rules? It might be argued that these commands encounter obedience on the part of the subjects because it is felt that such rules are reasonable, good and useful. Accordingly one might conclude that it is the persuasive force of the subject's own interest and conscience which bends the subject's will to lawful behavior. It is indeed true that every legal rule has to rely to a large degree on the support of those psychological forces which are known to be potent factors in human decisions. But is a legal rule only legal when it coincides with people's moral standards or common purposes? Moreover, are there not always conflicting notions of moral norms and of common intentions among the subjects of a legal order? And if that is so, what accounts for the binding force of legal rules upon those with whose aims or beliefs the rules do not happen to coincide? Finally: If a legal rule is binding only because it meets with our moral approval and serves our well understood (enlightened) self-interests, why should the capacity to issue those rules be reserved to one particular unit of will? Why could there not be competition among various units of will for the devising of the rules that best reflect people's moral standards and common purposes, with the people acting as the final judge as to which is the best rule of law? It seems that these questions cannot be answered satisfactorily by those who hold that the moral sense and the enlightened self-interest of the subjects causes them to accept legal commands as binding rules. The quality of law attaches to a command not only because of its conformity with certain principles, standards and aims, but also because it is the prescription of a unit of will *to which a specific qualification for law-giving is attributed.*[9a] It is the believed and accepted superiority of the commanding will which lends to its prescriptions that binding force which is the characteristic of law. Whence does the commanding will derive its superiority?

The simplest way of giving one will a strength superior to other wills is that of physical coercion. It can be directly applied or its application can be merely threatened. In the latter case the binding influence of the commanding will over the obeying will is achieved by fear. Fear is also the most important factor when the commands of a certain will are accepted as obligatory because of that will's connection with supernatural forces. This is the case with the priest or with the man whose successes give the impression of miracles (cf. Max Weber's notion of the *charisma*). But instead of religious awe or superstition, other emotional forces of an equally compelling strength may cause people to accept a certain will as superior to their own, e.g. deep-rooted beliefs, prejudices or fundamental ideals.

[9a] "An imperative theory, thinking of law as a body of laws established by a sovereign, excluded criticism and led lawmakers and courts to feel that the words 'Be it enacted' and 'It is considered and adjudged' justified whatever followed." R. Pound, "Fifty Years of Jurisprudence," 51 *Harvard Law Review*, p. 445.

There is only a difference of degree, not of kind, between accepting the superiority of a certain will by virtue of its supernatural qualities, and bowing to a unit of will by virtue of a social or political philosophy. It is no more irrational to look upon the will of the medicine man as a specially qualified and therefore binding one, than it is to consider the will of the majority as inherently superior. Fundamentally in both cases it is the compelling might of one will (or unit of will) which is taken for granted and which gives this will a force capable of binding "ordinary" wills. Undoubtedly the will of the majority owes its obligatory force largely to the myth that greater numbers also represent greater power, a myth which makes majority rule a device particularly fitting to the mentality of periods in which quantitative thinking is the general habit.

In its more subtle forms, the superiority of a particular unit of will does not depend on the possibility of physical coercion. The subjection of the obeyer's will is produced by his own conviction that the command issues from a will of superior force, whether this belief corresponds to actual facts or not. Thus the capacity of a unit of will to issue binding commands resides in the readiness of the subjects to be impressed by it, not in the possession of certain material instruments of force. The disposition to obey is produced by anything that will create the impression of the commanding will's inherent superiority, provided that impression is constantly working, as a subduing force, upon the subject's will. This acknowledged superiority of a will, which is accepted irrespectively of the prospects of physical compulsion, is called authority. Authority has been distinguished from power as such, because people considered the relation between a commanding will and a subjected will a special one if the subjection was not caused directly by physical coercion. However, the philosopher, Giovanni Gentile, rightly reminds us that "all force is moral force, because it is always directed at the will. Whether the argument used is preaching or the bludgeon, it can only be effective with the consent of him at whom it is directed."[10] Accordingly, for the purposes of legal theory, authority and power present fundamentally the same aspect: a concrete unit of will which for some reason or other has the capacity of regularly imposing its decisions on other wills. Authority is a reality in so far as the authoritative will has the superiority which actually compels people to accept its commands. Thus as long as the motive of obedience is the accepted superiority of the commanding will, the obedience results from force, whether that force consists in steel and lead or in the compelling effect of creeds, beliefs, prejudices or superstitions. It is a mistake to believe that the physical lever to human will is in itself more coercive or forceful than the psychological lever. The methods which Jesuits developed systematically, enabling them to find out and play upon the innermost spring of an individual will, has built for them a force superior to that of many an army[11]. And the student of the propaganda methods of modern totalitarian régimes will know how irresistable a force and how coercive a power can be built up by systematically exploiting human ideas and emotions. If authority therefore is characterized by the absence of resort to material means of power, it nevertheless is real might. Upon that might is based the binding force of legal rules.

Arguments which deny that the binding force of legal rules emanates from the might of the commanding will, can arise only

[10] As quoted by I. Silone, *The School for Dictators* (1938), p. 306. Similarly, Morris R. Cohen remarks: "Force may take subtle forms. The rulers may govern in the name of God, the Constitution, the will of the people, or the interests of the proletariat. But ultimately they must be able to exert some kind of physical compulsion." "On Absolutism in Legal Thought," 84 *University of Pennsylvania Law Review*, p. 697.

[11] Thus, e.g., the Spanish Jesuit, Balthasar Gracian, advised as follows: "Discover each man's thumbscrew. It is the way to move his will, more skill than force being required to know how to get at the heart of anyone: there is no will without its leanings, which differ as tastes differ. All men are idolaters, some of honor, others of greed, and the most of pleasure: the trick lies in knowing these idols that are so powerful, thus knowing the impulse that moves every man: It is like having the key to another man's will, with which to get at the spring within, by no means always his best, but more frequently his worst, for there are more unholy men in this world than holy: divine the ruling passion of a man, excite him with a word, and then attack him through his pet weakness, that invariably checks his free will." From Fischer's translation of Gracian's *A Truthtelling Manual and The Art of Worldly Wisdom* (4th Printing). Courtesy of Charles C. Thomas, Publisher, Springfield, Illinois.

through misunderstanding. It has been possible to overlook the intimate connection of imperative legal rules with the power of the imperious will, because might was identified with soldiers, policemen, bailiffs, prisons and guns. By defining power as the possession of material instruments of force it could be argued that restrictive legal rules had been known to exist without a powerful will behind them. Consequently, it was argued, the binding force of the law must be something entirely independent of will, power, might and coercion. However, this argument fails to consider that in all historic systems of law which operated without an organized material force, the binding effect of the legal rules was obtained by religious fear, superstition, taboos or other forms of non-material power. Thus the conclusion is inevitable that might, whether based on physical or on psychological methods of compulsion, forms the ultimate background of every legal rule which is construed as a command addressed to "free" wills. Whenever the submission of such free wills to external commands is sought, power of will over will is the only way in which that submission can be regularly secured, and by which declarations of will can become "binding rules".

THE LEGISLATIVE WILL IN INTERNATIONAL LAW

What is the relevance of these observations to the theory of international law? Paradoxical as it may sound, it is submitted here that even international law, in the present system, is ultimately based on the assumption of the might of a legislative will. This conclusion follows from the course of the entire argument. It was shown first that the subject of law is the center of the entire legal system, and that the subject's will is believed to be essentially free and independent. Then we demonstrated that this basic assumption of the "real" freedom of subjects makes it necessary to construe legal rules as restrictive commands. Finally we argued that these commands can be conceived as binding rules only by virtue of the authority of the will that issues them, and that authority is actually superior might of one will over other wills. It will be shown now that this theoretical construction also underlies the notion of legal rules which have been established by agreement or consent.

If the theory that legal rules in international law are based on agreement really meant what it said, it would imply that agreement between the subjects of law was required at every moment when the legal rule was applied. Consent, either in the form of international treaties or of tacit acquiescence, is often said to be the basis of the validity of existing rules. However, since the subject's will, by virtue of the premise, is essentially free, there is nothing that could prevent him from changing his mind and finding himself in disagreement. If agreement were really the basis of the existence of legal rules, disagreement would remove them instantly. Since this is not the case, it becomes clear that it is not the agreement between free subjective wills, but again a specific and authoritative unit of will, which gives the legal rule the force of a binding command. Accordingly, this particular unit of will has to be construed as superior to the wills of the legal subjects. Therefore the theory of international law must prove to the states that the will which by its decision has created the legal rule has an inherent quality of distinction which elevates it essentially above the will of the particular states. This and only this is the significance of the theory of consent. For what does the maxim *pacta sunt servanda* signify but this: the will that manifests itself in the form of treaties must be obeyed! *Pacta sunt servanda* does not mean: treaties ought to be kept because they contain good and just rules of law. The maxim "sanctifies" all treaties just and unjust, those concluded under pressure of force as well as those concluded by mutual concessions. It does not say that treaties must be respected because they are respectable, for it sanctions treaties good and bad alike. It simply postulates that all commands issuing from a unit of will constituted between different governments and within certain forms of procedure have the force of binding rules.

It must be remembered that the superiority of the law-issuing will does not have to be founded in actual material force. *Obedientia facit imperantem.* It is the submission of the legal subjects to what they consider to be a superior will which forms the essential condition of the binding force of legal rules. Accordingly not only the superiority but the very existence of a unit of will may be merely imagined by the subjects, without existing in reality. Even a will which is only fictitious fulfills the function of sanctioning the rules which are issued in its name, if only he who actually formulates the rules can create the impression that they ultimately issue from that fictitious unit of will. This is the significance of the concept of Nature in the earlier phases of international law when the "will of Nature" was accepted as an awe-inspiring command with binding force. Hence it is one of the most important tasks of a legal theory, which works upon the premise mentioned before, to establish, in the eyes of the legal subjects, the existence and inherent superiority of the will to which legal rules are imputed.

Thus the notion of the legal rule, as construed within the present framework of legal theory, rests on two main pillars. On the one hand it implies the idea of a will issuing commands which are addressed to the subject's "free" will. On the other hand it presents this will as an intrinsically superior one, as an authority to be respected for its own sake. This superiority of the law-issuing will must necessarily be an axiom of legal theory, admitting of no discussion. Legal theory cannot possibly admit a discussion of this point, for if there should be doubt as to whether the commanding will is of such quality that it must be obeyed under all circumstances, what factor could make the restrictive rules of law binding upon the subject's free will? Consequently the maxim *pacta sunt servanda* is posited as an indisputable *Grundnorm*.[12] In this way the unity of will reached by negotiations between two or more states is elevated to the rank of axiomatic superiority. That will, perpetuated in written

[12] See, eg., D. Anzilotti, *Corso di diritto internazionale*, vol. I (3rd ed. 1928), p. 43. The role of the axiom *pacta sunt servanda* is played in other schools of thought by similar formulas about the "nature" of the international community, etc.

form, is "sanctified" so as to impress the mind of the legal subject and to compel his will to obey the written command.[13]

Why should this unit of will be superior to the subject's particular will? The answer literally is: God only knows. For the superiority of this unit of will is based on a belief, a tradition, which makes the legal subject subordinate itself to that will. This is the reason international law so often recalls Sunday school exhortations. International lawyers cannot help talking and writing like preachers as long as they have to build up the special reputation of a "legislative" will by exalting it systematically, by creating the impression of its superiority. For since there is no machinery of material coercion behind the transitory units of will which set up international rules of law, their capacity to command can be secured only by surrounding them with a halo of extraordinary, even supernatural, qualities. Thus, for example, a terminology which speaks of "solemn covenants," the "sanctity of treaties," the "sacred obligations" etc. uses religious emotions in order to impress the subjects of law with the binding force of legal rules.

To what extent such appeals are effective depends entirely on the attitude of the public in a given period. In the seventeenth century the invocation of Christian and Stoic ideals was a mighty force for securing what effectiveness legal theory had at that time. But this was possible because a strong religious sense permeated the entire culture of the states to which international law was then addressed. The mere reference to morality certainly does not exercise a very strong pressure upon the will of people, unless there is also a strong belief in the ultimate sanction of an avenging God. Grotius was aware of this 250 years ahead of Nietzsche, for he points out that an act, according as it is or is not in conformity with rational nature, has in it a quality of moral baseness or moral necessity; and that, in consequence, such an act is either forbidden or enjoined by the

[13] "Nous pouvons dire d'une obligation juridique qu'elle naît du consentement, en ce sens seulement que l'occasion qui lui donne naissance est un consentement des parties, et sans vouloir impliquer que son fondement ultime, la règle juridique qui donne autorité au consentement, possède elle-même le caractère d'un consentement." Brierly, *Recueil des Cours*, vol. 23, p. 479.

author of nature, God.[14] However, the substance of the notions necessary to impress governments with the binding force of international rules of law is not our concern here. Whether the superior "legislative" will is symbolized as God, Nature, the Family of Nations, the International Community, or the *Vereinbarungswille*, whether submission to its commands is urged through the intellectualized appeal of a fundamental norm or by the more emotional way of solemn formulas invoking eternity and sanctity, the theoretical construction remains the same in all cases. For as long as the starting point of international law is the free and independent existence of separate states, there is no logical possibility of construing the notion of legal rules otherwise than as a body of commands which issue from a will of inherently superior quality and force.

THE ASSUMPTION OF POWER BEHIND INTERNATIONAL LAW

From these observations we may draw the conclusion that a legal system whose rules are construed as restrictive commands can function only if its commands are based on real power over the will of the subjects. It is irrelevant whether this power derives from physical force or from psychological compulsion, from a deeply rooted taboo or from a generally accepted philosophy. But it is indispensable that the will to which legal rules are imputed, should enjoy actual ascendancy over the subjects' wills, should be capable of producing a regularly compelling effect on them. In other words, although there is no need for material power, there must exist the impression of an inherently superior will from which the legal rules issue in order to secure the binding force of these rules. The problem is not identical with that of sanctions. A particular legal rule may be effective or ineffective according to the sanctions that support it. But the entire system of law which is composed of commanding rules presupposes as such the assumption of a "legislative will." And a command can appear as a binding rule of law only if to the will that issues it is attributed an inherent strength and superiority which gives this will a continuous ascendancy over

[14] De iure belli ac pacis, Prol. I, ch. 1, sect. X, 1.

the wills of the legal subjects. The real power of the "legislative will" behind the law is necessary not so much to make the subjects actually abide by the law—this being the function of sanctions—as to make them accept certain commanding axioms as binding rules of law. Without the elevation of a unit of will to the rank of legislator—an elevation which always presupposes the idea of power—it is not possible to have any legal rules, at any rate not in the form of commands.

Now international law is a body of commands addressed to those entities which have exclusive control over the material means of power in society. The most fundamental function of states is to operate as monopolistic units of collective power. A state would cease to be a state if its government were not in the position to exercise regularly the supreme and also the most efficient power within its territory. Thus, since all the material power of human society is potentially concentrated in the hands of the states, international law cannot rely on an ascendency based on material force. Consequently the problem of the binding force of international law is to create and maintain the impression that there is a permanent "legislative will" endowed with a superiority that does not derive from material force. The rules of international law have a binding force which comes from the compulsion of traditions, conventions, beliefs, taboos and prejudices which are commonly held among the nations.

In past centuries this problem was solved by a common religion embracing the different nations. Undoubtedly, the belief in and the fear of an omnipotent God engendered the conviction that there was a real power superior to that of the sovereign ruler, and therefore capable of binding the ruler's will by its commands. International law could be based on this conviction as long as every incident of private and public life was permeated with religion. Today religion no longer holds the key to people's wills. For this reason the invocation of morality as a "sanctification" of international law fails to bring forth a binding effect of international rules of law, because moral appeal is ultimately effective only through a belief in a supernatural power behind it. In more recent times, the belief in the International Community, the Family of Nations, the League of Nations, and so on was the source of the ascendency of international law over the will of the State. Again, these commonly held ideas produced the general impression of a real power superior to that of the particular states. But the spell was broken when, unfortunately, this power was put to practical tests which revealed its impotence. Therefore it is no longer feasible to impose the commands of international law upon the will of the State merely by referring to "The International Community."

The general implications of the problem present themselves more clearly when it is realized that the same difficulty exists with those commanding rules which are addressed to the highest commanding individuals. What could cause a supreme ruler, such as a pope, a generalissimo, a president, to recognize commands of a restrictive character if it were not the respect for a will which is superior to his? This ascendency of a higher will, however, can be founded only on non-material compulsion, because those who are highest in command have all the material means of force in their own hands, and they know it. Accordingly any will which in social hierarchies enjoys a top rank, can be subjected to commands only by the compelling effect which stems from firmly established beliefs and convictions. To the same degree to which such beliefs actually dominate these highest wills, there is a real binding force in legal rules which are based on those beliefs. But when taboos or religion or superstition or other beliefs fail to engender in the ruler's mind the conviction that there is a power superior to his own, he will never consent to be bound by any restrictive command, bowing only to the force of circumstances. The force of legal rules which derives from those convictions is a real one, because it operates as a real compulsion upon the will of those to whom the rules are addressed. But whenever the subject's will has thrown aside the fetters of his own convictions and beliefs, no amount of preaching can reestablish the authority of the legal rule. Therefore, to the degree to which powerful subjects of law cease to be impressed by the idea of some superior will from whom the law issues it becomes impossible to bind them by rules in the form of authoritative commands.

Our argument has led us to the paradoxical conclusion that the present system of international law is founded on the assumption of power superior to that of the particular states. It is impossible to conceive legal rules as authoritative commands over states without visualizing a "legislative will" to which an essential ascendency over the particular states is attributed. Thus the assumption of power is the necessary basis of command. Command is the necessary form of legal rules which are supposed to restrict the freedom of originally independent wills. The independence of will, in turn, is a necessary starting point for a personalistic system of law, which makes the notion of the subject the starting point and the center of juristic construction. Thus the circle of thinking within the framework of traditional international law, inevitably leads to the notion of the power, i.e. the ascendancy, of the will which issues legal rules.[15] In some form or other, international law in the past has lived on the authority which was generally assumed to make rules binding upon states, i.e. on the actually compelling force of the idea of a "legislative will" above the states. It is evident that this type of international law is bound to become an ineffectual set of paper-rules in proportion as the world ceases to be under the dominating influence of a common religion, or a common political philosophy.

THE BINDING FORCE OF LEGAL RULES

The original conception of legal rules as authoritative commands gives rise to numbers of insoluble problems, filling the

[15] "Un lourd atavisme fait de volonté de puissance, d'arbitraire et d'habitude du recours à la force (qui d'ailleurs est de leur compétence juridique) a créé pur les gouvernements une psychologie qui obnubile chez eux les considérations d'intérêts général. . . . La théorie classique du droit contractuel ou 'volontariste' est bien faite pour maintenir et développer un tel état d'esprit. Si vraiment la règle de droit international ne résulte que d'un compromis entre volontés gouvernementales, n'est point dominée par un ensemble de normes antérieures et supérieures à toute volonté humaine, qui s'imposent par leur valeur intrinsèque au détenteurs de la puissance lorsqu'elles sont objectivement dégagées,—aucun frein réel ne s'oppose au jeu brutual de l'équilibre des forces.

Dès lors, la question de la révision des traités n'est plus qu'une question de force." G. Scelle, *Théorie juridique de la révision des traités* (1936), p. 28.

polemic pages of professional literature. One of them has been analyzed on the preceding pages. It is the question of how to prove the intrinsic authority of the will from which the legal command is supposed to issue. The doctrine of the obligatory force of international law was no problem whatsoever to people in the sixteenth and seventeenth centuries, because the unquestioned omnipresence and omnipotence of God was evidently enough of a real power to lend authority to legal rules which were intimately connected with the idea of God's Creation. As soon as religion lost its dominating influence, however, legal theory had to make special efforts to prove that the law was the command of a unit of will the authority of which gave really binding force to its commands. The problem presented itself not so much in respect to those legal rules which corresponded to the will of all the states as in connection with the norms with which some of them disagreed. By what authority could those rules be presented as binding upon the unwilling states? Since there is no organized unit of will and power in society above that of the State, legal theory here faces the difficult task of concealing what is evident and of proving what is non-existent. Accordingly, all theoretical attempts to establish the binding force of international rules of law have something of tilting against wind-mills about them. They give the impression of ardent efforts to make commands binding upon certain subjects by persuading these subjects that they had better obey, "because it is unworthy of their own dignity to disobey;" "because to obey is the correct thing to do;" "because they believed in God;" "because they believed in Legal Theory;" "because one never knows . . .;" "because . . ."

In fact there exist only two means or ways of establishing the binding force of legal rules conceived as authoritative commands. One way is to rely on an ethical justification of such rules: Legal rules, it may be argued, are binding in so far as they coincide with the commands of human conscience; they are obligatory because they command only that which is felt to be "right" by the legal subjects. Hence since there is a compelling force in the dictates of human conscience, the coincidence of legal rules with the tenets of conscience would establish their binding character without the assumption of an "external" power.

However, no author of international law would maintain that the problem of the binding force of law is soluble by invoking an intrinsic quality of rightfulness in legal rules. For the issue presents itself above all because, and in so far as, the rightfulness of positive rules of law is not acknowledged, and the law is challenged by its subjects. Since no system of authoritative rules can be based entirely on the inner acknowledgment of its orders, the other, and only remaining, argument by which the binding force of commands can be established is to invoke a categorical respect for the power that wills the law. It is the very nature of a command that it cannot have a binding effect upon the subject except by virtue of the subject's submission to the commanding authority, however that submission may be brought about. Therefore, unless the governments of states subordinate themselves to legal rules because they actually do believe in a higher authority behind those commands, nothing can convince them that any command of international law has a regularly binding force over them.

The doctrine of the obligatory force of international rules of law is thus an artificial argument. There is no similar doctrine of equal importance with respect to domestic law within the different states, because the authority of the legislative will there is an established fact. Being insoluble in itself, the discussion around this problem will continue to present the spectacle of a purely academic controversy until it disappears together with the whole theoretical framework from which it originated.

THE REVISION OF THE LAW

Another of the insoluble problems resulting from the notion of the legal rule in the present theoretical framework is the question of revision. Legal rules, if construed as commands, "exist" as soon as the legislative will has issued the formal order. They continue to "exist" in this way as long as the authority of the commanding will is respected by the subjects and as long as the order has not been revoked. However, all authors on international law agree that a legal rule, once issued, has a tendency to become obsolete after some time. It prescribes a certain behavior in order to solve a specific difficulty of social relationships. But the conditions prevailing when the rule was issued will change after a time, and, instead of producing order and harmony, the legal rule begins to beget difficulties and friction. In such a situation the remedy is to adjust the formula of the rule to changed circumstances, to revise the law.

Since legal rules, within the present framework of theory, are conceived as commands emanating from an authoritative will, only one procedure is possible for revising legal rules: the "legislative will" which issued the legal rule has to decide anew and either to reshape or to revoke it. This procedure presents no problem whatsoever in domestic law, because here the "legislative will" exists continuously through a permanent organization of unified decision. Not only when a legal rule is enacted but also when revision is needed in domestic law, the will of the State exists and is ready to decide. It is different in international law. Here the "legislative will" is a unit which usually disappears as such after it has issued legal rules. The will which enacts rules of international law is the unified will which results from the negotiations of two or more governments. This unit of will is not permanently maintained between the states by an organized process of integration (except for the League of Nations and the International Labor Organization, which, however, produced between them only an infinitesimal part of international law). Thus in international law the legal rule, once it has been issued, "exists" all by itself. It is not supported in action by a continuous adaptation to changing circumstances through the help of a constantly deciding unit of will. Nor is there a permanently existing unit of will which could effect a revision of the rule when it is needed.

When the discrepancy between the "reality of life" and the legal rule becomes intolerable, the legal command has to be revised by what Scelle has called the *acte contraire*. By *acte contraire* he means the revocation of the legal rule by the same unit of will which enacted it. It seems that this procedure is the only possible way of securing a strictly legal revision of rules which are conceived as commands. Therefore it is of special significance that this method of revision encounters fundamental difficulties in international law. For here the formation of that unit of will which can decide about legal rules is a coincidence depending on many political circumstances. The "legislative" unit of will is not institutionalized or organized. It comes into existence only when the policies, interests and intentions of the nations happen to coincide, and when on the basis of common understanding the different governments happen to arrive at a unity of will. Accordingly there is no certainty that this interstate unit of will will make its appearance at the moment when revision of the law is necessary. If it fails to materialize, and if a unity of decision is not reached between the states concerned, there is no possibility of a revision of the law by strictly legal procedures. The only alternative left then is a revision by way of outright defiance of the legal "command."[16] This is clearly an illegal method of revision, but in international law this procedure is almost the normal rule. Although illegal, it is nevertheless revision. For, as has been stated before, legal rules that are construed as commands "exist" only as long as the "legislative will" continues to maintain its authority and ascendency over the subjects' wills. When a legal rule is not merely violated in a particular infraction but is rejected as such, the authority of the will that issued it is involved. If this defiance of the authority of command is successful, both the ascendency of the "legislative will" and the binding force of the legal rule are destroyed.

The argument that domestic law is violated countless times without losing its obligatory force and effectiveness, is a fallacy. For these infractions of domestic law are violations of its rules

[16] "Dans ce système, quelle est la signification de la signature exigée du vainceur? Elle est la reconnaissance authentique de la plus grande force du vainqueur, l'aveu du plus faible que sa résistance est épuisée et qu'il se resigne au rôle de minorité, c'est à dire à subir la loi de la force ou du nombre.

Il ne reste toujours que le renversement des positions, la conquête de la compétence majoritaire par la minorité ou de la force par le faible." Scelle, *Théorie juridique* etc., pp. 58*f*.

which do not reject the authority of the legislative will or its commands as such. They are merely attempts by the law-breaker to obtain a special personal exemption or advantage for himself. The burglar, while he fails to respect the property of others when he steals, would nevertheless protest vehemently against any such act against himself. He does not deny or reject the validity of the legal rules, he only tries to disregard them in his own favor. This sort of infraction, it is true, does not fundamentally weaken any sort of law, even if it be international. However, the "illegal revision" of international rules of law is not merely a casual infraction: it is a rejection of existing rules because of their obsolescence. It is a refusal to submit any longer to the authority of the will that issued the rule. It denies the obligatory force of the "legislative will" with respect to its commands. Consequently, if it is successful, it not merely infringes upon but actually removes the legal rule concerned.

The insoluble problem of revision is again a necessary feature of a system of theory in which the legal rule is conceived as a command. It is especially thorny in international law because of the absence of a permanent unit of will capable of adapting legal rules to changing reality. So long as the personalistic pattern of law dominates international law, the question of how to revise its rules will continue to be the object of an interminable, and therefore purely academic, discussion.

The features of the present system of international law which have been analyzed in this chapter have turned out to be direct consequences of the personalistic structure of that law. In a personalistic system of law, it was shown, a legal order can be conceived only in the form of commands. Every command requires a will which formulates and enacts it. In order to give legal rules a binding force this will has to enjoy authority over the subjects of law. Authority rests on an empirically established ascendency of one specific unit of will over the "ordinary" wills of legal subjects—in other words, a form of power.

These arguments might easily be misinterpreted as a plea for a revival of Austinian ideas. However, they do not involve any attempt to revive or establish any legal theory. Our analysis of personalistic law is not an interpretation of the phenomena of law as such, nor an attempt to construe the idea of the law in a particular way. Its purpose is merely to find out the tacit implications *of a specific way of legal thinking*. At the same time it is meant to throw light on the significance of theoretical constructions for the practice of international law and international politics. It aims at showing the inescapable consequences which stem from a personalistic conception of the legal community and its legal order. And it is designed to prove that these consequences are common to all schools of thought that have developed out of this personalistic conception of law, whether they are conscious of these implications or not. In this sense, Austin's views are not "true," nor are they satisfactory: they are symptomatic. They merely emphasize a fundamental feature of legal thinking which is inherent not only in the Austinian or any other version of voluntaristic positivism, but in the entire framework of theory which works with the premise of the original independence of the legal subject. Therefore even such thinkers as Erich Kaufmann ("*Nur wer kann, darf*": only he who is powerful has legal rights) cannot be considered as perverters but only as logical executors of the personalistic system of law.

It is true that the discussion of legal concepts and constructions does not solve the problems of international law and order in a crisis-stricken world. But let no one imagine that we could escape the iron law of power-worship and its tragic dominance over the practice of law and politics as long as we are not even in theory capable of conceiving a system of law and order other than one which is based on the sheer force of authoritative commands.

THE FUNCTIONAL CONCEPTION OF LEGAL RULES

The question now arises: is it at all possible to conceive legal rules otherwise than as a body of commands? And if it is possible, how can we arrive at such a conception? It is at this point that the findings of the two preceding chapters merge with the analysis attempted in this chapter to produce some fundamental conclusions regarding the notion of law.

When investigating the question of legal evaluations, we found that the personalistic system of law was characterized by its naturalistic conception of reality. If the reality of social life is conceived as a sphere of purely natural forces and relations, acts and objects, then logically law must be conceived as an equally closed sphere of purely ideal norms. Accordingly, the validity of its rules cannot be tested by any criteria derived from actual life, but has to be based on a delegation of authority from the next norm above. Thus the authority of legal norms is built up in successive steps, until we are finally referred to a norm which is considered fundamental and axiomatic, and from which the validity of all other legal rules is derived. In domestic law this fundamental norm says: Obey the "legislative" will! In international law it says: Treaties must be observed!, which, as has been shown, amounts to substantially the same thing in a different guise. In other words, legal rules which are conceived to represent the "ideal" as opposed to the "real" live entirely on the authority of the "legislative will" to which they are imputed. Accordingly, they cannot exist otherwise than in the form of commands. If "reality" is considered to be without its immanent values, the task of the law must be defined as that of imposing on reality an absolute and abstract set of values "from without." If "reality" is looked upon as a sphere of blind dynamic forces, then legal order must be conceived as a wall erected against the overflow of the stream of life, not as a system of channels through which it might run in creative directions. Thus the unfortunate dualism of the real and the ideal is closely connected with the fatal conception of law as a set of authoritative commands. Both of these theoretical difficulties ultimately spring from the same root: the atomic, or individualistic view of society, a view which focuses its attention primarily on the separate existence of persons and things, and construes all social phenomena as products of these independent entities.

It is at this critical juncture that change is introduced by the functional approach. In the two preceding chapters of this book an attempt has been made to outline the nature of this change in viewpoint. The first of these two chapters dealt with the problem of how to conceive values not in opposition to the reality of social life, but in terms of actual social relationships. The second chapter criticized the notion that society is a collectivity composed of so many single parts (the individuals, or persons), and showed social reality to consist of human behavior in so far as it is governed by transpersonal ends and is shaped by the experience of inter-personal connectedness. In these two chapters ideas were evolved which now have to be linked up with the functional notion of legal rules.

The functional conception of legal rules emerges from the basic assumption that the phenomenon of "connectedness" in social behavior is a reality of its own, which is not a product of "separate" individual wills, although it proceeds from their mingling. The inter-personal connectedness of activities enables individuals to create, in their relationships, an enduring essence, which stands apart from their subjective "purposes". Social behavior is always coordinate behavior, and all coordination is directed towards some constructive end. Law is the order of human conduct which is required to attain those ends. It is the inner lawfulness that governs the structure of social contexts. In other words, rules of law are inherent in social behavior, because all social behavior consists of individual acts which are commonly directed toward specific ends.[17]

The difference of this conception from the personalistic construction of law is obvious. On the basis of the atomic idea of society, law was conceived as an objective standard designed to keep the subjective wills and the personal interests of the independent entities within their due bounds. Therefore, the law had to operate as an authoritative command, and the legal

[17] "Men go about their business, and regulate their affairs with serenity and safety, though the principle or rule or standard to which they adhere for guidance or enlightenment is without the sanction of a judgment, and even more frequently without the sanction of a statute." B. N. Cardozo, *The Growth of the Law*, Yale University Press (1924), p. 33.

subjects had to be under the obligation to obey the authority which issued those commands. From the functional perspective, however, there is no difference between individuals as separate entities and their mutual relationships. Society is not composed of individual entities, but consists of behavior which is shaped by the realization of transpersonal contexts. Since it is not possible to act with social relevance except through such transpersonal contexts, since it is not possible to realize any such relationship without realizing its inherent meaning, and since every meaningful relationship embodies an immanent principle of orderliness, law is an integral part of social relationships. Accordingly, from the functional point of view it seems senseless and superfluous to try to impose legal rules upon social reality "from without." Since there is no social reality except that behavior which is governed by the immanent rules of coordinatedness, there is no need to look for a value system apart from actual social life, in order to clamp it down upon dynamic reality by the force of command. Thus the functional notion of law, discarding the idea that legal rules are commands, finds law to be the element of orderliness which is inherent in the actual behavior of individuals.

The elimination of the personalistic perspective also makes it possible to overcome the conception of legal rules as commands. Starting out from the person as the basic unit of society and the basic premise of law means assuming the independence of persons as an axiom. Legal subjects, when looked upon in their separate existence appear to be free-willed. Once we realize the functional connectedness of all social behavior, however, the will of individuals-in-society appears far from free. It is molded and channeled by the laws of reciprocal orientation and functional coordination. Individual behavior has social relevance to the extent that it is meaningful. It is meaningful to the extent that it is manifestly directed toward the achievement of some transpersonal end. Therefore the law is that rule of behavior which enables individuals to act in a meaningful and constructive way. It is not necessary to impose upon individual wills by an authoritative command a line of conduct which they must will anyway if they want to realize a meaning in their acts. What is necessary is to point out the functional ends of social behavior to individuals, to suggest the means of attaining them, to make them fully conscious of the immanent order which governs the structure of social conduct. Thus functional law provides the channels in which social relationships can mature. The function of law, therefore, is no longer to restrict and limit the forces of social life, but to further their constructiveness, to indicate the path toward the highest fulfillment of their functions, to formulate the element of orderliness inherent in them.

The functional concept of law might possibly be confused with the historical idea of an *ordre naturel.* Therefore it must be emphasized that it is not a natural[18] but a cultural orderliness to which this concept of law refers. This means, on the one hand, that the element of orderliness is inherent in a social context because of its "directedness" toward specific ends. For culture is the transformation of natural material with a view to ends that are conceived by human minds.[19] Therefore our concept of immanent order is a functional, not a natural one. On the other hand, this immanent orderliness of coordinate behavior is embedded in human culture as determined by time and space. Former centuries had to believe in a natural law, i.e. a law emanating from a superhuman source of legislation, and therefore valid beyond human differences in time and space, because it seemed impossible to explain the existence of immanent rules of social order in any other way. Modern sociology and psychology, however, have enabled us to understand how human beings can realize the inherent "lawfulness" of some behavior, even apart from statute law and regulation,

[18] In the terminology of this book, "cultural" phenomena are distinguished from "natural" phenomena. Culture involves always human activities aiming at the realization of human ends (see p. 251), activities which modify the given natural material to make it serve human purposes. Therefore the phenomena of culture cannot be measured, like those of nature, by "general laws" (Kant, *Prolegomena,* §4). Since "this social world has certainly been made by man" (Vico, *Scienza Nuova*), its laws vary with the "modifications of human consciousness" and the conditions of human existence. Cf. also Heller, *Staatslehre,* pp. 34*f.*

[19] See p. 253*f.*

by virtue of their own sense of orderliness. We know now that "a concrete form of action, arising out of concrete impulses of individuals, converges, in connection with the requirement of reciprocal understanding, with other forms of action into an ordered whole of an overwhelmingly logical structure."[20] This is what makes it possible for us to realize that there is an inherent element of orderliness in social reality, and yet to conceive this immanent order as being conditioned by the pattern of a specific culture. For the intrinsic order of social relationships is lived and experienced by concrete individuals in concrete settings. It is the element of transpersonal values in actual individual behavior which embodies the immanent law of social reality. In such a conception of law there is no place for abstract commandments hovering over time and space and enjoying a timeless validity separate and apart from concrete human experiences. According to the functional notion, there is no law except that which is actually experienced by individual beings in social behavior. It may or may not be observed integrally, but there is always inherent in human conduct the implicit acknowledgment of immanent standards, and accordingly an intrinsic tendency to conform to them.

The example of language has already been used several times to illustrate the functional concept of law. It may serve this purpose here once again. The law governing social relationships is to be found in the orderliness which is inherent in actual behavior, just as the rules of language are to be found in actual speech and its inherent standards of linguistic correctness. Grammar, after all, is only a consensus of opinion as to how language should be talked and written. As to the order of language, however, it is the talking and writing which actually matter. Similarly the rules formulated in statute books are not the legal order of social behavior itself. It is in actual conduct and behavior that the legal order exists. Law must be sought not apart from, but within the reality of social life as a structure "existing and changing as the behavior of individuals".[21]

[20] Hermann Heller, *Staatslehre*, p. 84.

[21] Lynd, *Knowledge for What?*, p. 27.

We know that children learn first how to speak, and only later take cognizance of the rules of language. Grammar always is an afterthought. Similarly, we know that nations with a creative gift for legal order, such as the Romans, first developed the actual orderliness of their daily conduct, and only then formulated rules about the standards of this inherent orderliness of behavior. With the Romans, however, these rules became authoritative prescriptions, instead of "afterthoughts" about the actual structure of social reality, only when their sense for the immediate reality of legal order had declined, and when, instead of interpreting the living law of actual relationships, they began to interpret the edicts of defunct praetors.

It may be expedient to at this point summarize some of the differences between personalistic law and functional law.

Personalistic Law	Functional Law
1. Idea of social reality	
The independent existence of separate persons	The coordinate behavior of individuals
2. The will of legal subjects	
Free subjective will	Individual wills governed by the necessities of reciprocal understanding and functional coordination
3. Idea of social relationships	
Determined by subjective interests of the separate persons	Determined by the trans-personal ends which constitute the meaning of each relationship or institution
4. Idea of legal order	
Objective limitation on the free action of the various subjective interests	The element of orderliness which is inherent in actual coordinate behavior of individuals
5. Legal valuation	
Value standards conceived abstractly and in opposition to social reality	Value standards derived from the functional "directedness" of concrete relationships
6. Materialization of legal order	
Authoritative commands imposing standards of abstract values upon individual wills	Promoting the individual's consciousness of law by pointing out ends and suggesting means, of social relations

In the following sections of this chapter, some of these more fundamental differences between the traditional personalistic approach to law and the functional approach will be explained in greater detail.

THE DISAPPEARANCE OF THE PROBLEMS OF REVISION AND OBLIGATORY FORCE

From the standpoint of functional law the problems of the obligatory force of legal rules and of their revision cease to have any significance. Both problems, as has been shown, result from the separation of legal norms from factual reality. In the personalistic theory of law the actual behavior of persons was considered to be a purely factual reality. On the other hand the concept of "ideal" law was applied to the formulas which ordered or forbade persons to act in a specific way. These formulas "existed" as long as they were upheld as commands by the authority behind them. The link between the command of the ideal and the facts of reality was the obligation of the personal will to behave in conformity to the law. This made the obligatory force of legal rules the keystone of the whole theoretical structure of law.

From the functional point of view law is no longer held to consist of mere formulas of command. Instead, we conceive law to be the inner lawfulness governing the actual behavior of people. Therefore a command which is issued without producing any actual effect on the behavior of individuals is not considered to be law. The Austrian sociologist Eugen Ehrlich has estimated that approximately 33 per cent of the Austrian Civil Law Code had remained ineffectual paper provisions. In a personalistic system of law these rules are considered nevertheless law, because the "obligatory force" of legal rules is conceived as something apart from the actual acknowledgement of legal rules in social life. Functionally conceived, these formulas would represent attempts to "make" law, or to set up ideas about law, but not actual law itself. Law consists only in the immanent orderliness which dominates the structure of individual behavior within the framework of social institutions or relationships. Since this conception of law does not postulate the "existence" of legal rules apart from the reality of behavior, the obligatory force of law is no longer a theoretical problem. Where there is a context of action and reaction, i.e. of coordinate human conduct, there are inherent criteria of lawfulness which attach to the idea of the context as such. The old truism *ubi societas ibi ius* thus appears in a new light. No social relationship is conceivable or feasible without its own standards of order; for only a common frame of reference makes it possible for men to act and react upon one another in a meaningful way.

When law is conceived in this way, it becomes clear that such immanent standards of social behavior cannot be made at will. No one would think of decreeing how a language should be spoken. In the same way, the laws of social behavior are part of ourself, as it is molded in its constant touch and reciprocal interaction with other selves. The necessities of reciprocal understanding and of effective coordination of action between individuals constitute the laws which condition all social behavior. In this sense it can be said that the existence of legal rules is a feature of social reality which can be recognized, furthered, protected and made conscious, but which cannot be deliberately "made". Since law is not conceived apart from social reality, there is no need for a specific category of "obligatory force," which is required only when law is embodied in a formula that has to be imposed on reality as an authoritative command.

Similarly, the problem of the revision of law owes its existence mainly to the antithesis between norm and reality characteristic of the traditional system of law. Legal rules, which have an "existence" apart from social reality, and which are meant to impose abstract standards upon the dynamic flow of life "from without," are bound to fall out of rhythm with the actual conditions of reality. If this discrepancy becomes unbearable, a violent rupture occurs between the norm and reality, and a new rule is established in closer contact with real circumstances. It is the absolute basis of its existence, and the abstractness of its value criteria, which exposes the legal rule in the personalistic system of law to violent corrections at the hands of dynamic life.

Again, the functional conception of legal rules removes this difficulty. From the functional point of view, the validity of legal rules does not derive from some abstract value standard maintained by the authority in command. It is tested and sustained by the actual behavior of individuals within the framework of relationships and social institutions. It would be erroneous, however, to assume that the validity of a legal norm could be derived from a descriptive analysis of the way in which people act empirically. A law of social behavior is not like a physical or other natural law which may be inferred from a number of experimental observations. Law as social order is a standard of "required behavior," not a formula for some factual regularity of behavior. Therefore, the factual behavior of people as such is not conclusive; what is important is the norms which people acknowledge, implicitly or explicitly, by the way in which they behave. The actual conviction that some pattern of conduct is *required* by the structure of social contexts, is the basis of the validity of legal rules. Required with reference to what criterion? The criterion of "requiredness" of behavior in functional law is the objective (transpersonal) end with a view to which individual acts are coordinated in a relationship or an institution. The transpersonal result, or effect, which constitutes the *raison d'etre* of coordinate human activities, is the criterion by which the "requiredness" of behavior is judged. Thus functional law "exists" only by virtue of the actual acknowledgment of legal rules as manifested in typical individual behavior. Hence, the legal conviction (the "faith") of people is the test of validity with respect to legal rules. Those rules are valid which individuals on the whole accept as guiding standards in their actual behavior. Since this conviction is open to change, the revision of legal rules is effected by the dynamic development of our consciousness. The problem of revision as a specific procedure ceases to be significant. Legal rules develop along with the changing convictions of what is "required" lawfully by individuals-in-society.

FUNCTIONAL LAW IS A FACILITATING NOT A RESTRICTIVE TYPE OF ORDER

We have seen that personalistic law works on the assumption that the free exercise of personal will and the satisfaction of personal interests are elements of social reality and at the same time form the basic premise of the legal system. It recognizes and acknowledges the subjective aspirations of legal persons, the competition between them, and their conflicting interests. It merely erects a buffer between the different subjects in order to prevent, as much as possible, the pursuit of each subject's interest from harming the interests of other subjects. Personalistic law therefore has restrictive and protective functions. In order to restrict the will of legal persons, it must command and prescribe limitations on their freedom; in order to protect the interests of legal persons, it must adjudicate titles, possessions, rights. The central problem of personalistic law is therefore that of distribution. "To whom shall this object belong?" "Who is entitled to protection in this conflict?" The entire orientation of this type of law is toward the interests and the will of persons, whom it endeavors to serve, to appease, to satisfy. Accordingly international law, being construed on the personalistic pattern, centers around the will and the interest of the states. Because it is supposed to serve the State, it is liable to become an instrument of state interests and power politics. At the same time it is liable to be rejected by the impulse-for-power, because it acts as a mandatory restriction and limitation on the same power-interests which it is understood to serve.

The insoluble problem of distribution, and the inner contradictions between service to personal interests and restrictions of these same interests, are left aside in functional law. For functional thinking recognizes that any legal order of social relationships can do no more than regulate the "connectedness" between individuals. It can never serve individual or personal interests without at the same time suppressing the liberty to pursue those interests. Thus functional thinking insists that the aspect of human life with which law can really deal is the coordinatedness of human behavior, not the integral existence of individual persons. The integral aspect of personality is a problem which faces, and a task which is incumbent upon, only individuals themselves. Social order can never do more than provide the framework of coordinatedness of human activities, regulating them with a view to the objective ends that they are meant to achieve.

Thus functional law serves a functional ideal[22], it serves the ends for which *the coordination of human behavior* as such is destined. In functional thinking it appears nonsensical to attempt to protect subjective interests by the means of the social system of order. For men necessarily act in coordination. It is a condition of human life, it is, moreover, necessarily the will of human beings. No man can possibly pursue subjective interests without bending his will to the structure of social contexts and relationships. Every purchase, all productive effort, every economic activity crystallizes in forms of social relationship which are determined not by subjective purposes, but by trans-personal ends. These structured contexts form the mold into which men have to fit their intentions and their impulses in order to give them social relevance. All human interests materialize only through inter-human coordination which cannot be realized otherwise than with a view to some trans-subjective end of its own. If law is the order that facilitates the coordination of human activities, it must necessarily be directed toward serving those trans-subjective ends of social contexts. The central problem of functional law therefore is not

[22] Feilchenfeld, in the book that has been quoted so many times already, establishes, as a criterion of judgment for legal rules and legal problems, what he calls an "objective ideal" (*sachliches Ideal*). His characterization of this ideal is significant: "The task established here posits an end which cannot be conceived as the specific purpose of any individual or of any community. . . . Not man, not even perfect man is the end, but only his works. It is not the technical achievement which is valued as such, . . . but only the *right* work. . . . This criterion is applicable to all relations, measuring everything by an impersonal ideal, which I should like to call 'objective ideal'" (p. 144).

a distributive, but a coordinative one. Its guiding question is: "How can this task be realized?"[23] It operates not to protect the separateness of personal existence, but to facilitate the functional coordination of human energies. Yet functional law cannot be considered just a means to an end. It is neither means nor end; it is the condition of coordinate behavior. Just as language is not merely the means to the end of communication, but an expression of the constructive and creative faculties of human beings, so the legal forms of coordinate behavior are products of human creativeness, which are valuable for their own sake.

THE ANTITHESIS BETWEEN LEGAL ORDER AND DISORDER

In personalistic law the "life" of the law was a struggle of objective standards against subjective wills, of the society against the individual, of collective interests against personal interests. Law was realized to the degree to which the standpoint of social interests and social standards prevailed over the standpoint of particular interests and subjective wills. The individual and his impulses represented the element of disorder, the collectivity and its norms represented the criterion of legal order.

In functional law the antithesis between lawfulness and lawlessness is not one between individual and society. Individual behavior can be lawful or unlawful, but the realization of the law is not a struggle between the separate subject and an equally separate collectivity: it is rather a struggle between the energies which are and those which are not coordinate within each individual. Human behavior is social in so far as it is coordinate. The coordination of human behavior is brought about by reference to transpersonal ends which are meant to be achieved by activity-in-coordination. The lawfulness in individual behavior therefore depends on the orientation of the

[23] Very interesting in this connection are Feilchenfeld's definitions of legal rules and legal science: "By a norm I understand an idea that posits a task." "The thinking which posits tasks is of the second kind: its aim is not the description of reality, but the setting up of ends" (pp. 37*f*.).

individual's will and consciousness toward those ends. There is a certain inner necessity of conduct, deriving from the functional coordination of acts within a social context. Thus, for instance, people desirous of negotiating a purchase must necessarily observe a form of conduct which is consistent with achieving the exchange of material values. Behavior which follows this inner necessity of coordination is lawful; conduct which is arbitrary from the point of view of the coordinatedness of behavior is disorderly.

Any individual action is motivated by some impulse of human significance. But from the standpoint of the connectedness of human behavior not all motives or impulses are equally significant. Those motives which derive from the impulse to realize the objective end of social contexts are coordinatable. They follow an inner necessity, for human relationships necessarily crystallize around these trans-personal ends. The motives which derive from a purely personal— or better, self-centered— purpose are not coordinatable. They are haphazard from the point of view of social order. They vary infinitely, emerging from the whims of individuals and the way in which individual desires happen to react to the material environment. One might also say that the incalculable motives and impulses of individuals (precisely their subjective interests) are not coordinatable because they are capricious. The necessary motives of individuals (those which men must have in order to act-in-coordination) are coordinatable because they obey an inner necessity, the inner necessity of all social behavior.

These are the two poles between which legal order materializes in social reality. The inner necessity of motivation on the one side, the arbitrariness of motivation on the other. Corresponding to these two extremes of motivation, the behavior of individuals-in-relationship may be inherently lawful or inherently lawless. But the struggle for the materialization of legal order is no longer fought between the individual on one side and society on the other, but between the lawful and the lawless elements in human personalities themselves. To the extent to which individuals are capable of achieving human order in the chaos of pure matter, of giving meaning to the factuality of nature, of realizing the laws of constructive action, there is legal order in their conduct. Between the pole of the inner necessity of social behavior and that of arbitrariness of conduct swings the pendulum of individual decision.

This is not the old antinomy between selfishness and unselfishness. The disregard of the intrinsic standards of order in social behavior also thwarts the full realization of all subjective purposes. Individuals usually have subjective purposes in mind when they are engaged in coordinate activities. But these purposes can be attained only through social contexts which are functionally directed toward ends of their own. Therefore, the subjective purposes of individuals can have significance for social order only through the medium of the functional ends of social relationships as such. Individuals cannot avoid willing those results which constitute the functions of social relationships and institutions. Whatever the subjective purpose of men may be, they cannot realize them without aiming at the accomplishment of those transpersonal effects with a view to which people's behavior is socially coordinate. Accordingly, functional law does not appeal to, or rely on, any altruism or the suppression of selfish impulses.

THE ROLE OF LEGAL STATUTES

The functional type of law is brought about not so much by a sweeping reorganization of the machinery of social order as by the growth of a new orientation of individuals in their behavior vis-à-vis its institutions. The abstention from any deliberate "making" of laws, and the tendency to find the law in social reality rather than to impose it on that reality is characteristic of the functional approach. It demands the focusing of attention on the phenomena of connectedness in behavior rather than on the features of separateness in existence. Since orderliness and lawfulness are to be found in the structure of social contexts as such, law from the functional point of view never can be enacted as an abstract rule opposed to living reality. It can therefore never convert itself into an instrument to which life is made subservient, in the sense of the defeatist formula *pereat mundus, fiat ius*. Neither can it become a means that has been dissociated from its ends and therefore is liable to be abused and perverted in its meaning. These assertions need to be discussed in more detail.

Legal order consists in the elimination of arbitrary conduct from social reality. The only agent who can bring about the orderliness of social behavior is the individual man who can weigh various possibilities of action and decide between the right and the wrong one. The orderliness of individual behavior will depend not so much on the pressure that is brought to bear upon his will as on his seeing his action in the right perspective, and on his selection of the right ends. As Father Walsh put it in one of his speeches: Human will is not governed by penalties, but by motives. Therefore, the behavior of individuals is lawful to the same degree to which the motives behind it are in conformity with the laws of coordinate activities. Right behavior presupposes right evaluation. Thus the sequence of processes by which legal order is realized, is: Right evaluation, from which results a right perspective, from which emerges a right "directedness" of action, which in turn conduces to right behavior.[24]

The problem of legal statutes is the problem of how to bring about these different processes in individuals. The personalistic type of law does not rely on the responsible decision of individuals and on individual initiative in the realization of legal order. It takes the decision out of their hands, trusting only the legislator, and imposing his selection of means for certain ends as an authoritative command upon the individual's will. The subject of law is supposed to obey these commands passively. He is kept unaware of the ends and motivations which have inspired the selection of those means, and he is discouraged from selecting his own means for the attainment of these same ends in accordance with varying circumstances. What the

[24] Bott-Bodenhausen, *Formatives und funktionales Recht*, p. 145.

subject of law is ordered to do is prescribed in detail and with strict rigidity, while the meaning of these prescriptions is hidden away in the minds of the legislators or in political documents; never, or seldom does it form part of the letter of the law. Accordingly, legal statutes in a personalistic system attempt to govern human wills essentially by penalties and not by motives.

However, this is true only of our formal law. There are countless prescriptions and instruments of direction which try to bring about a lawful behavior of individuals by producing in those individuals a lawful attitude, and by relying on this attitude to produce the order of actual behavior. Look, for instance, at the instructions that are used by post offices during the weeks before Christmas, relating to the problem of Christmas mail. The public is not told with minute detail what to do in every situation, but it is informed on those points which "matter" for the smoothest dispatch of the mail, i.e. the ends at which they should aim in their behavior. Or one might think of the instructions handed out by the sales manager of a big commercial enterprise to his salesmen. Again, these instructions do not contain commands or authoritative prescriptions, but they point out the important features of good salesmanship, in order to give each salesman the proper perspective. The ultimate decision about what is correct in each particular situation is then left to the salesman himself, and can be entrusted to him safely once his attention has been directed toward the right criteria of correct behavior. These two examples show that in many instances, even today, we do not rely on the force of command alone, but try to introduce order in human behavior by making people aware of the ends at which they should aim, thereby engendering in them a mental and emotional "directedness," a perspective of evaluation and judgment, which will result in a more secure and more stable order of behavior than any command could produce. Functional law therefore, instead of prescribing rigidly defined means, emphasizes the necessity of functional ends. The "directedness" of perspective which derives from those ends, the orientation of people's wills *and* minds *and* acts toward these ends, is the mainspring of lawful behavior. Once the right attitude prevails in individuals, the rest may be left to their creative initiative.

This is most important for rules of law which govern the behavior of those individuals who hold the highest positions of power. The only possible means of making the powerful on this earth observe rules of inherent lawfulness is by creating in them, through careful training and constant habituation, a perspective which works as a motive in all their relevant actions. This becomes clear when we realize what it is that makes a general conform to the rules laid down in military manuals. The manual certainly contains rules and prescriptions of military tactics. The general does not, however, work out the actual plan of battle by resorting to the prescriptions of the manual and trying to apply them obediently to the actual situation. It is the judgment of the general which produces the plan of the battle. Nevertheless the plan is not arbitrary. It should coincide with the instructions of the manual, and it usually does so because the judgment of the general has been governed by the same pattern of evaluation and by the same perspective which underlies the rules of tactics as set out in the manual.[25] No one would demand that the plan of battle should be derived from the book of instructions. Yet no one on that account fears that the general's actions and decisions will be arbitrary. This is because we are confident that the motives which dominate his mind and will spring from a "right" perspective, and therefore exercise a directing influence that makes arbitrary action unlikely, if not impossible. Discretion is not arbitrary and initiative is lawful in proportion as the motives and impulses behind them are channeled by a fundamental orientation towards constructive ends. Similarly, Feilchenfeld has analyzed the basis of those rules of law which apply to the highest priests of the Catholic Church. He points to the clerical system as a proof that "the prevalence of law in human be-

[25] "It never occurs to anyone as desirable that a judge should be free to work out situations practically, a freedom which we allow to arbitrators or even to administrative tribunals doing the same thing with a different attitude toward their task." Thurman Arnold, *The Symbols of Government*, Yale University Press (1935), p. 84.

havior is greatest when legal rules do not consist in a number of detailed prescriptions, but in the direction of motives of action toward . . higher ends."[26]

Written articulations of the law, such as statutes, treaties, etc. are thus simply means by which the judgment and the motives of individuals are directed toward lawful ends. Lawful ends are those which, by virtue of an inner necessity, pertain to the relationships and institutions of human behavior. The rules and sentences formulated in statutes, when functionally conceived, do not call for passive obedience, but for active initiative on the part of individuals in realizing legal order in their behavior. They aim at developing the awareness of necessary ends, at training the sense of judgment, at directing individual evaluations, while leaving the concrete shaping of orderly behavior to the individual's discretion. Thus the function of the judge in functional law will be more similar to that of a doctor than to that of an avenger. Just as the doctor adjusts pathological disturbances in the functional order of the organism, the judge will have to adjust pathological cases of arbitrary conduct in social relationships.

The function of these statutes and other written articulations of the law, however, will be decidedly secondary. In personalistic law, the formula set up as a prescription is itself the legal rule. In a functional system only the lawfulness which is inherent in actual behavior is considered to be legal order. Legal rules are found within the reality of life, not in abstract formulations opposed to it. Consequently a statutory formula may actually correspond to the law, but it is also possible that it may not coincide with what is actually acknowledged as being lawful. In this latter case, the statutory formula is at best a hypothesis about the law, and a wrong one at that, but it does

[26] Feilchenfeld refers repeatedly to the impossibility of binding a holder of supreme power by authoritative legal rules.

"The only possibility of assuming norms which are binding [upon the highest priest of the Catholic Church] is by realizing that the binding effect of legal norms is strongest when they do not consist in a series of detailed prescriptions, but in a general functional direction (*Zweckbindung*) toward a superior end." *op. cit.*, p. 128 (translation mine).

not represent law. It may also be characterized as an attempt to bring about the acknowledgment of certain rules in actual behavior. Such an attempt may be successful; it may also fail. Therefore a statutory provision may be disproved by evidence that it differs from the acknowledged rules of social behavior. The role of statutes in functional law has been compared to that of the grammar of a national academy. It is an articulation of the rules of language emanating from a highly authoritative source. But just as the grammar of the academy is not the actual order of the language, which we find only in the structure of actual speech, so the statutes in functional law are not the law, which exists only in the structure of actual behavior.

Between the actual legal order and its statutory articulations there is a relationship similar to that between the actual laws of warfare and the manuals of military strategy and tactics. The rules of warfare are not affected by what the manuals say. For the immanent lawfulness of military movements is contained not in formal instructions but in the inner necessity prevailing in such contexts as "defense," "attack," "retreat" and so on, and their concrete appearance in concrete circumstances. Therefore the prescriptions of the manuals are merely attempts to create, in soldiers, that perspective which will enable them to act under any circumstances according to the immanent laws of warfare. That is why the manuals are subject to correction by the actual necessities of warfare. They may turn out not to have represented the laws of military movements at all.

But even though statutory articulations may actually represent the laws of social order, their significance is only a secondary one. For individuals may be aware of the immanent laws of social relationships without having taken cognizance of statutory formulas. Since the validity of law is based on the conviction of the lawfulness of certain types of behavior, the individual sense of what is lawful and what is not may be just as good a guide for his conduct as the instructions of written instruments. The important thing is the inherent orderliness of behavior, not the source from which individuals derive their right perspectives. For law consists in the realization of lawful action, not in the obedience to letters and formulas.

Legal statutes represent attempts to formulate the laws which actually govern social behavior. Consequently, they compete with the actual experience of individuals with respect to the standards of law in their behavior. They are liable to be tested and measured by reference to the "inner necessity" which is the criterion of legal rules in social behavior. This makes it necessary to distinguish between legal statutes proper and what may best be called "regulations". Besides trying to give expression in written form to the laws of social behavior, the authorities often want to issue regulations in order to accomplish some practical purpose. Thus, for instance, it may be necessary to prescribe a certain behavior which is meant to prevent the flight of capital, or to secure the fairness of trial, etc. These prescriptions are of a technical nature. Their criterion is not the "inner necessity" of evaluation, but practical expediency. Traffic regulations, for example, are not representative of any inherent lawfulness in human relationships, they are a technical device to prevent collisions. The role of regulations in the process of legal order is entirely different from that of real laws and their articulation in legal statutes. Regulations do not correspond to the necessary structure of behavior which constitutes legal rules, and they cannot be tested by criteria of conviction and inner acknowledgment. Precisely for this reason it is imperative to distinguish between the two categories, and to call them by different names.

The question of how the change from an individualistic system of law to a functional system can be effected, will be only briefly touched upon here. We can do no more than indicate in a general way that the change will come more by way of a new orientation than by way of a new organization. The machinery of legal order will follow the needs which it is meant to serve. Consequently it is the thinking which has to be remodeled before any external devices are envisaged. What is needed is not so much a new mechanism as a new outlook of the men who handle the existing one.[27] In legislation and jurisdiction, for instance, emphasis on the functional ends of social relationships must replace the strict prescription of rigid means. Insistence on a perspective, an attitude of individuals which is in conformity with the meaning of coordinate activities, must supplant the expectation of merely external obedience to the letter of legal commands. The meaning of social relationships and institutions as such must be recognized as the guiding criterion of legal order, and the notion that subjective interests can properly be the ultimate ends of law discarded. And finally we must become more conscious of the fact that legal order consists in the lawfulness of actual behavior, not in a set of commanding formulas backed by physical force. These are the program points of a functional system of law.

It would be beyond the scope of this book to indicate the extent to which signs of a change in this direction are already noticeable today.[28] This task must be carried out through a number of more specialized studies investigating trends of functional thinking and actual functional forms of legal order in international as well as in domestic law. However, there can be no doubt, considering the more recent theoretical developments in science, philosophy, art and modern forms of social organization, that strong tendencies in our cultural pattern point in the direction of a legal order which is guided by the inherent functional laws of social relationships and which is realized by immanently lawful individual initiative.

[27] This idea was very appropriately expressed in a letter by John Foster Dulles to the *New York Times*, concerning the problem of administrative reform: "It is traditionally American to feel that, whenever abuses exist, the remedy is to pass a law. After considerable study of the subject, I doubt whether this approach will solve the abuses of the administrative process. . . . I have not been able to conceive of any law which will prevent private individuals from being irreparably injured if we have administrative commissions which act recklessly and without scruple, or which allow bureaucracy or lust for power to obtain the upper hand. . . . The proper functioning of the administrative process depends upon putting it into the hands of men, . . . who are sufficiently imbued with the American principle of fair play. . . ." *New York Times*, April 26, 1940.

[28] See Schindler, Heyse, Bott-Bodenhausen, *op. cit.*, and the authors quoted in the introduction to part III.

In the five preceding sections of this chapter an attempt has been made to outline the general ideas of a functional system of law. Much of what has been said on those pages is a repetition of arguments to be found in all parts of the book, but repetition was thought useful in the interest of clearness. For the sake of simplicity, the lines of functional law have been explained with reference to individuals and their relationships. Now the question arises as to how these ideas of a functional order can be applied to the affairs of states.

It seems difficult to fit the scheme of functional law into the problems presented by the institution of the State. On the one hand we have defined functional law as the immanent order of coordinate behavior. On the other hand we have analyzed the State and have found that the State as an organization exists only in so far as human behavior is coordinated within its specific framework. The State is a structure of coordinate behavior characterized by a specific function in human culture. Because of the very ends for which the institution of the State operates it is involved in contexts of functional activities with other states. Thus everything about the State seems to be structured, coordinate, patterned, ordered. Now if functional law is identical with the inherent order of coordinate behavior, does that mean that everything the State does is lawful? Is functional law really equivalent to an uncritical endorsement of every political policy?

When we discussed the process of the realization of a functional order of law with respect to interindividual relationships, we found that it took place in an antithesis between what is necessary and coordinatable in human behavior and human motivation and what is accidental and arbitrary. Certain impulses and urges of the individual's will were found to be coordinatable because they sprang from the inner necessity of what H. G. Wells has called the "socially constructive passion in any man." Other motives and initiatives could not be coordinated socially because they originated from the reflexes of human senses—reflexes which from the point of view of culture are entirely accidental. Any initiative which is relevant merely from the point of view of sensual reactions and any motive aiming at the gratification of the senses, are, in the widest possible meaning of the word, incapable of having more than a significance for the individual self. That is why they are not coordinatable.

If the "necessary" and the "accidental" impulses and motives of behavior constitute the poles between which the process of legal order occurs, then indeed it seems difficult to apply the idea of functional law to the phenomenon of the State. For while individuals may follow an initiative which is determined by the gratification of the senses and which, therefore, is addressed purely to the interests of the individual self *per se*, states do not have such impulses, because they are not animate beings. Actions of the State are decided on by individuals who, in so far as they behave "institutionally," are not inspired by purely self-centered motives. The very fact that they behave according to the requirements of a public office means that their behavior is motivated by constructive ends, is coordinate and is functional. Thus it is senseless to assume that there are motives of political action which originate merely in the accidental reaction of the senses. States have no passions, no appetites, no fear, no greed, no hatred such as would spring from the chance reactions of an individual. Yet, there are elements of arbitrariness in the conduct which is imputed to the State as well as in the behavior of single individuals. Only the arbitrariness of "institutional" behavior is of a different kind.

The notion of function, as we have analyzed it in the introduction to this part of the book, implies two elements: on the one hand the idea of a task to be performed, on the other hand the actual operation of coordinate units. That behavior of individuals which constitutes the State is functional behavior and accordingly is coordinate. But it is possible that the actual operation of this coordinate structure may not always correspond to the functional task which constitutes its ideal meaning. To illustrate the difference, one might think of the example of an automobile engine functioning in different contexts. Suppose some one has removed the top of the cylinders in order to use the rest of the engine as a flower vase. This evidently is not the function for which the engine was designed. The inherent functional meaning of an engine is to develop power by successive explosions. Nevertheless the engine is also "functioning" with the top of the cylinders off and flowers put in the borings. However, this "performance," measured by the intrinsic meaning of the engine, is not "fitting". It is not functioning in the "right" way.

Similarly it can be said that a social institution does not always function in accordance with its inherent meaning. The behavior which makes an institution is always structured and coordinate, otherwise there would not be any institution; but the structure and coordination can be inspired by motives which, from the point of view of the cultural meaning of the institution, are accidental and arbitrary. Thus not all of the ways in which an institution operates can be regarded as of equal value. Any institution by reason of its own coherence makes possible the use of its strength for ends which are essentially "non-fitting." From the point of view of social order and social constructiveness, these "accidental" uses to which institutions are put are just as uncoordinatable as the sensually relevant motives of individual beings.

The most conspicuous instance of an arbitrary operation in an institution is the idea (and practice) which views the State as a suitable tool for the promotion of collective interests. For the criterion of interest is an incalculable one. It stems from entirely self-oriented evaluations which do not have trans-personal validity or constructive "necessity." It is not possible to coordinate the operations of states if states are operated in accordance with collective interests, for these, after all, are never more than the interests of a particular pressure group or a ruling class. That is why functional law—nay, all international law—depends on the purification of our notion of the State and on our becoming clearly aware of the connotations of politics.

It is logically as well as practically impossible to have a system of international law which is based on precisely that element in the operation of states which is arbitrary, non-coordinatable, and self-centered: that is to say, the element of interest. But in so far as the operation of states is inspired by the criterion of objective tasks which the State is meant to perform in human culture, it becomes possible to coordinate the actions of various states and to realize order in their relationships. Interests represent "consumptive" values, tasks represent "constructive" values. That is why the evaluations relating to interests are "accidental" and the evaluations relating to tasks are "necessary". Actions based on "accidental" evaluations are arbitrary from the point of view of social order, actions based on "necessary" evaluations are lawful. Therefore a state, just as well as an automobile engine, may function so as to attain necessary ends, but it may also "function" so as to attain arbitrary ends. The first we call a fitting function, the second, a non-fitting function. From the point of view of international law as well as from the point of view of a satisfactory order within the State itself, it is necessary to distinguish clearly between these two possibilities of political action.

Therefore the primary condition of a functional system of international law is that the functional meaning of the State should be realized by all the individuals who act in relation to it. The inherently necessary ends of political institutions have to emerge clearly in the consciousness of individuals, freed from all accidental and arbitrary modifications. The notion of the political function has to be crystallized into a workable concept of legal order. It has to be realized independently of the subjective purposes of individuals who hold offices in the State. Only by reference to this transpersonal and necessary element of lawfulness in the structure of the State, disregarding the arbitrary element of interests, can a true legal order of international relations evolve.

FUNCTIONAL RECONSTRUCTION

The attempt of the present system of international law to impose authoritative commands on modern states must inevitably meet with failure. It is a hopeless undertaking to try to apply force to those whose position puts them in control of the organized force of society. In former times, the fear of God, and later, the respect for the incalculable power of an International Community were cloaks under which compulsion could really be exercised over the rulers of states. Today these spells no longer work as restrictive inhibitions on the wills of the powerful ones. Therefore, legal order can no longer rest on the authority of command assumed by abstract rules and prescriptions. The only way of securing legal order in the relationships of the supreme organizations of society is to emphasize the immanent laws which pertain to the activities of states, and to bring about a clear consciousness of these laws in the individuals who act on behalf of states.

It is not a new but a very old truism that in order to make the powerful observe lawful conduct, they must be imbued and motivated by a perspective which does not admit of any but a lawful initiative. The experience of the Catholic Church as well as the history of military leadership bear witness to this principle. Neither a pope nor a generalissimo can be held down merely by the authoritative force of commands; they themselves are too powerful. But their training, the molding of their personality through education in their profession, has produced in these individuals a general "directedness" of will toward those tasks which are lawful and "right." It is their total attitude, mental and emotional, which is oriented toward objective tasks and which begets actions of inherent lawfulness.

This, then, is the way in which international law can also be effectual. Legal order in international relations will not be secured by preaching, thundering, indicting, and threatening on the part of international lawyers, but by engendering a fundamental orientation of statesmanship in the direction of the functional tasks of the state as a cultural institution. The mainspring of legal order is this attitude of functional "directedness," an attitude such as that which causes a general to act, during a battle, according to the ends and the immanent laws of warfare and not according to his personal whims or interests. As for statesmen and state officials, such an orientation derives ultimately from their awareness of the necessary ends of the functioning of states. International law in the present world cannot be effectual as long as its rules are conceived of as in opposition to institutions which fulfill a necessary functional task in human culture. But when they are conceived of as in conformity with the meaning of the State and with the function of political institutions, international law can be realized as the intrinsic lawfulness of the behavior of individuals acting on behalf of states.

The task of creating this rightly oriented attitude in individuals is a function of the written instruments of legal order: treaties, conventions, protocols, and so on. By pointing out the functionally necessary ends of international relationships, by suggesting means for the attainment of those ends, by emphasizing the nature of the objective tasks to be solved, they cause individuals acting for the State (statesmen, diplomats, civil servants, soldiers, even civilians) to realize the meaning of coordinate behavior, to evaluate in the right direction, to act in accordance with the immanent laws of interstate relations. The words of the Jesuit priest, Father Walsh: "The human will is not ruled by penalties, but by motives," give the best characterization of the role of these written instruments. For there is no better safeguard of an intrinsically orderly conduct than the ultimate perspective which prevails in those layers of human consciousness that govern the impulses of our will. Therefore a functional order of law is based on the accentuation of those motives which are necessarily lawful from the point of view of the coordinated behavior of men. These "necessary" motives, as has been said before, are those which come from the visualization of the ends to which social relationships and social institutions are destined by virtue of their cultural meaning.

As to the question of who is to decide about the inner necessity of ends and motives, no concise answer can be given. This question can be answered just as much and just as little as the query: who is to decide about the criterion of correctness in a language? In the last analysis any system of order in social behavior is founded on the individual sense of what is inherently lawful, because only the particular individual experiences the inner necessity of acknowledging certain standards and values. In actual individual behavior these individual convictions become manifest and are found to be either insignificant or of transpersonal validity. Thus it is ultimately the single human being who, through his stewardship of social relations, contributes his share to the constant development of the criteria of lawfulness. The legislator, the diplomat, the acting statesman, the administering civil servant: all are agents of legal order, because legal order exists only in the inherent lawfulness of their conduct.

By pointing out what they can and should do, instead of decreeing what they are forbidden to do; by emphasizing ends and suggesting means, instead of prescribing blind obedience to narrowly defined rules; by facilitating the realization of the functions of institutions, instead of setting up restrictive dams against human energies, the impulses and initiatives of individuals can be formed into a living source from which the legal order of their behavior constantly flows. Thus conceived, international law will operate not as an obstacle but as the necessary channel for the energies that are coordinated in and through the institution of the State. In no better way can the spirit of this notion of law be expressed than in the words of Goethe's *Wahlverwandtschaften*.[29] "In the education of children, as well as in the conduct of nations, there is nothing more worthless and barbarous than laws and commandments forbidding this and that action. Man is naturally active, and if you know how to tell him what to do, he will do it immediately, and keep straight in the direction in which you set him. A man is really glad to do what is right and sensible, if he only knows how to get at it.

" 'Thou shalt not murder.' As if any man felt the slightest inclination to strike another man dead! Men will hate sometimes; they will fly into passions and forget themselves; and

[29] In the English translation published by *Collier's*, under the title "Elective Affinities."

as a consequence of this and other feelings it may easily come now and then to a murder; but what a barbarous precaution it is to tell children that they are not to kill or murder! If the commandment ran: 'Have a regard for the life of another—put away whatever can do him hurt—save him, though with peril to yourself—if you injure him, consider that you are injuring yourself'—that is the form which should be in use among educated, reasonable peoples."

CHAPTER IX

ORGANIZATION OR ORIENTATION

WHAT IS TO BE DONE?

EVERY critical analysis of the problem of international order today faces ultimately the one question which seems to be of exclusive importance to the public: "What is to be done?" This question is, in the eyes of the public, the supreme test of the soundness of any criticism of past or present institutions. It is the true justification of any study of international law and international relations. Any analysis which leads to no immediate practical conclusions, or only to those which are already known, is for this reason judged valueless and academic.

The public seems indeed to have a right to insist on this test. A scientific investigation of real conditions and of the laws governing real action should be instrumental in reaching practical decisions with respect to those conditions and actions. If the theory of international law and international relations does not enable us to achieve actual improvements, it is difficult to see what value it could claim aside from that of giving personal satisfaction to its authors. However, nobody would deny that the impatient demand for immediate "solutions" has led the students and practitioners of international relations to adopt those unrealistic plans that contributed essentially to the disillusionment of the world with regard to international order. Thus we come to the conclusion that while it is true that all theory is nothing but deep insight into the structure of real phenomena, and accordingly is tested by practical application, the theory of international order seems to be more "realistic" when it refuses to be applied in the form of practical solutions. How can this paradox be explained?

An explanation offers itself when, instead of yielding to the impulse of answering to it, we proceed to query the public's question itself. What sort of result do people expect when they raise the problem of practical action regarding international order? The fact that the question "What is to be done?" is regarded as the ultimate measure of soundness of analysis implies that to "do" something in the field of international order is considered not only desirable, but feasible and commendable. In other words, the public has already made up its mind that "doing" is the only form of progress in international order that is conceivable. This attitude prejudices scientific analysis because it anticipates the kind of "solution" that is expected and narrows the range of possible conclusions by declaring that only one type of conclusion is acceptable, that which proposes "action". The prejudice appears even more serious when we realize that action with respect to international order has a restricted meaning in our days. It refers to the action of governments and to that which governments can practically "do", viz. the setting up of machinery of international procedures. The hope for a stable order in international relations today has taken the form of a demand for more and better international organization. The public mind does not seem capable of conceiving progress in international order except in terms of a more effective League of Nations, a World Court, an International Police Force, or of other such organizations for securing peace and solidarity. For this reason the public, in demanding "practical solutions," tacitly bans any answer to its question that does not propose some sort of governmental action towards the establishment of international machinery. It is this prejudice that progress in international order is proportional to the effectiveness of international organization which puts the stamp of unrealism on most of "scientific" scheming in the international field. As an example, let us look at a recent investigation into our problem, the *Preliminary Report of the Commission to Study the Organization of Peace.* In this document, the Commission, after stating its theoretical premises, proposes the now almost traditional "limitations on national sovereignty" in favor of new international institutions, to wit: An international court with jurisdiction adequate to deal with all international disputes on the basis of law; international legislative bodies; adequate police forces; international machinery with authority to regulate international communication and transportation; and appropriate authorities to administer backward areas. On the other hand, the Commission recognizes that "the nation-state is the unit of world society. . . . Clearly the organization of international society with the greatest chance of success will be that one which will assure a dynamic peace with the minimum sacrifice of international sovereignty." This clearly indicates that the Commission expects the proposed international organization to emerge from the concerted action of the particular governments who are supposed to "renounce sovereignty for the common good." Yet the Commission is realistic enough to "deeply appreciate that mere form without substance is of little value. No system of laws and organization can be of value without the living faith and spirit behind it and in it."

Now neither the Commission to Study the Organization of Peace nor any other human being can foretell the kind of spirit that will prevail when peace finally comes. In spite of this the Commission proposes a definite scheme of international institutions. This can only mean that the spirit of the nations is expected to conform to the organization. The plan envisages first the instruments of solidarity and relies on the subsequent "growth" of the necessary common consciousness; it proposes a framework of international community and hopes piously for the faith that will make it work. This conception is typical not only of the so-called "practical" solutions that are being offered today to the problem of international order, but also of the attitude of mind that so insistently poses the question: "What is to be done?" It implies the idea that a scheme of international institutions as such is identical with "the common good." Organization is so completely identified with the quintessence of progress, solidarity, and order in international relations, that even the spirit of nations is considered secondary and is supposed to adapt itself to the plan of an international machinery.

To what extent are these hopes grounded in the real structure of international relations? Can we possibly envisage international institutions, procedures, and organizations without having reached agreement as to the common purposes which such a machinery is to serve? If such common ends among nations cannot be stated in advance, can we arrive at any conclusion as to the shape of the future organization? In other words, if we are uncertain about the "substance" of international solidarity, can we propose anything that "is to be done" about its form? These questions will be discussed on the following pages.

THE FEDERALISTIC FALLACY

The notion of international organization has been repeatedly criticized ever since it originated. For this reason it is here sufficient to restate only some of the most vigorous arguments against it. International organization connotes the institution of an agency above the states, such as a world court, an equity tribunal, a league, a union, an international police force, and so on. The essential characteristic of such an agency is that it would supposedly take over the task of preserving international peace while leaving most of the other governmental functions to the particular states. In other words, the idea is based on the assumption that sovereignty can be "divided." Pointing to the analogy of "civil society," people argue that states, like individual persons, ought to surrender "part of their rights" to the common agency, and ought to obey its decisions for the sake of peace and order. If nations were only willing to renounce the completeness of their sovereignty, such an agency could secure universal peace and stability in international relations.

This sort of argument is possible only on the basis of a fundamental misunderstanding of the functions of a state. Either it is forgetful of the fact that the State, too, is an organization aimed at securing peace and order; or, if it does remember this fact, it envisages the simultaneous functioning of two types of agencies, the national and the international organizations, for the same end. Now can there exist two classes of organization, side by side, in charge of law, order and security? If the existing states were left intact as units of govermental authority, each nation would be ruled by two powers: its own government and the international organization. But there would be a division of functions, people argue. The international agency would be in charge only of questions relating to peace and security, and all administrative functions would be managed by the national government. This is the point where the federalistic fallacy comes in.

It is possible for several organizations to work upon the same group of people if these organizations are instituted for concrete, definite and limited ends of social activities. Organizations, the ends of which are functionally defined in terms of concrete and limited purposes are not, however, political organizations. They are meant to achieve either economic, or cultural, or financial, or scientific or other non-political ends. That is why in the lives of individuals so many different organizations have a place side by side, because each individual and each group of individuals can pursue an almost unlimited number of different ends by differently "directed" activities which are not mutually exclusive. However in each group of people only one political organization (or hierarchy of organizations) can operate. For the scope of political organization is not limited to one kind of activity. It is the specific function of political organization to coordinate in a comprehensive way all social activities within a certain territory. Political we call the organization providing for general social order and synchronization, for the accomplishment of whatever unity and consistency is required in the social life of a group. For this reason political organization is necessarily monopolistic and exclusive. If there were duplication of political organization with respect to the same territory—that is if more than one organization were in operation with the end of securing the general unity of social order and cooperation—this end could certainly not be attained. Therefore, political organization necessarily calls for the existence of a supreme central unit of collective action and decision.

The highest and supreme unit of collective action and decision on each political territory is the State. In the course of four centuries, the State has acquired the social monopoly of legislation, of making the ultimate decision in social conflicts, and of maintaining and employing armed force. This exclusiveness of governmental functions exercised by the State is not an idea, it is an historical and cultural reality. From the point of view of the ends for which the State operates it is impossible to have in addition to the State another organization which also serves the ends of a general and comprehensive ordering of social relationships. Yet this would be exactly the function of an international organization for assuring peace and security. The organization of peace among the states would necessarily involve decisions regarding their general relations with each other. Hence any international agency for the maintenance of general order would have to weigh the interests of one state against those of another, it would have to forbid certain actions on the part of one state and command the modification of measures on the part of another etc. In other words, it would necessarily be forced to interfere with the functions of the states, by assuming the right to decide what shall be done within their respective territories. The international agency would thereby become a unit of command superior to the national governments, and one on whose decisions conditions, laws and order within the national territories would largely depend.

No agency can assume this rank of superior power without at the same time performing the functions which correspond to it. Therefore the operation of an international agency would amount to the simultaneous exercise of the functions of government by two organizations: the national government and the international agency. Now every agency exercising governmental functions must have the means to impose its decisions directly on individuals, the influencing of whose conduct is, after all, the sole objective of all governmental activities. Therefore a political organization presupposes, among other things, a permanent bureaucracy with direct powers over, and having access to, individual persons and their property. This is what all existing plans for international organizations fail to consider. They plan for an international agency which is supposed to decide the most vital and fundamental questions of government and order in human culture without having its own means of enforcing these decisions. For the essence of international organization as envisaged in most of these projects, is that they presuppose the continued existence of nation-states, basing the authority of the international agencies "on consent." In other words, international organization is expected to operate mainly through constitutional "rights" acquired by the "renunciation of sovereignty" on the part of the states. This means that the different states will continue to maintain their own bureaucracy, their own system of taxation, their own police force, their own army, and above all, their own system of legislation and jurisdiction governing social and private conflicts. Although the decisions of the international agency will affect fundamentally the social conditions and legal order within each state, it will have to rely on the various national governments for the execution of its orders. The utter impracticability of this idea has been convincingly demonstrated by Alexander Hamilton in No. XV of the *Federalist*.

Thus, a truly international agency, i.e. an organization built upon the consent of the different nation-states, cannot possibly discharge functions which require it to decide questions concerning the inner structure of states. The function of maintaining peace and security, however, is precisely of this nature. It necessarily involves the most fundamental affairs of each nation, its security, its social and political constitution, its laws, its finances, its administration, its prosperity. The organization of peace and security in human society is thus properly a political function. Being comprehensive in scope and effect, it cannot be discharged except by a supreme organization operating exclusively within its territory.

For this reason, some projects envisage an international organization that is genuinely superimposed on the national states. Such an agency would be given instruments of power which would enable it to exercise direct control over individuals, without being in need of the goodwill of the various governments. However, such an agency can no longer be termed international. It ceases to be based on consent, it becomes the State itself. To distinguish it from the existing nation-states it might be called a super-state.

Thus we come to the conclusion that the idea of an international organization for the maintenance of peace is unrealistic because it does not take into consideration the necessary social functions exercised by the State. An organization that took over these functions would itself be a new state on a larger scale, and unless this new state embraced the entire world it would not in fact eliminate the problem of international law and order. Short of the World-State, in other words, every project for international organization must fail to provide a solution.

THE WORLD-STATE

But is a world-state really a valid and desirable alternative to the present chaos of nation-states? Most people criticize the idea of a universal government on the ground of the improbability of its ever being realized in fact. When sufficient regard is had for the unbridgeable disparity of cultures, religions, languages, traditions, customs, temperaments and cultural levels, which separate the various parts of mankind from each other, the materialization of a world-state appears, indeed, very unlikely. For how can we expect within any reasonable length of time the growth of that community of values and standards, that minimum of common consciousness which is indispensable to any political unity? But the question of whether the world-state is likely or not to materialize is ultimately unanswerable. For, however it is answered, the answer given can be based only on generalizations derived from past experience, and these may be refuted at any moment by new and unexpected developments.

Leaving aside this consideration, however, it can hardly be maintained that the political unity of the world under one government is ultimately desirable. The demand for a world-state represents the point of view of a generation whom the horror of war has deprived of a sense of proportion. Driven into a one-sided pacifism, we are prone to look at war as the one calamity that must be avoided at the expense of everything else. We fail to realize sufficiently that war is just one specific kind of chaos and disorder in human society. We overlook the fact that the result of arbitrary power inside a system of government can be just as fatal to creative life, to human productivity and progress, and to the development of culture, as the fight between nations. In order to escape from war, the establishment of a world-state would subject the whole of mankind to the decisions of one single unit of power, from which there would be no appeal and to which there could be no alternative. Because of the vastness of the territory over which it ruled, a world government would be bound to be less dependent on consent, to be more mechanical, more standardized, and therefore culturally more oppressive, than any other government. Being able to rely on countless sources of support, against which the people of any particular nation would be in a hopeless minority, the power of a world government would inevitably be more absolute than that of any possible national government.

Thus, for the sole purpose of avoiding war, we propose to force upon the entire world the dubious security of a necessarily dictatorial world régime. Fundamentally, this means the disposition to do precisely what the now totalitarian nations have done: to sacrifice the values of personality and autonomous development for the value of security.

If considered rightly, the question of international order thus constitutes only one aspect of the general problem of the lawful and orderly exercise of political functions and political power. That particular form of disorder in the political relations of society which is called war is nothing but a specific instance of chaos in politics. Therefore the world-state would leave the problem fundamentally just as unsolved as the different projects of international organization. It would simply suppress one of the symptoms of disorder.

Possibly for this, possibly also for other reasons, not many people are ready to sacrifice national independence to a world Leviathan. However, unaware of the inner contradiction in their arguments, they continue to pursue, by means of international agencies, ends which could be realized only by a world-state. They desire the security of universal peace without wanting the ultimate subordination of all nations under a single government—which is the indispensable condition of such peace. Consequently, their projects suffer from an inherent inadequacy, a lack of balance between too ambitious ends and too modest means.

On these and similar grounds all the various projects for international organization have been criticized by competent authors. The critics of the idea of international organization have been extremely effective in uncovering the hidden fallacies and mistaken premises on which these different proposals are based. No one familiar, for instance, with Clyde Eagleton's *Analysis of the Problem of War* can avoid recognizing how utterly delusive and without foundation the hopes connected with pacifist panaceas really are.

Yet it must strike any observer that no criticism of this sort, however trenchant, has actually been successful in eliminating the idea of international organization from the schemes of statesmen and scholars. How can this phenomenon be explained? If a continued adherence to the vision of eternal peace is to be expected on the part of the emotional masses, it should certainly not continue to motivate the scholar in favor of unrealistic projects. The reason that it continues to do so, however, is that most criticisms of pacifist plans of international organization rarely criticize more than the plan as such. The critics confine themselves to cutting off the head of the magic animal without ever becoming aware that the torso will immediately produce new ones. For their criticism, aimed solely against the concrete details of the various plans, leaves untouched the underlying perspective of which such plans are merely the inevitable result. The best proof of this assertion is the fact that these critics themselves have been unable to offer any alternative to the idea of international organization except that of international anarchy. While realizing clearly the impracticability and the defects of the different plans, they are incapable of conceiving any other solution, because, in spite of their criticism, they still cling to the same basic ideas from which the postulate of international organization itself inevitably emerged.

Accordingly, if we are really to avoid unrealistic "solutions" we must criticize not merely plans and projects but their basic underlying assumptions. What are these assumptions?

The belief in the miracle of international organization has its roots in three fundamental notions which are closely interconnected, and which have already been discussed in different contexts throughout this book. These notions are: A mechanical conception of the phenomenon of "society" (or community), an atomic conception of the legal person, and a formalistic conception of legal rules. Any line of thinking which starts out from these three concepts must necessarily arrive at the conclusion that international organization is the only possible way of maintaining law and order in international relations. The logical inevitability of this result has already been indicated in the preceding chapters. By way of a final summary the argument will be briefly recapitulated here.

A *mechanical conception of society* leads to the postulate of international organization for the following reasons: According to this conception, international society is regarded as composed of a number of states, each of which is conceived as a material "body" governed by a will and interest of its own. Thus the particular "members" are considered to exist "really," and society is merely a composite entity, less "real," by definition, than the individual units which form its parts. Now the idea that the units have an individual and real existence prior to society must lead to the postulate of a machinery, an apparatus, technical devices of procedure, by which these separate units and the "forces" governing them can be held together in a system of common law and order. The mechanistic conception of the composition of society calls forth a mechanistic idea of the way in which society maintains itself.

The reasoning behind this demand for greater organization of the "Family of Nations" is that international society needs mechanical devices to be able to exist independently of the good will of its units. The notion that society is an aggregate composed of individual units involves the idea that these units are motivated by interests which are originally selfish, and the pursuit of which they partially abandon in favor of the "common good" upon entering society. But once national self-interest is postulated the existence of international society is bound to appear precarious, as being constantly endangered by that self-interest in the different states, which may at any moment threaten society by triumphing over the "social reason" of nations. From that point of view, therefore, international law and order cannot be regarded as secure until "society" as such is supported by an organization which will work independently of the good will of governments—which will work "automatically." "Set up a collective machinery and equip it with sufficient power, and the problem of law and order in international relations will be solved." So runs the argument. And this demand for a mechanism of collective force is supported by somewhat the following reasoning: "The problem really consists in nothing but devising a technique for keeping in bounds the dynamic 'forces' that are driving the members of international society, the states. Therefore it can be solved only by opposing to the 'forces' of the individual states a superior collective 'force'. This, however, is merely a problem of organizational technique."

On the basis of this line of reasoning, countless programs of international procedures and plans for organizations have been suggested: An international police force, a reformed league (this time with "teeth in it"), an international air force, disarmament as a way of weakening the "forces of the individual states," "automatic" procedures of jurisdiction, arbitration, conciliation, consultation, indictment before public opinion, boycott, schemes of collective assistance, etc. All these attempts to solve the problem of lawfulness in international relations by creating a self-reliant machinery have their logical and ideological root in the notion that every society is mechanically composed of so many individual units, each of which is characterized by its separate "body" and an independent will ruling it like a physical "force."

On the other hand, the foundation of legal theory on an *atomic conception of the legal person* likewise inevitably conduces to the unrealistic demand for international organization. To use the concept of the single person, be it the human individual or the individual state, as the starting point of legal thinking means to construe law essentially as a scheme for the protection of personal interests. However, society and its laws cannot represent the interests of one particular person, it can protect and advocate only those personal interests which are common to all the persons forming the legal community. On the other hand, the interests of each individual person are recognized both as a reality and as a value by force of the atomic conception from which legal theory started out. Thus an antagonism necessarily results between the unique and subjective point of view of the individual subject, and the standard and general point of view of the law. In other words, the problem of international order, seen from this perspective, is how to weigh and how to balance the interests of each individual state against the interests of "the many" embodied in the law.

Now the observer who compares the antagonism between "the one and the many" in civil society with the same conflict in international society is struck by the fact that in civil society the common interest is made vocal through an organization that defines and expresses it, defending the viewpoint of "the many" against the interests of each "one," while in international relations no such mouthpiece of the community as such is in existence. Therefore, in the international field, the interests of "the many" are not as evenly balanced against the interests of "the ones" as in civil society. The various subjective interests of the individual states are backed by the power, capacity of decision and readiness for action which are proper to the various states. But this weight of real force on the side of the particular subjects is not matched, on the side of the law, by an equally "real" force to back up the standards of common interest. Consequently, the different states are in a position to define the standards of collective order, often in their own particular interest, simply because the society of states has no "real" existence of its own which would put it on an equal footing with the individual subjects.

In order to make international society just as "real" as the subjects of international law, it is argued, it is imperative to establish a collective organization which will take charge of the common interest, defining it and representing it against the subjective interests of the various states. The lack of balance between the community and the subjective interests compels us, in other words, to postulate the creation of an international organization. For, if we conceive law as a means of protecting interests by balancing them against each other in case of a conflict, we cannot imagine that international law would be able to function unless the society of nations does have as real an existence of its own as its members. In short, the demand for international organization proves to be an inevitable conclusion of that theory of law which starts out from the notion of the single person and which centers its construction around the phenomenon of personal interests.

Finally, the *formalistic conception of legal rules* also compels us to resort to the idea of international organization as the only possible solution to problems of international law. According to this conception, legal rules are considered to be formal commands imposed upon the will of the subjects. Now it is possible to conceive of law as a set of commands without necessarily envisaging a machinery to enforce them. A system of law consisting of authoritative demands might well be imagined as operating efficiently even without a special apparatus for collective enforcement, for its operation could be based on privately handled sanctions.

While a system of law construed as a set of commands can

be envisaged without any machinery of enforcement, it cannot be imagined without a legislative will deciding upon and defining the norms which constitute the body of law. As Hermann Heller has shown in his monograph on Sovereignty, it is the formal certainty of the legal command, the "decidedness" of legal rules, that requires the unity of a common will. We cannot conceive of commands without assuming that there is a unit of will formulating the commands. As soon as it becomes impossible to attribute the declaration of the law to the will of God, or of Nature, or of a mysterious Community of some sort, as soon as our thinking about this will becomes entirely realistic, the collective organization is the only form in which such a legislative will can be envisaged. The legislative will that decides the law concerning individuals is the result of a complicated system of the organized integration of wills, culminating in the final unity of the formal law. A considerable number of international lawyers believe that a similar process of integrating and unifying single wills into a common unity of will also exists in the society of states. On the other hand, those who admit that there is no legislative or pseudo-legislative organization behind international law call it an imperfect law for precisely this reason. Thus the idea that law consists of commands induces them all to envisage the progress of international law mainly in terms of a future development toward the organization of a legislative unit. The basic premise inevitably conduces to the postulate of an organization which can promulgate international rules and issue precise and certain legal commands. Thus, again, it is obvious that against the background of this conception of the legal rule the only conceivable progress is that of an international organization "above" the states.

THE REVISION OF BASIC ASSUMPTIONS

We are compelled to criticize these basic assumptions because they lead to untenable results. We found that the idea of international organization is unrealistic and delusive, and for that reason dangerous. It must be rejected because it arouses false hopes and thereby is harmful to the materialization of a genuine and organic order in international relations. But it is not enough to attack this idea by showing that it is useless, infeasible or utopian. Even though the partisans of international organization must perforce acknowledge the validity of such criticism, they will continue to cling to their project as long as the fundamental premises to which they adhere force them by their inherent logic to continue to draw the same conclusion. For this reason the trap of the idea of international organization can only be avoided if the criticism begins at the very roots of the entire conception of international law, substituting new notions for the old ones.

The three preceding chapters were devoted to an attempt to outline the nature of such a conceptual renovation of international law. Functional thinking leads to new conceptions about the realities underlying the law of nations. Thus society is not "composed," in a mechanical way, of "bodies" which are driven by the "forces" of will and interest. Neither the single individual, nor any institution which is given the attribute of legal personality, can be regarded merely as a "body" with which society would have to cope as with a natural event. The State in particular cannot be conceived as a "body." The State is an organization, and like all organizations it consists not of men but of coordinate behavior. It is a structure of human acts, coordinated according to a plan and with a view to the attainment of certain functional ends.

This conception of the State makes it impossible to regard the unity of will, which is the result of the process of organized integration, as an arbitrary "force" which in itself cannot be orderly but needs to be curbed by the "laws of society." If the State is a coordinate structure of human energies, then inside this structure orderly energies must be at work as well as arbitrary ones, lawful forces must be effective side by side with blind impulses. In other words: it is an error to conceive the single State as the embodiment of "subjective," and accordingly "real," forces, and "the community" as the embodiment of the "objective," and therefore "ideal," norms. The elements of law and order are found not in the collectivity as opposed to the subjectivity of the single state; they are at work inside the very structure of the State itself, where they are contending with the inner forces which are unconstructive, chaotic, and disorderly.

If our conception of the person is revised in the light of the functional approach, it becomes equally impossible to adhere to the very notion of "collectivity." The mechanistic conception of society must go together with the atomic perspective which prompted it. Society is not made up of persons as such, but of the connectedness in their behavior. The element, the basic fact underlying all social phenomena, is not the existence of separate persons, but their reciprocal orientation and the coordinatedness of what they are doing. In other words, "society" does not consist of individual units, but of that which connects them. The "connectedness" between individual persons, however, does not lie in any external standard or machinery imposed upon their otherwise disjointed wills, but in the objective ends by reference to which human behavior is interrelated and coordinated. Thus it is unrealistic to assume that the spirit of order and the principles of law are linked with the collectivity, whereas the acts of the individual subjects are inspired only by "real" and "private" interests. The keeping of the law is not a privilege attached to the organization of the community: it is in actual human behavior that law is found. Legal order does not materialize in a struggle between the "one" and the "many," but as a struggle between the inner necessity of constructiveness and the capricious impulses toward arbitrariness within the structure of single persons. Collectivity in itself is not any more inherently lawful than individuality in itself is inherently arbitrary. The functional approach takes from our legal thinking the curse of the adulation of collectivity, and restores to the individual legal person of law the full responsibility for the realization of legal order.

Once the idea that collectivity as such is the guardian of legal standards is overcome, collective organization ceases to be the indispensable prerequisite of a system of law. The antinomy between the "one" and the "many" loses its significance once it is realized that "society" does not consist of bodies and forces, but is made up of coordinate and interrelated behavior. On the basis of this conception the process of ordering consists in eliciting those impulses and motives which are coordinatable, and of directing the energies of individuals into constructive channels. Since the struggle between the lawful and the arbitrary impulses, between necessary and incidental motives constitutes the process of ordering, and since this struggle occurs within the legal person, the idea of organizing collective power for the sake of legal order must appear meaningless. Not that power and its organization would be unnecessary as a part of human culture. But the idea that the realization of law is dependent upon collective power will disappear from the functional perspective. Power is an instrument for achieving ends which are inaccessible to the disjointed forces of individuals, but power cannot force legal persons to have lawful motives or to realize orderly ends of behavior. In this sense functional law is law without force.

This conclusion is confirmed by the functional notion of the legal rule and the conclusions to be drawn from it. If law is no longer conceived as a set of authoritative commands, but as the immanent lawfulness of actual behavior, legal rules cease to depend on the decision of a central legislative will. Legal rules that are construed as commands "exist" only in the form of a declaration of the will which is supposed to command. But legal rules that are found in the immanent orderliness of behavior do not "exist" by reason of an authoritative decision, but by virtue of being actually acknowledged in social relationships. This acknowledgement is not the consequence of commands imposed upon the legal persons, but of the inner orientation of the impulses and motives behind individual acts. Not the issuing of commands but the inner lawfulness of conduct is the test of positive law. Thus from this angle as well as from that of the new conceptions of person and society, collective organization appears irrelevant to the progress of legal order in international relations. Legal order, if it is to be more national sovereignty" in favor of new international institutions, to wit: An international court with jurisdiction adequate to deal with all international disputes on the basis of law; international legislative bodies; adequate police forces; international machinery with authority to regulate international communication and transportation; and appropriate authorities to administer backward areas. On the other hand, the Commission recognizes that "the nation-state is the unit of world society. . . . Clearly the organization of international society with the greatest chance of success will be that one which will assure a dynamic peace with the minimum sacrifice of international sovereignty." This clearly indicates that the Commission expects the proposed international organization to emerge from the concerted action of the particular governments who are supposed to "renounce sovereignty for the common good." Yet the Commission is realistic enough to "deeply appreciate that mere form without substance is of little value. No system of laws and organization can be of value without the living faith and spirit behind it and in it."

Now neither the Commission to Study the Organization of Peace nor any other human being can foretell the kind of spirit that will prevail when peace finally comes. In spite of this the Commission proposes a definite scheme of international institutions. This can only mean that the spirit of the nations is expected to conform to the organization. The plan envisages first the instruments of solidarity and relies on the subsequent "growth" of the necessary common consciousness; it proposes a framework of international community and hopes piously for the faith that will make it work. This conception is typical not only of the so-called "practical" solutions that are being offered today to the problem of international order, but also of the attitude of mind that so insistently poses the question: "What is to be done?" It implies the idea that a scheme of international institutions as such is identical with "the common good." Organization is so completely identified with the quintessence of progress, solidarity, and order in international relations, that even the spirit of nations is considered secondary pendent nations for certain defined purposes precisely stated in a treaty regulating all the details of time, place, circumstance, and quantity; leaving nothing to future discretion; and depending for its execution on the good faith of the parties. If the particular states . . . are disposed . . . to drop the project of a general DISCRETIONARY SUPERINTENDENCE, the scheme would be . . . at least consistent and practicable."

International organization as political organization, i.e. as an agency for the general coordination of interstate relations, is a chimera. International agencies, however, with tasks that are specified and concretely agreed upon in advance, represent a form of organization among states which is both theoretically sound and practically possible. It is significant in this connection that the breakdown of the League of Nations as an attempted "political" organization had very little effect on such of the League's non-political operations as were precisely defined by reference to specific ends. In so far as the League functions as an agency for the realization of concrete enterprises on an international scale, it is on the safe ground of reality. This reveals the definite limitation of the extent to which organization among states is possible. Of all organizations, only the political variety has the function of organizing social order with respect to *a certain territory*, embracing potentially all aspects of social life on that territory which require organization. Therefore political organization cannot be duplicated on a certain territory. If any political organization is to be superimposed on existing states, it can only be in the form of another, larger state. Otherwise interstate organization can only be organization functioning for limited purposes, not for the sake of comprehensive social order. It has to be an organization the functions of which do not compete with those of the only type of organization that tolerates no competition, political organization. Thus, as long as states exist in the present form, there can only be international organization of enterprises, but no international organization of "society."

The same essential limitation applies also to the second category of cooperative forms: regulations. While organizations are devices of coordination with a view to securing a permanent capacity for collective action, regulations are prescriptions of conduct with a view to attaining certain definite results apart from collective action. Instruments which prescribe a certain behavior in order to prevent wheat-prices from rising or to stop an undesirable migration of capital are regulations. It has been shown above that they do not represent rules of law because they emanate from a practical intention, not from an inner necessity of orientation. Their criterion is not immanent lawfulness, but practical expediency. Consequently they do not embody international law. Regulations are, like organizations, auxiliary means of administering international relations, but again, like organizations, do not represent the structure of international law. It is important that this be recognized. The case for international law will be better stated, if technical devices, procedures, organizational institutions and regulations are not confused with a genuine order of political relationship. On the other hand, institutions and regulations will be infinitely more effective in international relations, and will be enabled to secure a wider degree of international cooperation, if they are not burdened with exaggerated expectations of their success. It is imperative, therefore, to be clearly aware of the limited functions they serve, and to shape their form so as to fit these functions and to fit these functions alone. If international institutions and regulations function for necessary and not for arbitrary ends, no political conflict and no dissension among states will dislocate them from their position in international relations.

This leaves, as the true seat of international order, the third category of coordinating forms: legal rules. Laws of social relationships differ from organizations because they do not bring about a structure of collective action; they differ from regulations because they are not "made" for a certain purpose. Purpose does not affect them, any more than it affects the rules of language. They represent the immanently necessary line of conduct pertaining to social institutions or relationships. They cannot be wilfully made because they stem from the cultural pattern that governs our productiveness. Laws are the basis of every context of human activities. Where there is reciprocal orientation of human beings, there is also an inherent structure to such conduct. In this very structure exists the possibility of social intercourse. Therefore where there is "society" there are immanent laws of a transindividual scope.

There is nothing that can be done to "create" such laws. They originate not from planning action, but from the inner necessity of orientation in social relationships. It is in the way in which individuals empirically acknowledge certain standards of conduct that we find the lawfulness of behavior which contains the legal rules of social reality. Accordingly, no program of action can be proposed to further international law, to increase the number of its rules, to enact more of its provisions. No military academy can by deliberate action modify the rules of warfare. In the same way, nothing that might be planned in this respect would really affect the rules of international law and order. No amount of institutions, agencies, technical devices and procedures can promote the real scope of the law governing interstate relations. Only by reorienting our attitude to the problem of order can progress be made. We have to realize that rules of order are contained in the structure of social relationships, and not in the command of authority. We have to learn to eliminate the notion that persons are the units of social reality, and have to focus our attention on the interpersonal contexts of which society really consists. We have to become conscious of the fact that the order of social relationships is to be found inside the structure of acting individuals, not above them or even in opposition to them. It is this new orientation, the awareness of immanent laws, the criterion of transpersonal ends rather than personal interests, the insistence on the laws of connectedness rather than on those of separateness, which will open up the path toward further development of international law.

NOT ORGANIZATION BUT ORIENTATION

It has been and still is considered the task of international conferences to set up a mechanism designed to prevent international conflict, or at any rate the violence often connected with such conflicts. A conference of this kind which terminates a war will always try to achieve this goal on the basis of a definite historic theory about the causes of the last conflict. Looking back on the last conflict there will be an attempt to prevent another conflict from arising in the same way. Consequently there is always an innate tendency in these conferences to punish some state as the international wrongdoer or to hold down a "dangerous" nation, with the result that the pressure applied often engenders a counter pressure that finally leads to a new explosion. There is no escape from this vicious circle as long as states are identified with "elementary" forces governed by no law but the physical law of cause and effect. Force of this kind can be met only by force. Accordingly, there is no possibility of achieving order and stability in politics except through engendering in the incumbents of political power a fundamental orientation toward its functional ends. There is no lawfulness in international relations outside of the immanent lawfulness of the individual impulses of statesmen, and the only way to realize order is by creating in individual statesmen, civil servants, diplomats, civilians etc. that "instinctive" orientation toward necessary ends which makes generals act as generals and not as bandits, and makes popes behave like popes and not like medicine-men. Power which by its very essence is supreme can only be checked by the sense of its function, by the inner lawfulness of its use, but never by external limitations.

Therefore, it is more important to engender this orientation than to set up new institutions, checks, limits, and restrictions. What is needed is not organization but orientation, not a mechanism but organic order. It is not necessary to change the existing institutions in order to create the inner sense of order, but without that sense of order the best devices will be just tools for discord and disharmony. The only possible settlement in international relations—if the word "settlement" is to have any meaning at all—is the laying of the spiritual and practical foundations for a system of law which will enable states to function in the manner in which they necessarily must if they are to give expression to their inherent significance. It must be a system of law which will coordinate the respective functions of states—a system which, instead of restricting states, represents the conditions under which their functional ends can best be attained. It must be a system of law which by suggesting a frame of reference for the highest degree of constructiveness in coordinate conduct, stimulates an inherently orderly functioning, and thereby counteracts any arbitrary use of power.

To start this development by planning its external forms: organizations, institutions, regulations, would be putting the cart before the horse. More violence has been caused by imposing abstract intellectual blueprints on reality than by all the revolutions taken together. When the new outlook on the problem of law prevails, we shall detect by its light the solution of organizational problems as they present themselves. The laws of social reality cannot be speculated upon, they must be experienced. Therefore we conclude with the philosopher, John Macmurray: "What we have to do is to wait and be quiet; to stop our feverish efforts to do something. The next word is not with *us*, but with reality."

INDEX

INDEX

(See also topical table of contents.)

Volume 8 Gender, Culture and Human Rights
Siobhán Mullally

Volume 9 Monetary Remedies for Breach of Human Rights: A Comparative Study
Lisa Tortell

Volume 10 Judicial Review, Socio-Economic Rights and the Human Rights Act
Ellie Palmer

Volume 11 The Role of National Human Rights Institutions at the International and Regional Levels
Rachel Murray

Volume 12 Terrorism and the Limitation of Rights
Stefan Sottiaux

Volume 13 The Tension Between Group Rights and Human Rights: A Multidisciplinary Approach
Edited by Koen De Feyter and George Pavlakos